CAMBRIDGE SOUTH ASIAN STUDIES

THE POLITICS OF SOUTH INDIA
1920 – 1937

CAMBRIDGE SOUTH ASIAN STUDIES

These monographs are published by the Syndics of Cambridge University Press in association with the Cambridge University Centre for South Asian Studies. The following books have been published in this series:

1 S. GOPAL: *British Policy in India, 1858–1905*

2 J. A. B. PALMER: *The Mutiny Outbreak at Meerut in 1857*

3 A. DAS GUPTA: *Malabar in Asian Trade, 1740–1800*

4 G. OBEYESEKERE: *Land Tenure in Village Ceylon*

5 H. L. ERDMAN: *The Swatantra Party and Indian Conservatism*

6 S. N. MUKHERJEE: *Sir William Jones: A Study in Eighteenth-Century British Attitudes to India*

7 ABDUL MAJED KHAN: *The Transition in Bengal, 1756–1775: A Study of Saiyid Muhammad Reza Khan*

8 RADHE SHYAM RUNGTA: *The Rise of Business Corporations in India, 1851–1900*

9 PAMELA NIGHTINGALE: *Trade and Empire in Western India, 1784–1806*

10 AMIYA KUMAR BAGCHI: *Private Investment in India, 1900–1939*

11 JUDITH M. BROWN: *Gandhi's Rise to Power: Indian Politics, 1915–1922*

12 MARY C. CARRAS: *The Dynamics of Indian Political Factions*

13 P. HARDY: *The Muslims of British India*

14 GORDON JOHNSON: *Provincial Politics and Indian Nationalism*

15 MARGUERITE S. ROBINSON: *Political Structure in a Changing Sinhalese Village*

16 FRANCIS ROBINSON: *Separatism among Indian Muslims: The Politics of the United Provinces' Muslims, 1860–1923*

THE POLITICS OF SOUTH INDIA

1920 – 1937

CHRISTOPHER JOHN BAKER

Fellow of Queens' College, Cambridge

CAMBRIDGE UNIVERSITY PRESS

CAMBRIDGE

LONDON · NEW YORK · MELBOURNE

Published by the Syndics of the Cambridge University Press
The Pitt Building, Trumpington Street, Cambridge CB2 1RP
Bentley House, 200 Euston Road, London NW1 2DB
32 East 57th Street, New York, N.Y. 10022, USA
296 Beaconsfield Parade, Middle Park, Melbourne 3206, Australia

First published 1976

Photoset and printed in Malta by St Paul's Press Ltd

Library of Congress Cataloguing in Publication Data

Baker, Christopher John, 1948–
The politics of South India, 1920–1937.
(Cambridge South Asian studies; 17)
Bibliography: p. 339
Includes index.
1. Madras (Presidency)–Politics and government.
I.Title.II.Series.
DS485.M28B34 320.9'54'82035 75–2716
ISBN 0 521 20755 X

FOR JINNY

CONTENTS

MAPS AND TABLES

MAPS

TABLES

PREFACE

This is a study in the modern political history of India. It sets out to examine political changes in the Madras Presidency, the southernmost province of British India, at a crucial period in its recent history. In the years between the two world wars south India witnessed two political movements that have coloured its subsequent history; firstly a division of political forces along lines of caste and secondly the growth of nationalist organisation to a dominant position in provincial affairs. At the same time, the Madras Presidency, along with the other provinces of British India, had its first experience of many political institutions and practices such as large important legislatures, powerful local authorities, elections and election campaigns, political parties and ministerial office. In 1937, Indian politicians took this experience with them when they took over the entire government of the provinces for the only, brief spell of fully responsible government before the coming of independence ten years later. The experience of the inter-war years played a vital part in moulding political parties and political leadership.

Published works on India's modern history have concentrated heavily on the nationalist movement and on the all-India level of politics. There have been few forays into the provinces and into those areas of political life which were not closely bound up with the struggle for national freedom. The south has been conspicuously neglected, largely because it did not figure so consistently or so spectacularly in the nationalist saga as did other regions of India. M. Venkatarangaiya has compiled documents on the nationalist movement in Andhra, he and V. Venkata Rao have given excellent accounts of the history of local government, K. V. Narayana Rao has followed the formation of the state of Andhra Pradesh, Robert Hardgrave has described the changing fortunes of a single community, both he and Eugene Irschick have traced the genealogy of the more recent politics of Tamilnad and there have been several important biographies of political figures. It is no reflection on the scholarship of these works to note that they leave large tracts of territory untouched – so large indeed that this work cannot aim to be anything more than another voyage of discovery.

The events of the period are reasonably well known. The non-Brahman or Justice party, which emerged in 1916 to oppose Brahman domination of both the public services and political associations in the Madras Presidency, was awarded in 1921 the first ministerships under the new 'dyarchy' constitution and retained control over the ministry for all but a few months of the dyarchy period. In that time the party leaders formulated measures to improve the position of non-Brahmans in the public services and in other matters, while other party members equipped the non-Brahman movement with a set of social and political ideas. In the same period the south contributed to each of the different phases of the nationalist movement – to Gandhi's ascendancy in 1920, to the Non-co-operation campaign in 1921–2, to the Swarajists' attempt to invade and wreck the dyarchy constitution in 1923–7, and to the Civil Disobedience agitation in 1930–3. In general, however, south India was looked on as a backwater of Congress politics. Although Madras had shared with Bombay and Bengal in the foundation and in the early years of the Indian National Congress, the initiative had soon passed to the other presidencies and with the arrival of other provinces in Congress politics in the 1910s and 1920s Madras was pushed still further into the background. In 1937, however, Madras belied all generalisations that she was consumed with provincial and communal conflicts to the neglect of nationalism; in the first elections under the new constitution granting responsible government in the provinces the Congress in Madras swept to the most striking victory in any province, and annihilated the Justice party in the process.

In many ways these events in the south followed a pattern common to India as a whole. Political movements purporting to protect the interests of a particular caste, sect or community appeared in many different parts of India in the early twentieth century, and the ascendancy of the Congress in the 1930s was an all-India phenomenon. On closer examination, however, events in the south reveal certain oddities. To begin with, the victory in 1937 was not the only occasion on which the Congress in Madras had seemed to act out of character; in 1916 it had been a spate of political organisation in Madras that had helped to drag the Congress out of the deepest depression in its thirty-year history, and before that in 1887 it had been Madras that had staged one of the most successful of the early Congress sessions, even though in the intervening periods Madras had seemed to be fairly barren ground for the anxious patriot. The history of nationalism in the south has a waywardness all of its own. Similarly, both the emergence of the Justice party in the 1910s and then its eclipse in the 1930s were sudden and unexpected. Many politicians and government officials were still perplexed by the phenomenon of the Justice party long after it had firmly established itself, and both Congressmen and government officials were astonished by the conclusiveness of its defeat in 1937. Moreover, while movements which claimed to protect a minority were a common feature of the new politics of India in this period of councils, ministers, and electorates, it was unusual, if not paradoxical, to find a movement which claimed to defend a majority – a majority which included up to 98 per cent of the population and almost all the men of wealth and influence in local society. Clearly any straightforward explanation in terms of political movements and political ideas will not manage to unravel the complexities of this period.

This study sets out to examine the special character of political events in the southern province not by concentrating on any specific movement or institution, but by attempting to fit together the different pieces of the jig-saw of provincial affairs. The chief concern is with the province and thus with the obvious elements of provincial politics – the provincial government and legislatures, the provincial branch of the Congress and other provincial parties. However, in order to illuminate the narrative of events at the provincial level, it will be necessary to stray outside these narrow confines – on the one hand, into the affairs of the localities which constituted the province, and on the other hand into the affairs of the nation and the empire within which the province lay. The politics of both the wider world and of the worlds within impinged greatly on the political life of the province in this period. The Madras Presidency was a corner of Britain's empire, and many of the political and constitutional adjustments in the province were shaped by the changing position of Britain and the empire as a whole. The Madras Presidency was also a growing participant in a world economy, and was thus prey to economic influences that originated beyond its control. The Madras Presidency also formed part of a 'New India' and her politicians were drawn into allegiance with their counterparts in other parts of the nation. As for the localities, changes in communications and changes in administration which the former had facilitated had knitted them more tightly together as the fabric of a province than ever before. Provincial politics in this period were subject to many different pressures both from within and without.

In order to attempt such a broad view, many things will have to be left out. It will not, for instance, be possible to do justice to the great variety of the province and the great differences in the history of the different regions. From the beginning it has been necessary to neglect the areas at the periphery of the province in order to concentrate more effectively on the Tamil- and Telugu-speaking heartland. There is therefore no consideration of affairs in the part of the province which lay on the west coast. The languages, peoples, culture and geography of this area differed very sharply from those of the rest of the province, and its history both before and after the interlude of British rule had more in common with other parts of the west coast than with the rest of Madras Presidency. More particularly, since the concern is chiefly with the affairs of the province, the history of the locality, and the history of nation and empire, are dealt with briefly. The perspective on locality, nation and empire moreover, differs greatly from the perspective that would be expected of a specific study of such matters. Thus there is little consideration of the internal history of the all-India Congress and only a brief survey of changes in imperial policy. Similarly, there is little analysis of matters which would loom large in a local study – considerations of kinship, status and ritual, for instance, which undoubtedly played a large role in the ordering of local society, fade into a background when viewed from a vantage point of the province.

In other words, the tasks of selection and reduction which confront any historian have had here to be carried out with some ruthlessness, particularly since south Indian society in the early twentieth century was experiencing change in many different respects. Urbanisation, the growth of foreign trade, changes in the price structure and capital markets were transforming the economy; new institutions and new opportunities were making rapid changes to the style and purpose of politics; while adjustments to these and other novelties wrought changes in many aspects of society and culture. The purpose of this work is not to document such changes and to describe the interrelations between them, but to discover what factors played a part in the unfolding of political events and to examine the course of political development.

The story of course is far from simple and it will not yield to simple explanation. Two factors, however, loom large in the account, and those are administrative and economic change.

The later years of the Raj saw the creation of a novel form of state in south India, as the different fragments of a highly diverse region were drawn together more firmly than ever before. This development demanded new political institutions, new leadership and new forms of political organisation, and since the moving force was the fiat of government it was not surprising that many of the new phenomena were built around the ideas of government and the unities that government had created. This administrative integration in south India forms the background for the study of politics in the 1920s in chapters 1 and 2. The 1930s, as seen in chapters 3 and 4, witnessed a new direction in government policy as the British started to disentangle themselves from the details of government and administration and in doing so opened up new tracts of country to intrepid politicians.

Yet this study does not in any way set out to argue that administrative reform conjured up out of the mind of the Raj dictated the course of the region's modern history, or indeed that this was the tale of an energetic government imposing its will on a passive society. Government policy was not decided in a vacuum but was shaped to meet changing conditions and changing problems; in other words, government was often forced into actions even though the lines of force were generally indirect.

This was hardly surprising given the context and circumstances of imperial rule. The slim resources of the Raj were barely adequate to provide more than a skeleton for government, leaving others to furnish the skeleton with more solid matter. Madras remained a peaceful province – 'benighted' and dull according to British officers, backward and hopeless according to Indian nationalists – well into the twentieth century. This was not because government ruled with a firm hand but because for the most part it left a stable and well-ordered society to its own devices. The precariousness of government and its dependence on other leaders of society was thrown into sharp relief after 1930 when economic change began to undermine the stable foundations of Madras society; cracks began to appear in the edifice of government and in the gentlemanly façade of Madras politics. Through these cracks sprouted many new movements and organisations and the middle years of the decade saw the hitherto stunted growth of the Congress burst suddenly into bloom.

There are many people to thank for their assistance during the making of this book. I am indebted to the Hayter Foundation, the SSRC Modern Indian History Project at Cambridge and Queens' College for financial aid, and to the Committee of Management of the Centre of South Asian Studies, Cambridge for including this book in their series. For access to books and records and for much courteous help I am grateful to the directors, librarians and staff of the India Office Library and Records, the Madras Record Office (Tamilnadu Archives), the State Archives Hyderabad, the National Archives of India, the Nehru Memorial Museum and Library, the Centre of South Asian Studies Cambridge, the libraries of Cambridge, Madras, Andhra and Osmania Universities, the Sapru House library in Delhi, the Adyar and Connemara libraries in Madras, and especially the library of *The Hindu* newspaper in Madras. I profited greatly from conversations with K. V. Gopalaswamy, Sir Christopher Masterman, R. T. Parthasarathy, Mariadas Ruthnaswamy, P. S. T. Sayee, R. Sunderraj and R. Jayakumar. I am indebted to several friends and colleagues who helped in many different ways during research and writing, in particular to John and Karen Leonard, Susan Lewandowski, Pat Baker, Carolyn Elliott, Bob Church, Pandit K. J. Vethamuthu who struggled to teach me Tamil, A. Bapuji Chowdary who laboured to translate Telugu, B. Kesavanarayana, Jim Manor and B. N. Janarthanan Mudaliar, and to colleagues at some time in Cambridge including Chris Bayly, Jack Gallagher, Gordon Johnson, Peter Musgrave, Rajat and Ratna Ray, Eric Stokes, Tom Tomlinson and especially Anil Seal, without whom many things would not have been possible.

Finally my greatest debt is to David Washbrook with whom I have enjoyed close co-operation throughout research and writing. His book *Madras politics, 1870–1920* is published simultaneously with this one. While we have maintained a useful exchange of ideas and information about south India during research, our two works differ in many fundamental aspects. To begin with David Washbrook is concerned with the period before 1920, while I concentrate on the years after that date. Moreover, this chronological division has brought about great differences in style and approach. The nature of government and the style of politics in south India changed markedly in the period 1916–21, and our two works reflect this change. David Washbrook analyses in great depth the society and government of south India in the period from 1880 to 1920 and deploys that analysis to explain the complex events which transformed the face of politics during and immediately after the first world war. In parts of this study, I have to delve back into the earlier period and into the descriptions and analyses which have been made in much more detail by David Washbrook; yet primarily I am concerned with institutions which did not exist (or at least exist in the same form) in the earlier period and with a narrative of events in a provincial arena of politics which had had only a shadowy existence before the 1910s.

CHRISTOPHER JOHN BAKER

Cambridge
December 1974

NOTES ON REFERENCES, TRANSLITERATION & ABBREVIATIONS

1. GOVERNMENT RECORDS

All Government of India files are prefixed: GOI. The reference shows: department and where necessary branch; file number; date.

All Government of Madras files begin with 'G.O.' meaning Government Order. The reference shows: number of Government Order; (department and where necessary branch); date.

All references to government records end with an abbreviation (see below) describing where the file is deposited.

In most cases of references to Government of Madras files, the file as a whole is cited rather than a particular document in it. Most of these files are small and are specifically concerned with one incident or decision, and the account given in the text here is based on an evaluation of the different documents – petitions, newscuttings, official reports, Secretariat notes – in the file. Only in special cases does the reference cite an individual document.

Certain Government of Madras files dated after 1920 and relating to the area of the old Madras Presidency which now falls in the state of Andhra Pradesh are being moved from the Madras Record Office to the State Archives in Hyderabad. The references given here describe where the file was when viewed in 1970–1, and while the bulk of the transfer had then been completed some of the files shown here as being in Madras may by the time of publication have found their way to Hyderabad.

2. GOVERNMENT ANNUAL REPORTS

Certain annual reports are cited in a contracted form:

Settlement Report (annual)
  Report on the Settlement of the Land Revenue in the Districts of the Madras Presidency

Police Report (annual)
  Report on the Administration of the Police in the Madras Presidency

Forest Report (annual)
  Report on the Working of the Forest Department of the Madras Presidency

Abkari Report (annual)

Report on the Administration of the Abkari Department of the Madras Presidency

The titles of these and other annual reports differed slightly from year to year; the forms given here and in the bibliography were the most common.

3. NEWSPAPERS

All references to *The Hindu* are to the daily edition, unless shown as *Hindu*(w) which denotes the weekly edition. Unless the text or footnote refers to a particular part of the paper such as the letters page or editorials, the reference is to the columns of provincial and local news.

4. ABBREVIATIONS

(a) Departments and branches etc.

L	Local
M	Municipal
LSG	Local Self-Government
Misc	Miscellaneous
FR August (2)	Fortnightly Report of the Madras Government for the second half of August

(b) Archives

IOL	India Office Library and Records, London
MRO	Madras Record Office (Tamilnadu Archives)
NAI	National Archives of India, New Delhi
NMML	Nehru Memorial Museum and Library, New Delhi
SAH	State Archives, Hyderabad
SAS	Centre of South Asian Studies, Cambridge

(c) Other

AICC	All-India Congress Committee
MLCP	Madras Legislative Council Proceedings
NNR	Madras Native Newspaper Reports (see Bibliography)

5. TRANSLITERATION

Tamil and Telugu words and names in the text are not transliterated but are given in anglicised form. In the footnotes and the bibliography, Tamil and Telugu titles (but not authors' names) are transliterated, the former according to the system employed in the *Tamil Lexicon* published by Madras University, and the latter according to the Library of Congress system. There are no diacritical marks on transliterated words in the footnotes.

6. PROPER NAMES

There is no system used in the spelling of proper names in the text other than an attempt to copy the forms common in the period under study. Towns, districts and other geographical place-names are spelt in accordance with the forms used by the Madras Government in the *Census of India 1921* and the survey maps published in the 1920s. Personal names are spelt in the forms commonly used in the period, as far as possible in the forms used by the persons themselves. Where there is any doubt over a particular name, the simplest form is used. Thus, for instance, 'Iyer' is generally used in preference to the many other possible forms such as 'Aiyer', 'Aiyar', 'Ayyar'. The honorific '-ar' at the end of Tamil names has been omitted (thus 'Rajagopalachari' rather than 'Rajagopalachariar') except in the case of names which never appeared without it (for instance 'raja Annamalai Chetti*ar*').

7. BIBLIOGRAPHY

The bibliography includes a number of works – particularly biographies and political tracts – which are not specifically cited in the footnotes but which have provided important background material for this study.

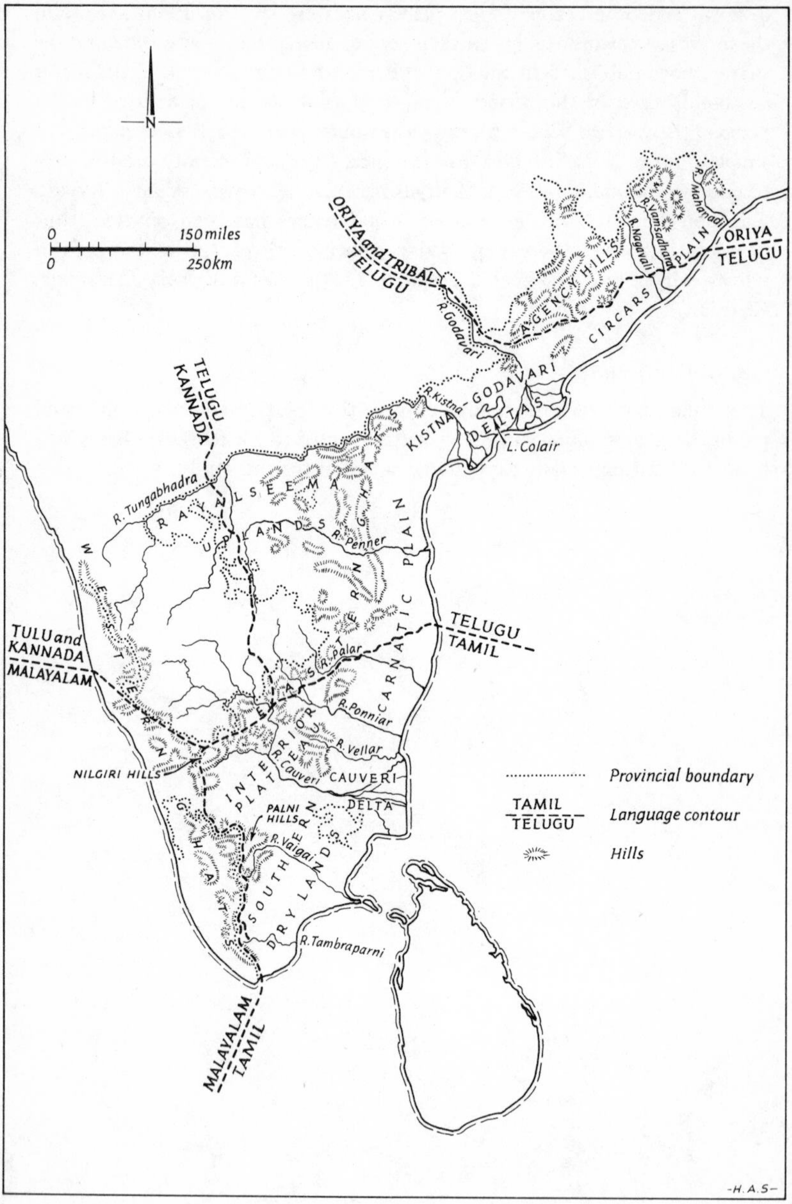

MAP 1. Madras Presidency—natural features, regions and languages

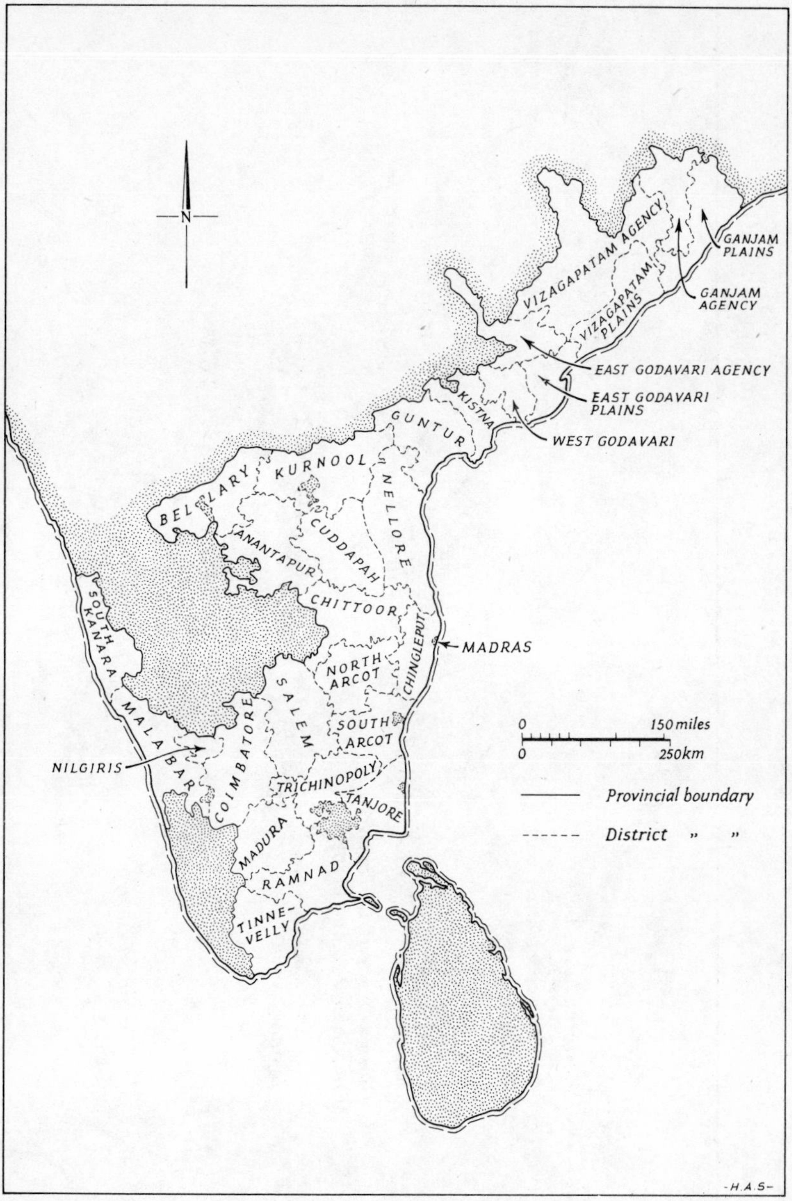

MAP 2. Madras Presidency—districts

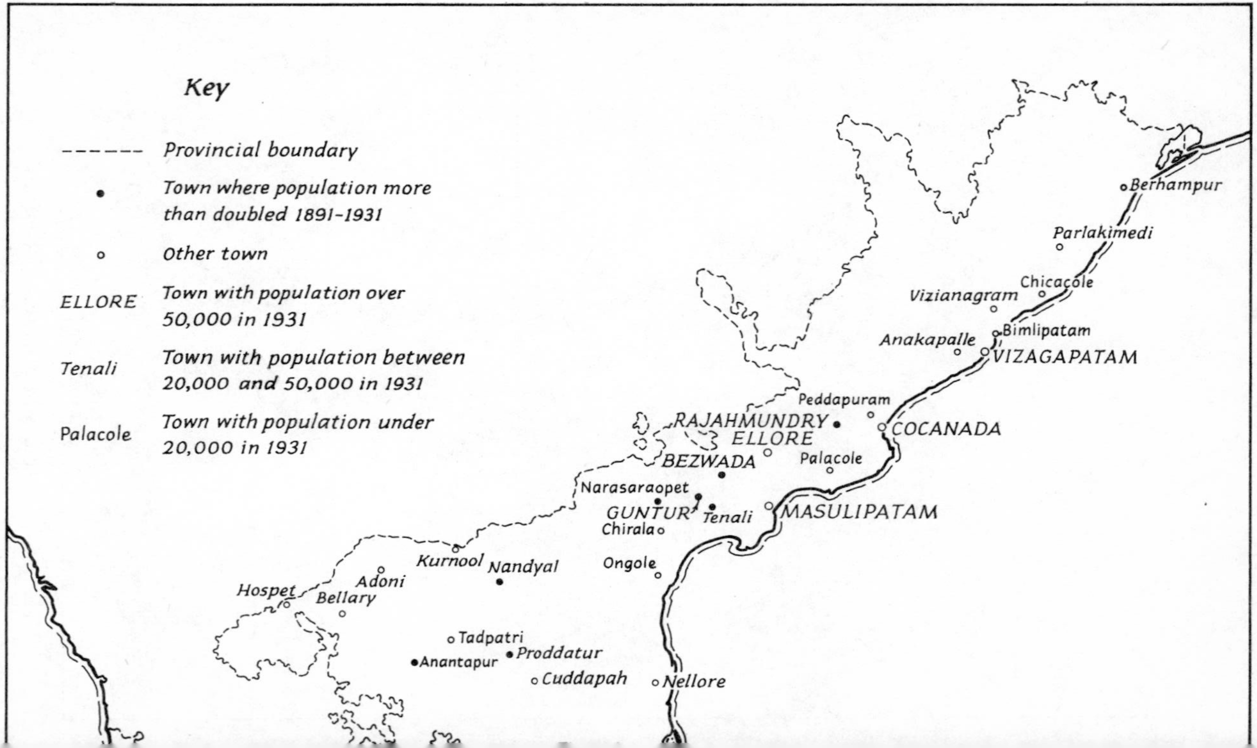
Key
Provincial boundary
Town where population more than doubled 1891–1931
Other town
ELLORE Town with population over 50,000 in 1931
Tenali Town with population between 20,000 and 50,000 in 1931
Palacole Town with population under 20,000 in 1931
Berhampur
Parlakimedi
Chicacole
Vizianagram
Bimlipatam
Anakapalle
VIZAGAPATAM
Peddapuram
RAJAHMUNDRY
COCANADA
ELLORE
BEZWADA
Palacole
Narasaraopet
GUNTUR
Tenali
MASULIPATAM
Chirala
Kurnool
Nandyal
Ongole
Adoni
Hospet
Bellary
Tadpatri
Proddatur
Anantapur
Cuddapah
Nellore

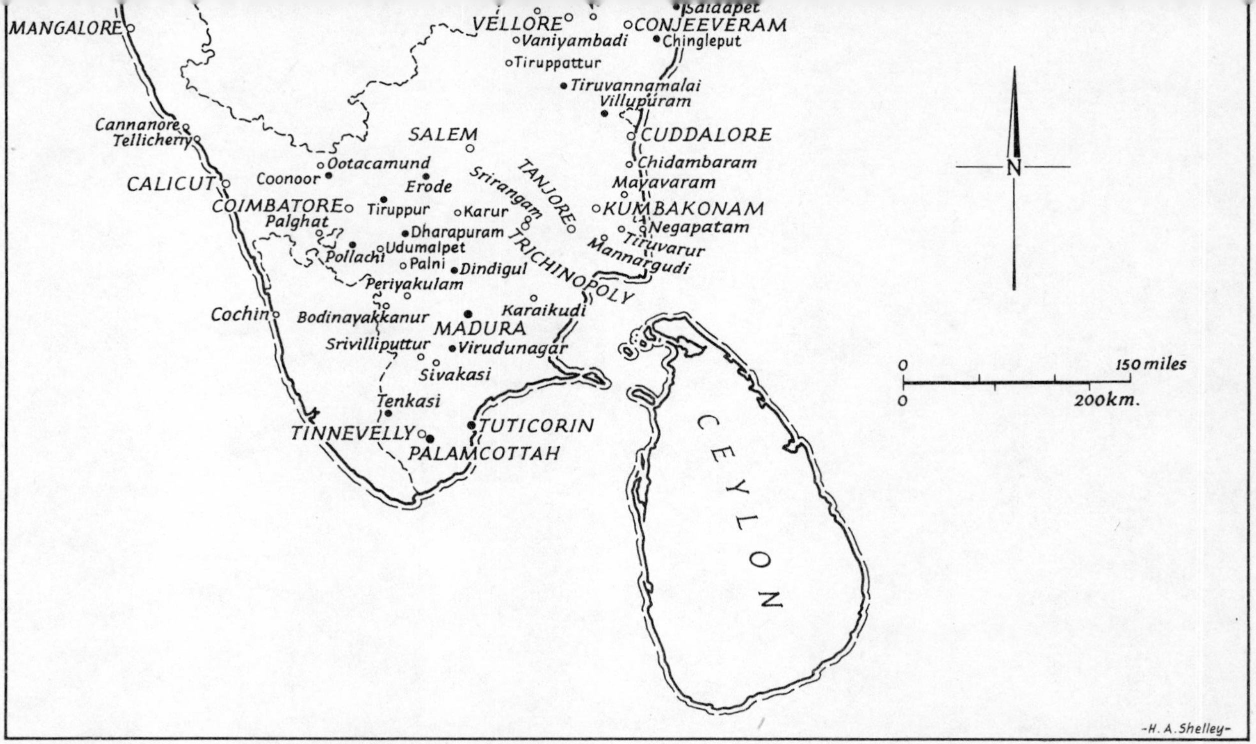

MAP 3. Madras Presidency—municipal towns

CHAPTER I

Politics and the Province: the Justice Party

In December 1920, general elections in the provinces inaugurated a new constitution for the Government of India. It created a new all-India Legislative Assembly at Delhi and made other changes in the central Government, but it was in the provinces that it introduced the most important changes. In the Madras Presidency and in the other British provinces, the constitution laid down a scheme of 'dyarchy' or dual rule. For the next sixteen years the Governor in Council shared the responsibility for provincial government with three Indian ministers. The ministers were selected from among the members of a new Legislative Council and they were responsible to it. An electorate of over a million people selected most of the 123 members of the new legislature. In many ways, this constitution marked a big change in India's political history. Since 1861 there had been Legislative Councils in the provinces, but never one which was this large, which was directly elected, and which possessed such wide powers. There had never before been responsible Indian ministers. Although many Indian politicians loudly dismissed the new constitution as inadequate, others showed that they understood its importance. It provided opportunities for Indians to participate in the administration of the province. In particular, the new legislature provided for the first time an arena for provincial politics.

The reform of the constitution was one of the main features of a quinquennium which transformed politics in the Madras Presidency. Firstly, the Home Rule agitations of 1914–17 had thrust Madras into the forefront of all-India politics. They were more determined than previous agitations, and they attracted considerable support in the up-country areas of the province. Secondly, a new political party had emerged during the negotiations over the constitutional reforms. This Justice party was to dominate politics in the region for much of the next two decades. Thirdly, Madrassis both from the provincial capital and from the hinterland came forward to contribute to the Congress' first nation-wide agitation in 1921–2. These events, and the opportunities provided by the reforms, cast provincial politics in a new mould.

Of course these events were not unique to Madras. The Home Rule Leagues, the agitations over reform, the Government of India Act and the Non-co-operation campaign of 1921–2 were all-India affairs. But many contemporary observers felt that the contrast between the events of these years and what had gone before was more marked in Madras than in other provinces. Previously, provincial politics in Madras had not been so lively. The Congress in Madras had not won the support that it had in the other two presidencies. The Government of Madras had not had to deal with provincial agitations or provincial political movements of any weight, and it had not had to arbitrate in political disputes of a provincial scale. Indeed Madras had become famous for its conservatism and for its political calm.

What then had made the Madras Presidency such a sleepy backwater in the later nineteenth century and why had it not remained so? What had led up to the constitutional reforms and the other changes of the years 1916–22? The answers to these questions provide the background to the development of provincial politics in the 1920s and 1930s.

TOWARDS DYARCHY: SOCIETY AND GOVERNMENT IN THE SOUTH

The British had not inherited a province in south India, they had created one. In much of north India they had been able to take over the administrative units, the machinery and even the personnel of the Mughal government, and to use them as the foundations of their own rule. In the south, they did not start with such advantages. Over the centuries, south India had seen many sophisticated kingdoms, but most of them were ephemeral and all of them were small. The region had never been drawn together as a political unit. The Vijayanagar kings had brought the whole of the south under a single government, but they had concentrated their energies on building a rampart against the Muslim north rather than integrating the varied parts of their empire. The Madras Presidency, then, was an artefact of British rule, put together piece by piece over forty years, and dismembered much more rapidly once its makers had departed. Not surprisingly the British found it was an extremely diverse and disparate province which was very difficult to govern as a unit.

It was, to begin with, by far the largest of the provinces of British India. It contained half the coastline of the entire subcontinent, it spanned both the east and the west of the peninsula, and it stretched from Cape Cormorin to the hills of Orissa. Climate and economic conditions differed widely between the shifting deserts of the far south and the steamy rain forests of the Western Ghats, and between the rich alluvial deltas of the major rivers and the barren uplands on the fringes of the Deccan.[1] The population, which reached 41,405,404 in 1921[2] contained a maze of different peoples and cultures. Of course none of the provinces was entirely homogenous, and indeed some of the disunities which marked other provinces were absent from Madras. The vast majority of the population of the southern province was Hindu. In 1921 only 3·2 per cent was Christian and 6·7 per cent Muslim,[3] and there was rarely any conflict between faiths. The bulk of the population spoke one of two mother-tongues. Forty-one per cent spoke Tamil and lived mostly in the districts to the south of the capital, Madras City, and 38 per cent spoke Telugu and lived mostly in the districts to the north.[4]

Yet Madras lacked other characteristics which helped lend unity to other regions of the subcontinent. Large agriculturist communities inhabited the rural areas of both northern and western India and helped to knit these regions together through kin ties, shared festivals and common customs. The Ganga acted as the one important trade route across the entire north Indian plain. The temples along its banks were centres of pilgrimage and worship for a large hinterland. The towns along its banks played a large role in the commercial life of the neighbouring rural areas. In the west and the east, Bombay City and Calcutta acted as true capitals of their regions. Each handled over 90 per cent of the foreign trade of its province and each became the most important centre of education, industry and culture in its region. The commercial networks which spread out from these capitals – Bengal had extensive cash-cropping and internal trade by the early nineteenth century, Bombay developed as the centre of the Indian cotton industry soon after – gave a clear focus to the economic life of their hinterlands.

[1] For descriptions of the province and its great variety, see E. Thurston, *The Madras Presidency with Mysore, Coorg and the Associated States* (Cambridge, 1913); O. H. K. Spate and A. T. A. Learmouth, *India and Pakistan: a general and regional geography* (London, 1967), pp. 683–782; and the several volumes of the *Madras District Gazetteers.*

[2] *Census of India 1921*, vol. XIII, pt. 1, p. 9.

[3] *Census of India 1921*, vol. XIII, pt. 1, pp. 64–6.

[4] *Census of India 1921*, vol. XIII, pt. 1, pp. 139–40.

In the south, conditions were very different. Settlement patterns and marriage customs had made the region a patchwork of different communities. In Tanjore district, for instance, at least nine different caste groups owned land. Although there was less fragmentation of this sort in the Telugu districts, the south had nothing to compare with the Kunbi, Jat and Rajput communities farther north. In northern India, exogamous marriages helped to spread family ties over a wide area. In the south, rural communities preferred endogamous marriages and confined their clans within very small circles.[5] A small group of Sengundars in Coimbatore, for instance, refused to marry their daughters outside the radius of three villages.[6] The 1891 Census in Madras set out to catalogue subcastes defined by interdining and intermarriage; it counted up to 25,000 before giving up and admitting that the list was far from complete.[7] Commerce and trade did little to help cement the villages together. Although they were hardly the self-sufficient republics beloved of the early anthropologists, the villages of the south cultivated mainly for their own consumption and sold what little surplus there was in the *sandai* or local market.

The disunity of the countryside showed up in the great variety of dress, diet and customs. Edgar Thurston's attempt to list the castes of the region and to describe their customs ran into seven vast and perplexing volumes, not only because there were so many castes, but also because the customs and habits of the different groups within any one caste were so varied.[8] In his account of local religion in the south, Bishop Whitehead noted that 'the number of different gods and goddesses worshipped all over the South is enormous and the variety of local customs almost infinite'. He added that 'often the deities worshipped in one village will be quite unknown in other villages five or six miles distant'.[9]

Towns did little to integrate the south. Indeed, the history and geography of the region had not encouraged the growth of important urban centres. The region did not produce the stuff of bulk trade, and

[5] F. J. Richards, 'Cross-cousin marriage in south India', *Man*, XCVII (1914); D. G. Mandelbaum, *Society in India* (Berkeley and Los Angeles, 1970), vol. I, pp. 156–7; L. Dumont, *Une Sous-Caste de l'Inde du Sud: organisation sociale et religion des Pramalai Kallar* (Paris and The Hague, 1957), pp. 12, 168.

[6] B. E. F. Beck, *Peasant Society in Konku: a study of right and left subcastes in South India* (Vancouver, 1972), p. 232.

[7] *Census of India 1891*, vol. XIII, pt. 1, index of castes.

[8] E. Thurston, *Castes and Tribes of Southern India*, 7 vols. (Madras, 1909).

[9] H. Whitehead, *Village Gods of South India* (Calcutta, 1921), pp. 12–13, 23.

it did not have a natural trade route like the Ganga. There were no natural features, other than a few river crossings and one gap in the line of the Western Ghats, which encouraged settlement at crossroads for internal trade. In the case of foreign trade, the long coastline was dotted with many different harbours, none of which had outstanding merits; as shipping technology changed and as river mouths silted up, old harbours had been abandoned and new ones sought, and the coastline was littered with ancient port towns which had lapsed back into villages. In the absence of commercial impetus, towns had grown mainly as administrative and cultural centres. Yet successive kingdoms had chosen different capitals and had patronised different centres of religion and learning, and this again interrupted urban growth. By the early nineteenth century the Vijayanagar capital had been reclaimed by the jungle. The spot which the British built into the third city of the Indian empire had been nothing but a sandy strip of beach in the early seventeenth century.

The region had remained overwhelmingly agricultural, and urban growth had been slow and diffuse. As late as 1931, 86·4 per cent of the population still lived in villages. There were 350 towns but only four had populations of more than 100,000, and three-quarters of them contained less than 20,000.[10] Many of the towns possessed impressive temples but they did not serve as cultural centres for the immediate neighbourhood. The Brahmanical deities worshipped in these temples were very different from the numerous gods and goddesses of the village shrines. Villagers paid respect to the Brahmanical pantheon as well as to their local deities and often made pilgrimages to the major temple towns, but these towns attracted pilgrims from far and near and in no way acted as a focus for the shire in which they stood.[11]

Madras City did not dominate and thus to some extent unite her province in the manner of Calcutta or Bombay City. Only 40 per cent of the foreign trade of the Presidency passed through Madras City. By the early twentieth century Madras had two cotton mills, but the rest of her industry was either government works such as the mint, armoury and railway workshops, or cottage enterprises such as tanning and handloom weaving.[12] Until well into the twentieth century,

[10] *Census of India 1931*, vol. XIV, pt. 1, p. 73; pt. 2, pp. 10–16.

[11] See Whitehead, *Village Gods*; R. K. Das, *Temples of Tamilnad* (Bombay, 1964); N. Ramesan, *Temples and Legends of Andhra Pradesh* (Bombay, 1962).

[12] J. Dupuis, *Madras et le Nord du Coromandel: étude des conditions de la vie indienne dans une cadre geographique* (Paris, 1960), pp. 220–1, 493–8.

Madras City was little more than the administrative centre of the region.

The completion of the rail network in the later nineteenth century began to impose some order on the chaos of trading patterns and on the haphazard growth of towns. A few railheads emerged as important trade entrepots. Railways and foreign trade also began to draw more goods out of the villages. New cash crops spread widely in some tracts. Cotton had been grown since the early nineteenth century; in the later part of the century tobacco and sugar were planted in the 'wet' tracts, those that were irrigated from the major rivers of the region, and in the early twentieth century the farming of groundnut increased dramatically in the 'dry' or unirrigated areas.[13] Yet only in the deltaic tracts, which were a small proportion of the province as a whole, did these developments cause significant change in urbanisation or in the relationship between countryside and town.[14] Elsewhere, the new crops were financed and marketed almost exactly as other crops were, and they were conveyed from village to town by itinerant commission agents who acted as insulation between the village and the wider economy.[15] None of the new crops had the same effect on the economic life and the economic unity of the region that cotton had had in western India. Groundnut, tobacco and most of the raw cotton were all produced for export. They did not form the staple for new industries in the region and they were taken straight from the field to the port with the minimum of processing. Industry grew very slowly. By 1921, less than 0.5 per cent of the population worked in factories.[16]

Although the British gathered the various bits of south India into one province, they could not easily make them function together as a unit. The resources at the disposal of the British at Fort St George (the site of the government offices in Madras City) were meagre indeed. The cadre of the Indian Civil Service (I.C.S.) stationed in the province numbered around 160.[17] In the early nineteenth century when they

[13] 1910–11: Net area cropped, 33,754,796 acres; cotton, 2,323,257 acres; oilseeds, 2,414,684 acres; sugar, 94,879 acres; tobacco, 221,677 acres; *Agricultural Statistics of British India* (annual) for 1910–11, vol. I, pp. 244–55.

[14] N. G. Ranga, *Economic Organisation of Indian Villages*, vol. I (Bezwada, 1926); vol. II (Bombay, 1929).

[15] D. A. Washbrook, 'Country politics: Madras 1880–1930', *Modern Asian Studies*, VII, 3 (1973), 475–531.

[16] *Census of India 1921*, vol. XIII, pt. 1, p. 190.

[17] *Royal Commission on the Public Services in India.* Appendix vol. II *Minutes of Evidence taken in Madras*, pp. 1–10.

were laying out the system of administration, their chief means of travel through the province were the horse and the bullock cart. Their predecessors had not left them much of a foundation on which to build a government. Faced with these disadvantages, they had little chance to overcome the fragmentary character of the region. In fact the disunity of the province overcame the British administration rather than vice versa.

The backbone of every provincial administration in the nineteenth century was its system for raising revenue from the land. The raising of revenue was the most important task of the provincial government and until the twentieth century land was the main source of revenue. As other functions of government developed, they tended to be built around the revenue system. In their first major experiment, the Madras administrators introduced the Bengal system of land settlement, in which the government dealt with zamindars or estate-holders. Government gave the zamindar a title to his estate in return for payment of a fixed sum of revenue each year. The system suited government since much of the burden of policing and administering the tracts within zamindari estates could be left to the zamindar, but the settlement worked badly in Madras and was soon abandoned as a general policy. Only a little over a quarter of the rural areas of the province, much of it in the Telugu coastal districts, remained under zamindari tenure. A small proportion of the rest was held under inam or preferential tenure. The beneficiaries of this tenure were mostly village officers, temples and charitable institutions. The rest of the province was settled under the ryotwari system.[18]

According to the theory of the ryotwari settlement, government assessed the revenue on each cultivated field. This assessment was adjusted every thirty years to take account of changes in prices, marketing opportunities, irrigation facilities and many other factors. The revenue demand was settled each year with each ryot or cultivator according to the extent of his holdings. The ryot could theoretically change the amount of land he cultivated from year to year. The system was widely heralded as a triumph for Ricardian principles since it maximised both justice for the cultivator and gain for the exchequer by cutting out all intermediaries between government and the tiller of the soil. It was also seen as a triumph of imperial administration.

[18] T. H. Beaglehole, *Thomas Munro and the Development of Administrative Policy in Madras 1792–1818: the origins of the Munro system* (Cambridge, 1966); D. Kumar, *Land and Caste in South India. Agricultural labour in the Madras Presidency during the nineteenth century* (Cambridge, 1965).

The business of fixing and collecting the revenue in each of the twenty-four districts of the province fell to the Collector, who also acted as District Magistrate. It was a cheap and apparently successful system of governing the interior.[19]

But the theoretical nicety of the ryotwari settlement made it almost unworkable in practice. The administration of the region was in the end shaped more by the lacunae in the ryotwari system than by its Ricardian principles.[20]

The British simply did not have the resources to assess the revenue on each piece of land, taking into account the soil, rainfall, proximity of markets and many other factors. Nor did they have the facilities to check each year who held the land and how accurate the local land records were. They could not deal with each cultivator and, indeed, it was often difficult to sift the claims of many different people for various rights in a certain piece of land and to determine who the 'cultivator' was.[21] The ryotwari system had to be bent to suit different conditions in different areas of the province. Later on, this was to produce great anomalies in the system. By the early twentieth century there were eight million south Indians who rented land from the people who paid ryotwari revenue to the Madras Government; because these revenue-payers were, in theory, the actual cultivators of the soil, there was no place in law for any tenants underneath them; government and the courts stolidly refused to acknowledge that these eight million people existed.[22] The ryotwari system required in theory a wealth of information in the revenue records in order to make the settlement fair; in fact such sophistication was beyond the facilities of government, the records contained more fiction than fact, and the courts refused to accept them as evidence.[23]

Far more serious than such petty eccentricities was the way that the authority of government was undermined. For much of the nineteenth century, Fort St George seemed to have little control over the branches of its own administration in the districts. The Collector, who was the head of a district, was almost autonomous in his adminis-

19 N. Mukherjee, *The Ryotwari System in Madras* (Calcutta, 1962).

20 See the chapters on 'land revenue' in the several volumes of *Madras District Gazetteers.*

21 N. Mukherjee and R. E. Frykenberg, 'The ryotwari system and social organisation in the Madras Presidency', in R. E. Frykenberg (ed.), *Land Control and Social Structure in Indian History* (Madison, 1969), pp. 217–25.

22 *Royal Commission on Agriculture in India.* Vol. III *Evidence taken in Madras and Coorg*, p. 292.

23 S. Y. Krishnaswami, *Rural Problems in Madras: Monograph* (Madras, 1947), p. 65.

tration and several Collectors behaved more like princelings than civil servants. As long as they forwarded the revenue to the capital, they were immune from too much pressure from their overlords.[24] Meanwhile, much of the real power in the district administration seeped down below the level of the Collector.

The Collector was the chief revenue officer and also the chief magistrate. If this were not enough, he was also burdened with responsibility for the police, for irrigation, for public works and for all other aspects of district administration. 'The Collector,' wrote one who had held the post, 'in fact with a jurisdiction larger in both area and population than the larger English counties, does the work undertaken in England by the Chief Constable and by the County and District Councils in addition to his revenue and magisterial work.'[25] The burden was patently too heavy and Collectors complained that they were little more than 'post offices'[26] for the vast amount of obligatory paper work. In most important matters they were utterly dependent on the information, advice and assistance furnished by their subordinates, and it was part of the folk-lore of the province that it was in these subordinate levels of the administration that the real power lay.

The Collector had a handful of Deputy and Assistant Collectors. Until the end of the nineteenth century, the rest of the administration was staffed mainly with Indians recruited in the district. Firstly, there was the staff of the Collectorate itself, and the tahsildars who were the link between the Collectorate and the countryside. Secondly, there were village officers. These were men who belonged to the villages and who stood at the point where government confronted rural society. In the early revenue surveys, the British relied heavily on information provided by the village officers. In day-to-day administration, the tahsildars and the sheristadars in the Collectorate controlled the records and the flow of information to their superiors. In the annual settlements of the revenue demand, the village officers did most of the work and the Collector or his assistants could make only a cursory check.[27]

The provincial administration housed a mosaic of little kingdoms.

[24] R. E. Frykenberg, *Guntur District 1788–1848; a history of local influence and central authority in south India* (Oxford, 1965).

[25] Sir Christopher Masterman papers SAS.

[26] G. O. 173 (Revenue) 20 Feb. 1902 MRO.

[27] For intimate descriptions of the revenue system at work see the papers of Sir Christopher Masterman SAS, and S. Wadsworth, 'Lo, the poor Indian', typescript memoir, especially pp. 120–32, 150–6 SAS.

Yet this did not necessarily bother the rulers. The chief goals of the provincial government were to collect the revenue and to keep the peace. In these respects Madras consistently performed better than other provinces. This was largely due to the flexibility of the ryotwari administration. The tahsildars and village officers did a good job of collecting the revenue for they did not want to place in jeopardy a revenue system which allowed them great opportunities for power and profit. On the surface Madras looked calm and contented, yet this did not necessarily mean all was calm beneath. Most men of importance in the districts could gain some purchase within the loose framework of ryotwari administration, and with so much power residing at the lowest levels of government, disputes over matters of revenue and local administration were generally settled within the locality. Few bubbled up and ruffled the tranquillity on the surface.

When disputes or scandals did appear, they were generally dramatic. Occasionally Collectors began to behave exactly like Indian rajas and ignored the governmental hierarchy altogether. Then government was forced to intervene and bring them to heel. At times government was obliged to investigate the revenue service in a particular district, and with relentless certainty these investigations uncovered a tangle of conspiracy and corruption in the lower ranks of the services.[28] The new and far more efficient revenue surveys undertaken from the 1860s onwards revealed startling discrepancies in the original ones. Vast tracts of land had lain hidden and thus untaxed, and others could barely be recognised from their description in the revenue records.[29]

For the most part, however, it was the policy of the Madras Government to let sleeping dogs lie. Government rested lightly on the people

[28] The case described in R. E. Frykenberg, *Guntur District* is the most famous but far from the only one of its kind. See D. A. Washbrook, 'Political change in the Madras Presidency 1880–1921', Ph.D. thesis (Cambridge, 1973).

[29] For an example see W. Francis, *Nilgiri District Gazetteer* (Madras, 1908), vol. I, pp. 227–82; 'I say, as far as can be ascertained, for it is impossible to find out with accuracy the rates really paid for the several descriptions of land. In the first place, the areas are incorrect . . . So much dry land is entered as wet; so much wet as dry; there have been such continual adjustments and readjustments of the shist on the whole rented area; so many additions have been made to the joint-rent in the lump, which additions have afterwards been distributed on the fields, more with reference to the circumstance and position of the ryot than to the value of the fields.' Papers relating to survey and settlement of Godavari district 1870, *Selections from Madras Government Records*, vol. XXII, p. 18.

and the people treated government with apparent respect. 1857 passed without incident, and the rural agitations which afflicted parts of northern, western and eastern India in the last quarter of the nineteenth century found no echo in the south. The Government of Madras grew complacent and conservative. It became a tradition for Fort St George to resist any initiative for change or reform stemming from Calcutta or London. When Edwin Montagu visited India in 1918 he reckoned that Madras was the most immovable of the many immovable governments on the subcontinent.[30] Indian civil servants christened Madras the 'benighted presidency' and avoided serving there if they wanted excitement or advancement.[31]

Fort St George seemed to be locked out of its own administrative system yet it did not see this as a cause for complaint. The Madras I.C.S. argued that the size and diversity of the province on the one hand, and the meagreness of government's resources on the other, made reform almost impossible. In the last quarter of the nineteenth century, however, circumstances began to change. The advent of the railway, the telegraph and later the motor car improved the government's chances of dealing with the sprawling province. Some of the administrators themselves began to express frustration at their inability to rule well and to do good in India. On a wider scale, many felt that at the high noon of empire, they should make India as rich and brilliant in fact as it was often portrayed in theory.

New sentiments and new opportunities could not change the dogmas of imperial rule. The dictates of finance could. The British had never found it easy to balance the books in India, and several factors conspired to make financial stability more than usually difficult in the last quarter of the nineteenth century. The problems arose both on the revenue side and on the expenditure side. Since the middle of the century, military and administrative costs had soared. The garrisons stationed after the 1857 revolt, the follies on the North-West frontier and other armed adventures had swollen the military budget. Rising prices and the slow but steady growth of

30 S. D. Waley, *Edwin Montagu* (London, 1964), p. 147.

31 See for example Willingdon's comments in a letter to Montagu dated 29 March 1920 in which he described his reaction to Madras: 'Of course down here one misses the cosmopolitan outlook of Bombay, the broader views which constant touch with the West has brought. Here we are much out of the world, and though many have intelligent brains, few find it possible to have any breadth of outlook. Nearly all are looking out for themselves.' Willingdon papers vol. IV IOL.

the bureaucratic apparatus had demanded increased spending on administration. Revenue, however, was less elastic than expenditure. In raising its revenues, the Government of India had to abide by two strict rules. Firstly, it could not burden the British taxpayer with any expense arising out of the Indian empire. Secondly, in India itself taxation had to be kept as low as possible since high taxes were deemed politically unwise. Yet land revenue, which remained the chief staple of the Government of India until the twentieth century, could not be raised as fast as prices. Salt, opium and stamp taxes, which were the other major heads of revenue, were little better.[32] By the 1870s it was clear that the Government of India would have to find some new ways of raising revenue and some cheaper ways of administering.

These financial pressures were bound to have effect in Madras for one simple reason: Madras was an important source of the Government of India's revenues. This was not because Madras was richer than other provinces, for arguably it was poorer than most, nor because the Madras revenue system was more flexible than those in other provinces. Madras was not strategically important in the way that the frontier provinces were; it was not commercially important in the way that Bombay and Bengal were; and it was not politically sensitive in the way that Bengal and the United Provinces were. Thus whenever the provincial contributions to the imperial revenues were reorganised in the late nineteenth century, Madras fared badly each time.[33] By 1922, a member of the British parliament called Madras the 'milch-cow' of the Indian exchequer.[34]

In the half-century beginning in the 1870s, a series of reforms at all levels of the administration gradually changed the shape and style

[32]

	Index of All-India Expenditure	% on Military	% of total revenue from: Land Revenue	Opium	Salt
1887–8	100	29	29	11	9
1897–8	130	30	26	6	9
1907–8	132	31	25	8	5
1917–18	201	33	18	3	5

Calculated from *Finance and Revenue Accounts of the Government of India* (annual) for the years shown.

[33] Ampthill to Hamilton, 11 June 1902, Ampthill papers vol. 7 IOL. I am indebted to David Washbrook for this reference.

[34] *Parliamentary Debates (Commons)*, CXVI (1919), 2379, quoted in E. F. Irschick, *Politics and Social Conflict in South India: the Non-Brahmin Movement and Tamil Separatism 1916–29* (Berkeley and Los Angeles, 1969), pp. 209–10.

of the British government in India. In Madras these reforms were particularly noticeable. This was partly because the reforms revolved around revenue and thus affected the revenue-giving province more than most, and partly because Madras had been so conservative before. The reforms ran along two paths. Firstly, they centralised the administration in the provinces. Secondly, they enlarged the scope and the functions of government.

Mayo's devolution order of 1870 prepared the way for reform in the province. It gave the provincial governments more autonomy to regulate their own affairs, particularly in matters of revenue and expenditure. Soon after, the Government of Madras took steps to improve its control over the lower reaches of the provincial administration. Mainly this meant dragging the subordinate branches of the revenue department out of the mires of local influence, and imposing more efficient supervision from the Secretariat. Fort St George relieved the Collector of some of his duties and thus freed him to be more efficient as a supervisor of the revenue system. Then beginning at the top and working down, it replaced most of the locally recruited revenue officers with members of the provincial civil service. The latter were examined, recruited, controlled and disciplined from the Secretariat. The process began with the appointment of many more Deputy Collectors in the 1880s and ended when the tahsildars were drafted into the provincial civil service in 1926.[35] It also made inroads on the power of the village officers. It curtailed much of their power to distribute the revenue demand within the village according to personal whim, reduced the number of their subordinate staff, subjected them to examinations, and even in some cases threatened to take away their jobs as a measure of retrenchment.[36] There were similar reforms in the police, the judiciary and in other departments of government. The result was to give the provincial government far more control over its own tentacles and thus to bring the provincial government more closely into the affairs of the locality.

The provincial and the imperial governments also took steps to secure a better flow of information from the periphery to the centre. Besides the Censuses which began in 1871, government started new statistical series on industries, cropping, banking, agriculture, industries, irrigation, joint-stock companies and co-operative enterprises. Between 1880 and 1930 there were detailed government

[35] D. A. Washbrook, 'Political change in the Madras Presidency'.

[36] G. O. 1958 (Revenue) 14 Aug. 1920 MRO.

enquiries into famine, labour, industries, banking, agriculture, co-operation, irrigation, railways, prices, taxation and many other matters. Government was equipping itself with the information it would need if it were to raise new taxes and undertake new tasks.

Both of these things the Government of Madras soon began to do in earnest. Between 1870 and 1910, it acquired new Departments of Agriculture, Statistics, Industries and Fisheries, a new Public Works Secretariat, a Commissioner of Forests and a Registrar of Co-operative Societies. Outside the capital, the expansion in the size of government's operations was even more marked. In the districts, it set up several advisory councils. These boards of non-official Indians advised and assisted government in the administration of forests, of the police, of irrigation, of the excise department and of the new income tax. More important than these were the new local self-government boards set up in the wake of legislation by Ripon in the 1880s. By the turn of the century, eighty towns in the province had municipal councils, each of the twenty-four districts had a district board, and each of the taluks (subdivisions of a district) had a taluk board. On these new local boards Indian non-officials, some of them elected, sat side-by-side with government officers and helped to administer roads, schools, charities, markets and other local facilities.[37]

The local boards and advisory councils invited many more Indians into the processes of government in the district. Fort St George was also drawing more Indians into the administration at the provincial capital. By 1920, sixty-two Indians had found their way into the Indian Civil Service in Madras, and another 320 into the provincial civil service. The number of Indians recruited into the lower ranks of the services rose from 4,912 to 12,388 in the first two decades of the twentieth century.[38] At the same time more Indians were taken on to the Senate of the Madras University, the body which administered higher education in the province, and into the High Court. In 1910, an Indian was for the first time appointed to the Governor's Executive Council, the 'cabinet' of the provincial government.

The reasoning behind these reforms was straightforward. The Raj could no longer balance the books by keeping government as cheap and skeletal as possible; the rise in military and administrative expenditure had put paid to such a policy. It had to raise new taxes

[37] K. K. Pillai, *History of Local Self-Government in the Madras Presidency 1850–1919* (Bombay, 1953).

[38] *Indian Statutory Commission*, vol. VI, Appendix pp. 607–13.

and to do this it would need more knowledge of Indian society and more collaboration from it. To begin with, then, government had to be more efficient. Next, government needed better sources of information, and new institutions which would attract Indian advisers and assistants. Finally, government had to think seriously about developing the economic resources of India. This would not only satisfy demands by both imperialists and nationalists that government should play a more positive role, but it might help solve the financial problems as well.

The new departments of the Madras Government set out to improve Indian agriculture and industry in order to bring prosperity directly to the people and indirectly to the exchequer. The local boards and advisory councils helped to associate prominent men in the districts with government's attempts to raise new taxes. By the turn of the century local rates, excise dues, forest and irrigation fees and income taxes supplied 24 per cent of the revenue raised in Madras. By the end of the first world war the figure had risen to 36 per cent.[39] The local self-government boards were the most important element in the new reforms. They raised local taxes and helped to ensure that the local elites acquiesced in the new imposts. They also relieved the bureaucracy of many administrative burdens particularly in education, sanitation, public works and the new development activities. They enlarged the scope of government without adding greatly to the costs of administration.

The administration was reformed, the groundwork for development laid, and the budget balanced. But the consequences went far beyond any which could have been imagined by the many people who had advocated and shaped these reforms. Government had begun to impinge on Indian society to a far greater extent than before. Previously the Madras rustic could expect an annual visit from the revenue officer and an occasional visit from some other government officer in connection with a local school or an irrigation work. Now government through its local boards, its advisory committees, its new departments and its more centralised administration was becoming more and more closely involved in day-to-day activities like sowing, marketing, washing and drinking. Government omnipotent was on the way to becoming government immanent as well. The institutions of local self-government with their responsibilities for many different local amenities were particularly responsible for this change.

[39] See table 1.

TABLE 1. *Madras Government revenue*

Year	Total revenue (Rs)	Index 1902–3 = 100	Revenue raised under major heads. Each entry shows amount in Rs millions and, in brackets, the proportion of total revenue. Land revenue	Salt revenue	Stamps	Excise	Customs	Income tax etc.	Irrigation rates
1882–3	94,627,560	60	45·1(48)	13·9(15)	5·2(6)	6·5(7)	1·0(1)	0·5(1)	3·5(4)
1892–3	123,787,420	78	46·5(38)	17·2(14)	7·4(6)	12·1(10)	1·7(1)	2·0(2)	5·5(5)
1902–3	158,739,566	100	53·7(34)	20·3(13)	8.2(5)	15·6(10)	5·0(3)	3·1(2)	8·2(5)
1912–13	155,166,589	98	58·1(37)	11·1(7)	13·6(9)	33·2(21)	8·0(5)	4·1(3)	11·2(7)
1917–18	182,973,952	115	59·5(33)	16·2(9)	15·4(8)	40·4(22)	11·5(6)	8·1(5)	11·5(6)
1922–3	226,333,544	143	60·9(27)	15·2(7)	22·0(10)	49·0(22)	31·0(14)	13·2(6)	9·5(4)
1927–8	243,734,753	154	62·4(26)	14·5(6)	25·0(10)	53·4(22)	43·1(18)	13·9(6)	8·6(4)
1932–3	258,977,037	163	50·3(19)	20·4(8)	24·2(9)	42·7(17)	53·3(21)	16·8(7)	10·9(8)
1937–8	264,529,344	167	49·6(19)	17·9(7)	19·3(7)	46·3(18)	64·6(24)	13·9(5)	8·5(7)

SOURCE: *Finance and Revenue Accounts of the Government of India* (annual) for the years shown. Table entitled: 'Account showing the estimated revenue (Imperial, provincial and local) in each of the provinces of British India and in England for [year] compared with the results of [previous year].'

TABLE 2. *Madras Government expenditure*

Year	Total expenditure (Rs)[a]	Index 1902–3 = 100	Expenditure under major heads. Each entry shows amount in Rs millions and, in brackets, the proportion of total expenditure: Administration charges[b]	Law, justice and jails	Police	Education	Civil works	Irrigation	Medical and sanitation
1882–3	44,111,310	64	14·8(33)	4·7(11)	4·0(9)	1·8(4)	6·1(14)	3·2(7)	1·5(3)
1892–3	68,788,490	97	19·1(28)	5·5(8)	4·2(6)	2·6(4)	7·2(11)	4·6(7)	2·5(4)
1902–3	69,181,409	100	22·3(32)	6·1(9)	4·8(7)	3·5(5)	8·1(11)	6·1(9)	3·2(4)
1912–13	86,130,941	124	30·2(35)	8·1(9)	8·8(10)	6·6(8)	16·3(19)	8·6(10)	2·1(2)
1917–18	89,046,708	129	29·7(33)	10·2(11)	11·7(13)	9·4(11)	8·0(9)	9·4(11)	3·8(4)
1922–3	137,307,242	198	48·0(33)	13·4(9)	20·2(15)	15·3(11)	10·6(8)	7·4(5)	6·5(5)
1927–8	164,750,389	238	51·0(31)	12·4(8)	18·8(11)	21·9(13)	14·1(9)	9·7(6)	9·2(6)
1932–3	180,923,772	261	57·5(32)	11·1(6)	16·1(9)	24·2(13)	15·9(9)	12·7(7)	10·5(6)
1937–8	184,246,498	266	65·5(35)	11·7(6)	16·1(9)	25·8(14)	13·9(8)	13·2(7)	13·9(8)

SOURCE: *Finance and Revenue Accounts of the Government of India* (annual) for the years shown. Table entitled: 'Account showing the estimated expenditure (Imperial, provincial, and local) in each of the provinces of British India and in England for [year] compared with the results of [previous year].' In both this and the preceding table on revenue, the *actual* figures for the previous year have been used rather than the *estimated* figures for the current year.

Notes:

[a] Up to 1908, military expenditure accounted for over a third of Madras Government expenditure; after that date, this head was transferred from the provincial to the central government accounts. To make this table more straightforward, military expenditure has been ignored and thus the total and the percentages for the earlier years have had to be adjusted.

[b] 'Administration charges' includes the amounts shown in the accounts under the following heads: General Administration, all Collection Charges, Stationery and Printing, Superannuation and Pensions, Territorial and Political Pensions.

More resources were being distributed through the machinery of government, and more people had to deal with government agencies in their everyday lives.

Government figured much more prominently than before as a controller of men as well as resources. The introduction of new posts at both higher and lower levels of the administration and in both the capital and the districts paved the way for new contests over power and influence. Finally, administrative change had begun to draw the province together. In attempting to tighten up the bureaucracy, the Madras Government had in many significant respects transferred the real seat of authority from the districts to the provincial capital. Governmental institutions in Madras City took on a new significance for the province as a whole. Changes in recruitment to the services, for instance, had made educational qualifications more important and had consequently focussed more attention on the University Senate and the Education Department in the Secretariat. Changes in the revenue system had moved the ultimate authority in many revenue matters from the Collectorate to the offices in Fort St George and people now had to direct their protests over administrative policies to the capital. In other ways too local men found that the provincial centre was invading the localities, and that matters that once could have been settled in the district now had to be settled at the provincial capital. Around the turn of the century, many local politicians literally packed their bags and moved to Madras City.[40] In order to serve local interests they had to move close to the hub of power. Administrative change promised in the end to transform the political life of the province.

This half-century formed a remarkable chapter in the story of British rule in south India. It was a period of administrative expansion and administrative aggression, sandwiched between periods in which the administration seemed to be going backwards rather than forwards. Before the 1870s, Fort St George had been concerned not to expand the role of the British administration. After the 1930s, it was busy disentangling the British from their commitments in India. Thus the reforms made the early twentieth century a time of great ferment. With the Government of India Act of 1919 the Viceroy, Lord Chelmsford, and the Secretary of State for India, Edwin Montagu, wrote the final paragraph in this chapter.

[40] See for instance V. K. Narasimhan, *Kasturi Ranga Iyengar* (Delhi, 1963), pp. 22–3.

Towards dyarchy: society and government

There were three main influences moulding the Montagu–Chelmsford reforms. All of them were bound up with the recent trends of administrative reform. In the first place, the provincial governments were calling for more autonomy. They wanted another devolution of power from the centre to the provinces, just like the one Mayo had initiated in 1870, so that they could have even more freedom to adjust internal affairs to the special circumstances of their particular regions. Thus the 1919 Act made a firm division between the heads of revenue which belonged to the centre and those which belonged to the province, and gave the provincial governments more responsibilities and more autonomy in financial affairs.

In the second place, the war had revived the financial problems of the empire with a vengeance. Britain had borrowed over £250 million from India to contribute to the war effort, and had pushed up military expenditure in India from Rs 233 million or 26 per cent of the entire Government of India budget in 1912–13, to Rs 365 million or 32 per cent of the budget by the last year of the war. This had saddled India with an enormous public debt.[41] To meet these payments and other spiralling costs, the Government of India had to discard the last of the nineteenth-century taboos about taxation. Income tax rates, which had been kept as low as possible until the middle of the war, were doubled in 1916. A new super tax was added in 1917, and in the aftermath of the war, income tax rates had to be raised twice more.[42] In the year before the war, income taxes had yielded 3 per cent of Madras revenues. By the end of the war, they contributed twice that amount. The actual amount raised by these taxes had tripled in five years. There were similar increases in other taxes which fell on enterprise rather than land. The yield of local rates almost doubled in the decade following 1912–13, excise dues increased by a half, and customs receipts multiplied four times. The overall change in the incidence of the revenue demand in Madras was quite dramatic. In 1902–3, excise, customs and income taxes had contributed 15 per cent of the total; by 1922–3, the total revenue had grown by almost a half, and those three heads of revenue now contributed 42 per cent.[43]

If they had to tax more, the British also had to find more ways

[41] *Statement exhibiting the Moral and Material Progress of India during the year 1917–18* (London, 1919), pp. 68–82.

[42] *Report of the Indian Taxation Enquiry Committee 1924–5* (Madras, 1926), vol. I, p. 189.

[43] See table 1.

to soothe the taxed. In 1917 Edwin Montagu announced that the aim of the British in India was now the 'increasing association of Indians in every branch of the administration and the gradual development of self-governing institutions'.[44] He was not planning the first step in a transfer of power. He was using the word 'self-governing' (which was included almost fortuitously in this famous announcement[45]) in the same sense that it was used in the term 'local self-government'. It implied the transfer of administrative burdens, but not executive powers, to reliable Indians. Thus the 1919 Act introduced a large Legislative Council with responsible Indian ministers; they could shoulder many of the tasks of provincial government but they would have no control over finance. The aim was simply to make British rule more stable and more efficient. The act was a pragmatic response to problems of government and administration, not a deed of charity. As Montagu insisted in a letter to Chelmsford in 1917: 'Fortunately or unfortunately, we are discussing a problem in the administration of an important part of the world, and we are not considering an abstract matter for debate in a lunatic asylum consisting of constitutional lawyers whose minds have given way.'[46]

Thirdly the Act was designed to counter growing discontent among important Indian citizens. The political temperature of India had risen dramatically during the war against a background of rising prices, higher taxes and increasing government controls. The decline in foreign trade, coupled with government's requisitions of foodstuffs and other materials in India needed for the war effort, had led to shortages in both local and imported goods. Everyday necessities such as salt, kerosene and cotton cloth were in particularly short supply. Shortages had pushed up prices. In the decade 1910–20, the general price index rose by almost 100 per cent. By 1917–18 this had helped to create a general wave of discontent, especially in the big cities where shortages and price-rises were worst and where discontent found expression in a wave of industrial strikes. For the wealthier sections of urban society there were special reasons for annoyance. The decline of shipping had cut into foreign business. Government had placed restrictions on internal travel and commandeered a lot of railway rolling stock, which hindered internal commerce. The new taxes hit especially at businessmen. Finally in

44 Waley, *Edwin Montagu*, p. 134.

45 *Ibid.*

46 Montagu to Chelmsford 21 Sept. 1917, quoted in Waley, *Edwin Montagu*, p. 137.

1917–18 government imposed strict controls on markets in an attempt to halt inflation and cut down profiteering.[47]

The war had thrown the changes in the relationship between government and society over the past half-century into sharp relief. High prices, new taxes and new controls sparked off a wave of discontent among the urban elites. This in turn fed into an upsurge of political activity. The Home Rule Leagues in Madras and Bombay re-invigorated the Congress by projecting a demand for more Indian control over the new leviathan.[48] Government was obliged to reform the constitution in a way that might win back the support of the 'moderates'. It designed the new legislatures to give representation to attract the men whose continued collaboration would be vital for the stability of British rule.

That such reforms were vital if the Raj was to remain firmly in the saddle in India was made starkly obvious when the Congress launched its first agitation on an all-India scale in 1920–2. The Non-co-operation campaign was initiated by Gandhi and by politicians who had been disappointed by the reforms; the agitations which contributed to the campaign in the southern province, however, were scattered and sporadic and had little to do with the politicians' aim of driving the British into the Indian Ocean. Many of them displayed an angry reaction to the recent changes in administration – in particular to new taxes and administrative incursions. Liquor manufacturers registered a protest against the new excise rules and taxes and helped to give weight to a temperance campaign. Cattle graziers and forest tribesmen, objecting to new regulation of the forests and to new taxes on forest produce, raised an agitation which temporarily undercut the tenuous hold of law and order in the forest tracts. In some areas, the village officers showed their resentment of the reforms which had deprived them of powers and privileges by refusing to collect the land revenue and thus creating a 'no-tax' campaign. In some towns the merchant groups who were angered by municipal taxes and by municipal regulation of their business interests, set out to sabotage the framework of municipal administration. These protests were mainly ephemeral. By 1922 they had dribbled away as most of the protesters found that there were opportunities

47 *Statement exhibiting the Moral and Material Progress of India during the year 1917–18*, pp. 68–82.

48 H. F. Owen, 'Towards nationwide agitation and organisation: the Home Rule Leagues 1915–18', in D. A. Low (ed.), *Soundings in Modern South Asian History* (London, 1968), pp. 159–95.

to be seized in the new style of government under the reforms.[49]

The architects of the 1919 Act were at pains to ensure that matters which affected Britain's larger imperial interests – foreign policy, trade and tariffs, the military – or matters which might seriously affect Britain's hold over the country – control over revenue and expenditure, the police and most communications – were kept firmly under imperial control. The Montagu–Chelmsford reforms were an attempt to put the Raj back on the rails, to take account of changed circumstances and changed requirements and yet recapture the stability of the later nineteenth century.

MYLAPORE, CONGRESS AND JUSTICE 1890–1920

As long as the province remained a miscellany of localities loosely marshalled together under an aloof government, it was difficult for a provincial politics to emerge. The disunity and the tranquillity of the Madras Presidency proved as stultifying for Indian politicians as it was for the foreign rulers. From the mid-nineteenth century there were activities which passed for provincial politics, but these were in fact strictly confined to Madras City.[50] Associations of the western-educated appeared from the 1860s and many of their members – chiefly lawyers, educators and administrators – attended the first meeting of the Indian National Congress in 1885 and organised one of the most successful of the early Congress sessions in Madras City two years later. The Congress returned to Madras three more times before the first world war, but it was soon clear that the initiative in nationalist affairs lay in Bengal, Bombay and northern India. The 'provincial politics' of Madras did not have much substance and thus could add little weight to the national cause. There were no agitations like those in Bengal and Punjab; there were no provincial disputes on the scale of those in Calcutta and Maharashtra which enlivened the nationalist movement; there was no leader to stand beside Tilak, Gokhale, Banerjea, Malaviya, Pal and Lajpat Rai.

From the last decade of the nineteenth century, however, circumstances in Madras began to change. Administrative reforms were slowly drawing the province together. Madras City was emerging as

[49] C. J. Baker, 'Non-co-operation in south India', in C. J. Baker and D. A. Washbrook, *South India: Political Institutions and Political Change 1880–1940* (Delhi, 1975).

[50] R. Suntharalingam, 'Politics and Change in Madras Presidency 1884–1894: a regional study of Indian nationalism', Ph.D. thesis (London, 1966).

more of a focus for the province than it had ever been before. District politicians trekked into Madras City to seek new ways to influence the bureaucratic machine; members of the Legislative Council raised campaigns over irrigation, public works and estate labour; the Congress from time to time demanded more power for Indians. The protagonists of the new politics in Madras City were the men who understood the principle of gaining power and influence in a state that was essentially bureaucratic, and who were equipped – largely through knowledge of the English language – with the skills necessary for promoting the interests of a wide clientele in the corridors of government. There were many people who needed to gain influence within the walls of Fort St George – managers of temples and charities, large landholders, big businessmen, directors of educational institutions. These were the interests which would want to have access to the pressure-points of any government. Previously, many of them had been content to have influence in the districts. Because of change in the administration, they now found they had to stake out a claim in Madras City, and to do this they had to work through the new politicians and their organisations.

Around the turn of the century, one group of men in Madras City emerged as pre-eminent in the business of mediating between the newly important institutions of the provincial capital and the many interests who needed to exert influence within them. These men were bound together by their success and were loosely referred to as the Mylapore set. At the core of the group were some of the most successful lawyers and administrators of the province. They were rich and highly educated, their families extended throughout the legal and service communities of the province, and their clienteles and personal networks stretched all over the region. Their knowledge and their wide range of contacts made them indispensable as advisers and assistants to the bureaucracy; their skills and their access to the bureaucratic ear enabled them to serve a plethora of different interests. By the 1910s, the influence of this tiny handful of men had become quite extraordinary. Some of their number had become judges in the Madras High Court, some had a powerful voice in the Senate of the Madras University, some sat in the Legislative Council and some had been invited on to government commissions; from 1910, when the Governor included an Indian on his Executive Council, a Mylaporean consistently filled the place. From these vantage points, they had found their way into other important positions in the capital as well. They had begun to replace the local merchants and contractors as the most important bloc in the Madras Corporation, gained a toehold in the Madras Port Trust and taken over the management of the wealthiest charitable foundation in the City, the Pachaiyappa's Trust. Their network also reached out into the mofussil. They could sometimes influence public service appointments in the districts and, from 1913 when a Mylaporean on the Governor's Executive Council was given the portfolio of local self-government, they could occasionally interfere in local politics; they had also formed a Dharmarakshana Sabha, a society for temple reform, which used the courts to place Mylapore's nominees in the management of some of the wealthiest temples of the province.[51]

Mylapore also counted the Madras provincial branch of the Congress amongst the instruments of its own provincial prominence. In its hands, the aims and organisation of the movement had been somewhat flexible. In the 1880s, when government was contemplating constitutional changes which would grant more jobs and more influence to Indians, the Congress became a powerful organ for agitation. Once devolution was secured and Mylaporeans had benefited, they brought the Congress smartly to heel. Thus during the all-India battle between Extremists and Moderates in the first decade of the twentieth century, Mylapore kept the Madras Congress firmly in the Moderate camp; and after the Surat split of 1907, the Mylaporean leaders locked the Extremists out of the Madras provincial Congress and virtually killed the Congress organisation in the districts lest it should disturb the political calm in which their influence was so secure. During the 1914–18 war, however, the Mylaporeans judged the time was right to press for a further devolution of power. Economic strains and the increased pressure of government interference had made many of Mylapore's clients restive and anxious for more power to influence government. Meanwhile the British government was penniless, anxious and susceptible, and it had hinted that it would, in return for Indian loyalty and assistance during hostilities, consider constitutional concessions once peace was established. Mylaporeans, and Indian leaders in similar positions in other provinces, decided to press a hard bargain for their continued assistance to government, in the hope that they could thus transform their undeniable influence into more formal power.

The vehicle for the Mylaporean demand was the Home Rule

[51] C. P. Ramaswami Iyer, *Biographical Vistas: sketches of some eminent Indians* (Bombay, 1960) portrays some of the leading lights of Mylapore; see also Washbrook, 'Political Change in Madras Presidency', pp. 273–317.

League in which Mylapore allied with Mrs Annie Besant, the remarkable Irish campaigner and adventuress who for some years had been settled in the Adyar suburb of Madras City where she dabbled in oriental religion and the occult. The Home Rule League linked Mylapore's influence in the City and its network in the mofussil with Mrs Besant's province-wide organisation of theosophical societies, a syncretist religious and cultural movement which had had great appeal to educated Indians. In 1916–17 the League, in parallel with similar organisations in other provinces, mounted an impressive campaign against the British government in India, and Mrs Besant was jailed and then chosen for the chair at the annual session of the Indian National Congress.[52]

The Madras Government was not a little distressed to find that its leading advisers had become the leaders of sedition. Several of the most influential men in Madras City now had one foot in the administration and one foot in a cantankerous nationalist movement. But the Mylaporeans had calculated that they were indispensable to government and partially at least they were right. They retained their influence at Fort St George, they were consulted on the form of the new constitution, and in 1921 the Madras Governor still wanted to give the first ministerships to them. They had calculated less well on the extent of Indian opposition to their antics.

For a brief time in 1916, the Home Rule League movement united all the political factions of Madras behind Mylapore and Mrs Besant. Before and after that time, however, the situation was far more complex. There were many groups who resented the remarkable growth of Mylapore's influence since the turn of the century. Firstly, there was a set of men in Madras City who once had been loosely known as the Egmore group. In background, profession and ambitions there was little to choose between them and the Mylaporeans; what they lacked, however, was the quintessential feature of Mylapore – success in gaining the confidence of both government and important elements in south Indian society. Without that they lacked influence, and this factor underlay the rather wayward course of their politics. Their position is best seen through the career of one of their leaders, Kasturiranga Iyengar. He had been educated in some of the best institutions in the province, had a successful legal practice in Coimbatore district and had gained some influence in local politics. Towards the end of the nineteenth century, like many others, he followed the scent of

[52] Owen, 'Towards nationwide agitation and organisation'.

power to Madras City. There, however, he never managed to break into the charmed circle of Mylapore and consequently never acquired more than a mediocre practice in a bar that was fast becoming overcrowded. He drifted towards journalism and in 1905 purchased *The Hindu*, an English language newspaper. He soon turned the paper into the chief organ of nationalism in the province and a constant thorn in Mylapore's side. In 1906–8 *The Hindu* backed the Extremist cause, in 1914–15 it ridiculed Mrs Besant, and in 1916 it was drawn rather reluctantly into the Home Rule movement. This last association was brief, however, and by 1917, *The Hindu* group, now known as the Nationalists, had turned back to ridiculing Mylapore for its two-faced strategy.[53] They aimed to embarrass Mylapore and force it out of control of the Congress by pushing the Congress towards a more extreme, intractable line on constitutional reform.

Secondly, there were many lawyers, merchants and local politicians in the districts who had grown to resent the monopoly of the City over the leadership of public affairs. Over the years, isolated groups and individuals in different localities had loosely allied together through the Extremist agitation in 1905–8 and again through the Home Rule Leagues in 1916–17. In the Telugu-speaking districts they also came together in the Andhra movement, an agitation for a separate province for the Telugu area, and in Tamilnad they had made a cause out of a mill strike in Madura in 1917. In 1918, the leader of this loose faction, Chakravarti Rajagopalachari, a lawyer and former municipal chairman from Salem, moved to the City. In 1908 they had allied with the Egmore group to push the Extremist cause against the complacent Mylaporeans; in 1917–18 they resurrected the same alliance in an attempt to wrest the Congress from Mylaporean hands.[54]

Neither of these factions could match the widespread influence of Mylapore, and they tried to make up for this by adopting radical policies and leading various agitations. The third faction, which was to become the Justice party, tackled Mylapore at its own game. When Mylapore in 1916 adopted the pose of sedition, they came forward to offer themselves as loyal alternatives to the Mylaporeans as government favourites, and begged to be allowed to supplant the Mylaporeans in the ante-rooms of government. This group was a very mixed bag indeed. It included several City merchants and politicians (most

[53] Narasimhan, *Kasturi Ranga Iyengar*.

[54] M. Venkatarangaiya, *The Freedom Struggle in Andhra Pradesh (Andhra)*, vol. II (Hyderabad, 1969); Kausikan, *Rajaji* (Madras, 1968); T. V. Kalyanasundara Mudaliar, *Valkkaik Kurippukkal* (Madras, 1969), pp. 258–61.

notably the weaving magnate Pitti Thyagaraja Chetty) who resented the way Mylapore had in recent years turfed them out of the Madras Corporation, Pachaiyappa's and other places of influence in the City. Then there were professional men (like the journalist and doctor, T. M. Nair) who had once been associated with Egmore and who had also been baulked in City affairs by the Mylaporeans' growing monopoly of influence. Several families which spread widely in the public services but which had not quite the same influence as the Vembakkam Iyengars or Chetpat Iyers (the two leading families of Mylapore) were also interested in this new group. These included the families of Arcot Ramaswami Mudaliar of Chingleput and Madireddi Venkataratnam of Godavari. Next came several of the biggest estate-holders of the province, particularly the rajas of Pithapuram, Ramnad, Bobbili and Kalahasti. Many of them resented the newfound power of these lawyer-administrators who had once been their own agents, while some had been directly disturbed by the Mylaporeans' success in deploying the Dharmarakshana Sabha to interfere in the management of temples which they had once considered virtually their own property. Finally there was a scattering of local politicians of all sorts who had all resented the growing influence of Mylapore in a central administration which had increasing influence in the affairs of the districts. The banner around which these various groups clustered was the cause of the non-Brahman community.[55]

In its widest interpretation, the non-Brahman community encompassed the 98 per cent of the province's population who were not Brahmans. The Non-Brahman Manifesto, with which the movement was launched in December 1916, argued with convincing statistics that Brahmans were unnaturally prominent in the public services, and also in the University Senate, the High Court and all the superior political jobs open to Indians; besides this they ran the Congress and thus dominated public life. The manifesto traced the Brahmans' success to their ancient literary traditions and their consequent 'skill to pass examinations'. It went on to point out that the Brahman Congress and many Brahman public servants had now espoused the cause of Home Rule, and it pledged the loyalty of the non-Brahmans to the British connection.[56] In the next few years this communalist polemic was considerably broadened. An English paper, the *Justice*, and the Tamil *Dravidian* and Telugu *Andhraprakasika*, were started and

[55] Irschick, *Politics and Social Conflict*, ch. 2; Washbrook, 'Political Change in Madras Presidency', pp. 337–47.

[56] *Hindu* 20 Dec. 1916.

several non-Brahman conferences were held; these organs argued that there was a fundamental political conflict between Brahman and non-Brahman, that the non-Brahmans needed to organise to achieve social uplift and political power, and that government should take special steps to promote non-Brahman interests in education, in the services and in politics.[57]

The polemics of the movement had obvious appeal for educated non-Brahmans and particularly for those families which, like many Brahman families, looked on the public services and the literate professions as their traditional careers. They also had a wider appeal to men who were feeling the brunt of the stronger administrative machine, staffed at the subordinate levels largely by Brahmans. They also drew on a more general resentment of 'Brahman arrogance', particularly on the arrogance displayed by many Brahman officials certain of whom were wont to claim that only Brahmans were suitably equipped for public service and only Brahmans deserved special patronage by government.[58] More specifically the movement fitted well over certain latent social and cultural divisions in different parts of the province. In Tanjore for instance there were several large Brahman landholders above non-Brahman tenants;[59] in Tinnevelly, a well-established 'literate aristocracy' of non-Brahmans vied with the Brahmans for cultural leadership;[60] in the Kistna delta there was a smouldering quarrel between non-Brahmans of agriculturist castes who wished to study the sacred Sanskrit texts, and Brahman pundits who wished to maintain a closed shop in such matters.[61] But these disputes were essentially local. Over the province as a whole, the Brahmans were little in evidence as landholders,[62] outside the districts of the far south, most non-Brahmans accepted the Brahmans' cultural leadership as a necessary part of the social fabric or ignored them altogether; outside the Kistna deltas, many non-Brahmans studied the

[57] T. Varadarajulu Naidu, *The Justice Movement 1917* (Madras, 1932).

[58] See for instance V. Anuntha Row Pantulu, *An Old Man's Family Record and Reference* (Madras, 1916), pp. 50–3.

[59] A. Beteille, *Caste, Class and Power: changing patterns of stratification in a Tanjore village* (Berkeley and Los Angeles, 1965).

[60] H. R. Pate, *Madras District Gazetteers: Tinnevelly* (Madras, 1917), vol. I, pp. 106–7.

[61] N. G. Ranga, *Fight for Freedom* (Delhi, 1968), pp. 28–9; S. Raghavayya Chowdary, *Brahmanettara Vijayamu* (Kollur, 1925) and *Brahmanettara Sangha Dharasyan* (Bapatla, 1927).

[62] In 1918, the Government of Madras collected information on a putative electorate in which the main qualification was a landholding worth over Rs 30 in annual rental or revenue-paying value; it contained 36,199 Brahmans and 200,837 others; see table 7.

Vedas and no-one objected.[63] The social relationships between Brahmans and others varied from area to area; while there were a few Brahmans who were rich and powerful, the majority, if it is possible to generalise at all, were employed in occupations that were essentially menial – as cooks, scribes and religious functionaries – and could be purchased by the wealthy of other castes for a few coins or a broken coconut. The upsurge of non-Brahman polemic might win fleeting sympathy from men involved in many dissimilar quarrels, but there was no social basis for a lasting movement.

Thus it was that in these early years the idea of non-Brahmanism was open to a wide array of different ideological interpretations. By 1920, the propaganda in Madras City emphasised the need to overcome the 'political Brahman', the Mylapore archetype, while a non-Brahman election pamphlet in up-country Godavari saw in non-Brahmanism the cause of the landholder against the townsman and of the mofussil against the capital.[64] As non-Brahmanism quickly became embroidered with cultural interpretations of Madras society, these too were greatly varied; while one school argued that the Brahmans and non-Brahmans stemmed from common racial stock and that the division was a fiction of quite recent history,[65] another school (which was to dominate in the 1920s) argued that the non-Brahmans were the native peoples of the south while the Brahmans were the descendants of later invaders.[66]

Besides all of this, any attempt to attach social and cultural dimensions to the non-Brahman cause ran immediately up against a dilemma over popular attitudes to the Brahman. A good many of the non-Brahmans in south India accepted the Brahmanical code and Brahmanical behaviour as the model of ritual purity. Many articulated their wish to rise up the social scale by adjusting their customs and habits to those practised by Brahmans, and many expressed their own, exalted view of their status by demanding to be called Brahmans.[67] Even for those not so greatly struck by Brahmanical manners – and

63 M. Singer, *When a Great Tradition Modernises* (London, 1972), p. 108.

64 P. Govindarow Naidu, *The Legislative Council Elections (1920): a critical study of party programmes* (Rajahmundry, 1920).

65 M. Venkataratnam, *The Non-Brahmin Origin of the Brahmins* (Madras, 1922) and *Reform of the Brahmins* (Madras, 1924).

66 J. S. Kannappar, *Cuttirarkal Yar?* (Madras, 1926); J. N. Ramanathan, *Akatu: Tiya Acarankal* (Madras, 1926).

67 For instance the Saurashtras wanted to be called Saurashtra Brahmans, and the Kammalans wanted to be called Viswa Brahmans. For the confusions that the Justicite campaign caused to some non-Brahmans see the statement by P. D. A. Anduperumal Pillai in *Hindu* 1 May 1920.

there were many of these in the south, particularly among prosperous agricultural communities[68] – there remained a fundamental ambivalence in any social or cultural opposition to the Brahman. Were those who opposed the Brahmans asserting that the position occupied by the Brahmans was irrelevant and thus worthy only of criticism or neglect, or were they arguing that they, rather than the Brahmans, should take over the position of social and ritual pre-eminence? These were two very different, and in many ways diametrically opposed, views. One appealed to those who wanted drastic reform in south Indian society, and this view found its most fervent expression in the late 1920s and early 1930s when the rejection of Brahmanism by the followers of the Self-Respect movement veered over into rejection of religion.[69] The other view was held by many of the scholarly and highly respected subcastes of Vellalas who believed that they were the true custodians of south Indian culture. Naturally enough, the latter looked rather askance at the iconoclasm of the former.[70]

The Justice party never faced up to these dilemmas, and its attempts to erect a social and political philosophy often seemed confused and self-contradictory. In the period 1916–20, this did not help the non-Brahman cause to develop into a mass movement. Its newspapers never gained a wide readership and were constantly in financial difficulties.[71] Few branch associations were formed and even some of these had disappeared before the legislature elections in 1920. Local politicians who tried to gain support for the cause amongst the rustics of Coimbatore district were run out of villages by farmers who resented propaganda which was disrespectful towards their local Brahmans.[72]

There was very little groundswell underneath the non-Brahman cause. As will be seen later, there was even very little evidence of a widespread demand among non-Brahmans for places in the public services. The root of the non-Brahman cause of 1916–20 was a campaign, fought inside the narrow world of City politics, to oust the overmighty subjects of Mylapore. The Justice party, as the non-

68 Beck, *Peasant Society in Konku*, pp. 8–17.

69 Kannappar, *Cuttirarkal Yar?*; Ramanathan, *Akatu*; see the burning of Hindu texts at a Self-Respect meeting, *Justice* 12 June 1928.

70 T. M. Arumuga Pillai, *Cuyamariyataikku Or Cuddukkos* (Madras, 1929).

71 A. C. Parthasarathi Naidu to P. Kesava Pillai, 9 Oct. 1919, Kesava Pillai papers NMML.

72 K. V. Srinivasa Iyer to P. S. Sivaswami Iyer, 18 June 1917, Sivaswami Iyer papers NAI.

Brahman faction soon became known, had a structure and a network of contacts shaped much the same as that of Mylapore, and had a similar set of political aims; it wanted to get the ear of government and then to profit from the coming devolution of power. As a contemporary pamphlet noted, it was only someone ignorant of the political circumstances of the time who would take the cause at its face value:

> Did you notice the great enthusiasm of the man to this non-Brahmin movement? I tell you, the whole thing looks very suspicious. I cannot for the very life of me, feel this wonderful enthusiasm, and why should he. Don't you think there is something selfish behind him? I think that he is trying to grind his own axe. He would have a position as the leading star among the non-Brahmins, and he would use that position in giving recommendation letters to his relatives and friends.[73]

The banner of non-Brahmanism was chosen for good reasons. Of course the Mylaporean leaders were Brahmans but this in itself did not mean their opponents should present themselves as non-Brahmans. These opponents were not, after all, objecting to the circumstances of the Mylaporeans' birth, and they had in recent years assailed Mylapore specifically as a 'clique' and then generically as 'lawyers'. What is more, most of the men who were ranged behind Mylapore and who profited from Mylapore's position were not Brahmans. Two factors made the cry of non-Brahmanism so apposite in 1916. Firstly, it had a potential appeal to nearly all the population and thus was a useful, uncontroversial rallying cry at a time of uncertainty about the political future. Secondly, it allied the Justice leaders with men in the Indian Civil Service itself.

Certain senior officers in the Madras I.C.S. were at least as worried as any non-Brahman about the growing influence of Brahmans within the governmental system.[74] Since some way back in the nineteenth century, the Madras Government had been trying to prevent the build-up of kin and communal networks in the public services. When the administration was centralised and more senior posts opened up to Indians, the problems of service recruitment became more important. Indeed the statistics on the public services on which the non-Brahman leaders based their 1916 Manifesto had been prepared by a senior I.C.S. officer for submission to the 1913 commission on the public services,[75] and two senior officers in the Madras Secretariat

[73] S. K. N., *Non-Brahmin Letters* (Madras, 1915), p. 80.

[74] Irschick, *Politics and Social Conflict*, pp. 96–117.

[75] *Royal Commission on the Public Services in India*, vol. III, pp. 85–133.

were actively involved in the foundation of the non-Brahman organisation in 1916.[76] In a wider sense, the whole idea of a caste-based political movement reflected a recent trend in Madras Government thinking. The early Censuses, and the work of the many government officers for whom amateur anthropology was a fashionable hobby, had done a lot to establish caste as a convenient means of dividing up the population of India. As administration became more complex, government was greatly in need of convenient categories into which it could divide the mass of its subjects. In the mid-nineteenth century, Fort St George had foresworn any use of caste as an administrative category, yet by the early decades of the twentieth century education grants, public works efforts, jobs in the services, places in local government and seats in the Legislative Council had all been subjected to considerations of caste.[77] A political demand for justice for the non-Brahmans appealed to the conscience, the fears and the administrative mentality of the Madras Government.

The years 1916–20 in Madras City witnessed a complex series of manoeuvres between the various groups who all wished to stand forth as the leaders of the province when the benefits of the reformed constitution were released. Radical posturing and all-India alliances enabled the Nationalists of *The Hindu* group to drum the Mylaporeans out of the Congress by 1918. In early 1920, however, just as they were preparing to use the Congress name and organisation to fight the first elections to the new legislatures, they in turn lost control of the provincial Congress to their erstwhile allies from the mofussil, who used exactly the same tactics that the Nationalists themselves had used against the Mylaporeans; that is, they forced the Congress to adopt a policy to which their enemies could not subscribe while at the same time pursuing their own real goals. Rajagopalachari, in alliance with Gandhi in the all-India forum, succeeded in committing the Congress to a policy of non-co-operation with government, a policy which included boycott of the elections and a resolve to undertake a real campaign of agitation. The Nationalists had to quit the Congress or they had to stay in it and ignore the elections; either way it was, for them, a step into the political wilderness.[78]

[76] Washbrook, 'Political Change in Madras Presidency', pp. 341–3, 355–9.

[77] Washbrook, 'The development of caste organisation in south India 1880 to 1925', and C. J. Baker, 'Figures and Facts: Madras Government Statistics 1880–1940', in Baker and Washbrook, *Political Institutions*.

[78] See the provincial conference at Tinnevelly, *Hindu* 22 and 23 June 1920; the

The battle for the leadership of the province under the dyarchy constitution was thus left to the Mylaporeans and Justicites. The Justice party attacked with a demand for the reservation of seats for non-Brahmans in the new Legislative Council. The demand itself was not really relevant. This was clearly shown soon after the Justice leaders had announced the demand, since in the elections to the old Legislative Council non-Brahmans won an astounding victory.[79] The Government of India sent down an officer to investigate the problem and he could make out no reason why the people who patently commanded most of the resources which would be important at elections and who were already strongly represented in local boards and the old Legislative Council, should ask for protection in the new electorate.[80] As a tactical weapon, however, it was superb. Behind the demand for the reservation of seats was a request that government should recognise the Justicites as the leaders of the non-Brahman majority in the province, and should admit that the non-Brahmans deserved special considerations. In this way the Justice leaders would become the main channels of government patronage. It was in this spirit that the Justicites conducted the agitation. They regularly raised the level of their demand to prevent the government from arranging a compromise between them and its old Mylaporean favourites.[81] They concentrated their energies on convincing the British government of the rightness of their claims by making appeals in Madras, in Calcutta and in London, and spent far less time organising support for their movement in the province.[82] By 1920 they had won a good measure of success. They had secured the reservation of seats, had succeeded in promoting the interests of several of their allies in the public services and in local government, and had even been asked

Madras Congress meeting, following Gandhi's visit to Madras, *Hindu* 25 Aug. 1920; the reaction in Madras following the special Calcutta Congress session, *Hindu* 23 Sept. 1920; and several confused letters in the Satyamurthi papers for 1920.

[79] G.O. 122 (Miscellaneous Legislative) 17 Oct. 1919 MRO.

[80] Meston to Willingdon, 8 Mar. 1920, GOI Reforms Franchise General A 31–43 May 1920 NAI; *Hindu* (w) 25 Mar. 1920; G.O. 122 (Miscellaneous Legislative) 17 Oct. 1919 MRO. In every 'general' constituency, one seat was reserved for a non-Brahman. The rule had to be invoked only once, and this was not in favour of a non-Brahman caste Hindu but a Buddhist. It occurred at the 1926 elections in South Kanara when the only candidates for two seats were two Brahmans and a Buddhist, and the latter was thus returned automatically in the reserved seat.

[81] GOI Reforms Franchise Deposit 7 Feb. 1920 NAI.

[82] Irschick, *Politics and Social Conflict*, pp. 137–42, 148–70.

to suggest suitable non-Brahman candidates for the I.C.S. examinations.[83]

The last stage of the battle came at the first elections to the new Legislative Council held in the last weeks of 1920. While Mylaporeans, Justicites and Nationalists had been manoeuvring in the City, they had also made occasional forays into the districts to recruit supporters and potential electoral allies. There was still a vast gap between the politics of the City – its factional divisions and its polemics – and those of the districts. Since the leaders from the centre were interested in recruiting enough supporters to establish before government their claim to leadership, they dished out party tickets to almost anyone who would receive them.[84] Since local men wished to appear to have a wide range of contacts among people of importance in the capital, so that they could impress the electors that they would be useful delegates to the provincial forum, they accepted party nominations from all and sundry. The result was a chaos of shifting allegiances. Local satraps cordially welcomed any Madras leader on tour, and accepted his gift of a party ticket, and when he had left they got ready to meet his opponent. One Tanjore magnate, for instance, who planned to stand for the provincial Legislative Council angled for an electoral alliance with a prominent Mylapore man who was standing for the all-India Legislative Assembly from the same constituency, while at the same time he fished for a Justice party ticket; he found however that the Mylaporean was not interested in his help, and that the Justice party had dished out more tickets in Tanjore than there were seats. Judging that his chances of election were slight he announced his sudden conversion to the cause of Gandhian Non-co-operation and withdrew his candidature.[85] Such electoral grasshopping was common.

In the actual conduct of elections in the districts, the polemical battles of Madras City, particularly the quarrel between Brahman and non-Brahman, mattered very little. The party labels did impose certain restrictions; the Mylapore man running in Tanjore was advised by his campaign manager not to publish lists of the prominent magnates in

[83] Diaries of K. V. Reddi Naidu, entry for 14 Aug. 1923.

[84] When Pitti Thyagaraja Chetty visited Salem, 'there was a discussion on choosing candidates for the new councils ... Mr P. T. Chettiar [explained] that it was not necessary that only persons professing the "Justice" principle should be returned to the councils.' *Hindu* 11 June 1920.

[85] P. R. Natesa Iyer to P. S. Sivaswami Iyer, 22 May 1920 and 31 Oct. 1920; M. D. Subramaniam to P. S. Sivaswami Iyer, 20 Oct. 1920; K. S. Venkatarama Iyer to P. S. Sivaswami Iyer, 7 Nov. 1920; Sivaswami Iyer papers NAI.

the constituency who had pledged him their support at the polls, as it might embarrass some of the non-Brahmans: 'While these are quite willing to render every sort of help practically in promoting our cause,' the manager reported, 'it is easy to understand that some at least among them might feel it very inconvenient and indelicate to be signatories.'[86] Despite this sort of sensitivity, few local politicians were really cramped by ideologies or by party loyalties. Many men who had been quite closely associated with the Congress before it slid into Non-co-operation and election-boycott in summer 1920, found it easy to cut their contacts and stand at the elections anyway. These included the two men who had organised the Congress provincial conference in June 1920, and ten others who had been appointed district organisers for the Congress ten months before.[87]

It was not after all an election of issues. As one City leader wrote to a friend: 'People know little about parties and what it is all about that people are quarrelling. Moderates and Extremists are, to the many, unintelligible terms.'[88] Elections were not fought from the hustings; in fact very few speeches were made in the district contests and almost no issues were raised. In the Tanjore constituency the only election promise was an undertaking to get land taxes reduced,[89] which was hardly a divisive issue in an electorate where the franchise qualification was based on the payment of such taxes. C. R. Reddy, an intellectual and political leader from Chittoor, observed shortly after the elections: 'The general politics of press and platform hardly affect the voting. The landlord, the merchant, and the lawyer have their clientele, and every man has his tribe, clan or creed behind him who follow with sheepish fidelity. In this medievalism, political conviction counts for little.'[90]

In any event it did not take very many votes to win an election. A million and a quarter qualified for the franchise (generally by paying over Rs 10 of land revenue in the rural areas, or over Rs 3 in municipal taxes in the towns) and these were divided into twenty-five

[86] M. D. Subramaniam to P. S. Sivaswami Iyer, 8 June 1920, Sivaswami Iyer papers NAI.

[87] The two were N. A. V. Somasundaram Pillai and T. N. Sivagnanam Mudaliar, both of whom became staunch Justicites in the Legislative Council after 1920. For the Congress election organisation before the boycott, see *Hindu* 17 Nov. 1919.

[88] T. R. Venkatarama Sastri to P. S. Sivaswami Iyer, 23 May 1920, Sivaswami Iyer papers NAI.

[89] Publicity Bureau to P. S. Sivaswami Iyer, 30 Sept. 1920; S. Parasurama Iyer to P. S. Sivaswami Iyer, 26 Nov. 1920; Sivaswami Iyer papers NAI.

[90] C. R. Reddy, 'Dyarchy and after', *Indian Review*, XXIII (May 1922), 296.

district constituencies. The turn-out in the rural areas was very low, averaging 23·8 per cent throughout the province, and thus three to four thousand votes were enough for victory.[91] The best strategy for a candidate was to win the support of men who could command many votes in a locality – managers of important temples, successful lawyers and businessmen, big landlords, the leaders of local government and petty officialdom.[92]

The election in Madras City was a rather different affair. Here the result might influence the Governor, Lord Willingdon, who after the elections would have to nominate three ministers from amongst those elected. By May 1920, six months before the polls, he reported that aspirants for ministerial office 'buzz round me like bees'.[93] Willingdon appreciated the talents of the Mylaporeans, indeed he had been thoroughly charmed by the leading light of Mylapore, C. P. Ramaswami Iyer, an immensely wealthy lawyer from one of the best Mylapore families. The Justicite campaign, however, had already forced Willingdon to admit that he could not hand the ministry to Mylapore. Yet he still clung to the idea of a ministry of all the talents, and the election result in the City would he hoped provide a useful gauge of party strength.

In fact, party organisation in the City was little better than in the districts. Ten people met in committee to choose the Justice candidates, and when they had selected four of their own number, two of those remaining defected and stood against the party. Moreover, the Justice party leaders did not seem worried about the past allegiances of their nominees. Their candidate for the Central Legislative Assembly seat had recently financed a Congress non-Brahman organisation which had been set up specifically to rival the Justice party. He was also an orthodox devotee given to patronising Brahmans on a vast scale.[94] Another member of the Congress non-Brahman organisation was offered the support of the Justice party in the special commerce constituency.[95] The candidates were generally selected for their personal wealth and influence, rather than their allegiance or work for the party, because in the City, as in the districts, election campaigns were for the most part conducted behind closed doors. Thus O. Kandaswami

[91] *Hindu* 23 Dec. 1920.

[92] For a fuller discussion of the legislature elections see below, end of ch. 2.

[93] Willingdon to Montagu, 23 May 1920, Willingdon papers vol. IV IOL.

[94] *Hindu* 29 Apr. 1926.

[95] S. Venkatachelam Chetty to P. Kesava Pillai, 14 June 1920, Kesava Pillai papers NMML.

Chetty, one of the Justice party's most assiduous workers and publicists, was turned down in favour of his half-brother, an influential merchant with control over temples and markets in the City who could afford to spend Rs 11,000 on his campaign.[96] Thus too, Pitti Thyagaraja Chetty the Justice party leader was offended to hear that the party had been displaying election posters in public places, since his tactic was to rely on the personal influence he had earned through a long career in the Corporation and in the political life of the City.[97] Yet there was more of a public campaign in the City than in the districts, with several meetings, bands of volunteer helpers and numerous articles in the press. Indeed, the campaign became quite violent. After his meetings had been disturbed and his campaign-manager had been beaten up, C. P. Ramaswami Iyer, the leading Mylapore candidate, took to carrying a pistol and brandishing it at election meetings. The campaign also became expensive. C. P. Ramaswami Iyer confessed that he had spent Rs 29,500 on his electioneering (whereas the average expenditure in a district contest was around Rs 1,000).[98]

The result in the City was a virtual draw. Thyagaraja Chetty headed the poll, followed very closely by C. P. Ramaswami Iyer. The other two seats were taken by the Justicite Tanicachalam Chetty, and Dr U. Rama Rao, a Brahman doctor from the West Coast. Accordingly the Governor summoned Thyagaraja Chetty and suggested that he form a ministry in coalition with the men of Mylapore. By now, however, the Justice leaders were experienced in the art of refusing to compromise with their Mylaporean enemies, and Thyagaraja Chetty refused to have anything to do with a coalition. The Justicites knew they were poised for victory. Thyagaraja Chetty and his lieutenants pointed out that fifty-seven of the seventy-four seats in general constituencies had been won by non-Brahmans, claimed all these were Justice party members, and persuaded the Governor to give them the ministry.[99]

It was a remarkable manoeuvre and by the time others began to point out the fallacies in the Justice leaders' arguments it was too late. A non-Brahman correspondent of *The Hindu* suggested that only fifteen of those elected could really be called Justicites and the editor concluded that 'Sir P. Thyagaraja Chetty was consulted as leader of a

[96] *Hindu* 29 Apr. 1926.

[97] Interview with K. V. Gopalaswamy (who was a Justice party worker in the City at these elections), Hyderabad July 1971.

[98] *Hindu* 6 Oct. 1920; A. Prakash, *Sir C.P.* (Madras, 1939), p. 35; for election expenses see *Indian Statutory Commission*, vol. VI, p. 339.

[99] Letter from Thyagaraja Chetty in *Hindu* 15 Dec. 1920.

party with the generality of the members of which he had no opportunity of consultation or conference'.[100] A non-Brahman barrister in the City doubted whether the Justice party would command a majority in the Council,[101] and the Madras Secretariat, after receiving reports from the District Collectors, calculated that sixteen of the M.L.C.s (Members of the Legislative Council) were really Justice party members, while most of them should be described as moderates or independents.[102]

These observations were technically accurate but they ignored the fact that political allegiances in such a precarious and rapidly changing political world depended more on opportunities than on antecedents. Thyagaraja Chetty and his Justicite cohorts had, it is true, won victory through diplomacy rather than through popular acclaim, but that was past history. What was now important was that once Willingdon had given Thyagaraja Chetty a free hand to compose a Justice ministry, the Justice leadership became the main channel of government patronage in the province. Mylapore was not totally eclipsed; throughout the 1920s Willingdon, and his successors in Government House, put Mylapore men into places on the Governor's Executive Council and into the important post of Advocate-General, and C. P. Ramaswami Iyer remained one of the most influential men in Madras. Nevertheless it was the Legislative Council and the ministerial portfolios which now became the main centres of political life. Political labels were now decided by a wholly new standard. Thus many different men, from diverse political backgrounds, now found it convenient to appear as Justicites. Even some of those who assumed important positions in the party and in the ministry from 1921 had little or no connection with the Justice clique before then. A. Subbarayalu Reddiar, the man whom Thyagaraja Chetty nominated to lead the Justice ministry, appeared as a 'moderate' in the Secretariat's post-election investigation of the background of M.L.C.s. A. P. Patro, who was to become the Justice party's chief organiser in 1921 and a minister after Subbarayalu Reddiar fell ill, was in the same list called a 'Liberal' which correctly denoted his association with the National Liberal League, an organisation set up and run by the leaders of Mylapore.[103] T. N. Sivagnanam Pillai, who became a Justicite minister

[100] *Hindu* 15 Dec. 1920.

[101] *Hindu* 17 Jan. 1921.

[102] See the notes on the background and affiliation of Madras M.L.C.s in GOI Reforms Franchise B 34–99 Mar. 1921 NAI.

[103] GOI Reforms Franchise B 34–99 Mar. 1921 NAI.

in 1923, had helped to organise a major Congress conference in June 1920. Dr P. Subbaroyan, who had been first an associate of Rajagopalachari and later a campaigner for the Congress Nationalists, became council secretary to the Justicite chief minister, the raja of Panagal. Despite these very recent allegiances, there was no doubt where these men's loyalties lay after 1920. 'The political party in India', as one observer noted, 'is the child of practical opportunism.'[104]

DYARCHY AND THE DISTRIBUTION OF POWER

The Legislative Council which the Montagu–Chelmsford reforms set up helped to create an arena of politics which included the entire province. Between 1880 and 1920, the increasing centralisation of the administration had focussed more political attention on provincial affairs, but there had been few avenues by which men from the districts could gain access to the politics of the province. It was this that allowed Mylapore to become so powerful, as most demands for a voice in matters of provincial administration had had to be funnelled through Mylapore. The 1909 Legislative Councils had been primarily advisory bodies which wielded little power. Their elected members were loudest in criticism of their lack of control over finance, their legislative impotence, and their subjection to the Governor's veto. Kasturiranga Iyengar called them 'pageants of mimic power'.[105] In the Montagu–Chelmsford Legislative Council, by contrast, there were ninety-two elected members. Each district sent two or three members, while thirteen Muslims, five Christians, six landholders, a European, a planter, five representatives of commerce and one representative of the University were chosen by special electorates. To these government added around twenty-three nominated members. In many different ways the members of the Council helped to bring the politics of the periphery into the centre. Firstly, government looked to them for information and advice on specific local matters. Secondly, government handed over to the Council particular thorny problems which arose in the distribution of provincial resources. A notable example of this in the 1920s was the question of siting the headquarters of the new Andhra University. Twenty of the thirty-three members of the Select Committee on the Andhra University Bill wrote

[104] N. Subramania Aiyar, 'Party politics in India', *Indian Review*, XXI (June 1920), 369–71.

[105] *Hindu* (w) 28 Dec. 1917.

dissenting minutes advocating different towns, and it was two years before the matter was finally settled.[106] Thirdly, the Council debated a wide range of issues, not only matters covered by the ministers' portfolios but also 'reserved subjects' which officially came under the sole command of the Governor and his Council. Fourthly, individual mofussil members sought influence with ministers and with other members of the government and worked to build up their stature as provincial leaders. Lastly, local agitations and disputes were sometimes aired in the Council and thus became confused with provincial matters. In 1925, for example, a feud between two factions of Reddi magnates from Anantapur district, which had been going on for some thirty years, became a provincial cause célèbre, when the lawyer of one faction tried to use his position as an M.L.C. to present the feud as a battle of Brahman against non-Brahman and thus persuade the ministry to intervene on his side.[107]

The ministers were the chief arbiters in this new arena and, as will be seen later, they had considerable patronage at their disposal. All the M.L.C.s were men of considerable local standing; they had been elected because of their range of contacts and command of resources. While some had sought election simply for the prestige which it conferred, most had positions to protect and causes to promote. They were concerned to fortify their local position, to promote their careers in provincial and national affairs, and to serve their constituency in general and the interests which had ensured their election in particular. Few had gone to the expense of getting elected merely to come to Madras and sit on the opposition benches. Few at the outset wished to be stamped as enemies of those who held the keys to power and patronage. Thus no ministry had difficulty in putting together a majority in the Council, or in commanding respect from the people of the province as a whole. The Justice leaders held their annual party confederation in Madras in January 1921, just as the new M.L.C.s were arriving for the first session of the Council and sixty-two of them attended the meeting.[108] By the time dyarchy had been in operation for two years, C. R. Reddy noted how quickly the ministers had become, like the idols in a temple, all-powerful and apparently unchallengeable:

[106] GOI Education Health and Lands Education 41 and 41B Feb. 1926 NAI; K. V. Narayana Rao, 'The Emergence of Andhra Pradesh', Ph.D. thesis (Madras, 1966), pp. 241–7.

[107] *Dravidian* 29 May 1925 NNR; *Hindu* 26 and 29 May 1925, 5 and 20 June 1925.

[108] *Justice* 10 Jan. 1921.

Eagerly do Associations, Communities and Societies desire to approach ministers to get this or that item included in their policies. Up to a limit there is nothing undignified in this; but a universal rush to Ministerial antechambers is hardly a sign of democratic self-respect. 'Seeing people' is a fine art in this climate; and the man who wants to get on goes on a pilgrimage to those that have; and the man who has got on would be offended if ceremonial visits are not paid to him and the proper quantity of incense burnt... Now that autocratic terror is over, people should give rest to their knees and not crawl so very much.[109]

The Justice leaders held the strings of ministerial power for all but a few months of the duration of dyarchy. The Justice party then was not so much an association of men with common ideas or common political interests as the meeting ground for all those petitioning for ministerial patronage. S. Kumaraswami Reddiar, a Tinnevelly magnate and leader in local government who was to become a Justicite minister in the 1930s, said at the party conference in 1927: 'Pretensions apart we are all job-hunters – our traducers more than ourselves; nobody need to be ashamed to confess it and be frightened by the sneers of interested critics engaged in the same pursuit though not by the same honourable and open means.'[110]

Thyagaraja Chetty considered that he was too old and too engrossed in the affairs of the Madras Corporation to fulfil the duties of a minister, and thus he nominated three others. A. Subbarayalu Reddiar, who took the education portfolio and led the ministry, was a landowner, businessman and local politician from South Arcot. P. Ramarayaningar, who was shortly to inherit the title of raja of Panagal, took over command of local self-government. He was a minor member of the Kalahasti zamindari family from Chittoor district, and, as all the prominent zamindar families of Velama caste had become linked together through marriage alliances, was thus related in some fashion to many of the great magnates of the Andhra districts – the raja of Venkatagiri in Nellore, the raja of Pithapuram in Godavari, the raja of Mirzapuram in Kistna and the raja of Bobbili in Vizagapatam. The third minister was K. V. Reddi Naidu, a lawyer and landholder from Ellore, who belonged to a prominent family with a long history in the public services. All three had figured prominently in the manoeuvres of the past four years. When Subbarayalu Reddiar fell

[109] Reddy, 'Dyarchy and after', p. 298.

[110] N. N. Mitra, *Indian Annual Register 1927* (Calcutta, 1927), vol. II, pp. 318–19.

ill a few months later, the raja of Panagal took over as chief minister, while A. P. Patro, a lawyer, landowner and crusading advocate of progressive farming, took over as education minister.

The ministers could feel sure that the exercise of their new power would not be impeded by opposition from other members of the Legislative Council. On most matters they could rely on the European official members, the nominated members, and the M.L.C.s who were anxious for patronage, to give them a majority. Yet their position depended, as had the Mylaporeans', on their ability to deliver the goods. Now that the Justice leaders had entered the promised land of ministerships, their followers expected a steady flow of milk and honey. The powers of the ministers under dyarchy, however, were not as clear-cut as had been expected. There was a long and impressive list of 'transferred subjects' in the ministers' portfolios, including education, health, development, local government, excise, transport, agriculture and industry, but the ministers were not necessarily in full control of these subjects. The departmental secretaries, who were senior I.C.S. officers, continued to run many of the departments exactly as they had before and it was difficult for the ministers to interfere. Besides this, the 'reserved subjects', those that remained in control of the Governor and his Executive Council, included finance. This of course was crucial. The Legislative Council was allowed to debate the budget each year and to pass token cuts, but these were immediately revoked by the Governor and after some years the budget debate ceased to be important. Meanwhile, finance could be used to wield quite a close control over particular actions of the ministers. Schemes in education, public health, development and any other of the matters in the ministerial portfolios could be, and were, vetoed on financial grounds.[111] Moreover, Madras was in its usual condition of financial crisis. The financial settlement which had accompanied the Montagu–Chelmsford reforms had been particularly swingeing on Madras. The province had to find 348 lakhs of rupees to help balance the deficit in the Central Government brought about by the new division of revenue-heads, and to find 17 per cent of the centre's annual deficit thereafter. Willingdon complained incessantly that the depredations of the Government of India were jeopardising the chances of working dyarchy satisfactorily, as the ministers sometimes found it difficult to justify their existence.[112] While this

[111] See the views of Panagal and Patro in *Views of Local Governments on the Working of the Reforms, dated 1924*, pp. 101–17.

[112] Willingdon repeatedly complained to Delhi about 'my three-and-a-half crores';

was an exaggeration, the development minister, K. V. Reddi Naidu, was privately lampooned as the 'minister without portfolio'[113] because he had insufficient funds to develop anything. He laboured to pass a State Aid to Industries Act which set up excellent machinery for passing government loans and grants to Indian industries, but the act never had a chance to operate properly since Madras lacked the funds to make loans or grants.

Willingdon tried to satisfy the ministers' desire for real authority by arranging that both halves of the government – ministers and Executive Councillors – met together in the Cabinet to consider issues arising under both the 'reserved' and the 'transferred' subjects. Willingdon broadcast that this Cabinet was a 'Happy Family',[114] but before long this family was riven with internal feuds as individual ministers, Indian and I.C.S. members of the Executive Council fought over the rather small stock of power and patronage. In 1923, C. P. Ramaswami Iyer was appointed the Law Member of the Executive Council. When Lord Willingdon was succeeded by Lord Goschen a few months later, Ramaswami Iyer capitalised on the new man's ignorance of Madras affairs and eased himself into the role of the Governor's chief adviser. For the next few years Ramaswami Iyer was probably the most influential man in Madras affairs, and when he opened a speech in the legislature with the words, 'My Government of which H.E. Lord Goschen is the head', many believed that this was exactly how Ramaswami Iyer himself saw it.[115] Ramaswami Iyer's position naturally caused the hackles to rise in Justice ministerial circles, but it also enraged Sir Charles Todhunter, a rather stiff-backed civilian who was now First Member of the Executive. 'The Todhunters', noted the third minister Reddi Naidu, 'hate C.P.R. [Ramaswami Iyer] like anything. They think, at least Lady Todhunter thinks, that [Ramaswami Iyer] is the greatest favourite of H.E. even in preference to Sir Charles.'[116] The position was further complicated by feuds between the ministers. The raja of Panagal, soon after he became chief minister, was anxious to drop K. V. Reddi Naidu from the ministry. To do so he allied with the other

for one such complaint see Willingdon to Montagu, 11 Feb. 1922, Willingdon papers vol. IV IOL.

113 K. Iswara Dutt, *Sparks and Fumes* (Madras, 1929), pp. 88–9.

114 MLCP, XIX (18 Aug. 1924), 128; *Hindu* (w) 1 Feb. 1923.

115 A. Ramaswami Mudaliar (ed.), *Mirror of the Year: being a collection of the leading articles in 'Justice', 1927* (Madras, 1928), p. 115.

116 Diaries of K. V. Reddi Naidu, entry for 26 May 1923.

minister, Patro, and with Todhunter; the latter had already quarrelled with Reddi Naidu over the responsibility for certain important appointments, and all Panagal had to do to win Sir Charles' support was to promise to immortalise his name on the next public building in Madras.[117]

These were court politics with a vengeance. The Governor appointed ministers and Executive Councillors alike and so was the ultimate source of power; precedence in these higher levels of government depended largely on influence with the Governor, and on manoeuvres within the Cabinet circle. Reddi Naidu, who was quietly dropped in 1923 in favour of a man who it was rumoured had lent Panagal Rs 30,000,[118] complained bitterly about the style of politics: 'Intrigue seems the only way of success. Everybody seems to indulge in it. What for? To get power, to get more influence, to please H.E., to be known to have a great place in H.E.'s heart.'[119] Thus despite the paraphernalia of the legislature and party labels, these politics were cut very much in the same style as in Mylapore's heyday. Thus too, the ministers, like the Mylaporean Congressmen in the 1910s, were soon pressing for more power. Most of the important issues which troubled the Madras Government and the Legislative Council in the early 1920s, although they may have begun as issues of principle, soon boiled down to struggles over the allocation of power within the government.

The chief legislative interests were land revenue and irrigation, both matters of considerable import to the province as a whole. Both issues became pawns in the contest between different parts of the government. It was the Secretariat which first proposed legislation on irrigation. Problems in the administration of irrigation works had previously been resolved by judicial decisions; the cumulative result of different court decisions in different districts was often chaotic. Ever since 1856, Fort St George had been thinking of putting this right by bringing irrigation law under a statute. In the war years, a ruling in the High Court on a vitally important irrigation problem went against government and, anticipating that far more problems would arise when it embarked on new schemes of irrigation development such as those planned at Pykara and Mettur, government prepared a bill and introduced it into the Legislative Council in 1922. This bill gave government full rights over irrigation water, even rain.

[117] *Ibid.* entries for 18 Mar. 1923, 5 and 11 May 1923.
[118] *Ibid.* entry for 24 Nov. 1923.
[119] *Ibid.* entry for 26 May 1923.

But just as Government was concerned to increase its power over matters of irrigation, so were the ministers and Legislative Councillors. The Council rejected the bill on the first attempt, and when government tried again a few months later, it inserted several significant amendments, including one that awarded the Council all power to make the rules under the act. The Governor took the bill back, rewrote the clauses savaged by the M.L.C.s and sent it back; inevitably it was thrown out.[120] The land revenue debate followed a similar course although this time it was started by the M.L.C.s who, in one of the first motions of the first session, demanded Council control over land revenue matters, in particular the resettlement rates. The Secretariat quietly composed a bill which, instead of giving the Council the power they had demanded, did in fact the exact opposite; it merely encoded all existing rules of revenue administration and thus confirmed executive control. The Council threw it out. Two years later, government tried again with exactly the same result. The M.L.C.s then wrote a bill which gave the Council powers to fix assessment rates, and the Secretariat sent it up to the Government of India for the inevitable rejection. In 1927 government had a last try to pass its codifying bill, and again it was unceremoniously rejected.[121]

The most prominent and most enduring of all these battles within the government, however, centred around the public services. Service jobs were always prestigious, while some were also lucrative and many conveyed real power. The Justice leaders had launched their campaign in 1916 with a demand for changes in service recruitment which would favour non-Brahmans. In the 1920s, the ranks of the party still included representatives of several non-Brahman service families, and it was hardly surprising that in August 1921 members of the Council tabled seven motions asking for steps to secure representation for non-Brahmans in the public services in proportion to their share in the population as a whole.[122] The issue was raised in almost every session of the Council, and was further trumpeted in the columns of the *Justice* and the *Dravidian*. The services were thus a prime issue for the Justice leaders, and the history of that issue gives many insights into the nature of the non-Brahman campaign and the nature of ministerial power.

120 *Hindu* 1 Feb. 1923, 20 Aug. 1925, 14 Jan. 1926, 2 Sept. 1926; Willingdon to Peel, 4 Feb. 1923 and 1 Apr. 1923, Willingdon papers vol. IV IOL; G.O. 47 (Law Legislative) 7 Feb. 1923 MRO.

121 *Hindu* 3 Apr. 1924, 25 May 1926, 3 Mar. 1927.

122 MLCP, II (5 Aug. 1921), 424–36.

TABLE 3. *Education and community*

		1889–90	1910–11	1920–1	1025–6	1930–1	1935–6
Arts colleges	Total students	2,688	3,741	7,580	12,258	12,419	11,627
	% Brahman	76·7	68·5	64·2	53·7	50·5	45·4
	% Non-Brahman	12·5	20·1	21·9	32·3	33·3	34·0
	% Muslim	1·6	1·6	1·8	2·8	3·4	4·3
	% Christian	7·6	9·9	10·8	9·6	11·2	13·7
Professional colleges	Total students	304	890	1,784	2,218	1,966	2,465
	% Brahman	46·4	67·2	69·6	58·8	47·8	46·0
	% Non-Brahman	27·0	18·5	19·5	25·9	33·7	31·9
	% Muslim	1·0	1·0	1·9	3·3	3·8	4·6
	% Christian	9·2	8·1	7·6	10·3	12·5	12·7
Secondary schools	Total students	68,370	152,413	161,796	176,144	198,074	202,902
	% Brahman	31·2	34·3	37·8	30·8	29·5	28·8
	% Non-Brahman	40·7	42·4	45·1	48·8	48·0	48·1
	% Muslim	4·9	5·5	5·1	5·6	6·0	6·1
	% Christian	14·4	13·8	10·8	12·7	12·3	12·8
Primary schools	Total students	381,916	922,911	1,492,666	2,213,965	2,638,108	2,867,000
	% Brahman	11·8	9·0	7·6	6·2	5·8	6·3
	% Non-Brahman	73·0	72·9	64·5	64·2	63·5	62·1
	% Muslim	7·8	9·7	10·0	10·4	10·6	10·9
	% Christian	7·0	7·6	7·6	7·2	7·2	7·3

SOURCE: *Report on Public Instruction in the Madras Presidency* (annual) for the years given; tables entitled: 'Return of colleges, schools and scholars in the Madras Presidency for the official year . . .', and 'Number of scholars on [date] classified according to sex, race or creed'.

TABLE 4. *The public services in Madras Presidency*

	Total	Brahman	Non-Brahman	Depressed classes	Muslim	European and Anglo-Indian	Christian	Other
(a) Gazetted, all-India Services								
1900	487	14	10	—	1	459	2	1
1910	489	17	13	—	3	447	8	1
1920	495	22	24	—	4	433	10	2
1927	490	75	38	—	9	350	15	3
(b) Gazetted, provincial services								
1900	497	201	86	—	13	177	19	1
1910	591	263	92	—	22	190	24	—
1920	926	439	182	—	51	198	56	—
1927	1,148	527	271	1	57	178	110	4
(c) Non-gazetted, over Rs 100 p.m.								
1900	1,623	758	433	2	91	244	94	1
1910	2,184	1,158	553	1	107	249	114	2
1920	2,961	1,665	722	2	133	238	198	3
1927	6,957	3,625	1,997	5	331	484	499	16
(d) Non-gazetted, Rs 35–100 p.m.								
1900	3,737	1,935	1,201	3	193	204	201	—
1910	6,423	3,561	1,895	11	255	399	297	5
1920	9,991	5,847	2,870	16	476	326	448	8
1927	20,610	10,213	7,349	57	1,723	93	1,139	36

SOURCE: *Indian Statutory Commission*, vol. VI, Appendix A, pp. 607–13.

TABLE 5. *Family background of students*

	Percentage of College students whose fathers/guardians are:					
Year	Officials	Petty-officials	Traders	Landlords	Artisans	Labourers
1895–6	33·8	5·1	5·6	46·9	0·4	0·1
1916–17	35·2	7·6	7·7	42·0	0·3	0·1
1926–7	31·4	11·5	9·2	39·6	0·7	0·9
1936–7	32·7	14·5	9·8	29·7	1·0	0·9

SOURCE: *Report on Public Instruction in the Madras Presidency* (annual) for the years given; tables entitled: 'Classification of scholars according to the occupation of parents or guardians.'

One of the chief obstacles in the way of the Justice leaders' campaign for more non-Brahmans to be admitted to the public services was the absence of a large number of non-Brahmans seeking the more subordinate administrative jobs. More non-Brahmans were seeking higher education – there were 526 in Arts Colleges in 1899–1900, 1,618 in 1920–1 and 4,126 in 1930–1 – but even in 1930–1 Brahmans still filled over half the college places. Meanwhile the number of service jobs, particularly at the subordinate levels, were increasing faster than college places. There was thus no great pressure on service employment. Moreover, around half of those who sought higher education were the sons of government servants themselves.[123] These figures suggest that sources of service recruitment were changing very slowly. This impression is confirmed by contemporary reports from those involved in service recruitment. A Collector in Anantapur reported in 1920 that:

> The few non-Brahmans that seek higher education in Anantapur mostly come from the Reddi caste which is the chief landowning caste in the district and which is traditionally averse to doing clerical work and filling subordinate posts in the Revenue Department. I have not had a single application all the time I have been in this district from a non-Brahman graduate for any appointment inferior to that of a Probationary Revenue Inspector.[124]

Thus when the Justice zealots in the Legislative Council demanded that the communal imbalance in the services be rectified in seven years, many officers doubted if this would be possible.[125] By 1926

[123] See tables 3, 4, 5 and 6.

[124] G.O. 986 (Revenue) 30 Apr. 1920 SAH.

[125] 'What will happen in seven years time is impossible to say but at present I

TABLE 6. *The growth of education and service jobs*

Year	Male students in 1st grade colleges	Base number	Base number	Gazetted and non-Gazetted posts over Rs 35 p.m.	Year
1899–1900	1,908	100	100	5,260	1900
1920–1	5,593	288	248	13,178	1920
1930–1	10,237	536	534	29,081	1927

SOURCE: *Indian Statutory Commission*, vol. VI, Appendix A, pp. 607–13.

government was finding it difficult to recruit sufficient qualified men for the expanded number of subordinate posts, and heads of departments resented any regulation which would complicate their recruitment methods.[126] Ten years later, the Public Works Department reported that the non-Brahman agitation had succeeded in discouraging Brahmans from competing for vacancies, but had not brought forward sufficient non-Brahmans to replace them.[127] From 1927, a Staff Selection Board had been empowered to examine candidates for subordinate posts and had been directed to select on the basis of fixed proportions from the different communities. It found this impossible. In 1927–8, for instance, it had to select 467 persons, and even if it had chosen every non-Brahman applicant who possessed the barest qualifications it could not have met the stated quota.[128]

The non-Brahman demand was evidently not the upshot of massive pressure from non-Brahmans. Few of them, it appeared, wanted the large number of clerkships. Nor indeed were Panagal and the other

should think it doubtful whether the number of duly qualified non-Brahmans was sufficient and there is no guarantee that the desired proportion will be forthcoming in future.' G. R. Paddison in G.O. 613 (Public) 16 Sept. 1921 MRO.

126 See the reactions of heads of departments to a proposal to abolish discretionary pay awards to graduates. The Director of Public Health reported: 'There has been no graduate applicants for clerks' posts in this office during the past three or four years.' The heads of the Police, Labour and Public Works Departments and the chief Presidency Magistrate echoed his views. Seventeen of twenty district Collectors who replied thought that the discretionary pay was vital to attract graduates of any sort; the Legislative Council offices and the Inspector General considered: 'Brahman graduates are available but non-Brahmans are hard to get.' G.O. 445 (Public) 16 May 1927 MRO.

127 G.O. 1065 (Public) 13 June 1936 MRO.

128 G.O. 439 (Public) 12 May 1928 MRO; see also G.O. 452 (Public) 16 May 1927 MRO; G.O. 1185 (Public) 21 Nov. 1927 MRO; G.O. 550 (Public) 9 May 1929 MRO.

Justice leaders mightily concerned over these menial posts. They were however, concerned about the plums of office, the few senior posts in the Secretariat, the Courts and the Collectorates, and above all about the right to wield patronage. Here, however, they were pitted not so much against the Brahman community as against the men who currently controlled these posts and that patronage, that is, the senior I.C.S. officers.

Members of the I.C.S. had colluded with the Justice leaders in their campaign in 1916–20 because they too feared the influence of certain Brahmans, particularly those of Mylapore. Since then, however, the position had changed. The Feetham Committee, investigating the role of the services under the reforms, had suggested that government should transfer the responsibility for all appointments below the I.C.S. grade to the ministers. The Madras I.C.S. was horrified.[129] In fact the proposal was never implemented, but the I.C.S. was considerably troubled by the prospect of losing power to the ministers. When the Justicites occupied the ministerial seats, began pressing for more patronage and demanding changes in the bureaucracy's hallowed methods of recruitment, they became as devilish in the eyes of the I.C.S. as the potentates of Mylapore had once been.

Many administrators, who did not understand the tactical nature of the demand, had been surprised at the Non-Brahman Manifesto and the subsequent demands about service recruitment. 'Surely,' noted a member of the Board of Revenue, 'there must be available facts to support the claim that of late years we have spared no pains to distribute appointments?' and pointed to four orders passed in the last few years.[130] When the agitation prompted the I.C.S. moghuls into action, they moved as little as possible. In response to a press campaign headed by the *Justice* in 1918, they publicly issued an order directing Collectors to keep separate lists of Brahmans and of others, to aid decisions over appointments and promotions. This order had in fact been already issued confidentially a couple of years beforehand and the move was nothing more than window-dressing.[131] In 1921 when the Legislative Council demanded firmer action, they issued an order which directed Collectors to beware of allowing influential families to monopolise subordinate appointments and to 'divide the appointments in each district among the several castes.'[132] This order

[129] G.O. 392 (Public) 3 July 1919 MRO.

[130] G.O. 19 (Home Miscellaneous) 6 Jan. 1920 MRO.

[131] G.O. 19 (Home Miscellaneous) 6 Jan. 1920 MRO; G.O. 986 (Revenue) 30 Apr. 1920 SAH.

[132] G.O. 613 (Public) 16 Sept. 1921 MRO.

had first been issued in 1851, had been re-issued many times since (most recently in 1912), and had been notoriously ineffective. It was no better this time, and in 1922 they were dragooned into issuing an order which directed Collectors to apply communal considerations to promotion as well as recruitment, and to send to government reports describing the community of all appointees.[133]

This 'Second Communal G.O.' (Government Order) was potentially quite effective, but the I.C.S., even before the order was passed, was already planning to scotch the whole affair. Judging fairly accurately that the non-Brahman agitation stemmed from the offices in the City, the Secretaries prepared an outrageous scheme to export Brahmans from the Madras Secretariat to the mofussil and to the central secretariat in Calcutta, and to replace them with non-Brahmans imported from offices in the districts. Offices in the City would thus display a nice communal balance, while offices in the mofussil would be even more over-loaded with Brahmans than before. Lists of men to be transferred had been prepared and Calcutta had been invited to co-operate before the Revenue Department stepped on the scheme. Another order was then issued emphasising that 'no hard and fast rule can be laid down which will fetter the discretion of the Secretaries to Government and Collectors in the matter of appointments'.[134] With this move, the Second Communal G.O. was unofficially, but effectively, cancelled. A few months later, when an M.L.C. asked whether government would consider directly limiting the recruitment of Brahmans, the Secretariat replied that 'the government cannot answer a hypothetical question'.[135]

The Justice leaders were more than a little piqued at their inability to get their hands on service patronage. Their dislike of C. P. Ramaswami Iyer stemmed at least in part from jealousy of his freedom as Law Member to make appointments to subordinate posts in the

[133] G.O. 958 (Public) 15 Aug. 1922 MRO.

[134] G.O. 855 (Public) 3 Nov. 1923 MRO.

[135] G.O. 12 (Public) 6 Jan. 1922 MRO; G.O. 32 (Public) 12 Jan. 1922 MRO. In 1928, government concluded that 'it is a fact that the returns compiled to exhibit the effect of the [Communal] orders do not show that there has been much change in practice in the years since the orders were issued'. G.O. 1129 (Public) 15 Dec. 1928 MRO. In fact the Communal G.O.s had been so vague and sweeping that they could not possibly have been applied to the complexities of recruitment and promotion in the various branches of the services. This was conclusively revealed in 1927–8, when government took a fresh look at the problem and found that the Communal G.O.s had simply been unworkable. See G.O. 1071 (Public) 4 Nov. 1927 MRO; G.O. 1115 (Public) 13 Dec. 1927 MRO; G.O. 751 (Public) 5 Sept. 1928 MRO.

judicial service, and the antipathy between Reddi Naidu and Todhunter began as a dispute over patronage. Moreover, the ministers were becoming increasingly embarrassed by the petitions and entreaties of their followers, many of which they were unable to satisfy. O. Kandaswami Chetty, a party worker and publicist, asked Patro, the Education Minister, to find a place for his daughter in the Educational Service and a job in the Publicity Office for himself. Patro, who could not bend the rules to accommodate the under-qualified daughter and could not influence the Governor who appointed to the Publicity Office, had to refuse.[136] C. R. Reddy pressed Panagal in turn for a district board place, the Presidentship of the Legislative Council and the Vice-Chancellor's post in the Madras University, and was refused each time.[137] Dr C. Natesan, one of the party's founder-members and leading organisers in the City, announced in the Legislative Council: 'I asked for a High Court Judgeship for a non-Brahman Hindu, another for an Indian Christian Protestant or a Ministry for him ... I asked for a chief Engineership for an Indian Catholic Christian (cheers), I asked for a District Board Presidentship for a Mukanadu (hear, hear). Sir, I have asked for appointments for partymen of various communities and sub-communities.'[138] None of these offices, with the exception of the district board places, was directly in Panagal's gift. It was Panagal's inability to give which brought these scandals into the open, laid the basis for opposition to the Justice ministry, and allowed *The Hindu* to taunt them by asking; 'Has not the whole of the energies of the Ministry been dissipated in an unseemly squabble for high and low posts?'[139]

The I.C.S. men made it clear that they were horrified at the notion of service appointments in the hands of 'politicians, probably men wedded to particular views of which the inefficiency and conceit of the bureaucracy will form a part, with no experience of administration or handling of men, changeable every three years';[140] but the Justice publicists could equally well reply, 'Are M.L.C.s the only sinners? Do not Secretaries to Government, Judges and even members of the Executive Council give recommendations?'[141] It had long been recognised that the passport to success in a service career was the kind regard of a senior officer. Most of the Indians who had risen in the services in the early years had been helped by particular senior

[136] *Hindu* (w) 29 Apr. 1926.
[137] *Hindu* (w) 7 and 14 Feb. 1924.
[138] MLCP, XVII (Mar. 1924), 145.
[139] *Hindu* 13 June 1923.
[140] G.O. 392 (Public) 3 July 1919 MRO.
[141] Ramaswami Mudaliar, *Mirror of the Year*, p. 209.

officers. The Justice leaders themselves pointed out that 'official patronage is only too full of jobbery and corruption'[142] and that there was nothing qualitatively different about ministerial favouritism. It was simply a battle over the power of appointment.

But the I.C.S. had all the advantages. Before the reforms had even been implemented, they had expressed fulsome approval for the idea of a Public Services Commission, an official body which would control service appointments and ensure 'the protection of the services from political influences'.[143] In the late 1920s government circles were treated to the unusual sight of the Government of Madras goading the Government of India into action over this very issue. In 1924 Fort St George hurried into existence a Staff Selection Board which scrutinised all candidates for subordinate posts, until in 1929 the Madras Services Commission was finally created. The Justicites opposed these moves every step of the way. They demanded, unsuccessfully, a non-official majority on the Staff Selection Board, inveighed that the constitution of the Board was 'contrary to the principles of Government' and accused the Board of failing to acknowledge the Communal G.O.s in its operations.[144] When the Services Commission Bill was before the Legislative Council, the Justice leaders proposed amendments which, according to the hostile *Hindu*, would have reduced the Commission's powers to 'that of merely issuing certificates of minimum fitness to the nominees of Ministers',[145] but these amendments were squashed. Moreover, the Secretariat called the Justice leaders' bluff over the non-Brahman issue. While setting up the Madras Services Commission, they also passed a series of orders laying down complex systems of communal proportion and communal rotation for recruitment, appointment and promotion in the services. Where the previous orders on communal recruitment had been vague and general, and thus both impractical and easily ignored, these were strict and specific.[146] It was a measure of their concerted and practical nature, that for the first time many Brahmans were moved to object. By arguing that the Services Commission was necessary to

142 *Ibid.* p. 9.

143 G.O. 327 (Public) 23 May 1921 MRO.

144 MLCP, XVII (21 and 22 Mar. 1924); G.O. 76 (Public) 6 Feb. 1924 MRO.

145 *Hindu* 15 Aug. 1929.

146 The rules frequently had to be by-passed, because there were not enough non-Brahman and Muslim applicants to fill the rotation, see G.O. 766 (Public) 10 Sept. 1928 MRO, and G.O. 1115 (Public) 13 Dec. 1928 MRO. Some years later government concluded that the rules had not been a great success, see G.O. 1063 (Public) 13 Mar. 1936 MRO.

ensure that these orders could be put into practice, the Secretariat hoist the Justice leaders with their own petard. In the first years of its operation, the Commission was locked in a battle to prevent the ministers ignoring and by-passing its procedures, and gradually the Commission won.[147] The I.C.S. had gained its immunity.

MINISTERS AND PATRONAGE IN THE MOFUSSIL

The ministers and their cohorts had had little success in their attempts to wrest power from the steel frame of the Raj in the vital matters of revenue, irrigation and services, yet they were coming under increasing pressure from their supporters to justify their position in the seat of apparent authority. The Justice leaders had been the staunchest advocates of the Montagu–Chelmsford reforms in 1918–19 yet by 1924, when the Muddiman committee came to inspect the progress of the reforms, they were the loudest critics:

> The Governor of the province [inveighed Patro] is made more absolute in the administration of transferred subjects than in the reserved subjects... Ministers are appointed by him in relation to transferred subjects to hold office during his pleasure and when he sees sufficient cause to dissent from the opinion of the Ministers he can overrule them ... Practical difficulties were experienced when the Governor assumed the absolute power of making appointments. There were occasions when there were serious disagreements between the Governor and the Ministers. In some cases matters reached a crisis which was averted by compromise ... Ministers repeatedly represented to the Legislative Council that they were unable to proceed with a certain proposal as the Finance Department would not sanction it... In practice, the Finance Department assumed powers of allocation of revenue quite foreign to its own constitution.[148]

But besides sulking in this way the ministers had also begun to seek ways to expand their stock of patronage, particularly in the mofussil areas. In this, they were able to capitalise on the now well-established trend of administrative decentralisation. More and more, government was devolving the responsibilities for the provision of local services on to committees of non-officials, and it considerably eased government's burden if it could also off-load the responsibility for selecting and supervising these bodies. The ministers were happy to inherit these powers.

The most important area of local patronage open to ministerial

[147] G.O. 231 (Public) 11 Mar. 1933 MRO; G.O. 1968 (Public) 12 Nov. 1933 MRO.
[148] *Views of Local Governments on the Working of the Reforms, dated 1924*, pp. 102–5.

exploitation was the structure of local self-government. In 1919–20 government had passed a series of acts which altered the framework of local government administration. As will be examined at more length in the next chapter, these increased the importance of local bodies and opened them up to a wide range of interests in local society. At the same time, the acts transferred the responsibility for supervising local government from the Collector to the Secretariat and ministers in Madras. This supervision was considered so important that after 1921 the chief minister in Madras regularly kept the local government portfolio for himself.

The 1919–20 Acts had made local boards considerably more liberal, throwing more places and presidentships open to election and in the first few months the ministry was caught up in this policy of liberalisation. In 1921 Panagal ordered that all taluk boards should elect their own presidents, unless there were special circumstances to discourage this, and after this order fifty-eight boards elected their presidents for the first time. Panagal also decreed that any district board which petitioned unanimously would be allowed to elect its own president.[149] As the ministers were driven into a cul-de-sac in their attempts to gain patronage in the public services, and as they came to realise the potential of local government, these liberal attitudes were quickly dropped. By the time of the next general election in 1923, Panagal had nominated district board presidents in no fewer than fifteen of the twenty-four districts; two boards which had followed Panagal's invitation and had asked for an elective president, were rewarded with nominees. When the presidential chair fell vacant in Ganjam, Panagal paid the district a personal visit and later nominated the zamindar of Kallikote, a fellow landholder and a distant relation who had no previous experience in administration or politics. In Kistna, Tikkani Balajirao, an M.L.C. who had reputedly lent Panagal money, was nominated president. In Coimbatore, the M.L.C., T. A. Ramalingam Chetty, occupied the presidentship; since 1921 Ramalingam Chetty had organised campaigns for more autonomy for local administration and had led a party revolt against Panagal's autocracy; when his three-year term expired, Panagal nominated one of his local rivals instead.[150] In his home district of Chittoor Panagal, according to the *Swarajya*, 'promised to

[149] G.O. 438 (LSG) 7 Mar. 1922 MRO.

[150] *Swatantra* 5 Aug. 1924, *Andhravani* 10 Sept. 1922, *Kistnapatrika* 6 Oct. 1923 NNR; *Hindu* 1 June 1923; G.O. 1131 (LSG) 17 May 1923 MRO.

throw the presidency of the District Board open for election and serious canvassing went on for two months. It was then found that the party's favourite had no chance of election with the result that the Minister had to go back on his word and resort again to nomination.'[151] The nominee was B. Muniswami Naidu, an M.L.C. whose family were hereditary estate-servants for Panagal's own family, and who had long been Panagal's henchman in district affairs.

The power to nominate presidents was not the only instrument of ministerial patronage. The minister also had the power to nominate a few members of each board, supposedly to provide for the representation of minority communities and minority interests. This power was often used to reward friends, or to build up certain factions in district affairs. O. Tanicachalam Chetty, a leading Justicite and by no means a member of a depressed community in the capital, was nominated to the Madras Corporation immediately after he had lost at the polls. In Guntur P. C. Ethirajulu Naidu, already an M.L.C. and the nominated president of the district board, was also nominated to the municipality. In Chingleput, C. Muthiah Mudaliar, a wealthy and influential landholder who had managed the electoral campaign of a leading Justicite in 1920, was put on the district board although ten of his fellow castemen were already members. In Guntur, five nominations to the municipality helped to swing the factional balance just a few days before the election of a new chairman. In 1926, Panagal ordered that the Chingleput taluk board be bifurcated, or divided into two; this move allowed him to nominate all the new members of the new temporary boards just a few months before his personal secretary was standing for election to the legislature from that constituency.[152]

Similar examples could be given for every district of the Presidency. Besides these obvious powers of nomination, the minister also had important financial powers, and the right to intervene in local disputes. Although local boards raised numerous local taxes, none of them was self-supporting. In fact the great increase in their powers and responsibilities that came in the 1920 reforms made them all the more reliant on doles from the provincial finances. Until the late 1920s there was no system for the distribution of these grants and the min-

151 *The Cult of Incompetence: being an impartial enquiry into the record of the first Madras ministry*, reprinted from the *Swarajya* (Madras, 1923), p. 7.

152 *Hindu* 17 Nov. 1925, 27 Jan. 1927; V. Venkata Rao, *A Hundred Years of Local Self-Government and Administration in Andhra and Madras States 1850–1950* (Bombay, 1960), pp. 77–8; *Cult of Incompetence*, passim.

ister had considerable personal discretion.[153] Finally local disputes were often referred up to the capital. Such disputes generally arose over procedural or legal points when two factions were locked in close combat. The minister had the power to decide the point for himself, or to let the dispute go into the courts. In Bezwada, for instance, the ministry allowed the municipal chairman, a known ally, to postpone the chairmanship elections three times when he was in a tight spot.[154] In Chidambaram, the minister intervened to cancel several court-cases charging the municipal chairman with corruption and maladministration.[155]

The ministers clung jealously to these powers. In 1925, government tried to cut back ministerial discretion over grants to local boards by introducing a grant-in-aid code, and issuing an order which emphasised that the nominated places in local boards were intended for minority interests. Neither move was fully effective and the ministers continued to wield the powers of nomination and of the purse with great effect.[156] The Legislative Council in 1923 demanded that all district board presidents be elected. Panagal, when he looked up the file and found that the terms of ten of his nominees would expire shortly before the 1926 election, was extremely reluctant to give way and he fended off the issue for over three years. In this case, however, Panagal had to give way grudgingly in the end and allow all but four of the remaining district boards to elect their own presidents, but not until the Governor himself had put considerable pressure on him.[157] In the same year, however, Panagal moved to increase his financial hold over the municipalities with a bill which put the responsibility for municipal taxation in the hands of special officers supervised by the government, and which placed firmer government supervision over municipal budgets.[158]

With other orders and other legislation, the Justice ministers sought to expand their powers and their patronage throughout the Presidency. In the early 1920s, government set up district education

153 *Hindu* 12 Aug. 1929; Venkata Rao, *Local Self-Government*, p. 298.

154 G.O. 919 (LSG) 24 May 1921 SAH; G.O. 945 (LSG) 30 May 1921 SAH; G.O. 167 (LSG) 24 Jan. 1922 SAH; *Hindu* 28 Jan. 1922, 24 Feb. 1922.

155 G.O. 151 (LSG) 11 Jan. 1933 MRO.

156 Venkata Rao, *Local Self-Government*, pp. 298–302; G.O. 4421 (LSG) 3 Dec. 1925 MRO; G.O. 3904 (LSG) 3 Oct. 1930 MRO.

157 G.O. 2316 (LSG) 19 Oct. 1923 MRO; G.O. 2406 (LSG) 29 Aug. 1924 MRO; G.O. 3391 (LSG) 4 Aug. 1926 MRO.

158 *Swarajya* 30 Jan. 1926 NNR; *Hindu* 11 Feb. 1926.

councils and secondary education boards which helped in the administration of schools.[159] Later it also set up selection committees which helped select candidates for the most important colleges in the province. Another similar set of committees were the district road boards, which advised on the building and repair of the highways. None of these bodies had direct control over any finance and thus they had limited executive powers; yet they undertook minor administrative work, framed schemes for new projects, and were the chief advisers of government in their sphere. Membership conveyed significant local influence. The ministry could appoint some or all of the members of these committees, and this patronage was important in the business of winning friends in the localities.[160] Patro's University Act of 1923 changed the whole balance of power in academic affairs by changing the composition and roles of the Senate and the Academic Council. Previously, the most important body had been the Senate, and the most important group of Indians in the Senate had been the representatives of past graduates, whose leaders tended to be of the Mylapore complexion. Patro's Act off-loaded some of the Senate's duties on to the Academic Council, which was run by the active teachers and administrators of Madras University, and it filled the Senate with representatives of the legislature and local government bodies, men whom they could expect to be indebted to the ministry in some way or another.[161] The ministers' biggest coup, however, was the Hindu Religious Endowments Bill which gave them great patronage in the politics of religion.

The temples of south India are not only beautiful and spiritual places, many are also extremely rich and influential. The larger temples such as the Sri Minakshi at Madura, the Brihideswara at Tanjore, the Rameswaram shrine and the Tirupati hills, own large tracts of land, lend money, own markets, employ vast retinues, issue lucrative contracts for repairing the fabric and for providing for festivals, patronise art and learning, run hostels, organise festivals

[159] *Indian Statutory Commission*, vol. VI, pp. 532, 540–1; G.O. 4443 (LSG) 3 Nov. 1928 MRO.

[160] 'The District Education Councils' authorities visit villages and centres of education to get mixed with the voters for local bodies or legislatures. Favouritism plays an important part in patching up "honest differences" and forming new centres for vote-catching. Most of the Presidents of District Education Councils are men of some local body or other who hanker after some honour, membership or office.' Letter in *Hindu* 8 June 1936.

[161] GOI Education and Health Education 35B May 1923 NAI.

and influence the hierarchy of status in their locality. Such vital parts of local society and economy had long been the focus of local politics, and had long attracted the attention of governments. Their internal politics were often Byzantine. The *maths*, monastic institutions of great wealth and influence, were often the scene of bloody succession disputes. Even many of the less wealthy temples were fought over with great zest. In pre-British days, the governments of the region had generally tried to regulate temple affairs. The Madras Government however, under pressure from Calcutta which believed the Raj should keep clear of religious entanglements, had withdrawn from temple affairs in 1863. While in some temples particular landholders, families or caste-groups were entrenched in control, in many the matter was open to local competition and even the courts were powerless to intervene. Control of a temple was important because it gave great power, patronage and status in local society. Moreover, temples could mobilise votes at local and provincial elections.[162]

Before 1920, the Justice leaders had vigorously opposed legislative interference in temple affairs.[163] At that time, any central interference in the temples would almost definitely have increased Mylapore's ability to interfere, since Mylapore was at that time best placed to profit at the centre. Once the Justicites had replaced the Mylaporeans at the Governor's right hand, their policy towards temples underwent a complete about-face. Pressed on by influential men like the M.L.C. N. A. V. Somasundaram Pillai of Tinnevelly and the Madura zamindar M. T. Somasundara Mudaliar, whose temple interests had suffered under the attacks of the Mylaporeans' Dharmarakshana Sabha in recent years, the Justice leaders pressed government to break its sixty-year-old policy of non-interference and to allow them to legislate in temple matters.[164]

The Justice leaders begged to be allowed to legislate on the grounds that many temples were badly administered and their funds squandered or even embezzled. This was undoubtedly true, and the Secretariat duly framed a bill which aimed to curb maladministration. It provided for local committees which could inspect temples, approve expenditure from temple funds, audit temple accounts and

[162] Chandra Mudaliar, 'State and Religious Endowments in Madras', Ph.D. thesis (Madras 1961); C. J. Baker, 'Temples and political development', in Baker and Washbrook, *Political Institutions*.

[163] G.O. 175 (L & M,L) 7 Feb 1918 MRO.

[164] G.O. 2317 (LSG) 25 Nov. 1921 MRO; *Hindu* 4 June 1921, 7 June 1923.

appoint temple trustees when there was a dispute over the post. The bill did not touch the *maths* and it made no attempt to interfere with the power of the courts to intervene in temple affairs.[165]

The bill as it emerged from the Select Committee of the Legislative Council looked completely different. Its new character showed that the Justice leaders were not simply interested in reforming temple management, but in imposing a large degree of central control on the temples and in bringing important patronage under their command. The new bill virtually annulled the power of the courts in temple affairs, included the *maths*, imposed a tax on temple incomes, gave a broader definition of the powers of the local committees and, most important of all, created a central Endowments Board which, along with the local committees, would 'do all things which are reasonable and necessary to ensure that *maths* and temples are properly maintained and that all religious endowments are properly administered'. The Endowments Board, in consultation with the ministers, was to nominate members to local temple committees, to arbitrate in temple disputes and to assume direct control of individual temples if it deemed it necessary.[166] Temples in the south had not been subjected to such a degree of supralocal control since the time of the Chola empire.

There was a huge outcry against this governmental aggression. Mylapore and its acolytes, who now saw the prize they had for so long coveted passing into rival hands, were the loudest in protest; one Mylaporean noted that 'the inevitable tendency of all central authorities like the Endowments Board is to develop their own control at the expense and the detriment of local control',[167] while another City politician noted that temples would 'become part of the great machinery which the Hon. Minister and his colleagues are blackening every day'.[168] The Justice leaders decried these protests as a Brahman reaction, but in fact opinion on the bill divided far more according to concrete considerations of political interest and political alignment than to diffuse considerations of community. N. A. V. Somasundaram Pillai, for instance, who had been the first to urge the Justice leaders to reform temple administration in 1921 and who was sufficiently

165 G.O. 85 (Law Legislative) 5 Mar. 1923 MRO.

166 GOI Home Judicial 427 1926 NAI; G.O. 85 (Law Legislative) 5 Mar. 1923 MRO.

167 M. Ramachandra Rao to P. S. Sivaswami Iyer, 13 June 1923, Sivaswami Iyer papers NAI.

168 S. Satyamurthi in MLCP, XXXII (17 Sept. 1926), 916–17.

well connected with the Justice leaders, welcomed the bill as a means to protect Saivism in south India; the head of the chief Saivite *math* at Tiruvadathurai, however, was among the bill's fiercest critics.[169] In all the important temple centres of the province, men of all communities feared that their local interest in temple affairs would suffer through this legislation; in Kumbakonam for instance, men of all castes from Brahman to Chetty and Udaiyar came forward to defend local autonomy.[170] Moreover, the Justice leaders faced a revolt among many of their closest supporters in the legislature, including men who had at first supported the idea of temple legislation but who shied away from the centralisation enshrined in the new bill. Many of the prominent landholders feared that government would now make some of the temples on their estates, which they had long considered their personal property and which were, among other things, a useful means to gain tax-relief, into public places.[171]

After much backstairs bargaining, submissions to the Government of India and interventions by the Governor, the Endowments Bill found its way onto the statute book. The act made only marginal differences to the character of temple administration since spectacular succession disputes and cases of embezzlement continued. The Endowments Board was simply not equipped to tackle those local interests which had a firm grip on the vast resources of the temples. The Board could not force temple managers to submit information about their buildings and endowments, let alone to pay their taxes, and for ten years both the Board and the local committees were either bankrupt or indebted.[172] The act, however, did give the ministers vast opportunities for patronage and considerable powers to intervene in local temple politics.

To begin with, the ministers had in their gift the nomination of the four commissioners of the Endowments Board and they made good use of this patronage. The first nominees included two relatives of ministers, the chief minister's solicitor, and the brother of a leading Justicite in the Madras Corporation,[173] and later choices showed similar favouritism.[174] Next, the ministers were empowered to exempt

[169] *Hindu* 14 June 1923; GOI Home Judicial 427 1926 NAI.
[170] *Hindu* 27 Nov. 1927.
[171] G.O. 3847 (LSG) 3 Sept. 1926 MRO.
[172] G.O. 1337 (LSG) 9 Apr. 1927 MRO; G.O. 328 (LSG) 24 Jan. 1928 MRO; G.O. 534 (LSG) 19 Feb. 1931 MRO; G.O. 1547 (LSG) 27 Mar. 1934 MRO; G.O. 4183 (LSG) 13 Sept. 1929 SAH.
[173] *Swarajya* 7 Apr. 1925, *Mitavadi* 16 Mar. 1925 NNR.
[174] G.O. 2107 (LSG) 19 July 1933 MRO; G.O. 2067 (LSG) 14 May 1935 MRO.

certain temples from the provisions of the act; this power was used in favour of temples controlled by many of the big landholders of the Circars and the Nattukottai Chetty bankers of Ramnàd who were the financial backbone of the Justice party, temples in the City many of which were managed by the Justicite leader O. Tanicachalam Chetty, and individual temples elsewhere.[175] Further, the ministers and the Board appointed all the members of the new district temple committees. This gave the ministers the power to bestow a useful favour – a seat on a temple committee conveyed great prestige and influence, and some opportunities for gain – on ten or twenty persons in each district. These committees were supposed to make arrangements to become elective after three years, but in almost every case the committee members decided they had neither the funds nor the inclination to risk an election, and the ministers were quite happy to go on nominating members up to 1932. Places on these committees were highly valued. Men offered to resign from temple trusteeships (since this disqualified them from committee membership) or to donate large sums for temple repairs if they were selected. In Negapatam for example, five magnates each boasting an annual tax bill in excess of Rs 10,000 begged to be appointed.[176] These nominations could be wielded to great effect. The minister in charge often selected candidates against the advice of the district Collector and the Endowments Board – P. C. Ethirajulu Naidu was twice put on the Guntur committee against the Collector's advice, and the Tirugnana Sambanda Pandarasannidhi was put on the Madura temple committee although the Collector had advised that he was a danger to the public peace[177] – and these nominations were considered so important that when the Endowments portfolio changed hands in 1930, the new minister in charge revoked all the orders passed by his predecessor but not yet implemented so he could substitute his own nominees.[178]

The Justice leaders had thus acquired a patronage bank. In many cases nominations to local bodies, temple committees and other boards were used to court M.L.C.s and to build up a party of men obliged to the ministers in the Legislative Council. District board presidentships

[175] G.O. 4905 (LSG) 12 Dec. 1927 MRO; GOI Home Judicial 38/28 1935 NAI.

[176] G.O. 3230 (LSG) 8 Sept. 1925 MRO; G.O. 4632 (LSG) 8 Nov. 1927 MRO; G.O. 2066 (LSG) 2 June 1932 MRO.

[177] G.O. 3334 (LSG) 20 Aug. 1928 MRO; G.O. 391 (LSG) 31 Jan. 1930 MRO.

[178] *India* 14 and 15 Oct. 1935 NNR.

were handed to several M.L.C.s including P. Kesava Pillai, B. Muniswami Naidu, P. C. Ethirajulu Naidu and T. Balajirao. Other M.L.C.s were nominated to the 'minorities' seats in municipalities and rural boards; Abbas Ali Khan and P. T. Rajan were put on to the Madura district board and S. Kumaraswami Reddiar on to the Tinnevelly district board, both times in the face of alternative suggestions from the Collector.[179] One historian of local government in Madras has calculated that at one point in time, 66 of the 125 sitting M.L.C.s had been nominated to some local body.[180] In the year 1926–7 alone, the ministry put twelve M.L.C.s on rural boards, three on municipalities, seven on district education councils, seven on road boards and six on temple committees.[181] After the ministry was reshuffled in 1927, twenty-three M.L.C.s were nominated to local institutions in ten months.[182]

Ministerial patronage and powers of interference were used more generally to make the power of the centre felt throughout the Presidency and to build networks of support in the different regions. The next chapter describes how local politics were brought into a loose alignment with the politics of the provincial centre, as men were forced to look to the centre both for nomination to important positions and for favourable decisions in factional disputes. Other City leaders were horrified at the way the ministerships had elevated the Justice leaders above other politicians. The *Swarajya*, a new Congress paper, ran a series of articles tracing the actions of the ministers, called rather inappropriately 'The Cult of Incompetence'. The climax of this series exclaimed that, 'with one foot firmly planted in mutts and temples and the other in local and district boards, the party hoped to stride the presidency like a Colossus',[183] and suggested that while 'political power may be distributive justice as Aristotle would have us believe', distributive justice should not be 'interpreted in the ministerialist sense of introducing patronage for party purposes into every department of national life'.[184] Yet with their armoury of governmental powers, the Justice leaders managed to spread a 'party' network throughout the province without the help of any substantial framework of organisation.

179 G.O. 1030 (LSG) 4 June 1921 MRO; G.O. 1181 (LSG) 23 June 1921 MRO.
180 Venkata Rao, *Local Self-Government*, p. 47.
181 G.O.s 4571 and 4572 (LSG) 25 Nov. 1927 MRO.
182 G.O. 4046 (LSG) 3 Sept. 1929 MRO.
183 *The Cult of Incompetence*, p. 2.
184 *The Cult of Incompetence*, p. 8.

THE ORGANISATION OF THE JUSTICE PARTY

The Justice party was born in the confined world of pre-1920 politics. It began as a loose faction in City affairs, whose chief aim was the obliteration of the influence of the Mylapore faction. Like Mylapore, it had a wide range of contacts outside the City, but the focus of its attentions was in the City and particularly in the politics and intrigue within the Governor's court. The nucleus of the Justice party in the City consisted, like the Mylapore nucleus, of service and professional families, and also of prominent merchants and politicians of the City. This nucleus remained throughout the 1920s, and its battle with Mylaporean influence also continued. The Justicites were largely successful since they now held most of the trump cards and by the end of the decade they had managed to root Mylapore out of many of the positions it had won in the years before 1916. The Justicites, led until his death in 1925 by Pitti Thyagaraja Chetty, dominated the Madras Corporation with the help of the European members. Even when government ordered that the Corporation chair should be occupied each year by men of different communities (Brahman, non-Brahman, Muslim, European, Christian, Depressed Caste) according to a rotation, it was still the alliance of Justicite and European merchants which effectively decided who would occupy the chair in any year.[185] Patro's Madras University Act drove a bulldozer through Mylapore's influence in the Senate, and this was not the only Justicite success in educational affairs. A Christian Justicite, Mariadas Ruthnaswamy, became the first non-Brahman principal of the Law College, and Justice nominees also appeared at the helm of the Engineering and Medical Colleges.[186] The Pachaiyappa's Trust and College, which Mylaporeans had captured in the 1910s, were recovered by lawyers and merchants of the Justice faction.[187] Finally, by the early 1930s there was a majority of non-Brahmans amongst the judges of the High Court.

These victories amounted to an undoubted success for the Justicites in City affairs. Yet the political world in which this party had been born had disintegrated as the province went to the polls in 1920. There was now a truly provincial arena of politics, which demanded

[185] See for instance Goschen to Reading, 8 Nov. 1925, Goschen papers vol. IV IOL; *Hindu* 16 Nov. 1926, 19 Aug. 1929, 6 and 7 Nov. 1933.

[186] Interview with Mariadas Ruthnaswamy, Delhi October 1970.

[187] V. Tiruvenkataswami (ed.), *Pachaiyappa's College Centenary Commemoration Book 1842–1942* (Madras, 1942), list of trustees.

provincial organisation. The Justice leaders slipped easily into the rhetoric of provincial party politics, but they never acquired the substance. For much of the time the full extent of their party organisation was a few tables in the Madras Cosmopolitan Club where the leaders met nightly to discuss affairs, and the 'durbars' held by the ministers in the style of maharajahs, to which M.L.C.s, local leaders and others came with requests for appointments, grants, nominations, legislative action and preferment of all kinds.[188] This was really all that, in the ministers' eyes, was necessary.

The South Indian Liberal Federation (S.I.L.F.) the party's organisation set up in 1916, functioned intermittently. It held meetings and kept records up until 1920, but these lapsed when the secretary, A. Ramaswami Mudaliar, left to take up a post in the legislature. A party branch was formed in Madras City in 1921 but in 1923 it could boast only sixty-three members.[189] Elsewhere branches appeared and disappeared according to political circumstance. One emerged in Tanjore when the ministry was on the point of selecting a president for the local district board, and one appeared in Salem when a local faction wanted ministerial help in a contest for the municipal chair. In other places, such as Nellore where E. Raghava Reddi tried unsuccessfully to start a branch to help him in his electoral campaign in 1923, there were no branches.[190] At the end of the 1920s, the party could list over 5,000 members in the province, but almost 2,000 of these came from Madras City or the adjacent district.[191] There were also sporadic local meetings, and an annual Non-Brahman Confederation. A regular feature of these annual sessions was a demand for a proper central party bureau, a party constitution, elected party leaders, a proper framework of party organisation, publication of the management of party funds, and a party programme and policy. The ministers regularly sidestepped these demands. The foundation of their leadership lay in their command of governmental power and patronage, not in any party organisation or support; party programmes and organisations could only embarrass and hinder them.

[188] 'Everything is left to be managed, rather mismanaged, by honorary workers, High Court Vakils, who have throughout the day enough of work to attend to and in the evenings have the equally, nay the more important duty, of answering the rolls at the Cosmopolitan Club.' *Hindu* 10 Nov. 1922. These 'durbars' were described by K. V. Gopalaswamy in an interview, Waltair July 1971.

[189] *Hindu* 17 Nov. 1921, 8 Apr. 1922, 15 May 1923, 19 May 1924.

[190] *Hindu* 7 Nov. 1922.

[191] T. A. V. Nathan (ed.), *The Justice Year Book 1929* (n.p., n.d.), pp. 52–5.

At the annual Confederation in 1924, the Justice leaders had to concede to an angry demand for more substantial party machinery, and they appointed a committee to draft a party constitution. The draft was published in early 1925, and it was evident that it had been designed to ensure that the clique of City leaders would remain in firm control. Even so, the constitution remained on the drawing board. In late 1925, the leaders announced that the question of implementing the constitution and electing an executive would be deferred for a year while the campaigns for the 1926 elections were in progress.[192] In 1927, the issue was conveniently forgotten, and in 1929 and 1930 there was not even an annual Confederation. The extent of party organisation by the end of the decade can be gauged from the fact that when in 1928 the leaders were in need of allies, they put an advertisement in the newspaper asking any local Justice party branches that might be in existence to get in touch with them.[193]

The ministers *were* the party leaders since the force that held the party together was the power of government. It was not long, however, before men began to resent the independence and the influence of the ministers. 'We have been holding conferences of one sort or another for a long time,' declaimed T. A. Ramalingam Chetty in 1923, 'and all these have only tended to make autocrats of a few people and help them in their own advancement'.[194] While in the first instance most M.L.C.s were anxious to align themselves with the ministers for there was the fount of all power and patronage, before long there was a growth of dissent. 'The party', as its chief whip later said, 'lived on patronage',[195] but patronage was always discriminatory and it was always finite, and soon the disappointed began to oppose the ministers.

The first rebels were some of the party workers, who had worked as publicists, agitators and electoral organisers between 1916 and 1920. Such men had been indispensable while the Justice leaders had been trying to impress the government and the electorate, but were no longer necessary once power had been won. J. N. Ramanathan, a prominent worker from Madura who had run local anti-Brahman

[192] The managing committee was to include sixteen from the City, four from each district and eight nominees of the president. Any gaps in the district quotas would be filled by co-option. *Hindu* 9 Jan. 1925, 21 Dec. 1925.

[193] *Justice* 25 Sept. 1928.

[194] *Hindu* 26 May 1923.

[195] R. V. Krishna Ayyar, *In the Legislature of Those Days* (Madras, 1956), p. 45.

campaigns, worked for the party newspapers, and organised the election campaign in Madura in 1920, led the protest. Since 1920 he had received no repayment for his services and he had been led to believe that he would at least get a place on the Madura municipality. In mid-1922 Ramanathan complained that the party was run from the Cosmopolitan Club, that the party papers received less party news than the European-owned *Madras Mail* and that he and his fellow propagandists had been grievously neglected.[196] J. S. Kannappar, one of Ramanathan's close associates, resigned from the editorship of the *Dravidian*, and together they criticised the management of party funds, including the collection set up for a memorial to the party's founder, the late T. M. Nair, the bloated salaries and allowances of the ministers, their personal manipulation of patronage and 'their extreme intolerance of outside criticism and their assumption of infallibility like the bureaucrats of the Civil Service to whom they bear a strong family resemblance'. In May 1923 they called a 'Non-Brahman Workers Conference' which launched such a scathing attack on the party leaders that Pitti Thyagaraja Chetty walked out in the middle of Ramanathan's speech.[197]

A more serious worry was a rebellion by important M.L.C.s and other men of influence who had failed to get their expected rewards from the party leaders. One of the leaders of this revolt was T. A. Ramalingam Chetty who, ever since 1921, had been fighting against Panagal's manipulation of central influence in local government and had been kicked out of the presidentship of the Coimbatore district board for this insubordination. C. R. Reddy and Dr C. Natesan, who also had been disappointed in their search for a place, were the other leaders of this group of dissidents. They were joined by up-country men who were distressed by the ministry's choice of favourites in their locality. Two of these, the raja of Ramnad and Pethachi Chettiar of Trichinopoly, both big estate-holders in the southern districts, helped to organise a 'Tamil Districts Non-Brahman Conference' in August 1923.[198] They sought help from others in the party, including the minister K. V. Reddi Naidu, who were personally linked to Pitti Thyagaraja Chetty and who disliked the way Panagal had captured the leadership of the party from the grand old man. The Tamil districts conference repeated the demand for a party constitution, pointed out that all the ministers came from the Telugu country and urged

[196] *Hindu* 27 June 1922, 21 Oct. 1922, 20 Oct. 1922.

[197] *Hindu* 12 Oct. 1922, 2 and 19 Dec. 1922.

[198] *Hindu* 26 and 28 May 1923.

the inclusion of a Tamil minister after the 1923 elections.[199] Finally in 1925, the growing problem of satisfying all the important men in the districts with a limited stock of patronage was thrown into clear relief when two antagonistic non-Brahman conferences were held simultaneously within a few miles of each other in Tanjore district. The ministers had built up A. T. Pannirselvam, a Christian lawyer and landowner, as their man in Tanjore district and Pannirselvam was now to organise a party conference. P. S. Rajappa and V. A. Vandayar, big landowners and leaders of the prominent Kallar community in the area, had until recently supported Pannirselvam, but his recent nomination to the chair of the district board and his organisation of this conference promised to make him far too powerful. Moreover, they had been disappointed by the Justice party leaders. Rajappa for instance had been refused ministerial help in his struggle to control the Tanjore municipality and in his attempt to raise an agitation over resettlement of the revenue. At first Rajappa and Vandayar tried to sabotage Pannirselvam's conference, and then held a rival one which attracted dissidents from the surrounding area.[200] This fiasco revealed how much the Justice leaders' network of contacts in some areas of the mofussil was already coming under great strains as more and more local politicians demanded crumbs from the table.

There were almost no fixed alignments in Madras politics in these years and individuals moved between the various party banners with little or no trouble. 'The changes', as Goschen remarked, 'are so kaleidoscopic that it is impossible to follow the various intrigues and issues from day to day.'[201] In this uncertain world, the Justice leaders possessed one distinct advantage – control over government spoils. They could usually log-roll a majority of support for any specific measure and buy off serious pockets of opposition. It was not necessary to please everyone all of the time and no set of people other than the ministers had the resources to bind together a coalition among men of such varied and conflicting aims as the M.L.C.s. The Justice leaders were thus little worried by the avalanche of invective from Ramanathan and the other party workers. Propagandists were always available at a price, and it was not long before Kannappar had been wooed back to the fold and persuaded to write articles damn-

[199] *Hindu* 18, 19 and 21 Aug. 1923.

[200] *Hindu* 17, 18, 24, 25, 29 and 30 July 1925, 3, 6, 20, 21, 22 and 24 Aug. 1925.

[201] Goschen to Birkenhead, 15 June 1927, Goschen papers vol. II IOL.

ing his recent ally Ramanathan.[202] The Tamil districts conference was also brilliantly sabotaged. Shortly before the conference Panagal met its two organisers Pethachi Chettiar and the raja of Ramnad and promised them help in local affairs. These two then rigged the conference programme so that the motion condemning the ministers, the whole point of the meeting, was never debated or put to a vote.[203]

Panagal was a master of the art of intrigue and his domination of the early 1920s owed as much to his personal skills as to the advantages he wielded as chief minister. At no time was this more in evidence than at the 1923 elections. Panagal seized on this opportunity to try and remove the most influential party dissidents from the political scene by using ministerial power to wreck their elections. C. R. Reddy found that he would be opposed in his Chittoor constituency by B. Muniswami Naidu, Panagal's henchman who, having recently been nominated president of the district board by Panagal, had considerable electoral advantages. Wisely, Reddy decided not to stand there. In the City, Panagal arranged that neither Dr C. Natesan nor R. Madanagopal Naidu, both party dissidents and followers of Thyagaraja Chetty, could get the Justice nomination. In Coimbatore, Panagal urged several people, including the son of the influential zamindar of Uthukuli, to oppose Ramalingam Chetty. K. V. Reddi Naidu, whom Panagal was planning to ease out of the ministry in order to accomodate a Tamilian and whom the dissidents hoped would become their leader, found that he had no chance of re-election in his old constituency of Kistna and had to switch to neighbouring Godavari where he had great difficulty since the man Panagal had recently put in charge of the district board also offered his candidature.[204]

In fact Dr Natesan, Reddi Naidu and Ramalingam Chetty squeezed in at the elections, and once elected prepared to attack Panagal with renewed vengeance. The manoeuvres that followed showed how 'Hanoverian' were the politics of this era, how fickle the ties of political allegiance, and how insubstantial the boundaries of party. Panagal repeated the trick that the Justice leaders had played in 1921. Immediately the election results were in, he summoned a meeting of several of those elected, including all those who had been elected for the first time and had no knowledge of City intrigue, and omitting all the recent dissidents. The meeting successfully confirmed his position as 'party leader' and thus ensured that the Governor would

[202] *Hindu* 2 June 1923.

[203] *Hindu* 24 Aug. 1923.

[204] Diaries of K. V. Reddi Naidu, entries for 27 Mar. 1923, 3 Apr. 1923, 5 May 1923, 2 and 4 Sept. 1923; *Hindu* 1 June 1923.

give him a free hand to compose his ministry.[205] He chose as his two fellow-ministers, his old ally Patro, and, as a Tamilian representative, T. N. Sivagnanam Pillai, a man who was not among the candidates put forward by the Tamil dissidents but who had reputedly lent Panagal a large sum of money.[206]

C. R. Reddy and the others immediately established a 'Justice Democratic Party', claimed the true mantle of the non-Brahman movement, and started to organise a motion of no-confidence in the new ministry.[207] They sought allies in all parts of political Madras, and paid no attention to their non-Brahman banner. Their chief allies were C. P. Ramaswami Iyer, now the Law Member and Panagal's personal enemy, and P. Rajagopalachari, a very successful Brahman civil servant who was currently president of the Legislative Council. They offered to make O. Tanicachalam Chetty, and K. V. Reddi Naidu into ministers if they would ditch Panagal and join their faction, but these two both thought it wise to steer clear. Panagal and Patro countered with great finesse and with notable lack of principle. They lobbied support from a Muslim who was known as the 'Prince of the Khilafatists' for his role in the seditious agitations two years before, and from *The Hindu* newspaper whose Brahman editor Kasturiranga Iyengar was a leading light in the Congress. Another pro-Congress newspaper man, Panikkar, was offered a job as Registrar of the Madras University by Panagal if he would refrain from supporting the dissidents, and another Khilafatist Muslim, Abdulla Ghatalla, was made a council secretary in return for his support to the ministry.[208] Panagal was thus apparently fighting off an attack by non-Brahmans (the constituents of his own 'party'), with the help of Brahmans, Congressmen and extremist Muslims (his avowed political enemies). In this way, the ministry narrowly survived C. R. Reddy's no-confidence motion.

In more mundane battles, Panagal and his cohorts displayed similar skill in the deployment of the advantages that they possessed. The Endowments Bill, for instance, was pushed through the Council despite strong opposition since the ministry could be assured that the official and nominated blocs would file out through the 'ayes' lobby, which meant that the ministry had only to woo a few other M.L.C.s

[205] *Hindu* 10, 12 and 13 Nov. 1923.
[206] Diaries of K. V. Reddi Naidu, entry for 24 Nov. 1923.
[207] *Hindu* 24 Nov. 1923.
[208] *Hindu* 28 Nov. 1923, 1 Dec. 1923, 24 Mar. 1924; Diaries of K. V. Reddi Naidu, entries for 21, 24 and 25 Nov. 1923, 12 Dec. 1923.

with promises to use the act to their advantage. Despite Willingdon's proud assertion that a two-party system had sprung up in the Madras Legislative Council almost immediately it was convened, in fact there was little organisation of government supporters and even less of the opposition. On the first session, Ramalingam Chetty remarked: 'There is at present a tendency to send too many questions and too many resolutions and not concentrate attention on important issues. This is due to the fact that there is no organisation and each member wants to play off his own bat.'[209] In the sessions following the 1923 elections and the no-confidence motion, C. R. Reddy and other dissidents tried to form a strong party opposition but the grouping never got off the ground because, as Goschen remarked, 'no political planks could be found on which to rest the party except discontent with the Government and because the constituent factions quarrelled over the allocation of party offices'.[210] In this system, only the ministers, and particularly the chief minister holding the local government portfolio, had the resources to cement together a political following. The allocation of power within this system could therefore be decided in isolation from the Council, in the intrigue, barter and manoeuvring of the Governor's court. Thus the Justice leaders gained power in 1921 through their astute persuasion of Lord Willingdon, and thus Panagal was able to drop Reddi Naidu from the ministry in 1923 because he had allied with Patro and Todhunter to convince the Governor this was necessary.

In 1926 Panagal and his allies were pushed into opposition. It might be argued that this was due to the poor showing of the Justicites at the elections in face of the contest by the Congress Swarajist party. It was true, as the 1924 no-confidence motion had shown, that the Justice party had lost many influential supporters in the capital and, as the Tanjore conferences of 1925 had shown, that the ministers were having difficulty pleasing their network of supporters in the mofussil. But Panagal still showed that he was equal to these difficulties. In April 1925, he used the occasion of Thyagaraja Chetty's death to put his house in order. Dr Natesan was wooed back with a promise of support for some of his friends in the coming Madras Corporation elections; Reddi Naidu formally returned to the party and refused to contest against Panagal for the leadership; other ex-dissidents were

[209] T. A. Ramalingam Chetty in *Indian Review*, XXIII (January 1922), 15–16.
[210] Goschen to Reading, 2 Aug. 1924, Goschen papers vol. IV IOL.

given posts in a new skeletal framework of party organisation; and, with an eye on the approaching elections, many mofussil leaders obliged to Panagal for help in local government were marshalled into an organising committee.[211] In early 1926, Panagal felt sufficiently confident to contemplate another shuffle of the ministry; he offered to make a minister of Dr P. Varadarajulu Naidu, a Salem politician and clan head who possessed a long pedigree for Congress radicalism, if he would throw in his lot with the Justicites. But the doctor declined and the idea of a re-shuffle faded away.[212]

The Justice party did not lose at the polls. Elections, as before, were fought in the localities with little reference to outside events. The attempt of the Congress leaders to identify the party allegiances of most of the candidates and list them in *The Hindu* before the polls, brought forth a storm of protests and denials. As one successful candidate, the raja of Ramnad, wrote: 'It is not correct to say that candidates who have come out successful in the elections belong to this or that party when many of them stood and secured success in the elections without any party label . . . My constituency . . . would have returned me with equal certainty if I had announced my candidature as a Justicite, Swarajist or Independent.'[213] The Governor, attempting a tentative assessment of the election results to help him in his choice of ministry, reckoned that twenty-three of those returned were firm Congressmen, seventeen definite Justicites and fifty-eight others floated in between.[214] Moreover, even some of the most confirmed leopards were ready, if not anxious, to change their spots if circumstances demanded; when it became obvious that the Justicites would not be handed the ministry this time, M. Krishnan Nair, a close associate of Panagal, hastened to the Governor's residence to ask if 'the fact that he belonged to the Justice Party would prejudice him if I [Goschen] had an idea of making him a Minister'.[215]

The Justice leaders had in fact lost before the polls. Goschen was far more realistic about the character of Madras politics than his predecessor Willingdon had been, and far less convinced about the non-Brahman cause. On his arrival he was quite warm towards the Justice ministers, yet he found many of the senior Europeans, who

211 *Hindu* 26 May 1925, 13 July 1925.

212 *The National Dharma: Life, Speeches and Writings of Dr P. Varadarajulu Naidu* (Salem, 1948), pp. 12–13.

213 *Hindu* 25 Nov. 1926.

214 Goschen to Reading, 3 Dec. 1926, Goschen papers vol. V IOL.

215 Goschen to Birkenhead, 18 Nov. 1926, *ibid.*

were now engaged with the ministers in disputes over service appointments, were openly unfriendly to them. In 1924 he watched his ministers forward to the Muddiman Committee a scathing attack on the nature of dyarchy and, in particular, on the overriding power of the Governor. Throughout his stay, he had been subject to the persuasive flattery of C. P. Ramaswami Iyer, the arch-enemy of the Justicite leaders. By late 1925 his attitude to the Justice leaders had visibly begun to cool.[216] Thus it was that in December 1925, observers noted the poor attendance at the annual Justicite conference, and in particular the absence of the big estate-holders who were the financial backbone of the party.[217] The reason for this absence was said by some to be the quarrel over the Endowments Bill, but it is evident that the Justice leaders had already settled this matter with the estate-holders. The truth was that these men felt they could not afford to be closely associated with a party leadership which had lost the confidence of the Governor and which was on the point of being consigned to the opposition benches. M. Krishnan Nair, when he hurried to the Government chamber in 1926, was just the last of a long line of erstwhile Justicites who had begun to hedge their bets.

Another reason for Goschen's coolness to the Justice leaders, was his wish to accommodate the Congress Swarajists in the ministry and thus hopefully to tame them and to reconcile them to dyarchy.[218] When the 1926 elections were over, it was clear that men of all political colourings were anxious to get a toehold in the ministry; the last six years had revealed without a doubt the importance of ministerial office. Goschen at first summoned the Swarajist leader C. V. S. Narasimha Raju and asked him to form a ministry. Narasimha Raju himself, who had been wooed into the Swarajist camp in the hope that the Swarajists would form a ministry, was keen; but the policy of the all-India Congress was to refuse office and obstruct the operation of dyarchy and Narasimha Raju did not feel he could fly in the face of this policy.[219] Goschen next turned to the idea of a ministry of talents, with the hope that the Congress would change its policy line at its imminent conference at Gauhati and a Swarajist would be able

[216] Goschen complained that instead of arousing the electorate, the Justice leaders 'like to stay in Madras and intrigue in the club'. Goschen to Irwin, 24 Apr. 1926, Halifax papers vol. XX IOL.

[217] *Hindu* 24 Dec. 1925.

[218] Viceroy to Governors of Bombay, Madras, Bengal and Central Provinces, 29 Nov. 1926, Halifax papers vol. XX IOL.

[219] Goschen to Birkenhead, 2 Dec. 1926, Goschen papers vol. II IOL.

to join the ministry then. C. P. Ramaswami Iyer came forward to organise a coalition of the talents.

Goschen had correctly reckoned that the differences of political aim and political policy among the various leaders in the Legislative Council were slight and that a coalition was a wholly realistic plan. He had not however taken into account purely personal differences. Panagal could not brook the idea of any form of co-operation with his deadly foe, C. P. Ramaswami Iyer, and he withdrew the Justice party from the proceedings. Many of his followers who were as anxious as anyone to have influence in ministerial circles, were furious when they discovered, much later, the reason for Panagal's withdrawal, but they were powerless to do anything about it as Panagal was their lead into these ethereal circles in the first place.[220] Ramaswami Iyer went on to engineer an 'Independent' ministry. The Swarajists had no representative in the ministry but, under Ramaswami Iyer's watchful eye, they helped to set it up, promised it support and were able to influence ministerial actions.[221] The chief minister was Dr P. Subbaroyan, an Oxford-educated estate-holder from Salem district who had been in the Congress, had served as a whip to the Justice ministry and who was soon to become known for his flexibility, vacillation and inconsistency. His two colleagues, A. Ranganatha Mudaliar and R. N. Arokiasami Mudaliar, were notable for having kept well clear of the hurly-burly of recent years. C. P. Ramaswami Iyer was generally recognised to be the eminence grise of the ministry.[222]

The ministry remained formally 'Independent' until after the next elections in 1930 but the Justice leaders did not in fact stay out in

220 Goschen to Birkenhead, 21 Sept. 1927, *ibid.*

221 A. Kaleswara Rao, *Na Jivita Katha – Navya Andhramu* (Vijayawada, 1959), pp. 440–1: C. P. Ramaswami Iyer, *'C.P.' by his Contemporaries* (Madras, 1959), article by Dr B. Pattabhi Sitaramayya, p. 58; G. Rudrayya Chowdary, *Prakasam: a political study* (Madras, 1971), pp. 64–6; Goschen to Birkenhead, 2 Dec. 1926, Goschen papers vol. II IOL.

222 C. P. Ramaswami Iyer always drew the best of the Justicites' poison, and his success in 1926–7 occasioned an explosion of vindictive rhetoric. At the Justice party conference in 1927, the president boomed: 'The dullness of Madras midsummer has been relieved by the kaleidoscopic scenes of naked exposure of the Mylapore sanctum sanctorum and the demi-gods within. It is one mighty individual, an adept circus-master, who holds the leading strings of the Ministerial lambs and the Swarajist lions, who have been domesticated by his magic influence into a most wonderful companionship for their mutual advantage (shall we add, and the country's welfare).' *Indian Annual Register 1927*, vol. II, p. 316.

the cold for more than eighteen months. The Justicites, unaccustomed as they now were to being excluded from influence in government circles, at first showed signs of acute confusion. At their meetings they stepped up their attacks on dyarchy and on the Governor, until at the annual confederation in Coimbatore in July 1927 they demanded the recall of the Governor, slated the power of C. P. Ramaswami Iyer, debated the question of joining the Congress, and resolved not to accept office again as long as the system of dyarchy remained unchanged.[223] At party functions during these months, Panagal unveiled portraits of Gandhi.[224] But if the Justicites were confused, no less were the other political leaders. The removal of Panagal and his cohorts, and the installation of a weak ministry, took away the guidelines which, however faint, had prevented the Madras political scene from fragmenting into many little pieces over the last few years, and created a power vacuum which many were anxious to fill. After the Congress session at Gauhati had failed to authorise open Swarajist collaboration with the ministry, the position of the Madras Swarajists became increasingly uncomfortable and many politicians deserted this loose Swarajist grouping. The Independent ministers soon began to feel the tensions between their obligations to the government and their alliance with the Swarajists. Individual leaders began making preparations to find their own way out of this maze. Satyamurthi, supposedly the leader of an increasingly aggressive Congress party, began to pay visits to the Governor, to send him Christmas presents and to make it known that he was always available for ministerial service.[225] S. Muthiah Mudaliar, another Swarajist M.L.C. from rural Tanjore, formed a splinter-group in the Congress with ambitions which were no less opportunistic.[226] K. V. Reddi Naidu formed a 'Justice (Constitutionalist) Party' and began to make desperate and fervid assertions of his loyalty to the Raj.[227] The chief minister, Dr Subbaroyan, who had already quarrelled with his fellow ministers over the allocation of patronage, began thinking of a cabinet reshuffle.[228]

The visit of the Simon Commission brought matters to a head.

223 *Hindu* 2 Apr. 1927; Ramaswami Mudaliar, *Mirror of the Year*, pp. 12–18.
224 *Hindu* 9 May 1927.
225 Goschen to Irwin, 2 June 1927 and 26 July 1927, Goschen papers vol. V IOL.
226 S. Srinivasa Iyengar to S. Satyamurthi, n.d. (probably November 1927), Satyamurthi papers.
227 *Hindu* 27 Oct. 1927, 16 Jan. 1928.
228 Goschen to Birkenhead, 20 Oct. 1927, Goschen papers vol. II IOL.

Sir John Simon was to visit India in the summer of 1928 as the first part of his investigation into the progress of the Montagu–Chelmsford reforms and into the possibilities of future constitutional adjustments. The Government of India was anxious that the visit should be a success. The Congress was equally anxious that it should be a fiasco. The Justice party, in their anger at the Coimbatore Confederation, had joined with the Congress in rejecting any co-operation with the Simon Commission on the ground that it included no Indian member. The Madras ministers were unenviably trapped in this crossfire. As Simon's visit approached, C. P. Ramaswami Iyer, perhaps because he knew that the ministry he had fathered could not survive, perhaps merely because he was more ambitious, began to fish for a job in the Government of India. With Ramaswami Iyer's attentions elsewhere, Panagal was in a class all of his own in Madras, and he capitalised on the crisis with great skill. After the Coimbatore conference when the Justice party had rejected the Simon visit, sworn to refuse office and insulted the Governor, Panagal went straight to the Governor and apologised for the attacks on him.[229] In the coming months, he also made it clear that he was himself moderately happy about the Simon Commission and that he was the one man in Madras who could prevent Sir John Simon's visit to the province becoming a complete fiasco. At the end of the year, he was the only major political leader in Madras (other than the chief minister) who had not signed Jinnah's letter rejecting the Simon Commission on account of its all-white composition.[230] Now Panagal opened up negotiations with Dr Subbaroyan on the possibility of a coalition, encouraged S. Muthiah Mudaliar's defection from the Congress, and weaned another section of the Swarajists away by supporting their faction leader in the contest for the chair of the Madras Corporation.[231]

When the Madras Legislative Council in March 1928 debated the issue of the Simon Commission, Dr Subbaroyan voted with the Government while his two fellow ministers embraced the Congress policy and voted for rejection. That very evening, Panagal sat down to dine with the Governor and Sir John Simon. A few days later, the Governor asked the ministers to resign and Panagal attended the meetings in the Secretariat which decided their successors.[232] Dr

[229] Goschen to Irwin, 8 July 1927, Goschen papers vol. V IOL.

[230] Goschen to Irwin, 16 Nov. 1927, *ibid.*

[231] FR October (1), GOI Home Political 32 1927 NAI; Satyamurthi to S. Srinivasa Iyengar, n.d. (probably November 1927), Satyamurthi papers.

[232] Goschen to Birkenhead, 1 Mar. 1928, Goschen papers vol. III IOL.

Subbaroyan remained as chief minister, along with Muthiah Mudaliar, whom Panagal had urged to defect from the Swarajists, and M. R. Seturatnam Iyer, who was both a Brahman and until recently a Swarajist, but who had long been associated in Trichinopoly local politics with men whom the Justice leaders considered as their staunch allies. In the next few months, Panagal persuaded the government to make minor alterations in the procedure laid down for the Simon Commission's operations so that the Justice leaders might use this as an excuse for a formal return to an attitude of constitutionalism and collaboration. In the nine months between this re-shuffle and his death, Panagal reputedly enjoyed more power and influence in government circles than he had done even while chief minister.[233]

MINISTERS, JUSTICITES AND NON-BRAHMANS

When Panagal died in December 1928, the party lost the man who without a doubt had dominated Madras politics in the 1920s. He was difficult to replace, and the next two years witnessed a struggle between nine main contenders to inherit Panagal's mantle. The struggle was fought on two levels. On press and platform, the aspirants adopted policies on two new questions – the possibility of admitting Brahmans to the party, and the possibility of letting Justicites join the Congress – while on backstairs and in backrooms, intrigue carried on apace. There was little consonance between the two battles. The apparent issues of principle had little substance and it was hardly surprising that while the rhetorical battle was undoubtedly won by the opponents of Brahmans and of Congress-entry, the man who emerged as leader was both pro-Congress and pro-Brahman; moreover, he clinched his victory by an alliance with the man who seemed to be the leader of the other ideological faction.[234] It was B. Muniswami Naidu who emerged as leader. He had been Panagal's chief lieutenant, and was thus best placed to assume his crown, and to maintain the influence over the ministry which Panagal had possessed.

The Justice party in the 1920s was a strange animal. It was born as a faction in the narrow politics of Madras City, and by 1920 it had won government favour and was handed the first ministerships under

[233] *Justice* 16 and 17 July 1928; *Hindu* 3, 6 and 18 July 1928, 29 Aug. 1928, 5 and 7 Sept 1928; interview with K. V. Gopalaswamy, Hyderabad July 1971.

[234] Nathan, *Justice Year Book*, pt. 2, pp. 3–4; pt. 4, pp. 30–54; *Justice* 27 Sept. 1929; S. Venkatachelam Chetty to C. R. Reddy, 3, 5 and 20 June 1930, C. R. Reddy papers file 53 NMML.

the Montagu–Chelmsford reforms. As it became the 'ministerialist' party it changed rapidly. The leadership unobtrusively passed from Thyagaraja Chetty to the raja of Panagal, from the man who had founded the party to the man who now controlled the strings of government patronage, the strings out of which the party network would henceforth be woven. The leadership was small – as there was only a narrow space at the Governor's right hand – and entirely dominant – no-one possessed the resources to challenge them. Their recent followers soon sneered at them as 'autocrats' and noted their 'strong family resemblance' with senior bureaucrats. This was an accurate observation. After all the ministers, like the top men in the I.C.S., were appointed to their posts by the Governor, were practically without responsibility to pressure from below, and manoeuvred among their peers in the high echelons of political Madras to get their hands on the levers of power and patronage. The ministry at times seemed little more than an extension of the services.[235]

This small group of ministerial leaders with their acolytes, and the City Justicites – merchants, lawyers and non-Brahman service families still engaged in combat with the old Mylapore connection – were the core of the party. Beyond this group, membership was loose and in constant flux. The M.L.C.s as a group were chiefly interested in gaining access to the ministerial ante-chambers, for only thus could they promote their own district, their own causes and their own career; they were less interested in other aspects of party affiliation. As the raja of Ramnad noted in 1926: 'Some of the . . . Ministerialists, at any rate, will be Ministerialists all the time there is a Council and a Ministry, be the Ministry composed of Swarajists, Justicites, Coalition or what not.'[236] Thus many members drifted quite comfortably from supporting the Justice ministers in 1926 to supporting the Independent ministry in 1927 and then the re-shuffled ministry in 1928. At times when the future source of leadership and influence was uncertain, careful men drifted away.[237] The estate-holders deserted

[235] 'Though responsibility has been introduced, it extends only to a part of the Government – the rest of it, which is the major portion, is still bureaucratic. . . . Thus a minister, supposed to be the leader of the most numerous though not a majority party, gravely thanked the house for its kindness in adopting his budget – the style of the old bureaucrats. . . . The Ministers ape the dignity and reserve of the Executive Councillors of the Old Regime – and have in fact become a reserved subject – very reserved indeed!' Reddy, 'Dyarchy and after', p. 297.

[236] *Hindu* 25 Nov. 1926.

[237] 'Once the present ministry is defeated, the Justice Party will gain in strength as the majority of the followers of the present ministry, who are only there

the sinking Justice ship in 1926, and many others cut their connections after it had sunk at the December elections. Similarly, while in 1928 and 1929 the choice of Panagal's successor was still open to doubt, many M.L.C.s and other political notables performed an epic of fence-sitting; at one Madras meeting, speaker after speaker got up to talk about the necessary qualities of the new leader, without one daring to back the claim of any one of the nine men who were currently contesting for the leadership.[238]

Men came into the party to petition for patronage and preferment; if unrequited they might drift away and return later when the time was riper. The party was a lobby for government assistance. Of course there were exceptions; there were some men of principle who never wished to come to terms with the ministers, and there were many dissidents. The members of the party were brought together not to pursue common aims but to fight for pieces of the same cake, and inevitably such a party was divided into warring factions. Moreover, it was never really possible to discern where, amongst the many factions that filled the stage of political Madras, the Justice party ended and something else began. Although this was the pattern throughout the 1920s, at no time was it more obvious than during the dispute for Panagal's succession. It was already obvious that the Justice party had regained its role as the chief ally of government, and the party leadership was therefore important and desirable; even the current chief minister of the Independents joined in the race, and there were nine contestants in all. Each commanded a small group of supporters. Amongst those clearly within the Justice party were B. Muniswami Naidu with his 'progressives' group, K. V. Reddi Naidu with the "Constitutionalists', the Circar estate-holders led by the raja of Bobbili, and P. T. Rajan from Madura who controlled the official party organisation. On the fringes were Dr Subbaroyan and his group of Independent supporters, the men S. Muthiah Mudaliar had led out of the Swarajist alliance and into the Independent ministry in 1928, and the following of Sami Venkatachelam Chetty, a prominent City merchant and politician who had hobnobbed with everyone from Panagal to the Gandhians and who until recently had led the Madras Swarajist party. Another group which did not join in the

because of the love of ministerial power, will cross the floor. There are still a few Independents who are evidently waiting for the budget session to decide which party they must join.' S. Venkatachelam Chetty to S. Srinivasa Iyengar, 12 Mar. 1927, AICC papers file 5 of 1929 NMML.

[238] *Justice* 21 Sept. 1929.

Justice leadership brawl, but which hoped to be included in any negotiations for forming a ministry which might follow from the leadership battle, was the Congress Democratic Party the heirs of the Nationalists of 1920, still led by Satyamurthi, who had formed this group to try and prevent the Congress lurching again into a policy of seditious agitation.[239] The manoeuvres of these various groups between Panagal's death and the choice of a ministry after the 1930 elections were extraordinarily labyrinthine. Almost every possible permutation of alliances was mooted, and it was this period that caused Goschen to fit the epithet 'kaleidoscopic' to Madras politics.

Individual politicians skated smoothly over the lines demarcating different parties. Sami Venkatachelam Chetty throughout the 1920s managed to stay in the grey territory between all the parties. He was elected to the Council both as a Swarajist and as an Independent, and he contested for the Justice leadership. His chief ambitions lay in the Madras Corporation and here he managed to win the support of staunch Congressmen and leading Justicites almost on alternate years. R. K. Shanmugham Chetty, a brilliant young banker and industrialist from Coimbatore, was another chameleon. Before 1920 he had toyed with the Congress, but he stood at the 1920 elections which the Congress boycotted and soon after he joined the Justice camp. In 1922 he became Panagal's council secretary but they soon fell out. When the Bengali Congress leader C. R. Das came to Madras in 1923, Shanmugham Chetty organised his tour and tried to use the opportunity to form a new political grouping outside Congress and Justice camps. After this had failed, he returned to the Justicites, but in 1925 went over to the Swarajists and was elected to the Delhi Assembly on their ticket in 1926. There he fell out with S. Srinivasa Iyengar, the Madras Swarajist leader, and moved closer to the Moderate grouping. On his return to Madras, he once again aligned himself with the Justicites and was elected on their ticket in 1930 and 1934. Shanmugham Chetty's career was by no means unique. Others toyed with various party affiliations simultaneously; Dr Subbaroyan, while leading the Independent ministry in the Council and contesting the Justice leadership at the Tanjore conference, announced with pride 'I am still a Congressman'.[240]

[239] 'Memorandum on the state of parties in Madras', dated 5 Jan. 1929, Goschen papers vol. III IOL; Nathan, *Justice Year Book*, pt. 1, pp. 3–4; *Justice* 1 Oct. 1929; S. Venkatachelam Chetty to C. R. Reddy, 3 June 1930, C. R. Reddy papers file 53 NMML.

[240] *Hindu* 24 Nov. 1928.

Party defined its members' attitude to government, not their political convictions or their individual aims. It was, if anything, a tactical consideration. In this sort of political system there was little room for ideologies. For one thing, the system was developing so rapidly that most political actors were loath to tie themselves to ideological standpoints which might cramp their freedom to manoeuvre in the face of new opportunities. For another, most of the issues which concerned political Madras provided no grounds for ideological differences. 'In a way,' noted C. R. Reddy, 'we are all nationalists',[241] while S. Kumaraswami Reddiar emphasised 'we are all job-hunters.'[242] The rulers were creating a new political structure, with new boundaries, new institutions and new arenas. In so doing they had set off a scramble which they would later find hard to contain. Whether the participants were advancing cautiously step by step, or massing to storm the citadel itself, their ultimate strategies differed little. In this mêlée, the Justicites' non-Brahman ideologies were an early casualty. Lord Willingdon accepted the non-Brahman rhetoric at first, but by 1923 he had become more doubtful. In that year he advised the Viceroy, 'please don't think that Brahman and non-Brahman are at each other's throats like Hindus and Mahomedans in the north. There is no violent antipathy in social matters, they meet and are quite friendly.'[243] Willingdon's successor was even more cautious. Goschen noted in the mid-1920s that the non-Brahman cause had little impact outside Madras City; in the City, the communal rhetoric remained useful to those who wished to oust the men, chiefly Brahmans, who had occupied so many positions of influence in the last decade, but in the districts, the style of politics did not fit into the communal mould.[244] Political alliances and political networks in the up-country areas took little note of community.

The Justice network when it reached outside the City was no different. Four of the men whom Panagal nominated to district board presidentships in the early 1920s were Brahmans. If their community were to be ignored, they were remarkably like all the other nominees; they were men with powerful connections in local society who had some sort of access to Panagal. One had been at school with Panagal, one was related by marriage to Panagal's secretary, and the other

241 Reddy, 'Dyarchy and after', p. 296.

242 *Indian Annual Register 1927*, pt. 2, p. 318.

243 Willingdon to Reading, 30 June 1923, Willingdon papers vol. V IOL.

244 Goschen to Irwin, 24 Apr. 1926, Halifax papers vol. XX IOL.

two were lawyers and political agents for powerful local estate-holders who gave support and money to the Justice party.[245] Brahmans benefited from other ministerial patronage as well. In Ramnad, the Collector was surprised to find the ministry forcing him to accept a Brahman as a nominated member of the district board although it was against the rules and against his specific advice; the reason lay in the fact that the Brahman was the legal and political representative of the powerful Nattukottai Chetty bankers who had influence with the Justice leaders.[246] In Salem the district board president got Panagal to nominate a Brahman to his board; the man was one of his estate servants.[247] In Kistna, the man Panagal had made district board head against local wishes, infuriated people further by putting Brahmans in important posts.[248] Even in the City, it was frankly impossible to force political affairs to suit the rhetoric. Dr C. Natesan, who had formed an association to help non-Brahman graduates and was one of the fiercest campaigners for the promotion of non-Brahmans in the services, allied with Brahmans when he fought elections to the City corporation.[249] And in 1928, of course, Panagal helped install a Brahman in the ministry. The non-Brahman ideology lingered, but it was always the first casualty in a time of strain or crisis. Panagal ignored it completely when manoeuvring to defend himself in 1923; the various contestants bidding for Panagal's succession between 1928 and 1930 made alliances which took no account of the very different rhetorical positions adopted by the allies at the same time. C. R. Reddy, who was happy to pose as a non-Brahman when it suited his immediate political ends, was even more scathing about the communal stance; he argued that 'party implies the possibility of converting an opponent into a supporter. Birth is not usually susceptible to change once it has occurred'.[250] Later he observed that if political divisions were based on community, political argument must turn round the question whether one's ancestors had decided to be shepherds or scholars. Mariadas Ruthnaswamy,

245 They were T. M. Narasimhacharlu (Cuddapah), N. Subba Rao (South Kanara), T. Desikachari (Trichinopoly) and A. S. Krishna Rao (Nellore); *The Cult of Incompetence*, pp. 37–8.

246 G.O. 545 (LSG) 19 Mar. 1921 MRO.

247 G.O. 4214 (Public) 18 Nov. 1925 MRO; for other examples of the Justice ministry's patronisation of Brahmans in Salem see G.O. 1295 (LSG) 5 July 1921 MRO; G.O. 1209 (LSG) 25 June 1921 MRO.

248 G.O. 582 (LSG) 27 Mar. 1922 SAH; *Kistnapatrika* 21 June 1922, 6 Oct. 1923 NNR.

249 *Hindu* 22 Sept. 1923; Kalyanasundara Mudaliar, *Valkkaik Kurippukkal*, p. 448.

250 *Hindu* 20 Mar. 1924.

who organised the Justice Party Confederation in 1924 (which four Brahman M.L.C.s attended) argued that communalism had been merely a 'temporary expedient' while 'it was with a policy of conservative progress that we started our career, and to that policy of cautious and slow political progress we must be faithful'.[251]

The idea of communal division had become firmly lodged in the political vocabulary of the province, and from the early 1920s publicists and philosophers had begun to put more ideological meat on the bare bones of opposition to the 'political Brahman'. Largely through the writings and preachings of S. Raghavayya Chowdary in Telugu,[252] and E. V. Ramaswami Naicker in Tamil,[253] non-Brahmanism acquired the makings of a social theory. Brahmans were accused of dominating south Indian society ever since the Aryan invasions and of maintaining that domination through caste rules and ritual practices. E. V. Ramaswami Naicker's Self-Respect movement, which began when he published a weekly *Kudi Arasu* (People's Government) from 1925, and which grew greatly in stature by the end of the decade, was the most febrile origin of the new ideology. In a series of conferences between 1928 and 1931, Ramaswami Naicker and his lieutenants laid down a programme of social and political action which included: condemnation of the 'theory of superiority and inferiority'; the abolition of untouchability and the right of access to temples and wells for all communities; the proscription of holy books which promulgated Brahman mythologies; diversion of temple funds for secular uses; abolition of priests and the conduct of marriages and other rituals without Brahman priests; the abolition of all caste suffixes in personal names; the uplift of women and a rational approach to all other excrescences of south Indian society.[254] Opposition to the Brahman had thus moved a long way from the criticism of his 'skill to pass examinations', the main thrust of the non-Brahman manifesto of 1916. The Justice leaders patronised the movement and helped make Self-Respect conferences into splendid affairs, especially the 1929 conference at Chingleput. But Ramaswami Naicker was irritated that the Justice leaders paid little more than lip-service to the ideas which they applauded at these conferences.[255] Some,

[251] *Hindu* 16 Oct. 1924.

[252] See Raghavayya Chowdary, *Brahmanettara Vijayamu*, and *Brahmanettara Sangha Dharasyan*.

[253] Chidambaranar, *Tamilar Talaivar* (Erode, 1960).

[254] J. N. Ramanathan, *Akatu*; *Justice* 12 June 1928; Nathan, *Justice Year Book*, pt. 4; copy of *Revolt* 20 Feb. 1929 in Jayakar papers file 36 NAI: *Hindu* 10 May 1930.

[255] Chidambaranar, *Tamilar Talaivar*, p. 122.

like K. V. Reddi Naidu, adopted the new form of priest-less marriage ceremony advocated by the Self-Respecters, but others continued to marry their progeny in orthodox fashion,[256] and hardly one bothered to drop his caste suffix. Meanwhile in the everyday business of politics, the Justice leaders did not allow their promotion of the idea of a non-Brahman movement to direct their actions. They continued to employ Brahmans as lawyers, to hand out political patronage to Brahmans, and to keep Brahmans as friends and political allies. Moreover, once the ghost of Mylapore dominance was decisively laid by the end of the decade, even the fierce antipathy between the Justice leaders and the Mylapore Brahmans crumbled away. R. K. Shanmugham Chetty, who became a staunch advocate of non-Brahman ideas and a close associate of Ramaswami Naicker, was quite ready to use the political influence he gained in the early 1930s to help place the sons of prominent old Mylaporeans in promising jobs.[257] Political ideology and political action had drifted apart, and a good deal of the blame for this anomaly lay with government. The non-Brahman idea had begun as an appeal to the government which had it in its power to make and un-make political fortunes. As time passed the idea gained a life and a momentum of its own. As C. R. Reddy noted: 'In India everybody who asked for special representation generally got it. Perhaps it would not be long before the country would be divided between "spectacled" and "non-spectacled" interests and representation in proportion to their numbers would be claimed for them.'[258]

[256] See for instance the marriages of A. T. Pannirselvam's daughter and the raja of Ramnad's daughter; *Justice* 20 Aug. 1935; *Hindu* 10 July 1929.

[257] The people whose relatives R. K. Shanmugham Chetty helped included S. Srinivasa Iyengar, M. Ramachandra Rao and P. S. Sivaswami Iyer; see Bobbili to R. K. Shanmugham Chetty, 5 Mar. 1936; N. D. Varadachari to R. K. Shanmugham Chetty, 22 Dec. 1934, S. Parthasarathy to R. K. Shanmugham Chetty, 20 Dec. 1934; R. K. Shanmugham Chetty to Managing Director Central Bank of India, 12 Jan. 1936; Shanmugham Chetty papers.

[258] *Hindu* 7 Nov. 1935.

CHAPTER 2

The Province and the Locality

'Politicians', as one prominent Madras politician told the Royal Commission on Agriculture in 1927, 'only take care of themselves. They want something which they call by various names, but they do not impart it to the villagers. The villagers' demand is only an ignorant demand; they do not know what it is the politicians are asking for.'[1] The speaker himself came from the mofussil, even owned land in the villages of Godavari district, and yet he felt that there was a great gulf between the world of provincial politics and the world of villages and up-country towns. Indeed the style of politics at the capital – the gentlemanly and sometimes not-so-gentlemanly court politics of Governor, ministers and legislators – seemed insulated from the hurly-burly of mofussil society. By deploying the patronage of government, the Justice leaders could just about satisfy all the up-country men whom they felt they had to satisfy. Like the administrators before them, the new politicians of the Legislative Council found the superficial calm of Madras society worked to their advantage; they were not pushed this way and that by agitations or by the whims of popular sentiment.

But below the surface, south Indian society was far from peaceful; indeed in many ways it was as violent as the legendary wild west. 'The principal cases', wrote a biographer about a legal practice in an up-country town, 'related to murders which were common. There were two types of murders, those caused by sex rivalry and those due to village feuds. One murder led to another as a matter of vengeance. This series was known as chain murder cases.'[2] In poor upland areas, particularly in the Ceded Districts, these feuds were exceptionally long and violent. One famous example in Anantapur district, which came to light during a court case in 1925, had a thirty-year pedigree and at its climax had entailed at least one murder a month.[3] The

[1] *Royal Commission on Agriculture in India*, vol. III, evidence of K. V. Reddi Naidu, pp. 358–9.

[2] K. Kasipathi, *Tryst with Destiny* (Hyderabad, 1970), p. 31.

[3] Details of the feud between Chinnarappa Reddi and Thimma Reddi appear in *Hindu* 20, 22, 29 and 30 June 1925, 16 July 1925.

British courts, where the decisions often depended more on the strength and daring of the parties involved rather than on the facts of the matter, were rarely able to contain these feuds; indeed the above feud had passed into the courts countless times before the sensational hearings in 1925; each time the case had been dismissed 'for want of impartial evidence'.[4] It was not surprising then that the parties took the law into their own hands. When a court had refused to convict an accused murderer in Narasaraopet, the dead man's sister declared in open court she would have him lynched and have his head displayed outside the cinema he owned in the town; she was only narrowly prevented from living up to her words.[5] In other parts of the province, crime had other purposes. In the rich agricultural areas in the deltas of the major rivers, landowners were sometimes prepared to fight and murder for the irrigation water that was the passport to prosperity. Meanwhile, in the far south cattle rustling was the vocation of several clan groups until well into the twentieth century, and a form of rural policing which verged on being a protection racket was the accepted occupation of others.[6] Dacoity had been in decline since its heyday in the early nineteenth century, but there were still notable exponents. The most notorious was Jambalingam Nadar, a real highwayman who rampaged round the southern districts in the 1920s. He was jailed, escaped and shot down in a police ambush.[7] Many people carried weapons. Feuding magnates armed their henchmen with stout sticks before sending them off to settle a dispute, while the Anantapur feud noted above came to a head after one faction had tried to gun down the leader of the other in the middle of the main road in broad daylight. C. Rajagopalachari, the Gandhian Congress leader, carried a gun with him in his younger days when he was a lawyer in rural Salem, and had the misfortune to kill a man when he mistakenly

[4] In his summing up after one court case which arose from the feud, the judge said: 'The evidence is a mass of contradictions, discrepancies and exaggerations and probably of fabrications as well. What you have to consider is whether there is a residue of truth on which you can convict.' *Hindu* 3 Sept. 1925.

[5] Kasipathi, *Tryst with Destiny*, pp. 31–2.

[6] W. Francis, *Madras District Gazetteers: Madura* (Madras, 1906), pp. 88–92; E. Thurston, *Castes and Tribes of Southern India* (Madras, 1909), vol. III, pp. 53ff., vol. V, pp. 22ff.

[7] H. Trevelyan, *The India We Left* (London, 1972), p. 151. An extraordinary missionary, Amy Carmichael, believed she had converted Jambalingam to Christianity shortly before his last shoot-out. After his death, she tried to make his life-story into a Robin Hood legend. See Amy Carmichael, *Raj, Brigand Chief* (London, 1927).

thought he was being attacked.[8] C. P. Ramaswami Iyer carried a gun with him during his election campaign in Madras City and brandished it when the audience turned nasty.[9]

Provincial politics, however, had floated above this. Elections were conducted with discretion, there was no organised political violence like that practised by the Bengali terrorists, and there were few violent agitations or disturbances; in Non-co-operation there had been nothing more than a few attacks on liquor shops by zealous advocates of temperance, and some scuffles involving the police with forest tribesmen. The largest and most undisciplined political demonstration in Madras before 1920 had been on Gandhi's Satyagraha day in April 1919 when 100,000 people gathered on Madras beach, largely because it happened to be a major public holiday in the region.[10] But government had begun to draw the province together in a new fashion, and had begun to push the different levels of politics – local, provincial and national – into closer accord. The tremors of Non-co-operation, and the way certain provincial politicians had capitalised on them, showed that just as the provincial government had thrust itself more firmly into the localities, so the concerns of the localities would soon impinge more on the political life of the province. In the 1920s, the periphery moved closer to the centre.

Yet until 1930, Madras retained its peaceful character, and politics remained polite, unlike in the U.P. where rural agitations gave questions of land tenure an acute importance or in Bengal where Hindus and Muslims began sparring for political precedence. The reasons lay in the character of Madras local society and in the nature of the institutions through which government was drawing the localities into the ambit of provincial affairs. Madras society, both rural and urban, was characterised by hierarchy – a hierarchy often buttressed by caste distinctions and ritual practices but founded on inequalities of wealth, and a hierarchy in which those at the top controlled the others with a firm hand.

LOCAL SOCIETY AND LOCAL GOVERNMENT

Around Coimbatore town, wrote one British officer, 'sprawled the sandy villages with the houses of the principal landowner, the money-

[8] The story is told in all biographies of Rajagopalachari. See for instance Kausikan, *Rajaji* (Madras, 1968).

[9] A. Prakash, *Sir C. P.* (Madras, 1939), p. 35.

[10] G.O. 318 (Public) 2 June 1919 MRO.

lender and the village official built of brick, the rest of dried earth with roofs of palm leaves'.[11] While there were great differences between the many villages in the 'dry' tracts (the areas which depended on rain rather than rivers or irrigation works and which formed most of the province) there were certain general features in common. This officer had noted the sharp division between the standard of living of the village elite and that of the rest. He had also noted that there were three principal ingredients for domination of the village – land, capital and office. Capital, was if anything, the most important of the three.

In most parts of the Presidency, despite a slow but steady growth of population there was still spare land that could be cleared and cultivated. Meanwhile that which was cultivated was rarely worth much more than the crops that could be grown on it; but land could not be cleared, nor crops cultivated, without capital whether in the form of cash or grain. More often than not, however, the landlord and the moneylender were the same person.[12] Urban moneylenders rarely risked their cash in the villages for they 'had learnt out of their narrow experience that it is profitable to lend only to their personal acquaintances',[13] while moneylending was the commonest, and probably the most profitable, way that a substantial landlord could deploy any surplus he made out of cultivation.[14]

The dominant men of the villages formed a very distinct elite in the rural areas. The size of this elite and the degree of dominance differed greatly in different parts of the dry tract. In the remote, upland areas of the Ceded Districts, one local baron, or 'sirdar' as they were often known in the area, might hold sway over several villages; Chinnarappa Reddi, a sirdar from Anantapur district, was referred to as the 'sole monarch' of forty villages.[15] In more prosperous areas the elite was somewhat broader. Some villages sported just one dominant family; N. G. Ranga found that in a village of upland Guntur 'most of the land is in the hands of a few big ryots most of whom belong to the family

[11] Trevelyan, *The India We Left*, pp. 119–20.

[12] C. F. Brackenbury, *Madras District Gazetteers: Cuddapah* (Madras, 1915), p. 91; numerous references in *Madras Provincial Banking Enquiry Commission*; see for instance vol. I, p. 81; vol. II, pp. 36, 187, 210, 286, 297, 357, 403, 425–9; vol. IV, p. 326.

[13] N. G. Ranga, *Economic Organisation of Indian Villages*, vol. II (Bombay, 1929), p. 109.

[14] N. G. Ranga, *Economic Organisation of Indian Villages*, vol. I (Bezwada, 1926) p. 37.

[15] *Hindu* 22 June 1925.

of Nannapaneni people'.[16] Elsewhere there were several big families; a Nellore farmer told a commission in 1914 that in his village 'there are ten houses under easy circumstances. All the rest have to borrow'.[17] It is difficult to estimate the size of this village elite throughout the province since not only did the Madras Government fail to collect statistics on the size of the landholdings, but also because dominance depended as much on moneylending as on landownership. However in 1918 the Southborough Committee collected statistics to help in calculating the level of the franchise for the new legislatures, and these give at least a rough indication. In the whole of the province, 237,036 persons or 0.63 per cent of the rural population held land for which they paid Rs 30 as revenue to government or rent to a zamindar. Assessment per acre differed markedly from area to area, but averaged around Rs 2 per acre, making these the men who roughly owned more than fifteen acres. Among them were a few with much larger holdings: the Southborough Committee reckoned that 12,517 persons, or 0.03 of the rural population paid over Rs 250 in revenue or rent.[18] These landholders were scattered among the 50,000 villages of the province.[19]

The members of the village elite loomed large in the rural economy. To begin with, most of the other members of the village in some fashion depended upon them for their livelihood. The village leaders were the chief patrons of the many different artisans and other service castes, ranging from potters to barbers and scavengers to priests, and employed many of the village labourers on their home farms.[20] Many of the other landowners of the village did not own enough to support their families, and thus supplemented their holding by renting land from the village elite.[21] Meanwhile, many of the villagers had at some time to come to the village bosses for a loan.

16 Ranga, *Economic Organisation*, vol. II, pp. 113–14.

17 *Report of the Forest Committee (Madras)* (Madras, 1913), vol. II, evidence of Giddulur Chenchayya, pp. 60–2.

18 See table 7.

19 The 1921 Census counted 52,708 villages in the province. This figure referred to 'revenue villages' – that is, the area under a village headman. This was not necessarily a residential unit. The character of villages differed very greatly in different areas of the province. It ranged from fortified settlements to completely dispersed communities with virtually no village nuclei and virtually no boundaries between different settlements. *Census of India 1921*, vol. XIII, pt. I, p. 42.

20 For one example of the relations between a particularly powerful rural notable and his neighbours see B. E. F. Beck, *Peasant Society in Konku: a study of right and left subcastes in South India* (Vancouver, 1972), pp. 42–9; see also pp. 193–9.

21 There were some eight million tenants of ryotwari landholders, *Royal Commission on Agriculture in India*, vol. III, evidence of N. Carmichael, p. 292.

TABLE 7. *The rural elite*

Community	Number paying annually in rent or revenue: Over Rs 250	Rs 100–250	Rs 30–100	Total over Rs 30	Income tax payers in rural area
Brahman	3,304	8,439	24,456	36,199	1,822
Non-Brahman	8,661	31,600	150,886	191,147	10,410
Non-Caste Hindu	14	150	1,272	1,436	12
Muslim	408	1,181	5,234	6,823	1,336
Christian	78	199	1,029	1,308	117
European	52	46	27	125	120
Total	12,517	41,615	182,904	237,036	13,817
Total as percentage of rural population	0·03	0·11	0·49	0·63	0·04

SOURCE: *Evidence taken before the Reforms Committee (Franchise)* (Calcutta, 1919), vol. II, pt. VII pp. 504–49. These figures were collected to assist estimates of the size of the electorate for the legislatures after the Montagu–Chelmsford reforms.

Moneylending was not always the cruel and parasitic business which the British administrators often thought it was. Indeed, by providing the capital for cultivation, the moneylenders fulfilled a necessary function in the village economy.[22] It was true that interest rates were often frighteningly high (up to 40 per cent), that many moneylenders made vast profits and some amassed enormous holdings by foreclosing on their debtors' lands. Yet in many cases the interest rates were simply unrealistic and the moneylender did not expect to recover the principal only the interest. Most moneylenders were not anxious to grab vast amounts of land, which they would then most probably be obliged to lease back to the original owner.[23] In lending money to their neighbours, the village bosses were often investing not in the hope of gain but in the hope of dominance. It was customary for a debtor to propitiate his patron in many different ways – by working

[22] The moneylenders were also bound by the sanctions that the other villagers could impose: 'If there is a vicious man in the village and if he insists on his independence, the village combines together and prohibits the washerman, barber, scavenger and other menials from serving him.' *Report of the Forest Committee (Madras)*, vol. II, evidence of R. Ramachandra Rao, p. 51.

[23] *Madras Provincial Banking Enquiry Commission* (Madras, 1930), vol. I, p. 81.

occasionally on his home farm, by sending his wife and children to work in his house on certain days, and by bringing him gifts at festivals.[24] The landlord-moneylender would count on the support of his clients in village politics and in the new wider arenas of politics as well; these bosses, one Indian revenue officer told the Banking Commission, 'control a large part of the population and this is felt at the time of elections'.[25]

The village bosses performed many important functions of government in the villages. Each village or group of villages recognised certain men as their leaders, and these were known in different parts of the region by names like *peddakarar*, *periathanakar*, *pettandar* or *pinapedda*, which all roughly meant 'big men'. Sometimes there would only be one, sometimes many, and in the latter case they often joined together in informal councils (panchayats). The choice of these leaders was made, usually informally but sometimes by a form of election, by the villagers themselves. In general they chose the men of substance, for they had the necessary status and resources to enforce decisions in matters of dispute.[26] The chief function of these village leaders was to settle quarrels, and also in certain cases to organise communal projects. 'In marriage troubles or in land disputes of a certain kind,' noted one European observer, 'they will meet together and appoint a pedda man to settle it.'[27] It was an efficient system, and one villager reckoned that in as many as 90 per cent of the cases the disputants accepted their arbitrator's decision.[28] In coastal Chingleput district, the tahsildar reported that the village leaders 'lease out fisheries and get money. They allow ducks to graze in the fields and for that they collect money and utilise it for general purposes.'[29] The organisation of communal projects was most common in villages with tanks or irriga-

[24] B. V. Narayanaswami Naidu and V. Venkataraman, *The Problem of Rural Indebtedness* (Annamalainagar, 1935), p. 14; P. J. Thomas, *The Problem of Rural Indebtedness* (Madras, 1934), p. 14.

[25] *Madras Provincial Banking Enquiry Commission*, vol. II, evidence of Mohammed Azamulla Khan, p. 178.

[26] *Report of the Forest Committee (Madras)*, vol. II, pp. 164, 309, 400, 440–1, 555; 'Two or three influential and big ryots sit and decide these matters.... Even when the High Court decide that a certain well should go to one brother the village people could set it aside by saying that the other brother must use it.' Evidence of C. Rama Rao, p. 133.

[27] *Report of the Forest Committee (Madras)*, vol. II, evidence of Rev. G. N. Thomassen, p. 156.

[28] *Ibid.* evidence of J. Lakshmaiah Naidu, p. 148.

[29] *Ibid.* evidence of V. K. Subbier, p. 587.

tion channels which needed to be cleared of silt each year. Here the recognised leader marshalled his neighbours to do the work and imposed quite strict fines if they were late or failed to appear.[30] Some of the really big rural bosses, particularly in the poorer areas of the province, performed these sorts of functions over a wide area. Chinnarappa Reddi, the 'sole monarch' of forty villages noted above, settled disputes over inheritance and land-rights throughout his extensive domain, and enforced his decisions with a private army of helpers.[31]

The village bosses managed to mark themselves off as a recognisable rural elite. Of course, membership of the elite was by no means fixed, since fortunes rose and fell often with remarkable speed; N. G. Ranga who traced the history of a village over half a century found that the two most prosperous families of the earlier period had been hopelessly wrecked, while five families who had been indebted to them had flourished and had themselves invested seven lakhs of rupees in moneylending.[32] Yet by forging links between themselves and by adopting a particular life-style, the village bosses marked themselves off from the run-of-the-mill. A European observer, as noted above, could not help but observe their tiled houses, while an Indian biographer illustrated the status of his subject's family by writing: 'In those days only the Kasus used to eat rice in Tubadu. All others ate coarse grain.'[33] At village festivals they commonly played a role which honoured and reinforced their local status,[34] and in their homes they generally adjusted their customs and habits to the model of ritual cleanliness recognised in the area. Although they often feuded violently among themselves (and it was this that caused much of the violence in the countryside), they would also in many cases band together against others. A witness before the Banking Commission said that although the moneylenders rivalled one another in many ways, 'they form a sort of union to enforce their claims and rights on the villagers and make common cause'.[35] As far as it was possible in the tessellated pattern of castes in the Madras country-

[30] *Ibid.* pp. 423–4, 452–3, 463, 471, 491–2.
[31] *Hindu* 29 and 30 June 1925.
[32] Ranga, *Economic Organisation*, vol. II, p. 100.
[33] Kasipathi, *Tryst with Destiny*, p. 17.
[34] Whitehead, *Village Gods of South India* (Calcutta, 1921), pp. 49–50; Beck, *Peasant Society in Konku*, pp. 118–20.
[35] *Madras Provincial Banking Enquiry Commission*, vol. II, evidence of B. Sitarama Raju, p. 45.

side, they married their daughters into families of equivalent status. Indeed where a bride who met the approval of caste rules was not available, rich landowners were more likely than anyone else to bend the rules in order to secure a decent marriage alliance.[36] In some cases these marriage alliances, coupled with changes in ritual practices, had marked the richer members of a local community off as a separate subcaste. 'While there are at least fourteen major and many more subcastes among the Reddis,' noted one Indian biographer, 'the principal division seems to be between the Prabhu or the ruling Reddis and the panta or the peasant class.'[37] The handful of Velama zamindari families who exchanged marriageable sons and daughters with one another and with hardly anyone else, had become known as the 'Rajya Velamas', although this was not a subdivision that figured in historical accounts of the various types of Velama. Moreover, these Velama zamindari families had managed one of the most remarkable changes in custom, which marked them off from all other Velamas; in imitation of the powerful Rajput families of north India, they kept their wives in purdah, a practice almost unique in south India.[38]

The framework of British rule had, if anything, strengthened the position of the village elite. Rural society had been sharply stratified before the arrival of the British, and the Pax Britannica and the ryotwari settlement had removed the adventurers and interlopers who posed the biggest threat to the position and the status of the village bosses. Of course, in some of the territory, the British left the zamindars in control and by allowing some of their political supremacy to rub off on the zamindars gave them a potentially powerful position. Some of the zamindars worked to realise their own power by taking over many of the roles of the village boss within their domains. They lent money to their tenants, settled disputes and governed their estates with a firm hand. For the most part, however, the zamindars were happy with the status they acquired from their role in the revenue system and from the recognition that government accorded them, and they left the villages and the village bosses to their own devices. Indeed, they often needed the help of the village bosses to collect the revenue from the estates and thus had to strike a bargain with them.[39]

The ryotwari settlement, while it cut away all intermediaries between government and villager, was not a great leveller. Indeed,

36 Beck, *Peasant Society in Konku*, p. 252.

37 Kasipathi, *Tryst with Destiny*, p. 5.

38 S. Wadsworth, 'Lo, the poor Indian', typescript memoir, p. 51 SAS.

39 For more detailed consideration of the zamindari areas see below ch. 3.

Thomas Munro, one of the chief architects of the system, recognised that the administration of Madras would depend on the existence of, and assistance from, big men in the villages; he wrote in 1817:

> Where there is no village establishment, we have no hold upon the people, no means of acting upon them, none of establishing confidence. Our situation, as foreigners, renders a regular village establishment more important to us than to a native Government, our inexperience, and our ignorance of the circumstances of the people, make it more necessary for us to seek the aid of a regular establishment to direct the internal affairs of the country, and our security requires that we should have a body of head men of villages interested in supporting our dominion.[40]

The ryotwari administration pivoted round the village officers – the karnam or village accountant and, more important than he, the village headman.[41] While the karnam was often a Brahman or other literate, the headman was generally drawn from the village elite. At the early settlements, the British administrators relied heavily on these men and their records while calculating the revenue on each field, and most of these calculations did not come in for scientific revision until new and more efficient surveys were undertaken after 1860.[42] The actual revenue demand was fixed each year at jamabandi, a process whereby a senior revenue official in two months of the hot season sped round several hundred villages checking on the extent of cultivation, revising land deeds, inspecting the village records and hearing petitions and objections. 'It struck me' wrote one Assistant Collector about jamabandi, 'as having become so overloaded with details as to be beyond the capacity of any single person to deal with efficiently . . . One just had to accept many answers on trust.'[43] The revenue official had to rely very much on what he was told by the village officers.

These village officers thus gained great opportunities for power and profit within the revenue system. The village officers parcelled out revenue demand within the village, collected the revenue instalments, kept the records and conducted any distraint proceedings for realising arrears. The new surveys in the 1860s revealed huge tracts of land which had either lain hidden and untaxed, or where the assessment bore little relation to the land itself, and of course it was the village officers and their cronies in the village elites who profited. It was part

[40] T. H. Beaglehole, *Thomas Munro* (Cambridge, 1966), pp. 116–17.

[41] *Village Officers and Ryots Manual* (Madras, 1931).

[42] See the chapters on land revenue in the various volumes of the *Madras District Gazetteers*.

[43] Sir Richard Tottenham papers, p. 17 SAS.

TABLE 8. *The urban elite*

Community	Number paying annually in property and profession taxes				
	Over Rs 50	Rs 20–50	Rs 5–20	Rs 1–5	Total over Rs 1
Brahman	544	1,803	8,588	15,417	26,352
Non-Brahman	1,957	4,802	26,548	78,631	111,938
Non-Caste Hindu	7	69	347	2,412	2,835
Muslim	492	1,088	4,624	16,713	22,917
Christian	138	336	1,405	4,824	6,703
European	374	249	276	231	1,130
Total	3,512	8,347	41,788	118,228	171,875
Total as percentage of urban population	0·15	0·37	1·83	5·18	7·53

SOURCE: *Evidence taken before the Reforms Committee (Franchise)*, vol. II, pt. VII pp. 504–49. These figures were collected to assist estimates of the size of the electorate for the legislatures after the Montagu–Chelmsford reforms.

of folklore that any land auctioned off to realise arrears went only to the men the village officers wanted to have it,[44] and at jamabandi it was a brave man who would speak out against the village officers and risk retribution in the coming year.[45] Besides, in other ways too, the British had lowered the great panoply of their government on to the shoulders of the village officers. They were officially recognised as village policemen and as magistrates in village courts. In the administrative reforms of the later nineteenth century, government had made strenuous attempts to qualify their powers by submitting them to examinations, depriving them of their subordinate staff, restricting their freedom with new bureaucratic rules, and improving the quality of supervision of their work by revenue officials. Yet it was still said in the 1920s that a man would pay Rs 5,000 to get the post of a headman although the official honorarium was only a handful of rupees.[46]

44 *Madras Provincial Banking Enquiry Commission*, vol. II, pp. 94, 302, 337.

45 'With the revenue powers vested in them ... they are still the demigods of the village.' K. Jayaraman, *A Study of Panchayats in Madras* (Bombay, 1947), p. 56.

46 The raja of Ramnad in a debate in the Madras Legislative Council on 17 Feb. 1922, copy in GOI Home Judicial 1–2 1922 NAI.

The urban areas of the province were marked by a similar pattern of acute economic stratification; they contained a few palaces and many cheris (hut quarters). The concentration of wealth was immediately noticeable when the British began to tax urban earnings and to base municipal and provincial franchises on tax-paying capacity. In 1911, only 469 manufacturers, 679 urban property-owners and 27,360 businessmen earned over Rs 10,000 and qualified to pay the income tax.[47] In 1918, the Southborough Commission found that 171,875 persons or 7·53 per cent of the urban population paid more than one rupee in municipal taxes, while only 3,512 or 0·15 per cent paid more than fifty rupees.[48]

The urban elite, while containing a sprinkling of administrators, professionals and others, was made up chiefly of businessmen. With the slow but steady growth of trade, cash-cropping and processing industries, the commercial sections of many towns were enjoying reasonable prosperity in the early years of the twentieth century. Those who were gleaning the best profits were the few who controlled the capital necessary for trade and manufacture. In some of the smaller towns, the lion's share of working capital was in the hands of one family alone, and even in some of the larger settlements a handful of families stood head and shoulders above the rest. In Ellore, for instance, a town with half a lakh of people, one family was said to control most of the capital, and thereby most of the other merchants.[49] Most traders and financiers were wary of lending money to anyone but kinsmen and acquaintances, and thus it was difficult for any newcomer to break into the charmed circle of the urban wealthy.[50] Venkatappa Naicker did; he rose from being a labourer to being one of the two magnates who controlled the town of Erode in Coimbatore district,[51] but it was a tough career and it was exceptional. Before 1920, there had been no significant changes in the capital market which might have made things easier for new men. The joint-stock company had been introduced, but most of the companies registered before 1920 were not new businesses but old family concerns taking advantage of a better legal framework. An attempt to start a stock exchange in Madras in the early 1920s faltered owing to lack of

[47] *Board of Revenue Madras, Income Tax Statistics 1911–12*, pp. 12–13.

[48] See table 8.

[49] G.O. 1011 (L & M, M) 17 July 1901 MRO.

[50] See for example *Minutes of Evidence taken before the Indian Industrial Commission*, vol. III, pp. 51–5, 124 (evidence of Mothey Gangaraju).

[51] Chidambaranar, *Tamilar Talaivar* (Erode, 1960), pp. 9–12.

interest.[52] New European-style banks had been introduced, and by 1920 there were nineteen joint-stock banks with paid-up capital of over five lakhs of rupees each. There was also the government-inspired Bank of Madras which had paid-up capital of fifty lakhs of rupees and which in 1920 was merged with the two other Presidency Banks to form the Imperial Bank.[53] The problems faced by these banks, however, were exactly those faced by any urban financier – the Bank of Madras in 1922, for instance, had its entire profits wiped out by one fraud case[54] – and thus they acted in a similar manner and lent only to safe enterprises and only under stringent conditions. This meant, in fact, that they lent chiefly to Europeans, and while many disgruntled Indian businessmen complained of racial favouritism, the bank directors explained that they were merely adhering to the conservative principles of the cautious banker.[55] Substantial Indian merchants in Madras City used the new banks, but up-country traders found their rules and conditions restrictive: banks in the locality could not provide exchange facilities, banks in the capital would probably not deal with such distant customers. The banks lent only to the most substantial of clients, and thus they helped to concentrate commercial capital in a few hands.[56] In the early 1920s, for instance, one Chetty banker who managed to convince the Madras Bank of his worth made a very profitable business out of borrowing from the Madras Bank, taking the funds 150 miles into the mofussil and lending them there at a rate of interest fractionally higher than that which he paid in Madras.[57]

The tightness of capital encouraged the growth of a few large and sprawling business empires, rather than many smaller ones. The Banking Commission in 1930 found that in Cocanada, one of the most flourishing port towns of the province, just twenty-four Vaisya firms controlled the seventy lakhs of rupees which financed local trade. Moreover, control was in fact even more concentrated than this suggested. One of these Vaisya merchants contributed fifteen of those seventy lakhs, and seven of the others, controlling another fifteen lakhs, were related to him.[58] The Motheys, the major Vaisya family

[52] J. Dupuis, *Madras et le Nord du Coromandel* (Paris, 1960), pp. 500–2.
[53] *Statistical Tables relating to Banks in India* (annual) for 1925, pp. 8–18.
[54] *Hindu* 23 Aug. 1923.
[55] *Minutes of Evidence taken before the Indian Industrial Commission*, vol. III, pp. 257–62, 275–7.
[56] *Madras Provincial Banking Enquiry Commission*, vol. II, p. 10; vol. III, pp. 404–5.
[57] *Ibid.* vol. IV, pp. 242–61.
[58] *Ibid.* pp. 374–416.

of Ellore, not only lent money to other merchants but also ran cotton and jute mills, an export business, bus companies and several wholesale trading concerns.[59]

Many apparently small-scale manufacturing concerns carried on in dozens of little workshops, were in fact floated on the capital of a handful of financiers. Some of the most important industries of the province were organised in this fashion – handloom weaving, tanning and cheroot manufacture in Madras City, which were the biggest industries there in terms of workforce, cloth-dyeing in Salem, and brass-manufacture in Kumbakonam.[60] The managing agency system, introduced by the European companies, had encouraged the lateral spread of business concerns. The system flourished because there was more European capital than European expertise invested in India, and experienced companies often managed the affairs of a diverse range of different concerns. Some Indian merchants had become party to the managing agency system; K. Suryanarayanamurthy Naidu of Cocanada, for instance had taken over Innes & Co. when the European partner died in 1910 and thus had a diverse export business as well as a substantial share in several local mills and other local enterprises.[61] In Madras City, the Europeans guarded their near monopoly of big business more jealously, yet European agency houses still needed to work with subsidiary Indian concerns; often they encouraged trusted Indian dependants to spread their operations throughout the many different concerns of the agency house itself. P. M. Balasubramania Mudaliar, who began as a contractor for Best & Co., eventually became a partner in a transport company, an agent for Burmah Shell, a director of several mills and a partner in several banks.[62]

Like the rural bosses, the urban magnates invested as much in their local status as in their financial future. By controlling capital they gained influence over the local economy, by funding charity and religion they won merit and status,[63] by providing jobs and social

[59] S. Playne, *South India: its history, peoples, commerce and industrial resources* (London, 1915), pp. 614–16.

[60] Dupuis, *Madras et le Nord du Coromandel*, pp. 220, 493–8; *Report on the Survey of Cottage Industries in the Madras Presidency by D. Narayana Rao* (Madras, 1929), passim.

[61] *Minutes of Evidence taken before the Indian Industrial Commission*, vol. III, pp. 88–91; Playne, *South India*, pp. 615–16.

[62] T. N. Satchit (ed.), *Who's Who in Madras 1938* (Cochin, 1938).

[63] See for instance the boast of Lodd Govindoss, a Gujarati gems merchant and landowner, that his family had given away over Rs 10 lakhs in charity and more in public benefactions. All over the province there were rest-houses and cattle-

services they acquired the position of patron.[64] Moreover, in the absence of close bureaucratic control by government, they took on most of the political management of the towns they lived in. Committees or urban notables settled many cases of local dispute, and often worked to restore order when the bazaar ran riot or when two communities started fighting.[65]

LOCAL SELF-GOVERNMENT AND THE REFORMS OF 1919–20

The British administration of Madras in the nineteenth century relied to a large extent on the fact that the society over which it was perched was quite capable of running itself. The regime, by imposing itself gently on the subject people, was able to draw on the strengths of the real governors. For the moment, the latter were quite satisfied with this state of affairs. The administrative changes of the late nineteenth and early twentieth centuries, however, extended the writ of government more deeply into society. This was not achieved with any new resources of money and manpower on the part of government, but rather by bringing informal structures of political control into closer association with the formal framework of government. This policy was pursued with particular enthusiasm in the Madras Presidency, since the Madras Government was unable to identify a class of landowners or administrators which it might set out to win over and then use as a buttress to British rule, and thus had to devise institutions which might attract the interest and collaboration of the most important leaders of society. That was what the ryotwari settlement had managed to achieve, and that was what the schemes of local self-government, it was hoped, would continue to achieve within a new and more extensive framework of rule. From the middle years of the nineteenth century, the Madras Government occasionally employed committees of non-officials to assist with certain aspects of local administration, but it was after Viceroy Ripon's local self-government acts in the 1880s

troughs bearing his name. B. V. Nancharya, *Biography of Lodd Govindoss Varu* (Madras, 1942), pp. 1–14; Satchit (ed.), *Who's Who in Madras 1934*, p. 64.

64 See for instance the boast of K. A. Shanmugha Mudaliar, a big yarn and cloth merchant, that he was 'helping many poor people by providing them with work and livelihood'. *Directory of the Madras Legislature*, published by the Madras Legislature Congress Party (Madras, 1938), p. 240–20.

65 See the panchayat formed to restore order after communal rioting in Salem, *Hindu* 3 July 1928.

that the new policy acquired momentum.[66] The primary aims of the new local self-government boards were to associate local notables with the touchy business of raising extra revenues, and to draw on their knowledge and assistance to help in the provision of better local services and amenities at the least possible administrative cost to the exchequer.

Local self-government first became important in the towns of the province. Following Ripon's acts, the Madras Government formed municipalitites in all the major towns of the province. At first it intended the municipal councils to be adjuncts to the Collector's personal administration. The Collector presided over them ex officio, and the members of the councils were hand-picked. Before long, however, government recognised that controlled elections were a more efficient way of choosing members of the local elite to serve on the boards, and that the Collector could not realistically deal with the rapidly growing business of the municipalities as well as his many other responsibilities. Government removed the Collector to a more elevated supervisory role, increased the number of elected members and handed the chairmanship over first to nominated and then to elected non-officials. With these changes, the municipal councils soon grew in stature and importance in local affairs.[67]

By 1918 there were seventy-two councils with 586 elected and 465 other members, and fifty of them elected their chairman.[68] The duty of these councils was to look after 'everything necessary for or conducive to the safety, health, convenience or education of the inhabitants'.[69] In practice this meant that they maintained roads, ran schools, provided water, organised sanitation, managed hospitals and dispensaries, controlled markets, fairs, slaughter-houses and burial grounds, licensed industrial enterprises, managed public property and supervised chatrams and charitable trusts. To perform these duties they had to raise taxes, to employ a retinue and to distribute contracts. Their chief receipt was rates on property, but besides this they taxed animals, vehicles, servants, professions and trades and levied fees on water-supply, schools, markets, slaughter-houses and

[66] For the early history of local boards in the province see K. K. Pillai, *History of Local Self-Government in the Madras Presidency 1850–1919* (Bombay, 1953).

[67] J. G. Leonard, 'Urban government under the Raj: a case study of municipal administration in nineteenth-century south India', *Modern Asian Studies*, VII, 2 (1973), 227–51.

[68] See table 9.

[69] *Indian Statutory Commission*, vol. VI, pp. 394–7.

cart stands.[70] Their retinue ranged from secretaries, office managers and revenue collectors to lighting attendants and scavengers. Their contracts covered removal of rubbish, repair of roads, construction of new public buildings and provision of water pipes.

The municipalities' duties brought government into almost every urban dweller's backyard, while their powers and their patronage attracted the attention of several of the townsmen. Municipalities were already the scene of lively politics before reforms in the years immediately following the first world war transformed them yet again. The Madras Government, fearing that the Montagu–Chelmsford Legislative Council after 1921 would introduce unacceptably radical reforms of local government, rushed through five major acts relating to local government in the last eighteen months under the old constitution.[71] These acts made the municipalities wholly elective except for a few seats reserved for backward communities and minority interests; they lowered the franchise qualifications (based on ownership of property and payment of taxes) so that 5.4 per cent of the municipal population was included in the electorate; they deprived the Collector and other officials of ex-officio membership of the councils and diminished the Collector's supervisory powers; they increased the councils' duties and their taxes – the rates or property were raised, and new taxes on entertainments, pilgrims, lighting, education, conservancy and scavenging were introduced.[72] After these reforms, few could ignore the importance of the municipalities, and many had a chance to gain power in them. By 1925 all but four of the eighty municipal councils had elected chairmen; there were 1,284 elected members, over double the number in 1918; and the budgets handled by the municipalities had tripled in fifteen years.[73] The importance of this speedy opening up of urban administration can be gauged from the immediate response. On the one hand, there was a widespread reaction against the march of government which was most often expressed in a distaste for paying taxes. The local self-government department in Madras spent a lot of time in 1921–2 cancelling resolutions passed by municipalities to abolish or reduce the property or professional taxes; Rajahmundry municipal council

[70] See table 11.

[71] *Views of Local Governments on the Working of the Reforms, dated 1923*, p. 23.

[72] V. Venkata Rao, *A Hundred Years of Local Self-Government and Administration in Andhra and Madras States 1850–1950* (Bombay, 1960), pp. 11–13, 85–6; G.O. 973 (LSG) 30 May 1921 MRO.

[73] See tables 9 and 10.

TABLE 9. *Constitution of local government*

		Members				Chairmen			
	Number	Total	Ex-officio	Nominated	Elected	Ex-officio	Nominated official	Nominated non-official	Elected
(a) District municipalities									
1892–3	55	863	na	na	383	—	4	9	32
1899–1900	60	931	na	na	446	—	9	8	32
1910–11	61	954	74	416	464	—	9	10	35
1919–20	73	1,082	99	315	668	—	3	11	59
1929–30	81	1,684	—	407	1,277	—	2	2	77
1934–5	81	1,769	—	—	1,769	—	—	—	79
(b) District boards									
1894–5	21	658	78	277	303	21	—	—	—
1899–1900	21	660	79	272	309	21	—	—	—
1909–10	23	702	109	272	321	23	—	—	—
1919–20	25	803	125	195	483	20	—	5	—
1924–5	25	896	116	215	565	1	1	12	11
1929–30	25	971	129	232	610	—	1	2	22
1934–5	26	1,322	—	4	1,318	—	—	—	26

SOURCE: *Report on the Working of Local Boards in the Madras Presidency* (annual) and *Report on the Working of District Municipalities in the Madras Presidency* (annual), for the years shown; tables entitled: 'Statement showing the constitution of the Local Boards and Union Panchayats in the Madras Presidency during the year ...', and 'Statement showing the constitution of the municipalities in the Madras Presidency during the year ...'

TABLE 10. *Local government expenditure*

	Expenditure by municipalities (Rs)	Expenditure by rural boards (Rs)	Total as Index
1890–1	3,331,210	8,107,420	100
1899–1900	6,249,745	9,204,376	135
1909–10	9,368,505	15,577,995	218
1919–20	18,044,565	26,650,800	391
1929–30	29,657,109	53,917,926	731
1939–40	42,279,987	50,557,457	812

SOURCE: *Statistical Abstract for British India and the Indian States* (annual) for years shown. Tables entitled 'Expenditure of Municipalities' and 'Income and Expenditure of District and Local Boards'.

even resolved to close the local high school so that it need not raise more taxes.[74] Several small towns resisted incorporation into the municipalities for the first time, largely because their merchant communities had no wish for their businesses to be subjected to government controls and their pockets to be taxed. The inhabitants of Chirala town in Guntur district went so far as to stage an exodus from the new municipal limits and thus became the rather bewildered heroes of Gandhian Non-co-operation.[75] Non-co-operation agitation in Bezwada, Repalle and many other towns harvested similar movements against local taxes. It became a common practice for a party who had just won control of a municipality to take the tax registers off the shelves and rewrite them to the advantage of their friends and the detriment of their enemies. Evasion of municipal taxes, and non-payment of arrears, rose steeply throughout the 1920s, while 'a common electioneering practice' according to the 1925 Tax Commission, 'is for a candidate to distribute to voters printed forms of appeal against the assessments to the municipal house tax and to promise remissions, if elected'.[76]

On the other hand, some local interests rushed to occupy the new places of power in the municipalities. In the years before 1920, many urban interests had been unable to find a place in municipal affairs either because the franchise was so high (only 2·4 per cent was enfranchised) and the number of elected places so few (an average of eight

[74] *Hindu* 19 Feb. 1923.

[75] G.O. 583 (LSG) 28 Mar. 1921 MRO; *Hindu* 28 July 1921; G. V. Subba Rao, *Sree Gopalakrishnayya* (Amalapuram, 1935), pp. 45–73.

[76] *Report of the Indian Taxation Enquiry Committee 1924–5*, vol. I, pp. 307–8.

TABLE 11. *Local government taxation*

Heads of revenue	Aggregate revenue in thousands of rupees		
(a) District municipalities	1900–1	1925–6	1935–6
Property tax	857	2,768	3,890
Animals and vehicles tax	198	576	521
Professions and trades tax	196	728	656
Menials and servants tax	4	—	26
Education tax	—	155	406
Entertainments tax	—	—	60
Pilgrim tax	—	110	65
Conservancy rates	—	—	593
Lighting rate	—	23	982
Water rate	154	1,239	1,974
Tolls	398	1,508	859
Market and slaughter-house fees	214	739	1,116
Licence fees	45	308	510
Education fees	124	472	591
Cart stand etc. fees	30	97	175
Rent and sale of municipal property	74	383	472
Fines	39	334	431
Grants from Government and local funds	284	2,727	2,030
Total (including other heads)	3,250	16,382	20,949
(b) Rural boards	1894–5	1914–5	1934–5
Land revenue cesses	6,022	1,039	1,727
Local rates		6,747	11,363
School fees	208	371	1,059
Rent of choultries etc.	408	775	2,383
Income from railways	—	6,932	13,445
Total (including other heads)	8,165	22,751	51,778

SOURCE: *Report on the Working of Local Boards in the Madras Presidency* (annual) and *Report on the Working of District Municipalities in the Madras Presidency* (annual). Tables entitled: 'Statement showing the revenue of the several Local Boards and Union Panchayats in the Madras Presidency for the year . . .' and 'Statement showing the income of the municipalities in the Madras Presidency during the year. . .'

per council) or because the Collector had deliberately excluded them. In some places, the Collectors were too busy to intervene; in others, however, they had deliberately excluded certain interests, generally merchant communities, and had favoured the landowners and the educated whom they felt to be more trustworthy. In Guntur town, for instance, the rich Komati merchants found it very difficult to get control of the municipality, although they were its chief source of revenue; this was one reason why the Guntur Komatis with Brahman lawyers as their representatives had made their town the centre of agitation and nationalist organisation in the Andhra district.[77] In Madura town the Saurashtras, a community of dyers and weavers who had migrated from Gujarat, formed almost a third of the population and dominated the trade and manufacture of cotton products.[78] In the 1910s, the Collectorate had set its face against 'Saurashtra tyranny in municipal affairs' and kept many Saurashtra merchants and their Brahman, Muslim and other allies out of power in the municipality.[79] After the franchise was widened and the Collector's powers reduced in 1920, there was a race for power which showed itself in agitations, new ratepayers associations and dramatic factional struggles. In Madura, in the space of four years there was a major mill-strike, a non-Brahman agitation, a Non-co-operation campaign and a tussle to control the Minakshi temple; two ratepayers associations, railway and postmen's unions, a branch of the Khilafat committee and a Congress Sabha were formed, and the Saurashtra community organisation was revitalised; and between 1920 and 1923 municipal affairs were in complete uproar and the municipal chair changed hands four times.[80] In Ellore, there was a concerted attempt to break the power of the Mothey family, the rich Komati merchants who were the chief financiers of local trade and industry, and who had run the municipality since the 1880s.[81] In Bezwada, merchants and lawyers formed a ratepayers association and tried to destroy the power of one Appalaswami, a low-caste merchant and contractor who had reputedly been the king-maker of all the municipal chairmen and most of the councillors for the past decade; when Appalaswami's men resisted, the opposition disrupted a major temple festival, fuelled a Non-co-opera-

[77] K. Venkatappayya, *Sviya Caritra* (Vijayawada, 1952 and 1955), pp. 156–8; K. Kotilingam to P. S. Sivaswami Iyer, n.d. (probably 1919), Sivaswami Iyer papers NAI.

[78] K. R. R. Sastri, *The Madura Sourashtra Community: a study in applied economics* (Bangalore, 1927); A. J. Saunders, 'The Sourashtra community of Madura, south India', *American Journal of Sociology*, XXXII (1926).

[79] G.O. 1384 (L & M, M) 16 Aug. 1917 MRO; G.O. 1074 (L & M, M) 12 June 1912 MRO; G.O. 1203 (L & M, M) 1 July 1912 MRO.

[80] *Hindu* 22 and 28 June 1920, 22 Aug. 1920; G.O. 1150 (LSG) 7 July 1923 MRO.

[81] *Hindu* 28 Apr. 1921; G.O. 667 (LSG) 10 Feb. 1928 MRO; G.O. 600 (LSG) 31 Mar. 1922 SAH.

tion campaign in the town and forced the British to call troops into the district.[82] In Salem, the municipal chairman himself started an agitation in the hope that he could thus stay ahead of his rivals.[83] Although such agitations and factional battles were not a new feature of municipal politics, in the years immediately following the 1920 reforms they were more widespread, less contained than ever before.

Before 1920, local government in the rural areas was far less advanced than in the towns. In each of the twenty-four districts, there was a district board; under each of these were ranged five or six taluk boards, and beneath these there were panchayats and union boards in some of the villages and small towns. Their administration extended to all the areas not covered by municipalities and their brief was exactly the same. In practice their chief responsibilities were the construction, maintenance and management of roads and sometimes railways, the administration of schools and hospitals, the supervision of markets and fairs, and the control of charitable endowments. The chief source of income was a land cess. Until well into the twentieth century, the Collector presided over the district board and his Revenue Divisional Officers over the taluk boards, and the boards acted as little more than useful adjuncts to official administration. P. Kesava Pillai, a prominent political figure from the later years of the nineteenth century, described in 1908 how successive Collectors had put him on the rural boards, taken him off and put him back on again and how he could 'not be free to talk in the presence of the Collector'.[84] In 1910, over half the members of the district boards were government nominees or ex-officio members, while the rest were elected from taluk boards which in turn had a high number of officials and nominees.[85] But while the rural boards devolved little concrete power on to Indians, the boards undertook important duties and offered some opportunities for local notables to influence the Collector and other officials.

The speed with which rural boards were made over to Indian control was quite remarkable. The first non-official was appointed head of a taluk board in 1912, and the first elections for four of these

[82] A. Kaleswara Rao, *Na Jivita Katha – Navya Andhramu* (Vijayawada, 1959), pp. 291–2, 350–1; G.O. 109 (L & M, M) 23 Jan. 1917 MRO; G.O. 2028 (L & M, M) 10 Dec. 1919 MRO.

[83] *Hindu* 9 Aug. 1921, 26 Feb. 1922; G.O. 169 (Public) 22 Feb. 1922 MRO.

[84] *Royal Commission on Decentralisation*, vol. II, *Evidence taken in Madras* (London, 1908), pp. 167–8.

[85] See table 9.

posts were granted in 1917. By 1923, 111 of 125 taluk boards elected their presidents. 1917 also saw the first four non-officials nominated to the head of district boards and 1923 the first elected head. Four years later, all but four district board presidents were elected. Acts in 1920, similar to those of the municipalities, took the Collectors and Revenue Divisional Officers off the rural boards, and made the boards predominantly elected bodies, although the district board members continued to be elected indirectly via the taluk boards. The 1920 Acts also increased the duties of rural boards, broadened the electorate, raised their revenues, and gave them more independent control over their own budget.[86]

The reaction was similar to that in the municipalities, only more marked as the rural board had truly been transformed within a decade from a bureaucratic appendage into an institution of unprecedented importance in rural politics and administration. As in the municipalities, the outcry against the new taxes revealed how greatly local government impinged on local society. The doubling of the maximum rate of the land cess caused a major storm in the Legislative Council.[87] Opposition to the profession tax, newly introduced into the rural areas by the 1920 Act, grew and grew until government had to admit that the expenses of collection almost exceeded the returns.[88] Meanwhile the sleepy character of the local board meetings was transformed as important men began to take an interest.

These new institutions supplanted the individual local bosses in the business of governing the locality. They provided more public services and they wielded far greater patronage than the old local bosses had. The latter quickly became aware that it was both possible and necessary to seek much of the prestige and power, that they had previously gained through their personal role as arbiters and benefactors, through membership of these new institutions. Moreover, the new bodies ruled over areas much larger than those which the individual bosses controlled. They thus offered new and more attractive avenues of influence, and brought many of the old bosses together to dispute for these higher prizes.

The men who were taken into municipal administration were chiefly drawn from the ranks of the professional and mercantile communities. There were some retired administrators, some astrologers and other

[86] GOI Education and Health Local Boards 5B August 1921 NAI.
[87] GOI Education and Health Local Boards 5B August 1921 NAI.
[88] *Report of the Indian Taxation Enquiry Committee 1924–5*, vol. I, pp. 308, 317.

queer fish, and some people whose influence came from managerial activities. In the latter category, there were often men who held important positions in the big European companies in the town; Guntur municipality included the clerk of a European-owned company which managed much of the export of tobacco from the district; M. Abboy Naidu, cash-keeper at Madura cotton-mills, was a prominent figure in Madura municipality for many years; a railway employee, F. G. Natesan, was municipal councillor and sometime chairman in Trichinopoly, site of the South Indian Railway workshops. Professional people, chiefly doctors and lawyers, had played a large part in the early days of municipal administration since the Collectors had often nominated them; they expected doctors to help with sanitary work, which the British hoped would be one of the main contributions of municipal administration, and believed that most educated men would be keen about the provision of public services and public facilities. Many professional men held their places in later years through election. Some came in as representatives of the 'professional wards', the urban areas where the professional men lived together and apart from the mercantile quarter. Some of them acted as the legal and political representatives of influential parties in the town. An example is K. R. Venkatarama Iyer, who worked as a lawyer for an important group of Madura townspeople interested in the affairs of the Minakshi temple, and worked as the political agent of the same group in municipal affairs. Some had forsaken their first profession to enter the profession of municipal politics, and were returned because of their skills. An example here is N. V. L. Narasimha Rao who had a long and exciting career in Guntur town. He was a lawyer who had almost no cases, and a businessman with a penchant for promoting failures, but his local political career was not based on his personal substance but on his ability sometimes to reconcile and sometimes to manipulate the many diverse interests in the complex and highly volatile affairs of the town.

Most of the seats on municipal councils, however, were filled by those who controlled the property and the wealth of the town. They were there in the first place because they commanded the resources which brought success at elections. Although the municipal electorate had been expanded by the 1919 Act to include all tax-payers, in the mid-1920s the average electorate in a municipality was only 2,700. This electorate was divided into ten or so wards and although the poll at municipal elections was usually very high, most ward seats could be won with at most a couple of hundred votes. In an electorate this small, defined by wealth and property ownership, it was inappropriate if not difficult to mount a popular electoral campaign. Few elections were fought over issues. Many contests were settled privately before they reached a vote, and nearly always the campaign took place out of sight as individual notables deployed their wealth, their contacts and their private store of influence to secure the election of themselves or their placemen. Bankers, property-owners, merchants and industrialists therefore took most of the places on municipal councils. Some were sufficiently powerful to fill not one but several seats. The Motheys, the Komati trading family who dominated the commerce of Ellore, regularly had four or five seats on the municipality filled by their relatives or dependents.[89] In Bezwada, a contractor, G. Appalaswami, was for many years known as the 'king-maker' in municipal affairs,[90] and in Chidambaram the landowner and businessman P. Venugopala Pillai had by the 1930s got himself, three of his relatives, his lawyer's clerk, his tailor, his doctor and his dancing girl on to the municipality.[91]

The exact composition of the municipal council generally reflected the particular characteristics of the town. In Tenali, a marketing centre for rich, agricultural hinterland, the municipality was dominated by cash-crop cultivators and commission agents.[92] In the municipality of a much larger and more diverse town such as Madura, the council in 1931 included eight merchants, three contractors, six property-owners, six lawyers, two doctors, a teacher, a tinker and a document writer.[93] In Erode, a small but flourishing trading town, the municipality in the 1920s contained a missionary teacher, two lawyers, a retired government servant, six men with various banking, commercial and property interests, and an astrologer. The Erode councillors also afford a glimpse of the real substance of municipal politicians. Seven of them were remarkably wealthy landowners, paying over Rs 500 a year in land revenue, and eight of them paid over Rs 500 a year in income and municipal taxes. This meant they were very wealthy indeed.[94] Such men were hardly re-

[89] G.O. 1011 (L & M, M) 17 July 1901 MRO; G.O. 667 (LSG) 10 Feb. 1928 SAH.
[90] G.O. 2028 (L & M, M) 10 Dec. 1919 MRO.
[91] Petition of C. V. Srinivasachari, dated 21 Jan. 1932 and Report of the Inspector of Municipalities and Local Boards dated 7 Nov. 1932, in G.O. 151 (LSG) 11 Jan. 1933 MRO.
[92] G.O. 4833 (LSG) 5 Dec. 1928 SAH.
[93] G.O. 2592 (LSG) 27 June 1931 MRO.
[94] G.O. 1768 (LSG) 25 Sept. 1922 MRO; G.O. 4302 (LSG) 5 Dec. 1926 MRO.

presentative of the bulk of the population of a small town in upland Coimbatore.

Some of the men sought council places chiefly for the status they conveyed; membership associated the man with the 'sirkar' and allowed him to participate in the pageantry of municipal meetings. A few, usually professional men, crusaded to provide better social facilities in the town. Some councillors were anxious to use the municipal machinery to continue in the style of the urban notable of old. T. Srinivasa Mudaliar, chairman of Erode, devoted a lot of his energies and, his enemies thought, a lot of municipal money to build a public park and name it after himself.[95] Many more councillors, however, were attracted by the fact that it was their interests which were at stake in municipal administration. Businessmen especially found that the municipality taxed their profits, placed restrictions on their commercial practices and also provided facilities like roads and markets which could be of use to them. They were thus anxious to get as closely involved in municipal administration as possible, and often this meant taking a direct interest in the councils' patronage. The councils provided jobs, services and contracts, usually on a larger scale than any other body in the town, and for many councillors the attractions of petty malfeasance were simply too great. Perhaps the most glaring example of the pork-barrel in the province's municipal politics emerged in Madura towards the end of the decade. Here a government inspector found that one councillor supplied books to the municipal schools, another councillor's brother held the contract to clear away nightsoil, the chairman's son was the municipal vakil, a Muslim councillor had 'quite a number of relatives' in the employ of the municipality, and one councillor, who as a municipal employee had been dismissed for operating a huge fraud in the lighting department, had now been put in charge of municipal lighting. The inspector also noted that local people alleged that many other councillors were similarly involved but he had no time to verify, and he added: 'What distresses me more than anything else is the atmosphere of corruption that surrounds the chairman and the councillors and the openness and freedom with which the man in the street and the respectable citizens take this corruption for granted and talk of it.'[96]

[95] Petition from the Erode Municipal Franchise Protection Association dated 22 Oct. 1927, and Audit report for Erode Municipality 1925–6, in G.O. 4444 (LSG) 16 Nov. 1927 MRO.

[96] Report of Inspector of Municipalities and Local Boards dated 8 May 1931, in G.O. 2591 (LSG) 27 June 1931 MRO; see also various petitions in G.O. 4443 (LSG) 3 Oct. 1929 MRO and G.O. 4438 (LSG) 13 Nov. 1930 MRO.

Madura was a particularly large and unmanageable municipality, but similar conditions prevailed elsewhere. Throughout the 1920s petitions reciting councillors' involvements in municipal contracts poured into the Secretariat in Madras. Government passed orders emphasising that such involvements should disqualify men from council membership, and occasionally such councillors were faced by suits for removal taken out by the local opponents. For the most part, however, government was insufficiently equipped to cope. Towards the end of the decade, government appointed an inspector of local bodies who toured the province investigating such allegations. Within months of his appointment, however, his engagements diary was fully booked up for almost a year ahead and the Madura scandal cited above was one of the very few cases he managed to reach while the controversy was still alive.

The rural boards were not honey pots like the municipalities. On the one hand, there was far more government control over appointments and contracts through District Health Officers, Public Works Department officials and other members of the civil service than there was in the municipalities.[97] On the other hand most of the members, being chiefly landowners, were not themselves as interested in appointments and contracts as were the merchants, lawyers and traders of the towns. The attraction of the rural boards was for status and power, not profit. Members had a chance to influence the contracts and appointments of others, and to influence the management of schools, charities, markets and other public services.[98] They could also, as will be seen below, use local rural affairs as a springboard into provincial politics.

In the rural boards, many of the places in the early 1920s were filled by lawyers, other professional men and even officials. In the early days when rural boards had wielded little independent power and had been important chiefly as channels through which men might be able to influence official decisions, the rural electors had often chosen the men whose English education and legal skills enabled them to prosecute their constituency's case in the halls of the bureaucracy.[99] This attitude lingered long after the transformation of the rural boards into more independent and powerful institutions. Following the

[97] Venkata Rao, *Local Self-Government*, pp. 465–82.

[98] M. Venkatarangaiya, *The Development of Local Boards in the Madras Presidency* (Bombay, 1939) p. 72.

[99] Many of those elected to these early district boards were just interested in the prestige of the post rather than in actual administration; see the satirical sketch in A. Madhavaiah, *Thillai Govindan* (Madras, 1913), pp. 118–20.

paternal pattern even further, many rural constituencies chose to elect their Revenue Divisional Officer to the boards.[100] Moreover, the areas governed by rural boards were larger and more diffuse than the towns, and the rural magnates were unused to the techniques of competing with one another in the new institutions. The arbitrator, the professional middleman who stood apart from any one rural interest and was able to mediate the interests of many, was a useful exponent of the new politics in the countryside.

Yet the franchise for the rural boards was based squarely on the ownership of land and, as the powers and opportunities of the rural boards became more obvious during the decade, the landowners moved in and tried to displace other occupants of rural board seats. 'Landlords with local influence', observed one historian of local government in the south, 'discovered that, as presidents and members of local boards, they could wield a large amount of influence in their locality, and exercise greater power over their neighbours'.[101] Indeed, one of the dominating themes of the dyarchy period was the movement of rural notables, the controllers of most of the vital resources of this predominantly agrarian society, into positions of power in the new administrative structure. One observer in Guntur district in the mid-1920s, noted with obvious distaste the mobilisation of the local peasantry of the Kamma caste:

> The Reform Act and the subsequent legislation relating to the Local, Municipal and Panchayat bodies lowered the franchise and broadened the electorate. The Kammas of the district who are mostly landowners, big and small, came to possess the 'Vote' which they had neither known nor heard before. A section of Kammas therefore cultivated a taste for politics and elections ... the Kammas saw the absolute need to capture all or at least the majority of the elective seats in all the local bodies so that they might... usher into them all grades of men belonging to their own community from the President down to the peon.[102]

In 1925 and 1926 several of the taluk boards in Guntur fell under the control of the Kamma landlords and in 1927 the landlords also captured control of the district board and elected their leader into the presidential chair.[103] Similarly in Coimbatore district in 1925,

[100] *Royal Commission on Decentralisation*, vol. II, pp. 163, 268.

[101] Venkatarangaiya, *Local Boards*, p. 67.

[102] Petition of O. G. R. Singh, submitted by the president of Guntur district board on 12 Mar. 1927, in G.O. 2357 (LSG) 23 June 1927 SAH.

[103] G.O. 3891 (LSG) 8 Oct. 1927 SAH; G.O. 4927 (LSG) 13 Dec. 1927 SAH.

the Collector noted that for the first time members of the dominant agricultural caste of Vellala Gounders contested the taluk board elections in force.[104]

It would be a mistake, however, to see these takeovers as peasant victories. The rural board franchise was fixed at payment of Rs 10 in rent or in land revenue. Government figures suggest that this would have excluded about three-quarters of all landowners, as well as all the landless population of the rural areas.[105] Most of the electorate was in the control of the rural bosses who at elections could command the votes of their many dependents, relatives and debtors.[106] They could even create new electors who were bound to be tame. Lease-holders and subleaseholders under ryotwari landholders were not recognised in revenue law and revenue administration and government had no records on such people; they were, however, enfranchised for local elections, and big landlords were able to include many partisans on the electoral roll as fictitious sublesses.[107] Few of those elected to rural boards were simple ten-rupee landholders. Jagarlamudy Kuppuswami, the Kamma leader in Guntur, owned 2,400 acres of agricultural land and 2,000 acres of plantation and paid government Rs 8,000 a year in land tax.[108] A West Godavari barrister, viewing the elected members of the local rural boards, complained that 'most of them happen to be the village munsiffs of this taluk'.[109] As in the municipalities a large number of local elections contests were settled before the polls by the powerful men who came to be known as the 'election bosses' of the district. Those which were fought, were fought privately. The biographer of Kasu Brahmananda Reddi described his first local election in Guntur, by stating that 'there was about four thousand voters who had to be approached person-

[104] G.O. 3838 (LSG) 21 Oct. 1925 MRO.

[105] Of the total of 5,414,515 pattas (land deeds) registered in 1925–6, 4,023,359 or 74·3 per cent were for holdings which carried a revenue demand of less than Rs 10. *Settlement Report* (annual) for 1925–6, pp. 41–7.

[106] 'Most of them were influential landlords who kept within their grip not only their tenants but all other classes of people in the villages.... Under a system of election, a landlord could issue mandates through his agents to the voters in the neighbourhood and use his influence as a holder of land and as a money-lender to get through the contest easily.' Venkatarangaiya, *Local Boards*, pp. 66–7.

[107] Venkata Rao, *Local Self-Government*, p. 89.

[108] GOI Reforms Franchise B 34–99 Mar. 1921 NAI.

[109] Objection petition from A. Venkataratnam dated 25 May 1927, in G.O. 2274 (LSG) 20 June 1927 SAH.

ally. There were no meetings or campaigns, no party symbols or canvassing.'[110]

The strength of this magnate elite and its jealous protection of its own status and powers is glimpsed in the attempts of a less substantial rustic to seek election to the Anantapur district board in the early 1930s. Before putting forward his candidature he consulted his village munsiff, the current district board president and other influential men, all of whom came from the Reddi caste as did most of the agricultural population of the district. He received their blessings. After these peregrinations he was surprised when the president's own brother stood against him. He had discovered that the local magnates would stick together and ignore all others for, as one of his earlier advisers now told him, 'we were all like members of one family and it was not fair to contest among ourselves.'[111]

There was indeed in the 1920s a tendency for the most powerful rural magnates within a district to draw together and, particularly in those districts where one cultivating caste was dominant, to strengthen their relations through marriage ties. In most cases, this meant extending the marriage circle beyond the narrow areas that were customary. A similar process had begun in the nineteenth century among the most successful families in the services (chiefly Brahman families) and in commerce (chiefly Komatis). Such extended marriage contacts helped to extend their network of influence, whether bureaucratic or financial, over a wider area.[112] With the establishment of the new politics of local and legislature elections many influential rural families began to marry over a wider area. The Kasu Reddi family of Guntur, for instance, had for several generations married within the adjacent group of villages; however the three brothers who grew up in the 1920s and 1930s and became active in local and provincial politics, chose their brides from far-off East Godavari and other distant parts of the Circars.[113] In Coimbatore, the inter-marriages were more complex. The Pattagar of Palaiyakottai a clan-head and religious leader of the Vellala Gounders, married a son and daughter to a daughter and son of the zamindar of Uthukuli, one of the biggest

[110] Kasipathi, *Tryst with Destiny*, p. 28.

[111] M. Chenna Subba Rao, *Myself and Rural Life (Autobiography)*, part 1 (Anantapur, 1951) pp. 22–3.

[112] D. A. Washbrook, 'The development of caste organisation in South India', in C. J. Baker and D. A. Washbrook, *South India: Political Institutions and Political Change 1880–1940* (Delhi, 1975).

[113] Kasipathi, *Tryst with Destiny*, pp. 1–2, 12–19, 42.

Gounder estate-holders. Palaiyakottai married another son into the Vellaikinar family, who were probably the biggest ryotwari holders of land in the district as well as moneylenders, traders and industrialists. V. C. Vellingiri Gounder, the head of the Vellaikinar clan and the district's M.L.C. and district board president for many years, married one of his daughters to S. G. Sengodaiyan, the first Vellala Gounder to get into the I.C.S., and another female member of the clan to V. K. Palanisamy Gounder, another powerful local board politician who became an M.L.A. in 1937. Between them these four interlinked families – Palaiyakottai, Uthukuli, Vellaikinar and Palanisamy – had influence in all four corners of the district.[114] Some of these wider marriages can be directly related to local politics. Carolyn Elliott has described how an influential Reddi magnate in Chittoor district found his base of power being undermined in the 1930s and so contracted a marriage alliance with another Reddi family influential in the other half of the district and successfully rehabilitated his political fortunes.[115]

Perhaps the most extensive and labyrinthine of these marriage networks existed among the Kammas of the Kistna delta. Nineteenth-century observers had noted that these agricultural families from the north of the province married in wider circles than those farther south anyway; even so, a remarkable network grew up in the early twentieth century among the most influential members of the Kamma caste. Jagarlamudy Kuppuswami, the district board leader, was one of its key members. His brother was also important in local boards and in temple politics. His lieutenant, P. V. Krishnaswami Choudhary, was a village officer from the southernmost part of the Kistna deltas. He was related to N. G. Ranga who emerged as a Congressman, caste leader and peasant agitator in the 1930s. Ranga had gone to England to be educated with the scions of two other influential families – Velgapudy Ramakrishnayya, who went into the I.C.S. and whose brother was in temple politics in the district, and V. S. Krishna, who became private secretary to the Justice chief minister in the 1930s and later influential in the Andhra University and whose family, the Vasireddis, were zamindars of Muktyala and one of the oldest established families of the region. Velagapudy Ramakrishnayya of the I.C.S. married the daughter of Adusumilli Gopalakrishnayya, an

114 Interviews with R. Sunderraj and R. Jayakumar, Coimbatore February 1971.

115 C. M. Elliott, 'Caste and faction among the dominant caste: the Reddis and Kammas of Andhra', in R. Kothari (ed.), *Caste in Indian Politics* (New Delhi, 1970), pp. 139–42.

influential clan leader and local board politician from Gudivada in the northern part of the Kistna delta. This man married other of his progeny into the Kondula family, who were influential in the neighbouring area of Kistna, and into the Yarlagadda family who were influential across the Kistna river in Guntur district. N. G. Ranga was also a close associate of B. Muniswami Naidu, the Chittoor politician who became chief minister in 1930. Muniswami Naidu married his daughter to D. Muniratnam Naidu, who became important in Chittoor local politics in the 1930s, while his brother, Narayanaswami, was both lawyer and estate manager to the leading Kamma zamindar and patron, the raja of Chellapalle. Chellapalle married his daughter to Kommareddi Pattabhiramayya, who was elected to the Legislative Council from Kistna in 1930. Thus it is possible to trace a network of influential families, which stretched from Chittoor district in the south up to the Godavari river almost two hundred miles to the north. At crucial points, this network had been cemented in the early twentieth century by marriage alliances. Before 1920, this network had not existed at all.[116]

There is no evidence to suggest that this pattern of marriages spread widely in rural society. It was limited to the stratum of wealthy and influential magnates who were being pulled into a wider political world. The character of these linkages illustrated how the political organisation of the countryside was adapting itself to new arenas and new practices. Politicians were forging wider political associations not by making appeals to constituencies based on class, caste or region, but by linking together existing political networks in the different localities. Each of the Kamma, Reddi or Gounder magnates seen above could mobilise a considerable following among tenants, debtors, neighbours, clients and dependants of various kinds. These local connections were linked together by alliances among their leaders. In the areas of the Reddis, Gounders and Kammas one of the most visible of these linkages was the marriage tie, but this was only possible because each of these particular castes formed the sole dominant agricultural caste in its region. Elsewhere, in the Madras Presidency, rural caste groups were far more interspersed and thus many of the alliances in these areas were necessarily intercaste and thus could not be confirmed by marriage ties.

This sketch of the pattern of rural political alliances helps to

[116] N. G. Ranga, *Fight for Freedom* (Delhi, 1968); K. Bhavaiah Chowdary, *A Brief History of the Kammas* (Sangamjagarlamudi, 1955); C. Ranga Rao (ed.), *Andhra Desa Directory and Who's Who* (Bezwada, 1939); G.O. 2608 (Revenue) 13 Dec. 1927 MRO; *Hindu* 26 June 1928, 15. Jan. 1935.

explain the sporadic appearance of the rhetoric of caste in local politics. In West Godavari in 1928 there were complaints that a 'Kshatriya oligarchy' had captured the district board; in Guntur in 1927, men talked of the 'Kamma scare'; and in Anantapur in 1926 there was said to be 'a raging and devastating campaign night and day that Reddies and Reddies only should be voted for'.[117] On closer inspection it is clear that these protestations did not mean that the rural population was being mobilised in communal blocks by caste leaders. In each case the local rural bosses were moving in to grasp the new opportunities of the rural boards and rural franchises for themselves and it was often useful for those displaced by this movement to cry out that they were the butt of a communal campaign. In Anantapur one observer noted that the Reddi communal campaign was in fact the work of some very influential village officers.[118] In Guntur, it was the network of rich and powerful families noted above which formed the 'Kamma scare'. In all the instances, the 'communal' campaign was helped by men from other communities; in Guntur a Brahman lawyer spearheaded the Kamma campaign,[119] and the lieutenant of the leading Kshatriya in West Godavari was not a Kshatriya himself but a Kamma.[120] The solidarity of each of these campaigns soon disappeared once the rural magnates occupied positions of local power. The 1930s found Kammas in Guntur leading Congress and Justice parties, pro- and anti- zamindari movements, and fighting with one another for local board and legislature seats. The Coimbatore Gounders split into two distinct factions after the 1930 elections to the Legislative Council.

Of course many politicians did make appeals based on caste. At the point in time in the 1920s when rural leaders were being forced to mobilise political supporters over an area wider than that to which they were accustomed, an appeal to fellow members of a dominant rural caste naturally seemed attractive. Such campaigns were, however, ephemeral, rarely successful and never institutionalised. Gounders, Reddis, Kammas and Kshatriyas held communal conferences, but never established permanent communal organisations.[121] An

[117] G.O. 1552 (LSG) 30 Apr. 1927 SAH; G.O. 2357 (LSG) 23 June 1927 SAH; P. Kesava Pillai to Dr Subbaroyan, 5 Dec. 1926, Kesava Pillai papers NMML.

[118] P. Kesava Pillai to N. Marjoribanks, 19 Nov. 1926, Kesava Pillai papers NMML.

[119] Gade Simhacahalam; G.O. 2357 (LSG) 23 June 1927 SAH.

[120] Maganti Sitayya; G.O. 1552 (LSG) 30 Apr. 1927 SAH.

[121] There was a Reddi Mahajana Sabha, but its main activity was providing scholarships for students and it had no political role.

appeal based on sentiments of caste could never be as satisfactory as political alliances based on mutual interest, and caste campaigns faded away when rural bosses began to create more efficient political groupings. Moreover, it is difficult to find evidence of rural politicians actually striving to marshal their caste-fellows as a political following; it is much easier to find disappointed or dispossessed politicians protesting that they had been the victim of the communal campaign of their opponents. Many politicians who were pushed aside by the influx of rural bosses into district politics raised the demon of a communal scare. In Anantapur it was P. Kesava Pillai, the lawyer who had until 1926 served as political middleman for the Reddi bosses, who complained of a Reddi caste tyranny when the bosses suddenly decided to forego his services. In Guntur, it was a dislodged taluk board president who complained of the Kamma scare, and in West Godavari it was the demoted Kapu minority who protested against the Kshatriyas. In the conditions of rural Madras, where caste communities were greatly interspersed and no single community was numerically dominant in any area, an appeal *against* the tyranny of a particular caste was attractive as a means to bind together a following over a wide area, and potentially far more successful than a campaign which sought the solid support of one particular caste.

THE LEADERSHIP OF LOCAL GOVERNMENT

One factor shaped the style of politics in local government and that was that within local boards real power was concentrated in very few hands. The constitution of the municipalities placed most of the power in the hands of the chairmen, and the constitution of rural local self-government placed most of the power in the hands of the district board presidents. To begin with, neither municipal chairman nor district board president could be removed from office by the vote of the other members; this enabled the board heads to be somewhat casual about the business of building and maintaining majority support. Most of their power came, however, from the fact that the presidents and chairmen acted as both chief executive officers and chief election officers for their boards.

As chief executive officers, the chairmen and presidents had almost exclusive control over the distribution of contracts and over appointments; furthermore they managed the finance, looked after the records and implemented all the decisions of their boards. They thus had virtually sole control over the most important patronage of local government. With this patronage and with the powers of the executive, the board head could build a majority of support in the board. Executive acts were bargained for support. In some municipalities especially, the transactional empire built up by the chairman was quite extraordinary. In Guntur in 1928, people complained that: 'The [Chairman's] party is no political party bound together by a definite programme. The party has to be strengthened by people of all castes, creeds and principles. Nothing but personal favours pleases them.'[122] They went on to describe how most of the municipal councillors were bound under ties of obligation to the chairman. To begin with, the chairman could influence the elections in all the wards of the towns and many of the councillors had only come in under his kind auspices. 'To get a friend into the Council', continued the complainants, 'the task begins with the voter's list, its preparation and its consolidation before the revising authority. The matter is then made the subject of collusive suits and later on it develops into many tricks of the trade.' The chairman also had an election organisation run by a contractor, who was in his debt for municipal contracts, and by the schools, who were at the mercy of his executive powers. 'The schools', wrote the complainants 'are election Bureaus' and teachers who refused to co-operate risked their jobs. Besides this the chairman could woo a constituency with municipal patronage, as the complainants noted:

> Vote-catching is thus the primary cause of all maladministration. There are instances where lamp-posts have fetched voters. Again a vote is obtained by means of a licence for a bench. A street is captured by a new tap. A road is laid to facilitate obligation pending. Encroachments on public streets are overlooked to secure the sympathy of voters.

On the council, individual members were tied to the chairman by the grant of favours which could be withdrawn if support for the chairman ceased. In Guntur, the complainants alleged that the chairman had ensnared councillors by leasing them municipal land, by extending the municipal water-supply to their homes, by delegating them executive powers over lighting, schools and dispensaries, by juggling with the municipal staff at their behest, by selling them municipal materials on the cheap and by constructing roads to their convenience.[123]

Some of these allegations were substantiated by a government

[122] G.O. 3416 (LSG) 6 Sept. 1927 SAH.
[123] Printed memorial against the administration of N. V. L. Narasimha Rao dated May 1927, in G.O. 3416 (LSG) 6 Sept. 1927 SAH.

inspector, while some were not.[124] Guntur was a particularly volatile town, but petitions describing similar transactional empires in other municipalities were received almost daily by the local government department in the Secretariat in Madras. In rural boards there were similar allegations – in 1927 Salem petitioners complained that the president of the district board had given contracts to several board members,[125] and in 1924 Tanjore petitioners complained that a taluk board president was misusing the funds of a charity controlled by the board[126] – but these were less frequent and less dramatic. However, both district board presidents and municipal chairmen made good use of the advantages they gained from their official control of local elections. As early as 1923 the Secretariat noted that in local government 'much of the trouble, if it exists, lies in the fact that persons interested in the results of elections have considerable share in the conduct of elections under the rules. It is the chairman of a municipal council or the president of a local board that has to fix the date of an election, receive nomination papers and scrutinise them. It is he who is to appoint polling officers and their staff and identifying officers. It is he who is to count the votes, declare the invalidity of any voting paper and finally to declare the result. Presidents and chairmen are interested in introducing persons likely to support them in the boards and councils and in putting off elections of casual vacancies to prevent their adversaries stepping in. They are already autocrats under the Acts which were designed to be democratic.'[127] Further to this, the board head could influence the electoral roll. The local board franchises depended on the payment of local taxes, and men could be disqualified for getting into arrears. The chairman could include new voters by illicit means; the Ellore chairman in 1926 put eighty new names on the electoral roll, all of whom were relatives, clerks, grooms, tenants, gardeners and sundry retainers of a political ally who had paid certain sums of tax on their behalf.[128] The chairman could also forget to collect the taxes of his opponents, which could keep them off the electoral roll and also get them disqualified from membership of the board. One pamphleteer described the regulation which permitted this as the 'Satanic Bye-Law' for it placed a 'saint, a genius, a Col-

[124] Report of the Inspector of Municipalities and Local Boards dated 22 July 1927, in G. O. 3416 (LSG) 6 Sept. 1927 SAH.
[125] G.O. 3019 (LSG) 9 Aug. 1927 MRO.
[126] G.O. 1893 (LSG) 1 June 1925 MRO.
[127] G.O. 1346 (LSG) 12 June 1923 MRO.
[128] G.O. 5384 (LSG) 22 Dec. 1926 MRO.

lector, a Judge, a Munsiff, a Doctor, a Merchant-prince, a patriot... at the beck and call of the municipal servants'; it allowed anyone to pay spurious taxes on behalf of 'butchers, cobblers, barbers and washermen to buy whose sympathy it indeed costs him so little'; and it could cause a wealthy man who had paid hundreds in taxes to be disqualified for not paying a few annas tax on his son's dog or bicycle.[129] Many municipal elections were effectively fought out before the polls as the chairman and the opposition faction wrestled to change the electoral roll in their favour.[130]

The district board president had yet another advantage. The taluk boards acted as electoral colleges for the district board and the district board president not only nominated a few members to the taluk boards, but also had some control over their funds and some power to arbitrate in their internal disputes. Besides this he arranged taluk board elections, and mediated in all matters between the taluk board and the government. The district board president was thus extremely well placed to influence the membership of his own board.[131] In the early 1920s, many district board heads secured a majority and ensured that they would be re-elected for a second term as president, by using their powers over the taluk boards. The Guntur district board president, P. C. Ethirajulu Naidu, was adept at this. In one taluk board under his command he delayed government confirmation of the election of new members until after the elections for new executive officers were completed. In another, he managed to get government to support election suits taken out by two of his supporters against the current regime. In another, he squeezed out an unresponsive president by nominating one of the president's chief opponents as vice-president, by putting another leading opponent in charge of local elections, and sending his rowdies to picket meetings and paralyse the administration. Within a few months, Ethirajulu Naidu's nominees controlled most of the Guntur taluk boards.[132]

Other factors helped to concentrate power in the hands of the

[129] A. K. Muni, *The Moral Victory* (Proddatur, 1925), pp. 2–3.

[130] The Inspector of Municipalities and Local Boards gave a detailed account of one such contest, in G.O. 3416 (LSG) 6 Sept. 1927 SAH.

[131] Venkatarangaiya, *Local Boards*, p. 62.

[132] Letter from the president of Guntur district board dated 7 Oct. 1922, in G.O. 140 (LSG) 17 Jan. 1932 SAH; letters from the president of Guntur taluk board dated 14 and 31 Oct. 1922, in G.O. 1346 (LSG) 12 June 1923 SAH; letter from president of Tenali taluk board dated 4 Jan. 1926, letter from president of Repalle taluk board dated 6 July 1927, letter from vice-president of Guntur district board dated 23 July 1927, in G.O. 3891 (LSG) 8 Oct. 1927 SAH.

district board heads. In 1923, in an attempt to stimulate the co-operative movement in the province, government allowed local government boards to invest their surplus funds in co-operative societies. The heads of the local boards who took advantage of this provision, often thereby became the biggest single investor in their local co-operative and many took this opportunity to win control of the co-operative society and thus strengthen their local position.[133] Within a few years, the elections of the officers of co-operative societies, particularly urban co-operative banks, had become intimately tied up with local politics.[134] Another measure which further increased the powers of the district board president was the reform of village panchayats. Before 1930, government encouraged villages to form panchayats to look after irrigation, markets and other local services. These bodies were purely voluntary. In the 1920s many new panchayats were constituted, and most were considered very successful. In 1930 however, the panchayats were brought within the structure of rural self-government, constituted on the same franchise, and placed under the supervision of the local board. Panchayats quickly became instruments of district board politics, usually as satellites of the district board president.[135]

'The Chairman', wrote an indignant petitioner in 1924, 'has succeeded . . . in making the municipality of Trichinopoly identical with himself.'[136] In Chidambaram the dominance of the chairman weighed even more heavily on his enemies, who complained that he was 'managing the Municipality as his private estate'.[137] This man, P. Venugopala Pillai, had compounded the advantages he possessed as chairman with a form of terrorism that was all his own. Men who dared to oppose him, it was said, could expect to find the full power of the municipal machinery turned against them, and could even find their lives and their property placed at risk. A young doctor who managed to win the chairmanship away from Venugopala Pillai for a few months was stabbed, and another opposition councillor was

[133] *Annual Report on the Working of the Madras Co-operative Credit Societies Act* for 1924–5 p. 17. The report for the following year noted that district board investments already formed a quarter of the entire working capital of district co-operative banks.

[134] *Annual Report on the Working of the Madras Co-operative Credit Societies Act* for 1931–2, p. 5.

[135] Jayaraman, *Panchayats in Madras*, pp. 30–2, 120.

[136] Petition of D. A. G. Ratnam in G. O. 1771 (LSG) 30 June 1924 MRO.

[137] Petition of C. V. Srinivasachari dated 21 Jan. 1932 in G.O. 151 (LSG) 11 Jan. 1933 MRO.

stabbed by Venugopala Pillai's own brother-in-law.[138] The inspector sent to look into municipal affairs in Chidambaram was fascinated by Venugopala Pillai's self-assurance: 'As the councillors harangued or quarrelled,' reported the inspector, 'the chairman sat in unconcerned silence, secure in his strength and grim as Destiny, with scoffing indifference to the vanity of the opposition's endeavour to upset his pre-ordained decrees.'[139]

Often the only men in local government to rival the power of the board heads were, not other councillors or district board members, but the top men on the permanent staff of the local boards. Only they had access to the records and only they were involved in executive acts of the boards to anything like the extent of the board heads. Often the office managers of local boards became very influential, as in Srirangam in 1922 where an inspector suspected that the manager of the municipal office was the real ruling force in local politics and the chairman only his cipher.[140]

This concentration of power in the hands of the heads of local boards did not mean that they could hang on to their office for as long as they liked, although many district board presidents and municipal chairmen did in fact hold their posts for several three-year terms. Many of those who were originally installed by government nomination because they suited government's purposes and not because they were the most influential men in the locality, managed to deploy the advantages of their administrative powers to great effect and secured re-election several times. Many, however, were less resourceful. The concentration of power, however, had far more important effects in forming the style of local board politics.

The patronage wielded by a local board head was always finite, and just as the distribution of patronage could weld a following together, so its denial could create an opposition. Most boards quickly became the scene of acute factional rivalries. The form in which these factional rivalries were played out was not, however, the set-piece battle at election time or at important council meetings; rather it resembled the politics of palace revolution. Small factions, constantly aligning and re-aligning, strove to dislodge the man in power. Opposition was

[138] See numerous petitions in G.O. 151 (LSG) 11 Jan. 1933 MRO and G.O. 499 (LSG) 6 Feb. 1933 MRO.

[139] Report of Inspector of Municipalities and Local Boards dated 7 Nov. 1932, in G.O. 151 (LSG) 11 Jan. 1933 MRO.

[140] Report of the Assistant Examiner of Local Fund Account dated 3 April 1927, in G.O. 2044 (LSG) 17 Sept. 1923 MRO.

technically difficult because the board could not remove its leader by a vote of no-confidence. In many cases they tried to limit his powers by passing resolutions which deprived him of his exclusive powers over matters like contracts and appointments, but such resolutions fell foul of the rule-book and were always annulled by government.[141] In other cases, councillors challenged the board head's acts in the courts, but the latter had control of the board records and usually managed to vindicate himself.[142] Thus a favourite opposition tactic was to secure the election of their leader as the vice-chairman or vice-president; in the temporary absence of the board head, all the latter's responsibilities fell onto this deputy and he could easily reduce the administration to a shambles.[143] More often, the opposition tried to lure the board head into a breach of the constitution or of the rules of procedure and then set about persuading government to remove him for this transgression. In this form of battle, skill in intrigue was at a premium. 'It is an irony of things', wrote one local politician who had just been tripped up, 'that in matters of local self-government human ingenuity is allowed to triumph over popular will.'[144] This made lawyers an indispensable part of local factions since so many quarrels were fought out in the courts rather than at the polls. An observer of local politics in Guntur noted the way a poor and inexperienced but resourceful vakil, Chellasani Satyanarayana Choudhary, had become very important to the Kamma landlords:

In the opinion of several Kammas he could nicely prepare cases for them, advise them as to the kind of evidence to be let into the law courts.... Most of these Kamma leaders being men of very little education and such of them as came into responsible positions having had no other desire than to be styled big men and be privileged to thrust in their own people into all positions regardless of their qualification and fitness ... they had always to run great personal risks, and to them also Mr Satyanarayana Choudhary

[141] See the motions passed by the opponents of the Trichinopoly municipal chairman, in G.O. 1771 (LSG) 30 June 1924 MRO.

[142] See for example T. Sivasankaram Pillai's fight against dismissal from the presidentship of Penukonda taluk board, in G.O. 2233 (LSG) 13 May 1929 MRO.

[143] See for instance Tinnevelly where the vice-chairman reversed all the chairman's policies and appointments whenever the chairman went to Madras to attend sittings of the Legislative Council. During one absence of six days, the vice-chairman cancelled two appointments made only days before, transferred nine teachers who had been only recently appointed and dismissed a clerk; G.O. 728 (LSG) 12 Feb. 1929 MRO; for similar events in Palni see G.O. 1259 (LSG) 16 Mar. 1930 MRO.

[144] G.O. 5129 (LSG) 23 Dec. 1923 SAH.

was ready at hand with all the knowledge he had of law, politics and trickery to suggest all plausible ways and means either for excuse, defence or justification, and to interpret and misinterpret the Acts, the code, the rules and the G.O.s.... Mr Satyanarayana Choudhary therefore became an indispensable asset to the Kamma fold of politicians.[145]

The framework of local government administration worked according to much the same principles as the revenue settlements of the nineteenth century. It relied on recruiting a few powerful men who, in return for the grant of a position of considerable status and power and the opportunity to manipulate the system to personal advantage, would collaborate with the rulers and carry out many of the functions of government and administration in their stead. Such a system worked well when it was mounted on a firm and stable base, where the collaborators were strong and secure. Ryotwari, as Munro had realised, rested on the broad shoulders of the village elites while the loose government of the towns in the nineteenth century had depended on the existence of urban magnates who would keep the peace. In a similar manner local government drew on the strengths of local notables. The elective principle, linked to a limited franchise, ensured that only men of considerable local influence would fill the local boards, while the constitution of the boards concentrated power in a few hands. It was a fiercely hierarchical system, which corroborated the power of the local notables. Therefore the latter were happy to make it work. South India accepted local government without much disruption and, barring some Non-co-operation campaigns and the inevitable disgruntlement of taxed businessmen, without much opposition.

Yet as with the ryotwari administration, it was not always clear that government was in complete command of its own outposts. Throughout much of the province, the local boards were soon taken over by a handful of local magnates who ran them with a firm hand. This was particularly the case in the smaller towns and in the 'dry' rural areas, where the local elites were small, cohesive and entirely dominant. In Salem, for instance, the district board in 1920 came under the command of G. F. F. Foulkes, a member of an adventurous European family which had bought up the Salem zamindari and had thus become the biggest landholder in and around Salem town. His chief lieutenant was S. Ellappa Chetty, a merchant, a landowner and a

145 Petition of O. G. R. Singh, forwarded by president of Guntur district board on 12 Mar. 1927, in G.O. 2357 (LSG) 23 June 1927 SAH.

moneylender. While Foulkes presided over the district board, Ellappa Chetty topped the poll in the Salem district constituency in all four legislature elections of the dyarchy period, ran the district Secondary Education Board, and was elected Foulkes' vice-president in 1922. When Foulkes retired in the late 1920s, he smoothly handed the headship of the district board over to Ellappa Chetty, who held the post until 1935; meanwhile Ellappa Chetty's brother became vice-chairman of the Salem municipality.[146] Similarly in South Arcot, A. Subbarayalu Reddiar, the first non-official president of the district board, handed over the charge to his friend, henchman and election agent, K. Sitarama Reddi, and Sitarama Reddi held the post until 1931.[147] In Anantapur, there appeared to be a change of command in 1926 when P. Kesava Pillai lost a seat in the Legislative Council and the presidentship of the district board at the same time as his lieutenant, Sivasankaram Pillai, was removed from the command of the taluk board; in fact, however, the changeover was more apparent than real; Kesava Pillai was succeeded by Reddi rural bosses who had been the foundation of his political career over the last thirty years and who had merely now decided to take over the reins of power for themselves.[148]

In each district, the nature of the ruling group was slightly different but the effect was the same. In Coimbatore, a clique of large landowners and moneylenders ran the local boards, and this clique was easily identified and talked of by other inhabitants of the district. They saw to it that any struggles for power in the district were decided in calm consultation among themselves, rather than through the expensive hurly-burly of the ballot box. Some weeks before local and provincial elections in 1930, for instance, they met and decided on a share-out of all the important posts in the district to the satisfaction of all, and rendered the subsequent elections somewhat nugatory.[149] In Ramnad, the family of the raja of Ramnad, which had once held most of the district in fief, was clearly in command. One raja held the district board presidentship from 1921 until his death in 1928, and his heir took over the post as soon as he came of age in 1931.

146 G.O. 437 (LSG) 7 Mar. 1922 MRO; G.O. 1876 (LSG) 23 Aug. 1923 MRO; G.O. 1756 (LSG) 14 May 1927 MRO.

147 G.O. 82 (LSG) 18 Jan. 1921 MRO; G.O. 2193 (LSG) 5 Nov. 1921 MRO.

148 P. Kesava Pillai to Dr P. Subbaroyan, 5 Dec. 1926, Kesava Pillai papers NMML; *Hindu* 19 Feb. 1927; G.O. 344 (LSG) 23 Jan. 1926 MRO.

149 See the evidence in the zamindar extortion trial, *Hindu* 20 Mar. 1935, 11 and 12 July 1935; *Justice* 10 Apr. 1936.

The board was run in the 1920s as a department of the raja's estate; he had placed one taluk board in the hands of his personal secretary, another in the hands of his cousin, and used the equipment of the district board to control the temples and markets of the district in the style of an old princeling. His writ ran through the district, as he himself announced, 'because I am the Raja of Ramnad and not only the President of the District Board'.[150]

In many of the smaller towns, too, it was common for one man, one family or small clique to take a firm hold on the municipal machinery and to use it to corroborate their local dominance. In Ongole, for instance, V. Sriramulu Naidu was municipal chairman continuously from 1920 until the mid-1930s, in which time he put five of his relatives into important posts in municipal service and conducted municipal business in a highly personal manner. His leadership went unopposed at every re-election until 1932, when the rival was not a serious threat but merely a trouble-maker.[151] Similarly in Walajapet, one family dominated the municipality for three generations. W. Vijiaraghava Mudaliar, a wealthy proprietor, banker and entrepreneur, whose father had been a municipal councillor, became chairman around the turn of the century and held the post for nearly three decades; he was re-nominated four times, and re-elected four times, each time unopposed, and spent some time as an M.L.C. and as president of the district board. On his death, his son succeeded him in the municipal chair.[152]

Local politics, however, could no longer be confined to the parish. In 1909 local boards had been constituted into electorates for the Morley–Minto Legislative Council; in 1910 the local government portfolio had been handed to an Indian member of the Governor's Executive Council; in 1919–20, the portfolio took on greater importance when more of the responsibilities for supervising local boards were transferred from the Collector to the provincial government, and in 1921 local government came under the control of the Justice ministry. The minister in charge of the portfolio had considerable power and patronage in local boards – he could nominate members to seats reserved for minorities, allocate grants, appoint chairmen and presidents in boards where elections had not yet been conceded,

150 G.O. 162 (LSG) 27 Jan. 1921 MRO; G.O. 1984 (LSG) 7 Sept. 1923 MRO; G.O. 4139 (LSG) 25 Sept. 1926 MRO; G.O. 1027 (LSG) 5 Mar. 1928; MRO; G.O. 4234 (LSG) 20 Oct. 1928 MRO; G.O. 288 (LSG) 27 Jan. 1931 MRO;

151 G.O. 2719 (LSG) 13 July 1932 SAH.

152 G.O. 1850 (LSG) 7 May 1936 MRO; G.O. 3028 (LSG) 13 July 1936 MRO.

arbitrate in disputes over rules and procedure and, moreover, was the only agency who could remove an erring local board head or dissolve a whole board in mid-term. As noted above, the ministers used these powers energetically.

But while the ministers had considerable formal power in local government, and made valiant efforts to use it effectively, their influence over local affairs was by no means clear cut. There were over two hundred rural boards and municipalities, and roughly the same number again of union boards and panchayats. Government relied for its information about local government on the observations of the Collector (who was generally too busy with his many other duties), on the occasional remarks of the peripatetic inspector, and on the petitions and submissions of the board heads and members themselves. With such great responsibilities and such slim resources, government was ill-equipped to fly in the face of local realities. Government had to settle with the forces of power in local society much as they stood. In certain instances, government could create a local politician of great power – as it did with some of the district board presidents appointed in the early 1920s – and sometimes bring about the downfall of a local potentate; for the most part, however, government could only interfere up to a limit laid down by local circumstances. Some of the less sophisticated interventions by the ministers in their first months of office prompted dramatic agitations that became linked to the Congress' campaign of Non-co-operation. For instance, minister K. V. Reddi Naidu, by manipulating local government nomination, succeeded in placing one of his henchmen in the municipal chair of his home town of Ellore, and gave him orders to destroy the power of the Mothey family who had run Ellore for the last half-century. The Motheys responded by financing Congress agitations, building khaddar factories, decking Non-co-operation processions with their elephants, funding a 'National College', and using the labourers from their jute mill as a Non-co-operation mob. For five years Ellore local affairs were in complete uproar, and Reddi Naidu found in 1923 that he would have no hope of returning to the Legislative Council from the Ellore constituency and had to look elsewhere.[153] As Foulkes of Salem reported when government tried to interfere with his own plans for the development of district affairs, 'if government is going to nominate members without reference to responsible local opinion, it

[153] *Hindu* 28 Apr. 1921, 6 and 7 May 1921, 9 Aug. 1923; G.O. 600 (LSG) 31 Mar. 1922 SAH; Diaries of K. V. Reddi Naidu, entries for 24 Mar. 1923 and 3 Apr. 1923.

is not long before government is going to land itself in difficulties'.[154]

Even so, local politicians were aware that the ministers could pose a greater threat to their position than most of their local opponents could. Ministers and local opponents working together could be very serious indeed. Once the ministers had shown their teeth in local politics almost every one of the different factions in local affairs began to compete to bring government into the locality on its particular side. At first many local men resented government intrusions – the Motheys' Non-co-operation campaign expressed their desire for local autonomy – but gradually all came to realise that government was an element that could not be ignored – by 1926 a Mothey figured prominently in the negotiations over ministry formation, and by 1930 a Mothey sat in the all-India Legislative Assembly at Delhi. Politicians at the periphery had to come and make a settlement with the men at the provincial centre.

As the ministers delved further into local affairs, so local politics were gradually suffused with the rhetoric of Madras City affairs. A dispute arose in Madura in 1921 over control of the Minakshi temple; the roots of the dispute stretched back over two decades, the factions ranged on either side contained men of various communities, and ideologies of nationalism or communalism had never before played any part in the affair. When the matter erupted in 1921, however, one faction hired professional agitators to portray the dispute as loyal non-Brahmans against the Brahman Non-co-operators – a careful copy of the current rhetorical alignment in Madras City – and sent petitions along these lines to the Secretariat in the hope that the ministers would bring the power of government into the dispute to their advantage.[155] In Repalle, one faction of merchants told government that the enemies who had just outplayed them in town affairs were Congressmen and begged for help.[156] In Erode even the Collector announced that Congressmen and Khilafatists had won most of the municipal seats in the hope that this would induce the ministry to confirm the names of the 'loyalists' whom he wished to nominate to the municipal council.[157] Local disputes quickly squeezed themselves into the pattern of conflict between non-Brahman and Congress. In Bezwada, local politics for the five years leading up to 1920 had revolved around the attempts of a diverse faction of lawyers and

154 G.O. 1295 (LSG) 5 July 1921 MRO.
155 *Hindu* 15 Apr. 1921; G.O. 477 (Public) 27 July 1921 MRO.
156 G.O.s 367 and 368 (LSG) 28 Feb. 1921 SAH.
157 G.O. 1482 (LSG) 30 July 1921 MRO.

merchants to disrupt the empire of the contractor, Appalaswami, who was the undisputed power behind the municipal chairman and most of the councillors. In 1921, Appalaswami began to paint his faction as the local Justicites and even formed a local non-Brahman association (despite the fact that his current placeman in the municipal chair was a Brahman), and got enough help from government to fend off the opposition's challenge for another two years. The opposition was driven into acts of agitation which were identified as Non-co-operation and began to appear as the local Congress.[158]

Most of the really big men of local politics struck discreet deals with the ministry. Those that reached the Legislative Council generally sat on the Justicite benches,[159] while some gave more useful service to the ministerial faction. The raja of Ramnad's cousin served as the whip of Dr Subbaroyan's ministry in 1926, K. Sitarama Reddi helped the Justice leaders in many ways and was rewarded with a post on the Endowments Board in 1930, and W. Vijiaraghava Mudaliar was always a good Justicite. Such men lent substance to the Justice leaders' claim to lead the province, while the ministers' support put the last few touches to the politicians' local empires. The story of P. Venugopala Pillai illustrated the nature of the compact between local satraps and the ministry. Venugopala Pillai, the Chidambaram municipal chairman, cultivated three men who were influential in Justicite circles – his lawyer and a local political ally, both of whom were nominated to the Legislative Council as representatives of the Depressed Classes, and A. Ramaswami Mudaliar, Panagal's secretary and a leading Justicite publicist, with whom Venugopala Pillai had business dealings. By manipulating these contacts, Venugopala Pillai got government to cancel criminal proceedings taken out against him by local enemies, to nominate him to the municipality when he was tripped up at elections, and to help dispose of an interloper who

[158] Kaleswara Rao, *Na Jivita Katha*, pp. 291–2, 350–1; G.O. 109 (L & M,M) 23 Jan. 1917 MRO; G.O. 919 (LSG) 24 May 1921 SAH; G.O. 945 (LSG) 30 May 1921 SAH; G.O. 167 (LSG) 24 Jan. 1922 SAH; G.O. 2322 (LSG) 27 Nov. 1922 SAH; *Hindu* 28 Jan. 1921, 24 Feb. 1922, 7 Dec. 1922.

[159] 'A president who was a member of the Legislative Council found it advantageous to support the minister as this would ensure his renomination as president on the next occasion and the appointment of persons belonging to his party to the few nominated seats on the district board.' Venkatarangaiya, *Local Boards*, p. 65. T. A. Ramalingam Chetty's career offered a warning to all M.L.C.s who opposed the ministers; when his term as president of the Coimbatore district board ended in 1923, he was unceremoniously kicked out by Panagal; see G.O. 1131 (LSG) 17 May 1923 MRO.

managed to seize the municipal chair.[160] As a local government inspector noted, 'he is . . . said to employ with telling effect the boast that he has influence with the Government and no local combination however powerful could restrain his return to power',[161] or as a ratepayers' petition complained when Venugopala Pillai had survived a crisis, 'it is freely broadcast here by the Chairman . . . that everything had been squared up with the help of a few thousands and [a Justicite minister]'.[162]

POCKETS OF LOCAL INSTABILITY

In most of the province local government functioned smoothly in the 1920s, and the Justice ministers used the framework of local administration as foundations of a provincial network of political influence. But in some parts of the province, the conditions which made for success elsewhere were absent. In the most fertile rural tract, the Kistna–Godavari deltas, and in the bigger and more prosperous towns (particularly Madura, Tinnevelly and Trichinopoly in the Tamil districts, Guntur, Bezwada, Ellore, Rajahmundry and Cocanada in Andhra), the question of local political leadership was far more open than it was in the 'dry' countryside and the small towns.[163] In these areas, local boards did not provide a satisfactorily skeletal framework through which the accepted men of power could exercise their poli-

[160] Petition dated 3 Nov. 1931, petition from C. V. Srinivasachari dated 21 Jan. 1932, report of Inspector of Municipalities and Local Boards on his interview with the deputation of shopkeepers, in G.O. 151 (LSG) 11 Jan. 1933 MRO; ratepayers' memorial dated 31 Jan. 1933, in G.O. 499 (LSG) 6 Feb. 1933 MRO.

[161] Report of Inspector of Municipalities and Local Boards dated 7 Nov. 1932, in G.O. 151 (LSG) 11 Jan. 1933 MRO.

[162] Deputation of shopkeepers, in G.O. 151 (LSG) 11 Jan. 1933 MRO.

[163] The division into 'wet' or irrigated tracts and 'dry' or unirrigated tracts is by no means exact. There were of course irrigated lands near tanks and rivers in the 'dry' region. The division is merely meant to point up the difference between the Kistna–Godavari delta area, which was dominated by the cultivation of 'wet' crops, and the rest of the province where 'dry' crops were common and 'wet' crops cultivated only on exceptional pieces of land. The Cauveri delta (the districts of Tanjore and Trichinopoly) had also profited from irrigation works built by Cotton in the 1860s, yet these works did not have the economic and social impact of the works on the Kistna and the Godavari. This was largely because the Cauveri area was dominated by a few very big landholders who remained largely in control, and because the pattern of marketing remained dispersed. See D. A. Washbrook, 'Country politics: Madras 1880–1930', *Modern Asian Studies*, VII, 3 (1973).

tical dominance; rather they proved to be a wholly inadequate arena for the staging of fierce political battles.

The tract that lay near the deltas of the two major rivers of Andhra, the Kistna and the Godavari, had experienced an agrarian revolution in a manner quite unlike any other part of the province. It had begun in the 1860s when the engineer, Arthur Cotton, had thrown major irrigation works across the two rivers, and spread a network of canals and irrigation channels into the surrounding countryside.[164] The arrival of abundant and reliable supplies of irrigation water raised the productivity of the land at a stroke. Previously most of the land had been given over to the coarse millets which prevailed throughout the province, and much of it had been forest or grazing land. By the end of the nineteenth century, the tract looked like one enormous paddy field criss-crossed by canals, and every available inch was planted with rice or one of the valuable cash-crops like tobacco and sugar which required constant irrigation.[165] The value of the land had rocketed; N. G. Ranga, an inhabitant of the area who in 1926 wrote an Oxford dissertation about changes in his village over the past sixty years, reckoned the price of land had risen from Rs 40 to Rs 1,000–1,500 per acre. The distribution of landholdings had remained roughly the same as it had been before, but a much larger slice of the population had been raised to levels of prosperity. The real income of the inhabitants, Ranga reckoned, had multiplied two and a half times.[166]

The changes in social and political organisation which followed were immense. To begin with, even the stability of the village unit had been undermined. Whereas 'dry' cultivation had kept the farmer busy throughout the year, 'wet' cultivation demanded two spells of frantic activity interspersed with long dormant periods. Not only were the latter an invitation to the inhabitants to indulge a taste for politicking, litigation and mischief,[167] but the whole new cycle of the year brought even greater instability to the local population. In the active periods, labourers flocked in from the neighbouring, less prosperous tracts; in the slack periods these returned home, and many of the inhabitants of the deltaic villages also went off to seek work in

[164] A. V. Raman Rao, *Economic Development of Andhra Pradesh 1766–1957* (Bombay, 1958), pp. 86–90.

[165] O. H. K. Spate and A. T. A. Learmouth, *India and Pakistan: a general and regional geography* (London, 1967), p. 690.

[166] Ranga, *Economic Organisation*, vol. I, pp. 20–5; vol. II, pp. 95–100.

[167] *Madras Provincial Banking Enquiry Commission*, vol. II, pp. 593, 596; vol. III, p. 743.

factories, railways and public works.[168] The constant traffic of persons undercut the village unit.

At the same time, the conditions making for strong village leadership had also disappeared. A handful of village bosses no longer had a monopoly on credit and on patronage. The rise in prosperity had made many villagers less dependant on the village boss's credit. Debts there still were – indeed the debt per head and per acre in the deltaic tract was far higher than in the rest of the province – but this was not a debt contracted through necessity, but a debt contracted in the hope of gain. Many farmers now borrowed, on the security of their valuable land, capital to invest in the profitable cultivation of cash-crops.[169] Besides, more people in the villages now had the funds to lend to their neighbours; in N. G. Ranga's village, the number of moneylenders had increased from four to forty.[170] Artisans and labourers had also escaped from the village elite's patronage. The labourers were patently better off than their counterparts elsewhere – Ranga noted that their wives were better dressed than the wives of landowning farmers in the 'dry' region – while many of the artisans had sold up their small plots at a good profit and left for the town.[171]

The villages had also lost much of their separateness, and in marked contrast to the villages in the rest of the province, had been drawn into close relations with the towns of the region. The prosperous farmers came into the towns to sell directly to the mills or exporting agents; at the same time, merchants and moneylenders from the town ventured out into the countryside to lend money directly to the cultivators, now that the latter could offer their valuable land as security.[172] Many landowners, in attempts to employ their new-found capital, had by the early twentieth century entered into business partnerships – in wholesale trading, shops, rice-mills, and export – with merchants from the towns.[173] Meanwhile, the level of trade in the tract had risen considerably and the towns had flourished.

With no stable villages, considerable urban influence, and no pre-eminent village elites, the area had grown turbulent and difficult to

[168] *Royal Commission on Labour in India, Evidence*, vol. III, pt. 1, p. 5; Ranga, *Economic Organisation*, vol. I, p. 7.

[169] *Madras Provincial Banking Enquiry Commission*, vol. III, pp. 739–40.

[170] Ranga, *Economic Organisation*, vol. II, p. 95.

[171] *Ibid.* vol. I, p. 189.

[172] *Madras Provincial Banking Enquiry Commission*, vol. III, pp. 739, 750–1; vol. IV, p. 24.

[173] Ranga, *Economic Organisation*, vol. I, pp. 35–6.

govern.[174] Crime rates were high, agitations common, village officers recalcitrant and it was not uncommon for the lower strata of rural society to rebel against the men who, in other areas, were meekly accepted as overlords; in 1922, for instance, village service groups in large parts of East Godavari district refused to bear their masters around on palanquins.[175] Since government's administration system depended so much on the village elite, it was hardly surprising that the deltas were a constant headache to the rulers. Village officers from the Kistna–Godavari tract staged a revolt against the diminution of their powers in the 1890s and repeated it during Non-co-operation in 1921 and Civil Disobedience ten years later.[176] The agitations in northern India in 1907 found an echo in the south only in the Kistna–Godavari area.

Political leadership in this tract required something beyond the ties of clientage and dependence which were the stock-in-trade of politicians from the 'dry' region, and politics had from an early stage taken on a public aspect. By the 1920s, there was a flourishing local press in the deltaic area. The *Kistna Patrika*, published from Masulipatam, was one of the earliest vernacular papers read by a largely rural audience. By the mid-1920s it had been joined by the *Chittaranjan*, *Swatantra*, *Telaga* and *Sri Sujanaranjin* in Rajahmundry, the *Hitakarini*, *Kapu* and *Satyagrahi* in Ellore, the *Swarajya Patrika* in Bezwada, the *Durbar* and *Navayuga* in Guntur, and the *Janmabhumi*, *Kammakula Patrika*, *Kaliyuga* and *Sarada* in Masulipatam. Excluding Madras City and the western coastal districts, the Madras Government could only identify four other papers with political content in the province.[177] The elections in 1920 saw the publication of electioneering pamphlets in Kistna and Godavari, but nowhere else outside Madras City. Non-co-operation propaganda in the Kistna–Godavari deltas a year later was helped along by dramatic performances, bhajan (*singing*) parties and itinerant speakers.[178] There were far more political campaigns. Government knew it would have an agitation on its hands

174 See the remarks on East Godavari in Chief Secretary, Government of Madras, to Secretary of the Home Department GOI, 15 July 1933, in GOI Home Police 13/1 1932 NAI.

175 *Godavaripatrika* 30 May 1922, 4 July 1922 NNR.

176 G.O. 1075 (Public) 20 Oct. 1931 SAH; G.O.s 938 and 939 (Public) 11 Sept. 1931 SAH; G.O. 760 (Public) 16 July 1931 SAH; G.O. 690 (Public) 22 June 1931 SAH; G.O. 639 (Public) 5 June 1931 SAH.

177 GOI Home Political 261 1926 NAI.

178 M. Venkatarangaiya, *The Freedom Struggle in Andhra Pradesh (Andhra)*, vol. III, (Hyderabad, 1965), p. 7.

when it resettled the revenue rates in the Kistna–Godavari deltas in 1928–30, and it began to take precautionary measures months beforehand; nevertheless the agitation here lasted five years.[179] The Kistna–Godavari deltas were also the cradle of the agitation against zamindari tenure in the 1930s and later the first stronghold of the communists in the south of India. Communal politics were also more public, more agitational. Unlike the Reddi campaign in Anantapur, the Kamma campaign in Guntur and Kistna needed propagandists and spawned a three-volume history of the community. One of the agitators 'frequently harped upon the past greatness and glory of the Kammas as Zamindars and influential personages in these places, their present neglect and decadence, and the need they now have to regain their influence in order to raise the community as a whole to the top'. Others attached themselves to the Non-co-operation movement in order 'to carry the message to the plough-man and the cow-boy in the far off and neglected corners of the whole district'.[180]

Political organisations were more common in these districts than elsewhere. Guntur and Godavari both possessed District Associations from the later nineteenth century, Kistna was the site of one of the few mofussil branches of the Justice party founded before the 1920 elections, and the Congress was a more vital organisation at the local level than it was in most of south India. District Congress committees in the deltas had a fairly continuous life from the 1910s, whereas in most districts of the province they waxed and waned with remarkable speed. These committees discussed each new issue of Congress policy in some depth – the Guntur district Congress spent four days in 1918 discussing the Congress' official policy towards the Montagu–Chelmsford reforms[181] – and they attracted men of considerable local influence: the annual election of officers was often heartily contested.

While this was a great difference in political idiom from the neighbouring dry areas, the difference in the personnel of politics was less marked. Big landowners, merchants and moneylenders still dominated the political stage, although they were likely to buttress their position through political organisation and political campaigning, which politicians elsewhere generally ignored. The local leaders could not rely on the methods – chiefly control of debt and administrative office – which were sufficient for the rural bosses of the dry areas; thus the village officers of Guntur, Kistna and Godavari did not only

[179] See below ch. 3.
[180] G.O. 2357 (LSG) 23 June 1927 SAH.
[181] *Hindu* 13 Aug. 1918.

object to the government's attempts to qualify their powers but they also rebelled, and in the 1920s many of them went looking for new bases of political leadership. Local political organisations in the deltas, far more than elsewhere, were littered with men from village officer families. Bikkani Venkararatnam, who became a prominent Congress leader and later a minister, Mallipudi Pallamraju who abandoned his village office in 1926 to go into the Congress, the Legislative Council elections and district board politics, A. Kaleswara Rao, a Bezwada Congressman, C. V. Venkatachelam, a Rajahmundry Congress leader, Penumetcha Peddiraju, an M.L.C., district board leader and Congressman, and P. V. Krishnayya Choudhary, an M.L.C., district board politician and ardent Justicite, all came from village officer families in the deltas.

One difference was that there were many professional men, particularly successful lawyers, in the political forefront. There were, of course, many such men in local politics in the dry areas, but in the deltas they were more numerous and more prominent. They also maintained their role throughout the 1920s when, in much of the rest of the province, professional politicians were being squeezed out by the influx of powerful landowners and moneylenders. The wide clientele of lawyers gave them the range of contacts necessary for a politician in such a fluid area, and enabled them to mediate among the many who desired to gain representation in the political process in the deltas; their professional skills were useful in the tight factional struggles which so often flowed outside the bounds of the political process and into the courts; their education helped them to act as publicists. Most of the lawyers and publicists who led the Congress in Andhra came from the heart of the Kistna–Godavari deltas – Kaleswara Rao, T. Prakasam, Konda Venkatappayya and Pattabhi Sitaramayya. In local politics, lawyers and publicists often figured prominently in the strategy of particular factions. In East Godavari, Bulusu Sambamurthy, a retired lawyer dedicated to asceticism and nationalism, moved in the front rank of local board politics as the agent for a diverse faction of landowners and businessmen.[182] In West Godavari, Dandu Narayana Raju, the scion of a prominent landed family, moved into Ellore town to study and then practice law and to serve an apprenticeship in municipal politics, before moving out to become one of the chief Congress leaders in the rural areas.[183] Kasu

[182] *Hindu* 8, 12 and 18 Sept. 1925, 6 July 1934.
[183] *Hindu* 6 Jan. 1921, 11 Sept. 1925, 15 Jan. 1935.

Venkatakrishna Reddi, a village officer from Guntur district, wanted all his sons to be lawyers; the three of them in the 1920s planned to set up separate legal practices in the three major towns of their area so that they might, in the words of a biographer, 'control the highland areas of western Guntur'.[184]

In the delta areas local politics were not so confined as in the 'dry' tracts. In most districts, the Legislative Council elections in the 1920s attracted four or five candidates for the two or three seats available. In the deltas, the numbers were almost invariably higher. In East Godavari in 1920 there were seven, in Kistna in 1923 eleven, and in Guntur in 1926 and again in 1930 there were seven. The negotiations which preceded the elections were more complex and more fragile than elsewhere. Kaleswara Rao, who tried to mediate between the prospective candidates before the polls in Kistna in 1926, had to deal with seven influential men who wanted to contest for the two seats; one of them, a rural faction leader, set up his lieutenant as a candidate, and then decided to stand against him himself; the Congress organisation in one half of the district actively campaigned against the Congress candidates chosen by the Congressmen of the other half; and Kaleswara Rao and the raja of Mirzapuram, who at the outset had concluded an electoral pact and who had hoped to manage the electoral contest between them, emerged at the end as bitter enemies and took out vindictive lawsuits against one another.[185]

The local boards of the area were also prey to the uncertainty of political control. In direct contrast to the situation in most of the province, the rural boards in Kistna, Guntur, East and West Godavari districts were the scene of rapid changes of regime, fierce public politicking and regular bouts of agitation. While in most districts, the district board presidentship changed hands only once or twice in the decade, Kistna had five presidents and East Godavari four. Taluk board elections were fought with more gusto; after the polls in West Godavari in 1928, there were objection petitions and court suits in every single taluk.[186] Taluk board politics were occasionally conducted in the streets; the members of one faction in Guntur taluk board, in order to enforce their point of view, 'paraded the streets with their motorcars and practised picketing by dissuading members from attending meetings'.[187] No district board president in the deltas

[184] Kasipathi, *Tryst with Destiny*, p. 35.
[185] Kaleswara Rao, *Na Jivita Katha*, pp. 434–9.
[186] G.O. 2900 (LSG) 14 July 1928 SAH.
[187] G.O. 1346 (LSG) 2 June 1923 SAH.

was as safe as his counterpart in the dry districts; T. Balajirao was drummed out of the headship of Kistna district board in 1923 by a noisy public campaign which accused him of loaning money to the chief minister to get the nomination as president, of abusing the distribution of district board contracts, and of waging a political campaign against Kamma rural leaders; the matter ended with Balajirao's resignation and a clutch of lawsuits.[188]

Local politicians in the deltas had to devote considerable attention to securing their local base. The polite methods of negotiation between the magnates, and rigid control of the elections would not work in an area where there were many anxious to challenge the claims of anyone who set himself up as a local leader. Some local politicians responded by making an expansive use of the tools of local power. The transactional empire established in West Godavari by Penumetcha Peddiraju had many parallels in municipalities but none in rural boards. He put his election agents into the nominated seats on taluk boards, and was thought to have the Revenue Divisional Officers who ran the taluk board elections in his pocket. He distributed contracts to a powerful clique of friends, which included the cousin of a taluk board president, and managed to find a place for his lieutenant's kinsman in municipal service although he was unqualified. To mollify his own vice-president, he got the board to purchase his old house for a school at a price that would save the vice-president from the debtors court.[189]

Besides this, many local leaders in the deltas felt that they had to take a leading role in agitational politics in the locality. For some, this meant that they took a fervent interest in non-Brahmanism. East Godavari was one of the few mofussil areas to possess a fairly constant Justicite branch organisation, which held meetings, published pamphlets and occasionally produced a newspaper. For most, however, it meant an involvement in the politics of nationalism. Although the Congress could claim, at most, to have won only forty-three of the ninety-eight elected seats at the 1926 elections, it won seven of the ten in the Kistna–Godavari area. M. Pallamraju and P. Peddiraju, who became presidents in East and West Godavari district boards respectively in the late 1920s, were both avowed Congressmen, while no

[188] *Kistnapatrika* 6 Oct. 1923 NNR; government notes on court cases in G.O. 475 (LSG) 10 Feb. 1925 SAH.

[189] Petition of T. Achutaramaiah and D. V. Narayanamurthy dated 6 Dec. 1931, report of Collector dated 5 Feb. 1932, and report of Inspector of Municipalities and Local Boards, in G.O. 900 (LSG) 6 Mar. 1933 SAH.

district outside the deltas sported a Congress president before the mid-1930s. In Civil Disobedience, as noted below, government was horrified to find that local politicians in the deltas were using the machinery of local government to carry out Congress agitations.

The fluidity of local politics also gave the ministers more opportunities for intervention. There was no obvious individual, or clique, in local board politics of the delta districts, with whom the ministry simply had to deal. Indeed, in the tight factional conflicts which characterised the local boards of the delta districts, the powers wielded by the ministers assumed great importance. The contrast between the two regions in this respect was illustrated in the attempts by Dr Subbaroyan in 1927 to interfere in the internal politics of Kistna and Salem districts. In Salem, Subbaroyan's home district, his efforts to disrupt the control of local boards by the dominant faction of Foulkes and Ellappa Chetty failed miserably.[190] At the same time, he was able to turn the local politics of Kistna upside down. He divided the old Kistna district into two new districts – Kistna and West Godavari – abolished the old district board and thus gave himself the power to nominate all the members of the new boards.[191] In selecting these members, he completely ignored the wishes of the faction, led by the raja of Mirzapuram, which had been in command of the old board and had confidently expected to continue to rule the two new ones. 'From what supernatural agency did he get the names?' protested an article written in the *Justice* on Mirzapuram's behalf.[192] Only four members of the old board had been chosen, the Collector's suggestions as well as Mirzapuram's had been ignored, both of those newly installed as presidents were Mirzapuram's enemies, and one had not even sat on the old board. There was a huge uproar, but Subbaroyan's placemen survived, at least until Subbaroyan was replaced as chief minister by a man more amenable to Mirzapuram's wishes. After this the ministry again demonstrated its ability to tinker with the affairs of the deltas and re-installed Mirzapuram.[193]

But while the fluidity of local affairs in the deltas gave the ministry more opportunities to intervene, it also ensured that such interventions were beset with problems. To begin with, the ministry had

[190] G.O. 1756 (LSG) 14 May 1927 MRO; G.O. 2412 (LSG) 25 June 1927 MRO; G.O. 3019 (LSG) 9 Aug. 1927 MRO.

[191] G.O. 1551 (LSG) 29 Apr. 1927 SAH; Kaleswara Rao, *Na Jivita Katha*, pp. 457–8.

[192] A. Ramaswami Mudaliar (ed.), *Mirror of the Year: being a collection of the leading articles in 'Justice', 1927* (Madras, 1928), pp. 20–37.

[193] G.O. 459 (LSG) 25 Jan. 1934 SAH; G.O. 900 (LSG) 6 Mar. 1933 SAH.

difficulty identifying its most useful allies. No obvious candidates, like Foulkes or the raja of Ramnad, presented themselves, and so in its choice of men to patronise in the locality the ministry could be swayed by other factors. Subbaroyan's intervention in Kistna politics had been carefully planned, but Panagal's management of local boards in Kistna earlier in the decade had had all the marks of a man fishing in the dark. His first choice for the presidentship of Kistna district board had been T. Balajirao, whose recommendations were not that he was obviously influential in the district but that he had once served as a dewan for Panagal's relative the raja of Venkatagiri and that, it was alleged, he had lent Panagal some money.[194] When as noted above, Balajirao's administration proved chaotic, Panagal chose Mirzapuram, one of his relatives, who again had a stormy time. In East Godavari, the district board was handed to a non-Brahman service family associated with the raja of Pithapuram, another of Panagal's relatives. In Guntur, the ministry gave backing to P. C. Ethirajulu Naidu, a recent immigrant to the district who won this patronage by ingratiating himself with the Collector and with the Justice leaders in Madras. He was soon at odds with the premier landed families, because they resented his usurpation of the district board which they thought they should control, and with powerful local merchants, since he was the agent for a European tobacco firm which competed against them for business. Naturally enough, Ethirajulu Naidu had a very rough ride.[195]

Thus the ministry found it had to give more solid support to its chosen agents in the delta tracts. Just before Subbaroyan had stepped in and ruined Mirzapuram's regime in Kistna, the Justicites had allowed Mirzapuram to gerrymander all the electoral circles in the district.[196] In Guntur, the ministry helped Ethirajulu Naidu along by twice nominating him to the temple committee although each time the Collector tried to veto the nomination.[197] In East Godavari, the nominations the ministry made to local boards to help their friends on the eve of local and Legislative Council elections in 1926 caused

[194] *Andhrapatrika* 21 June 1922, *Kistnapatrika* 6 Oct. 1923, *Trilinga* 19 July 1924 NNR; G.O. 475 (LSG) 10 Feb. 1925 SAH.

[195] GOI Reforms Franchise B 34–99 March 1921 NAI; G.O. 776 (L & M,M) 21 June 1919 MRO; K. Kotilingam to P. S. Sivaswami Iyer, n.d., Sivaswami Iyer papers NAI.

[196] Letter from raja of Mirzapuram dated 28 Feb. 1926, petition of C. K. Reddi dated 20 Feb. 1926 and associated notes in G.O. 1003 (LSG) 9 Mar. 1926 SAH.

[197] G.O. 4450 (LSG) 3 Oct. 1929 SAH; G.O. 3394 (LSG) 20 Aug. 1928 SAH.

Madras journalists to coin the term 'Panagalism' for the misuse of ministerial patronage.[198]

The wide channels which the ministry cut into the politics of these districts also served to convey the problems and disputes of their local politics back to the ministerial ante-chambers. The affairs of the delta districts thus had a disproportionate influence on events in provincial politics. In 1926, Kistna politics played a large part in the re-shuffling of the ministry; the Kistna politicians, A. Kaleswara Rao and Mothey Narasimha Rao, two of Mirzapuram's fiercest local opponents, colluded with C. P. Ramaswami Iyer to set up Dr Subbaroyan's ministry in order to pull down Mirzapuram.[199] Again, as seen below, the Justicite leadership changed hands in 1932 partly because of the politics of the deltas; two factions transported their supporters hundreds of miles in special trains from the deltas to the Tamil districts in order to fight a pitched battle at the annual Justicite confederation, after which Muniswami Naidu ceded the leadership and the chief ministership to the raja of Bobbili.

Many politicians in the deltas found that they had to adopt the aspect of Janus and to foster at one and the same time the image of a local democrat and the image of a ministerial satellite. In the politics of East Godavari in the 1920s it would be hard to find an important figure who had not at some time associated himself with the Congress, but equally it would be hard to find men who had not at some time tried to gain ministerial favour. Madireddi Ventataratnam, district board president for many years, was the staunchest of Justicite allies while his son-in-law Govindarow Naidu wrote Justicite pamphlets in 1920, ran a Congress campaign to get into the district board in 1926, was aligned with the Justicite faction in 1929, and formed a committee to meet Gandhi on tour in 1933.[200] Many families chose to spread their political loyalties over the widest possible area in this way. The Motheys of Ellore, after their flirtations with Non-co-operation and Swarajism in the early 1920s, decided to deploy their talents better; in 1930 Mothey Narayana Rao was a local Congress leader, Mothey Gangaraju helped the Collector to run a loyalist association, and

[198] *Swarajya* 14 July 1926 NNR.

[199] Kaleswara Rao, *Na Jivita Katha*, pp. 440–2.

[200] P. Govindarow Naidu, *The Legislative Council Elections (1920): a critical study of party programmes* (Rajahmundry, 1920); *Hindu* 16 May 1925, 12 Sept. 1925, 28 Aug. 1929, 16 Dec. 1933; G.O. 3087 (LSG) 31 July 1930 SAH; G.O. 1413 (LSG) 20 Apr. 1931 SAH.

Mothey Narasimha Rao, recently elected to the central assembly, was expected by the Collector to 'decide which party to join after going to Delhi'.[201] Other politicians took on all the different roles personally; N. V. L. Narasimha Rao in the early 1930s ran the Guntur municipality in the name of the Congress while working as the agent of the Justice ministry in the Guntur district board.[202]

The problems of political control and political organisation in the deltaic area were surpassed only by those in a few big towns of the province. Urban growth and urban prosperity were virtually confined to two areas of the province.[203] Firstly, in the Kistna–Godavari delta area, there were several towns which flourished on the trade and manufacture of the produce of their rich hinterland, in particular the port of Cocanada and the railheads of Guntur, Bezwada, Rajahmundry and Ellore. Secondly, there was a scattering of towns in the far south, most with a long history as administrative and cultural centres under past empires, and all with some modern prosperity from trade and manufacture, particularly in cotton; the most important of these were Madura, Trichinopoly and the Tinnevelly–Palamcottah conurbation. In the half-century before 1941, the populations of Ellore, Cocanada, Tinnevelly and Trichinopoly had roughly doubled, those of Rajahmundry and Madura had roughly tripled, while Guntur's population had multiplied three and a half times and Bezwada's more than four times.[204] These towns contained a large number of labourers, many of them migrants; as a Collector complained, 'in . . . Cocanada and Rajahmundry, there has always existed a large proportion of the "rowdy" element which is at the beck and call of political agitators'.[205] Fortunes could be made and lost more rapidly than elsewhere, and the elite of such towns might be transformed quite rapidly. Appalaswami, the eminence grise of Bezwada politics, came from a low-caste and low-income family and had built his wealth and

[201] GOI Home Public 325 1930 NAI; *Hindu* 17 Oct. 1931, 18 Jan. 1932, 19 Feb. 1932, 11 Mar. 1933; M. Narayana Rao to V. Patel, 17 July 1930, AICC papers file G40(i) of 1930 NMML.

[202] A. Kaleswara Rao to J. Kripalani, 4 Jan. 1935, AICC papers file 7 of 1934 NMML.

[203] Most of the other towns which were growing rapidly were little more than railheads. The pattern of the railways in the region made the immediate hinterland of Madras City into a major crossroads and there were many flourishing railtowns there; see map 3.

[204] *Census of India 1931*, vol. XIV, pt. 2, pp. 10–16; *Census of India 1941*, vol. II, pp. 26–36.

[205] GOI Home Police 13/1 1932 NAI.

political status through trading and contracting;[206] Tulsiram, who came to lead the Saurashtra mercantile community in Madura, was not born into the community's aristocracy but had travelled abroad and learnt new dyeing techniques which brought prosperity to himself and to the community in general. K. Nageswara Rao, a leading figure in Bezwada affairs, was the son of a poor country priest; he had built up an economic empire through patent medicines, cinema management and a host of other enterprises.[207] The entire profile of such towns might change quite quickly. Guntur had acquired twenty-two new factories in forty years, and had become a major centre of the tobacco industry;[208] Madura had become the site of the biggest cotton mill in India, and of two further cotton mills built in the 1920s.

As in the deltaic tract, rapid economic change and the absence of a secure elite impaired the working of local government. The municipal chair in Rajahmundry, for instance, changed hands fourteen times between 1908 and 1930, and only one occupant lasted his full three-year term. Legislature elections (five seats in the Montagu–Chelmsford Legislative Council were elected from urban constituencies) did not attract a particularly large number of candidates, but they were generally bitterly contested. 'They say,' noted the Collector on the subject of elections in Tinnevelly in 1923, 'it is going to be very expensive.'[209] By the later 1920s, it was becoming obvious that the structure of municipal government under the 1919 Act, although adequate for the many small towns of the region, was hopelessly inadequate for the larger towns. In Trichinopoly, tax collections were two lakhs in arrears, 300,000 square feet of municipal property was illegally occupied, further municipal property worth Rs 25,000 had been assigned away without sufficient reason, and a bloated staff which included even a 'microscope doctor' gobbled up over a third of municipal revenues.[210] In many of the big towns, it proved difficult to collect taxes and rates. 'The total realisations of the property tax', wrote a government inspector in 1932, 'do not indicate that Bezwada is a busy, flourishing city, the heart of the fertile deltaic districts',[211]

206 G.O. 2028 (L & M,M) 10 Dec. 1919 MRO.

207 K. Iswara Dutt, *Sparks and Fumes* (Madras, 1929), pp. 75–8; GOI Home Public 311/34 & Kw 1934 NAI.

208 G.O. 732 (L & M,M) 8 May 1919 MRO.

209 Tinnevelly municipal chairman to Governor, 12 Sept. 1923, in G.O. 2290 (LSG) 16 Oct. 1923 MRO.

210 Report of Collector dated 23 Dec. 1930, in G.O. 879 (LSG) 16 Mar. 1931 MRO.

211 Report on Bezwada by the special officer for the stabilisation of finances of local boards, in G.O. 4974 (LSG) 12 Dec. 1932 SAH.

which it certainly was. In Madura by the end of the 1920s there were nine lakhs of tax arrears, 4,000 petitions outstanding against the property tax assessments, and 1,000 subjects pending on the municipal council's agenda. The Collector urged that Madura, the second city of the province, needed a more elaborate framework for local government, but government was deaf to such appeals. Only the intervention of a cholera epidemic prompted government to take special action to unravel the mess that Madura municipal affairs had fallen into.[212] Major scandals were a feature of municipal affairs in these towns. The Bezwada council lost Rs 7,000 through an ingenious defalcation whose perpetrators used parallel sets of tax registers.

Madura lost a similar amount through corruption in the lighting department.[213] In Trichinopoly, the ratepayers urged stricter supervision of both councillors and municipal staff for, they insisted, 'if immediate steps are not taken, the Belly Gods in the Municipality will swallow the Ratepayers' money'.[214] Government had to dissolve the municipal councils in both Guntur and Madura at the end of the decade because faction and maladministration had reached such a height, and the head of the local government department in Fort St George urged: 'Actually I have no doubt that there is a case for supersession in the Guntur, Bezwada and Rajahmundry municipalities, all three of which are faction-ridden to a degree.'[215]

With reference to the Trichinopoly municipality, the Collector noted in 1931: 'So long as the Chairman and the Councillors depend for their success at the next election on the vote of the taxpayers, certainly no revision of assessment, no eviction of encroachments, no cancellation of objectionable assignments and no retrenchment can be expected from them.[216] The municipal chairmen who proved most successful in the administration of the large towns were those who indulged in the most flagrant exploitation of the tools at their disposal. Only thus could they override the opposition and keep the administration moving. Those who were either more nervous or more pious, generally could not cope with the problems they faced. F. G.

212 Report of Collector dated 11 Oct. 1930, in G.O. 4438(LSG) 13 Nov. 1930 MRO; Report of Inspector of Municipalities and Local Boards dated 8 May 1931, in G.O. 2591 (LSG) 27 June 1931 MRO.

213 Copy of court proceedings in the case of the five bill collectors, in G.O. 38 (LSG) 4 Jan. 1929 SAH.

214 Petition of C. Ponnuswamy Pillai dated 4 Jan 1928, in G.O. 4424 (LSG) 2 Nov. 1928 MRO.

215 G.O. 5129 (LSG) 23 Dec. 1932 SAH.

216 Report of Collector dated 23 Dec. 1930, in G.O. 879 (LSG) 16 Mar. 1931 MRO.

Natesan who was chairman in Trichinopoly in the early 1920s was accused by his opponents of malfeasance, autocracy and high-handedness towards the staff and the other councillors; but the government inspector, after detailing Natesan's highly personal administration of contracts and his disdain for the municipal constitution and rules, concluded that he had done a lot more than any other chairman towards getting the basic work of administration under way.[217] The Congressman, A. Kaleswara Rao, who was chairman in Bezwada for many years, boasted that he by-passed the rules and often ignored other councillors in order to get things done.[218] If judged by the ability to hold onto the chairman's post and to keep the wheels of administration turning, N. V. L. Narasimha Rao was undoubtedly the most successful chairman in Guntur. His opponents insisted that he was 'steeped in the most stinking and loathsome cesspools of maladministration, mischievous electioneering and heartless self-aggrandisement'[219] and sent petition after petition to the Secretariat detailing the webs of interest with which he held down most of the councillors. The government inspector verified most of these accusations, but suggested that he be allowed to continue since he was at least skilful and effective.[220] Similarly in Madura, the inspector praised the work of L. K. Tulsiram in 1931 for he had at least got the clogged wheels of administration to begin to turn:

> By the judicious distribution among doubtful councillors of the small favours which he could offer as chairman – such as appointment or retention of persons who are related to councillors or in whom they are interested, giving a new tap or additional tap, licensing temporary encroachments, accepting recommendations for the disposal of contracts and so on – he has been able to get through the business in the council with ease.[221]

As in the deltaic areas so in the big towns, local politicians supplemented their personal networks and their transactional empires by participating in the public agitational politics of the town. Most of these big towns possessed fairly permanent Congress committees while

[217] Report of Examiner of Local Fund Account dated 21 May 1923, in G.O. 1545 (LSG) 7 July 1923 MRO.

[218] Kaleswara Rao, *Na Jivita Katha*, pp. 387–92.

[219] Printed memorial dated May 1927, in G.O. 3416 (LSG) 6 Sept. 1927 SAH.

[220] Report of Inspector of Municipalities and Local Boards dated 22 July 1927, in G.O. 3416 (LSG) 6 Sept. 1927 SAH.

[221] Report of Inspector of Municipalities and Local Boards dated 8 May 1931, in G.O. 2591 (LSG) 27 June 1931 MRO; letter from Madura municipal chairman in G.O. 1969 (LSG) 30 May 1932 MRO.

some like Bezwada and Madura also had somewhat less permanent Justicite branches. These committees were not simply outposts of provincial and national organisations; they were often also intimately involved in local politics. The Bezwada Congress committee agitated over a municipal tax on sunshades, the Rajahmundry and Madura Congress committees agitated against rises in the property tax assessments,[222] and in Tinnevelly, according to the disgruntled municipal chairman, 'S. Palaniyandi Mudaliar is a great Congressman of subtle type and he eggs on the rougher elements of the town to throng in great numbers in the Municipal office whenever he thinks it necessary for his purpose'.[223] Kaleswara Rao and his allies were propelled into control of the Bezwada municipality on the impetus of Non-co-operation agitation. N. V. L. Narasimha Rao, throughout his long career in the Guntur municipal chair, struggled to keep a toehold in the local Congress although he was opposed bitterly by many other local Congressmen who thought his municipal regime prejudiced the Congress image.[224]

The ministry found it difficult to secure a stable base of support in these towns. The difficulties that this caused were most graphically illustrated in the political snakes and ladders of Madura town. Here the two most prominent men who came forward to mediate in the relationship between ministry and locality in the 1920s were a lawyer, R. S. Naidu, and L. K. Tulsiram, one of the leading figures of the Saurashtra community. Tulsiram had ventured into provincial politics before 1920; he had attended several Congress sessions but in the late 1910s he was quick to spot the rising star of the Justice leaders and he aligned himself with them. However, Tulsiram was soon confronted by the great difficulties of straddling the gap between the centre and the periphery. The members of his community, who were currently claiming that they should be recognised as Brahmans, would have nothing to do with the non-Brahman agitation which Tulsiram tried to import. Tulsiram thus quickly dropped the latter, adopted the cry for Brahman status, and added that if government ignored their claims, the Saurashtras should join the Non-co-operation movement. Thus within the space of a few months, Tulsiram had run through the

222 FR March (2), GOI Home Political 112 1925 NAI; *Hindu* 19 Feb. 1923; *Andhrapatrika* 16 and 20 Feb. 1922 NNR.

223 Letter from C. Alagirisami Naidu in G.O. 1969 (LSG) 30 May 1932 MRO.

224 See for example A. Kaleswara Rao to J. Kripalani, 4 Jan. 1935, AICC papers file 7 of 1934 NMML. See also the trouble over Congress conferences organised by Narasimha Rao in 1928, *Hindu* 30 and 31 July 1928, 1 Aug. 1928.

whole gamut of Madras City's political attitudes. Once the Justice ministers were installed he switched back into his Justice incarnation and conducted Panagal on a tour of Madura in early 1921. A few weeks later, Panagal nominated Tulsiram to the Madura municipality along with seven others, which was enough to get Tulsiram elected chairman immediately afterwards. R. S. Naidu had in the meantime become Tulsiram's chief opponent. He also had vague Congress connections, which he strengthened in early 1920 when he planned to contest the legislature elections on a Congress ticket. He prudently withdrew from the elections when three others announced their candidatures for the Madura seat, and became a prominent organiser of Non-co-operation. He also got elected to the municipality and led the opposition to the chairman's regime. Tulsiram was soon in trouble in the municipality. He depended on the support of his fellow Saurashtras, who had made it abundantly clear that they wished to control the municipality in order to neutralise it, and in order to evade its taxes and its controls on their commercial activity. Tulsiram could not accede to their wishes and retain the support of his ministerial patrons at the same time, and this made his position intolerable. Harassed in the municipal council, he finally hurled the minute book at an opponent and resigned. Soon after, he stood at the elections to the Legislative Council and lost. Over the next three years, Tulsiram and Naidu changed places. Naidu was elected municipal chairman in the wake of Tulsiram's fall, and he also fell foul of the merchants. He was still anxious to call himself a Congressman, but this proved difficult when he found that his merchant enemies were building their opposition to him round a Congress flag. By 1926, he had to seek ministerial help in order to stay in command of the municipality, in the Legislative Council elections of that year he contested as a Justicite, and immediately after he organised a big Justice party conference. Tulsiram, in the meantime, had become a Congressman again, had grasped the leadership of the merchants, and had stood as a Congressman at the 1926 elections. In six years, Naidu and Tulsiram had swopped political hats three times.[225]

In order to get some sort of purchase in this situation, the ministry had to choose its allies and then give them firm support. In Trichino-

[225] *Hindu* 17, 18 and 28 June 1920, 20 and 22 July 1920, 19 Jan. 1921, 4 and 7 June 1921, 14 June 1922, 15 Aug. 1922, 17 May 1923, 28 June 1923, 28 Aug. 1925, 1 Sept. 1925, 25 Dec. 1926; G.O. 919A (LSG) 24 May 1921 MRO; G.O. 1150 (LSG) 7 July 1923 MRO; FR March(1), GOI Home Political 112 1925 NAI.

poly, they marked out P. Khalifullah, head of a wealthy and influential trading family and political leader of the local Muslims. He had become an M.L.C. and he moved closely with the ministers in Madras. By 1924 his ministerial contacts had given him such a position that the Collector complained that Khalifullah knew about government decisions on matters relating to Trichinopoly even before he did.[226] In 1929 when the chief minister called off an investigation instituted by the Secretariat into the affairs of Trichinopoly municipality, many detected the hand of Khalifullah behind the scenes.[227] Finally in 1931, Khalifullah requested quite brazenly that government should conduct all its relations with Trichinopoly municipality through him, although he was currently not even a member.[228] In Tinnevelly in the late 1920s the chief minister repeatedly brushed aside petitions alleging malfeasance on the part of Ch. K. Subramania Pillai, the ministerial favourite in the municipal chair, and even looked on with equanimity when it was revealed that several of these allegations, in particular those describing how the chairman had manipulated the tax registers to favour himself, his family and his political allies and to hurt his enemies, were undoubtedly true.[229] When Subramania Pillai's neighbour and close friend, M. D. T. Ranganatha Mudaliar, succeeded him in the municipal chair, the ministry abetted his use of the municipal machinery to undermine the influence which his political rivals had in the temples and markets of the town, until the manipulations became too flagrant and the secretary of the local government department in Fort St George stepped in and overruled the chief minister.[230] In most of these politically wayward towns, the ministry found that it became tied to men whose bases of local support were uncertain and whom the ministry had to continue to support by increasingly em-

226 Letter from Collector dated 2 Oct. 1924, in G.O. 3038 (LSG) 30 Oct, 1924 MRO.

227 P. Khalifullah to chief minister, 19 Oct. 1928, in G.O. 4424 (LSG) 2 Nov. 1928 MRO.

228 Letter from P. Khalifullah dated 2 Feb. 1931, in G.O. 879 (LSG) 16 March 1931 MRO.

229 Petition from M. Sivakolundu dated 15 Feb. 1929, petitions from A. Kumaravelu Pillai dated 27 May 1929 and 11 Feb 1930, notes by chief minister dated 26 Mar. 1929 and 27 Mar. 1929, letter from Tinnevelly municipal chairman dated 8 Aug. 1929, and associated papers, in G.O. 2615 (LSG) 8 May 1929 MRO.

230 Numerous petitions and report of Inspector of Municipalities and Local Boards dated 26 Aug. 1933, in G.O. 1673 (LSG) 8 May 1934 MRO; petition from E. R. Authimoolan Chettiar dated 4 June 1934, in G.O. 4104 (LSG) 15 Sept. 1934 MRO; notes by Secretary of LSG department dated 10 May 1934, in G.O. 2525 (LSG) 25 May 1934 MRO.

phatic and precarious interventions. The alternative was to abandon such towns and as affairs in Rajahmundry and Guntur, which the ministers by the end of the 1920s had given up as hopeless, showed the effect was disastrous; Rajahmundry and Guntur led the way in Congress organisation, and in the campaign of Civil Disobedience.

The extension of local government had brought a large slice of the population into the political system of the province. Between 1919 and 1927, the number of electors registered in municipalities had multiplied almost four times (from 58,554 to 215,348), and the number in the rural boards almost eight times (from 112,414 to 862,025). Interest in local elections had also grown; the average poll in rural board elections had risen from 32 per cent in 1920–1 to 52 per cent in 1925–6.[231] Through common participation in one structure of administration, the affairs of many disparate and separate localities had been drawn far closer together. All local politicians had in some fashion to negotiate with the ministers in Madras City. Moreover the local boards were closely linked to the Legislative Council, not only because local government matters formed the substance of much of the debating and politicking in the Legislative Council and because the Legislative Council acted as a channel of communication between ministers and local politicians, but because M.L.C.s and local politicians were generally the same people and because local politics formed one of the springboards for a prospective M.L.C. The style of the elections to the Legislative Council helps to illustrate what men and what interests found a place in the politics of dyarchy.

ELECTIONS TO THE LEGISLATIVE COUNCIL

Electioneering began with negotiations between influential men in the constituency. Members of the local elite wished if possible to avoid the expense of contesting against their peers, and in some cases these preliminary conferences resulted in members being returned unopposed. Sixteen candidates succeeded in this way in 1926. In other cases these negotiations merely resulted in electoral pacts. The district constituencies each returned two or three members, and each voter had as many votes as there were seats. Candidates often tried to lessen the electioneering load by allying with other candidates and sharing their support. These preliminary negotiations were often

[231] *Indian Statutory Commission*, vol. V, pp. 1116–19.

quite complicated. In Trichinopoly in 1926, M. R. Seturatnam Iyer, a Brahman who was recognised as a Swarajist, ran in harness with T. M. Naryanaswami Pillai, who was recognised as the Justicites' local ally.[232] In Coimbatore in 1930, the local magnates shared out the seats and when they found there was still one hopeful left over, they arranged that one man should resign half-way through his term and allow the other in.[233] In Kistna in 1926, A. Kaleswara Rao and the raja of Mirzapuram tried to mediate among the many hopeful candidates who included the agent of a prominent zamindar, two big rural faction leaders and a politician from the district town.[234] Ministerial influence could be useful at this stage. In 1923, the ministry made sure that the third minister, A. P. Patro, would be returned unopposed in Ganjam, and in Godavari K. V. Reddi Naidu wanted Panagal to offer the district board presidentship to one prospective candidate in return for his withdrawal from the contest.[235] In the later elections of dyarchy, it became quite common for men to come forward as candidates chiefly in the hope that other candidates would offer some bargains in return for their withdrawal.

There were some attempts to fix the election in advance of the polls by manipulating the electoral rolls. In keenly contested elections, it was common for both parties to try and bolster up their number of supporters in the electoral registers. In Tinnevelly in 1926 there were 1,759 claims against the original electoral roll and 348 objections.[236] In Kistna in the same year, a government officer admitted he included 3,500 new names on the electoral rolls at the request of one of the candidates.[237]

The contests were rarely conducted through open, public campaigning. Generally, candidates attempted to win the support of men who controlled a large number of voters. There were many different instances of these vote-banks or 'election-bosses'. Some of the most important were the leaders of local government, and it was no coincidence that a large number of the seats in the legislatures were won by district and taluk board presidents and by municipal chairmen. Of the 140 persons who served as district board presidents between 1917

232 Statement by M. R. Seturatnam Iyer, *Hindu* 30 Mar. 1928.

233 *Hindu* 20 Mar. 1935, 11 and 12 July 1935; *Justice* 10 Apr. 1936.

234 Kaleswara Rao, *Na Jivita Katha*, pp. 434–9.

235 Diaries of K. V. Reddi Naidu, entries for 2 and 4 Sept. 1923; Annamalai Chettiar to R. K. Shanmugham Chetty, 22 Dec. 1934, Shanmugham Chetty papers.

236 *Indian Statutory Commission*, vol. VI, p. 319.

237 Kaleswara Rao, *Na Jivita Katha*, p. 439.

and 1946, sixty-five also sat in the Legislative Council.[238] Shortly before the 1923 elections, a correspondent of *The Hindu* noted: 'These candidates who are Presidents of District boards have developed a sudden fit of travelling through the whole district.... To keep up their state they travel about with the District Board engineers and his subordinates or other employees.'[239] In Kistna, in 1920 villagers anxiously begged the district board president to stand for the Legislative Council, while in Godavari a conference demanded that all the executive heads of local boards should be banned from contesting because, as one speaker explained, 'they apprehended that Presidents of District Boards who wielded enormous influence over hundreds of teachers, dozens of Union Chairmen, overseers and other subordinate engineering staff etc. might abuse their power in canvassing votes for their election'.[240] These fears were fully justified. Almost every petition filed against an election during dyarchy alleged some manipulation of local administration. In South Arcot the district board president was accused of admitting to the board school the son of a prominent rural leader and giving him a discount on fees.[241] In Kistna a long petition alleged that the president of the district board had given and promised nominations to taluk boards, given licences to motor buses, promised new roads, schools and bridges, remitted district board fines, loaned district board funds and given contributions to charities in return for votes.[242] Many board heads used their staff as an electioneering organisation. One district board head was alleged to have instructed all the board staff to use 'their latent but magically successful influence'[243] to secure his election. Teachers were often used as agents, as a correspondent of *The Hindu* noted: 'The unfortunate or designing schoolmaster . . . is made to cajole or coerce the parents of his students in to the pleasant task of voting for their master', and if the teacher refused to co-operate he placed his job in jeopardy.[244] Candidates who were not themselves in district boards often took a taluk board president or a union board chairman with them on their election tours.

Temple patronage could also be put to good use. In Tinnevelly P. Nelliappa Pillai rewarded his election agents and most influential

[238] Venkata Rao, *Local Self-Government*, p. 113. [239] *Hindu* 28 July 1923.
[240] *Hindu* 2 June 1920; *Andhrapatrika* 17 Aug. 1920 NNR.
[241] G.O. 186 (Law Legislative) 11 Oct. 1922 MRO.
[242] *Hindu* 6 Jan. 1927, 28 Mar. 1927, 4,5,20,23,24 and 25 Jan. 1928.
[243] G.O. 186 (Law Legislative) 11 Oct. 1922 MRO.
[244] *Hindu* 28 July 1923; see also *Hindu* 29 Oct. 1923.

supporters in 1920 by arranging for their elevation to the local temple committee. When he was then defeated at the next elections he well knew the name of the game; he put in a petition alleging that his opponent had used two temple trustees as his election agents and that these two had, among other things, threatened to stop payments to contractors employed by the temple until the latter had promised their support.[245] In Tanjore in 1920, the Legislative Assembly candidate P. S. Sivaswami Iyer made sure he won the support of the leading *maths* in the area, arranged to hold meetings with the local aristocracy on their premises and also contacted the trustees of all the major temples in the constituency. When Sivaswami Iyer's agents tried to by-pass these men they often found great difficulties; they were told that they had to consult the head of the *math* as 'many of the non-Brahman voters say that they will do what he says',[246] and that one temple manager commanded the votes of two taluks.[247]

The powers wielded by local officials and by village officers made them important forces at elections. In 1920, one candidate came in from outside the district to contest in North Arcot because his brother was sub-Collector and Deputy Magistrate with influence in one half of the district, and this brother's brother-in-law was a tahsildar in the other half.[248] K. S. Venkatarama Iyer, who contested in Tanjore in 1920, conducted his campaign through village officers and branch postmasters.[249] K. V. Reddi Naidu in Godavari in 1923 arranged meetings with the village officers before taking his campaign into any new part of the district.[250] Government had in fact rushed a bill through the legislature in 1919 limiting village officer's privileges, in the fear that the electorate after 1920 would be in the village officers' pockets and that thereafter such a bill would never get passed.[251]

Beyond these official and semi-official sources, candidates contacted men who, through a command of land, money and dependants,

[245] G.O. 289 (Law Legislative) 15 Dec. 1922 MRO.

[246] Letters to P. S. Sivaswami Iyer from his election agents: from G. Venkatesan dated 22 Nov. 1920; M. D. Subramaniam dated 14 May 1920, 8 June 1920 and 31 Aug. 1920; from K. V. Rangaswami Iyengar dated 17 Oct. 1920; From R. P. Moorthy dated 16 Dec. 1920; Sivaswami Iyer papers NAI.

[247] M. D. Subramaniam to P. S. Sivaswami Iyer, 14 May 1920, Sivaswami Iyer papers NAI.

[248] *Hindu* 13 Oct. 1920.

[249] S. P. Natesa Iyer to P. S. Sivaswami Iyer, 6 Nov. 1920, Sivaswami Iyer papers NAI.

[250] Diaries of K. V. Reddi Naidu, entry for 25 July 1923.

[251] G.O. 1958 (Revenue) 14 Aug. 1920 MRO

could control several votes. Bankers and moneylenders figured prominently. In Tanjore in 1920 the secretary of the Tanjore Permanent Fund, the leading local bank, was said to control 800 votes.[252] In Tinnevelly in 1922, one candidate had the manager of the branch of the South Indian Bank as his agent, and this man had allegedly threatened to start collecting outstanding loans unless men promised their support.[253] In the towns, big merchants and moneylenders were the chief vote-banks. In Kumbakonam in 1920, the two merchants who led the town's opposing factions were said to control 100 votes each.[254] In the rural areas, it was the big landed magnates. In the Ceded Districts, where the power of the Reddi sirdars was enormous, it was said that no one would vote at all unless he received instruction from his local sirdar.[255] The election agents of Sivaswami in Tanjore in 1920 reported, 'we ... saw all the leading mirasidars – they have promised to secure all the votes in their jurisdiction'.[256] A. Ramaswami Mudaliar, campaigning in Chingleput, toured round with the district's leading zamindars and it was said to be folly for any opponent of his to attempt to hold an election meeting or conference.[257] A. Rangaswami Iyengar, campaigning in 1926, attended the weddings of big magnates in order to meet many local landholders.[258] Agents campaigning in Tanjore in 1920 made sure that they were present at weddings, sessions of the temple committee and meetings of the rural boards so that they could meet members of the local elite. Campaigning in Kistna in 1926, A. Kaleswara Rao looked for support to the zamindars who had been his legal clients, and to an assortment of rural clan-heads and faction-leaders.[259] Perhaps the ultimate example of a vote-bank was raja Annamalai Chettiar, an incomparably wealthy banker and landowner from Ramnad. When he stood for election in 1923, his agents collected all the voting papers for the Ramnad area from the post office, took them round

252 M. D. Subramaniam to P. S. Sivaswami Iyer, 29 and 30 May 1920, Sivaswami Iyer papers NAI.

253 G.O. 289 (Law Legislative) 15 Dec. 1922 MRO.

254 T. R. Venkatarama Sastri to P. S. Sivaswami Iyer, 23 May 1920, Sivaswami Iyer papers NAI.

255 Kaleswara Rao, *Na Jivita Katha*, p. 333.

256 M. D. Subramaniam to P. S. Sivaswami Iyer 29 May 1920, Sivaswami Iyer papers NAI.

257 Kalyanasundara Mudaliar, *Valkkaik Kurippukkal*, p. 386; *Hindu* 13 Oct. 1920.

258 A. Rangaswami Iyengar to S. Srinivasa Iyengar, 12 June 1926, AICC papers file G57(ii) of 1926 NMML.

259 Kaleswara Rao, *Na Jivita Katha*, pp. 434–9.

for the voters to sign, and then delivered them to Annamalai Chettiar to fill in.[260]

There were some appeals to caste at elections. In Godavari in 1923 Telagas were exhorted to vote for Telagas, and in Kistna Kammas encouraged to vote for Kammas. Similar calls were heard among the Gounders of Coimbatore, the Padaiyichis of South Arcot and the Reddis of Anantapur. Undoubtedly many voters were influenced by caste identity and caste pride when they placed their vote, yet it was difficult for a candidate to turn his caste into a firm political base. Rural castes were greatly interspersed with one another, and an appeal for a caste following stood to lose more votes of members of other castes than it could possibly gain; this was the case argued by a Nadar candidate in Tinnevelly in 1926 when his caste-fellows urged him to run on a communal ticket.[261] Besides, the networks of magnate influence, which cut across all considerations of caste or community, were far more persuasive as mobilisers of support at elections. As a result, candidates who invested heavily in caste support generally did badly. The man who ran as a Kamma candidate in Kistna in 1926 lost to a Brahman and a Velama; Kammas probably formed the majority of the electorate, but the successful candidates had canvassed the support of influential Kamma notables and had thus managed to trounce the man who made a public appeal to a Kamma identity.[262] Similarly, the two who ran as Padaiyichi candidates in South Arcot at the same elections lost to another Padaiyichi who had not tried publicly to cultivate his community.

The election campaign carried on right up to the moment of polling. The number of voters who cast their vote was generally below 50 per cent, and a candidate could make quite a difference to the size of his support if he just managed to get more of his known supporters to the polling booth. The Governor attributed the Swarajists' victory in 1926 in part to their success in commandeering cars on polling day.[263] A. Ramaswami Mudaliar went further than this and in 1923 provided food and refreshment at the polling booths to lure more supporters.[264] Sivaswami Iyer's agents in Tanjore in 1920 performed a remarkable coup when they secured the support of one influential landowner for, as they reported to their employer,

[260] *Hindu* 22, 29 and 30 April 1926, 3 May 1926.

[261] *Hindu* 9 Apr. 1926.

[262] Kaleswara Rao, *Na Jivita Katha*, pp. 434–9.

[263] Goschen to Birkenhead, 11 Nov. 1926, Goschen papers vol. 2 IOL.

[264] *Hindu* 12 Mar. 1924.

'the polling station is his bungalow and he has agreed to do the needful there'.[265]

Elections were fought not through public campaigns, but through a manipulation of existing sources of power in local society. Shortly after the first election in 1920, one M.L.C. suddenly exclaimed in the Council: 'I do not see why members should pretend to represent the ten-rupee landholder in this Council ... [for they] really represent what I should call the oligarchy of this country.' When another M.L.C. objected, he replied: 'I should like to ask ... the honourable member ... how many of the people who voted for him knew what they were voting for?'[266] According to the government's calculations, landholders, businessmen, retired officials and professional people (chiefly lawyers) filled the seats in the Legislative Council, and most of them had a background in local government.[267] In another outburst an M.L.C. exclaimed: 'The will of the people never prevails in the Legislative Council, but it is the will of the District Board Presidents that influences the people.'[268]

THE SWARAJISTS

The legislature elections provided the final link between the affairs of locality and province. The Legislative Council and the local boards housed a new provincial political elite which, founded on a stable base of local magnates and regimented through the powers concentrated in the hands of ministers and leaders of local government, promised to carry on the traditions of stable and secure government in the southern province. There was, however, one serious challenge to the complacency of the rulers and their satellites, and this came from the Congress in the middle years of the decade.

While the years 1916–21 had witnessed a dramatic reorientation of provincial politics, they had also seen a major turning-point in the

[265] M. D. Subramaniam to P. S. Sivaswami Iyer, 27 Nov. 1920, Sivaswami Iyer papers NAI.

[266] Dr Subbaroyan in MLCP, Ia (1921), 752.

[267]

M.L.C.s in:	1920	1923	1926
Lawyers	48	43	36
Landlords	28	27	38
Businessmen	26	30	27
Other professionals	10	8	12
Officials	17	19	15

Source: Indian Statutory Commission, vol. XV, p. 5.

[268] *Indian Statutory Commission*, vol. XVI, p. 222.

history of the Congress. So long as the government possessed little or no machinery through which to listen to the representations, petitions and demands of its subjects, the Congress had gained considerable status simply by acting as a channel of communication between rulers and ruled. Government, albeit unwittingly for the most part, helped to make the Congress important. This had particularly been true in the Madras Presidency since 1900 when the Congress and the Mylapore group, from which government drew most of its senior advisers and administrators, were virtually synonymous. But after the ministers and the linked institutions of local boards and legislature had been introduced in 1920, government had machinery which enabled it to dispense with the rather questionable services of the Mylaporeans and their Congress. The Congress needed a new role. Gandhi had offered one possibility in the policy of Non-co-operation, a spirited opposition to British rule, founded on stern moral principles and prepared to use agitation and mass participation to make itself felt. In the economic and financial confusion that followed the first world war, the crisis in Muslim political society over the issue of the Khilafat and the overheated political atmosphere generated by the negotiations over reforming the constitution, Non-co-operation attracted many politicians.[269] By 1922, however, as the Non-co-operation movement crumbled away and its fundamental limitations and its short-sightedness became apparent, an alternative policy emerged. The protagonists of this policy, who became known as Swarajists, argued that in constitutional rather than agitational methods lay the quickest and best path to national freedom; that the Congress should be taken into the legislatures and local boards, should thus regain its status inside the framework of British rule, and should use this status to press for further constitutional concessions.

The core of the Swarajist movement in the province was the Madras City Nationalists, the group who had captured the Congress in 1920 and had planned to take it to the polls then, but had been forced by the triumph of Gandhi to acquiesce in Non-co-operation or be consigned to a political wilderness. They remained reluctant about the idea of Non-co-operation and took the first opportunity to guide the Congress back towards an electoral strategy. From late 1921, their most active member, S. Satyamurthi, was writing to politicians in other provinces who were known to be dissatisfied with Congress

[269] C. J. Baker, 'Non-co-operation in south India', in Baker and Washbrook, *Political Institutions.*

policy, who rankled under Gandhi's leadership and who wanted more freedom to adjust Congress policy to the particular conditions of their region.[270] In mid-1922, Satyamurthi made his dissension public[271] and at the Congress annual session at Gaya at the end of the year, the Madras Nationalists joined with other dissidents to lay the foundations of the all-India Swarajya party. In the next two years, the Swarajists gradually managed to prise the control of the all-India Congress away from the Gandhians. In that time, however, the Bengali C. R. Das and the Allahabadi Motilal Nehru emerged as the all-India leaders of the Swarajist cause and pushed the southerners into the background.[272]

In the province the Swarajists slowly gathered support. The supremacy of the Justice party and the ministers' use of governmental patronage had been one of the most important factors prompting the Madras Nationalists to try to revive the Congress and take it into the provincial political forum. Indeed the party organ, the *Swarajya*, exclaimed that: 'The gaunt spectre of the blood sucking party vampire has its stranglehold now on the public life of this Presidency.'[273] Satyamurthi and the Nationalists were not alone in this fear and were not the only Madras politicians anxious to find a new base from which to challenge the Justicite hegemony. C. R. Reddy, who had joined forces with the Justice ministers in 1921 but had soon quarrelled with Panagal over patronage, had also begun to put out feelers.[274] By 1924 when he had failed to fell the ministry either by fomenting dissension among party supporters, by intriguing in the top circles of Madras politics, or by bringing a motion of no-confidence against the ministers in the Legislative Council, he threw in his lot with Satyamurthi. Satyamurthi was in fact doing an excellent job of courting all the dissidents in Madras politics. Besides C. R. Reddy, he had wooed other

[270] M. R. Jayakar, *The Story of My Life*, I (Bombay, 1958), 487; N. C. Keikar to S. Satyamurthi, 27 May 1922, T. B. Sapru to S. Satyamurthi, 18 June 1922, M. Malaviya to S. Satyamurthi, 1 Sept. 1922, Sarojini Naidu to S. Satyamurthi, 17 Dec. 1922, V. Patel to S. Satyamurthi, n.d., Satyamurthi papers.

[271] 'Drop the fatuous and suicidal boycott of the Legislative Councils in the country, and concentrate on capturing them and using them as a potent means for compelling the early advent of Swaraj.' *Hindu* 4 May 1922.

[272] See R. A. Gordon, 'Aspects in the history of the Indian National Congress with special reference to the Swarajya Party 1919 to 1923', D. Phil. thesis (Oxford, 1970) and D. E. U. Baker, 'Nation and region in Indian politics: a study of the Swarajya party 1922–6', M. A. thesis (University of Western Australia 1966).

[273] *Cult of Incompetence*, p. 9.

[274] C. R. Reddy to M. R. Jayakar, 7 Oct. 1921, Jayakar papers file 12 NAI.

Justicites like T. A. Ramalingam Chetty, who had also quarrelled with Panagal over patronage, and had even tried to win over A. Ramaswami Mudaliar, one of Panagal's chief lieutenants. Among the M.L.C.s he had got the support of C. V. S. Narasimha Raju, who after 1923 led the 'Independent Party' in the Council, and Sami Venkatachelam Chetty, an influential businessman and City politician. He had also picked up several refugees from the Non-co-operation Congress like the Salem clan-head Dr P. Varadarajulu Naidu and the Andhra leaders A. Kaleswara Rao and Konda Venkatappayya.[275]

The Swarajist cause attracted these men because it promised to provide a vehicle for displacing the Justicites in the seat of power. C. R. Reddy had made it quite clear that he would only make his organisation 'scaffolding for the Congress edifice' if the Swarajist Congress was prepared to take its challenge right into the ministries.[276] It was at this point that the difficulties inherent in forming such a ramshackle coalition of dissidents became obvious. The nucleus of the Madras Swarajists' organisation had been their connection with allies in other parts of India. This connection gave them status, and helped them with party funds; Satymurthi and his allies got important financial assistance from C. R. Das and Motilal Nehru, which enabled them to start a party newspaper and build up a cadre of party workers and publicists.[277] By 1924, however, Das and Nehru were committed to a policy of entering the legislatures in order to obstruct their operation and consequently to compel constitutional reform. Thus on the question of the aims and strategies of the Swarajist party after it had entered the legislatures, the views of the Madras leaders' patrons and the views of their supporters were diametrically opposed; Satyamurthi and his allies were obliged to adhere to one set of policies when they were inside the province and another set when they were outside it. Men like C. R. Reddy were aware of this contradiction but they were also aware that it was necessary to have strength, even if not agreement, in order to defeat their enemies: 'Three or more parties', he wrote, 'will perpetuate the regime of Justicites.... Two bad parties

[275] Dr P. Varadarajulu Naidu to S. Satyamurthi, 1 July 1924, M. K. Acharya to S. Satyamurthi, 7 Apr. 1924, C. R. Reddy to S. Satyamurthi, 22 Apr. 1924, Satyamurthi papers; Kalyanasundara Mudaliar, *Valkkaik Kurippukkal*, pp. 322–6.

[276] C. R. Reddy to S. Satyamurthi, 22 Apr. 1924, Satyamurthi papers.

[277] M. Nehru to C. R. Das, M. Nehru papers file C7 NMML; A. Rangaswami Iyengar to M. Nehru, 24 Nov. 1924, AICC papers file 60 of 1924–8 NMML.

are better than four logical groups', and he worked to prevent tours of the province by all-India leaders whose disquisitions about Congress strategy might shatter the fragile coalition of interests in Madras.[278]

The City Nationalists had by 1924 won control of the provincial Congress organisation and had attached a variety of political dissidents to their new Swarajist Congress. Control of the Congress did not, however, automatically make them a force in provincial politics. Since the collapse of Non-co-operation, the machinery of Congress in the province had run down, local committees had faded away, the coffers had emptied, and many Congress leaders and organisers had gone off into other fields of interest.[279] The Swarajists still faced the problem of building up substantial political support. They did so by plumbing in the localities and by tapping resentment of the new denizens of local government and of the ministers that stood behind them. From 1921, Satyamurthi had urged that Congress should aim to capture local boards as well as legislatures, and in 1923–4 Satyamurthi, Srinivasa Iyengar, A. Rangaswami Iyengar and other Swarajist leaders began visiting districts and offering to assist local politicians to contest elections to local boards under the Swarajist flag. In April 1923, an Andhra Swarajya party was formed to organise these elections in the Telugu districts,[280] and in February 1924 the Tamilnad Swarajya party appointed a special subcommittee to organise local election campaigns in the Tamil districts.[281] The Swarajists' rallying cry in the districts was straightforward. They promised to free local bodies from 'autocratic chairmen, secure behind the support of bureaucrats and ministerial partisanship, ignorant irresponsible councillors anxious only to please the nominated President or local officialdom, [and] communal or personal squabbles resulting in constant deadlocks and inefficient administration.'[282]

In the localities, they found a useful groundswell of dissent. As noted above, many local inhabitants had been moved to protest against the new dispensation of local government after 1920, particularly against higher taxes, the tyranny of a few men in command of local boards and the interference by ministers in parochial affairs. Some of these protests had become identified with the Congress campaign of Non-co-operation, while in many places merchants had

[278] *Hindu* 9, 10, 12 and 27 July 1926.

[279] Report of the General Secretaries of the Tamilnad Congress in AICC papers file 7 of 1920–6. In August 1924, the Tamilnad Congress was Rs 5,000 in the red; *Hindu* 5 Aug. 1924.

[280] *Hindu* 26 Mar. 1923. [281] *Hindu* 9 Feb. 1924. [282] *Hindu* 25 Apr. 1924.

organised themselves into ratepayers associations or local Congress committees to protest against increased taxes and against administrative encroachments. The introduction of a new education cess in the municipalities of the province in 1922, for instance, evoked new Congress organisations in Coimbatore, Kumbakonam, Cocanada, Guntur, Rajahmundry and other towns. The Swarajists were able to reach down and draw on these movements of protest.

They found most of their support in the areas of local instability, in the Kistna–Godavari deltas and in the big towns. In these places politicians were more prepared to deploy the techniques of organisation and public agitation and, besides, the flagrant interference of the Justice ministers in the affairs of these areas had shown local politicians who did not profit from these interventions that they needed to gain political influence beyond the locality. Dissidents in Guntur even wrote to the all-India leader Motilal Nehru asking for advice and help over the problems they were facing in local government,[283] while the Andhra Swarajya party was in fact formed by men already deeply involved in local politics in different parts of the Kistna–Godavari tract.[284] Local elections were fought under the Congress banner in Tinnevelly and Cocanada in 1922, in Guntur and Madura in 1923, and in Bezwada and Godavari in 1924.

In a few other places of the province, men who resented the overbearing command of the leaders of local government looked to the Swarajists for help. In the small town of Virudunagar, for instance, a merchant Sankaralinga Chetty, who had been harassed by the municipal administration for almost a decade, had had half of his house demolished on the ground that it encroached on municipal land and had been kept out of municipal politics by the chairman's manipulation of the electoral roll, failed to win any redress through the High Court and started a local Swarajist branch in 1924.[285] In the same year politicians in Nellore who wanted some means to prevent the municipal chairman conducting the next municipal elections in the same esoteric manner in which he had conducted the last, looked to

[283] P. V. Subba Rao to M. Nehru, 19 May 1928, AICC papers file G57(i) of 1926 NMML.

[284] The man who convened the first meeting of the party had just lost in the taluk board elections; *Hindu* 26 Mar. 1923.

[285] Notes on suit between Kailasam Chettiar and Virudunagar municipal chairman in G.O. 1086 (LSG) 17 June 1922 MRO; letter from V. Dhanushkodi Nadar dated 2 Nov. 1925, in G.O. 4167 (LSG) 13 Nov. 1925 MRO; report of Collector dated 19 Feb. 1926, in G.O. 2767 (LSG) 29 June 1926 MRO.

the Swarajist leaders for help.[286] In Ramnad district, a coalition of men irritated by the raja of Ramnad's use of the local board machinery to interfere with their interests in temples and markets, formed a Swarajya party and invited the Madras leader S. Srinivasa Iyengar, a native of the Ramnad district, to come and assist them.[287]

In practice the provincial Swarajist leaders could give little concrete assistance to local politicians. Only one third of each board came up for election each year, and thus it proved virtually impossible for the Swarajists to capture control of a board in one year; many elected to oppose the current administration in one year were compromised before the next year's elections came round; and ministerial interventions could upset the best-laid plans. Although the presence of Congress leaders often lent colour and excitement to local elections, they were rarely able to impose a strong framework of organisation. In the Kumbakonam municipal elections in 1924, the Swarajist leaders had to search hard to find enough men to stand as Congress candidates; in the following year, there were more aspirants than constituencies and in several wards avowed Congressman stood against avowed Congressman.[288] In Cocanada in 1925 everyone wanted the Congress nominations and there was chaos when the visiting Congress leader published a list of candidates; once the elections were complete, the successful candidates, irrespective of their party colouring on polling day, settled back into their old factional alignments.[289] In Madras City, the Swarajists captured control of the Corporation, but then found their inability to enact any startling reforms in Corporation administration was an acute embarrassment.[290] In some of the large towns of the province and in parts of the deltaic tract, the Swarajists secured the support of influential men in the localities and did well at the elections. The taluk boards of Ramachandrapuram, Cocanada, Ellore and Bapatla, all in the Kistna–Godavari tract, fell to Swarajist campaigns between 1924 and 1926, as did the East Godavari district board for a short time and the municipalities of Madura, Bezwada, Rajahmundry and Guntur. Elsewhere the Swarajist resurgence could not match the power of

286 *Hindu* 13 Feb. 1924, 6 Mar. 1924.

287 G.O. 1462 (LSG) 26 June 1923 MRO; G.O. 1984 (LSG) 7 Sept. 1923 MRO; G.O. 1027 (LSG) 5 Mar. 1928 MRO; *Hindu* 8 and 9 Apr. 1921; A. K. D. Venkata Raju, *A Brief Life Sketch of P. S. Kumaraswamy Raja* (Rajapalaiyam, 1964); P. S. Kumaraswamy Raja, *My Induction as a Gandhite* (Rajapalaiyam, 1956).

288 *Hindu* 6, 16, 18, 19 and 27 Sept. 1924, 18 and 19 Sept. 1925.

289 *Hindu* 21 July 1925, 7 Aug. 1925.

290 *Hindu* 10 and 15 Feb. 1926.

local government bosses and the ministers that stood behind them. All this, however, only served to emphasise that local politicians needed to attain influence in higher places and that they should thus help propel the Swarajists into the legislature and the ministry.

The Swarajist party was an extraordinary monster; at the all-India level it contained a variety of dissident politicians, each with his particular reason for joining the alliance; in the province, it embraced City Nationalists, jaded Non-co-operators, independent M.L.C.s and disillusioned Justicites; in the localities it attracted a plethora of different interests pitted against the status quo in parish and province. By 1926 it was being led in Madras by S. Srinivasa Iyengar; in all-India affairs, he was aligned with Das and Nehru, supported the strategy of entering the Councils in order to obstruct them and was bidding for the post of Congress president on the basis of that policy; in the province, however, he had informed the new Swarajist recruits like T. A. Ramalingam Chetty and C. V. S. Narasimha Raju that the Swarajists aimed to enter the Councils in order to capture control of the ministry;[291] in his tours of the local areas, Srinivasa Iyengar and his lieutenants promised the Swarajists would help in a miscellany of local problems, such as a dispute over the management of Srirangam temple, trouble over the issue of bus licences in Chingleput, and complaints about the actions of the Port Trust in Tuticorin.[292] It was not chance that had cast the Swarajist party into this extraordinary mould; the party was put together to oppose those who had profited most under the new framework of British rule, and as such it had to be shaped to fit the new unities of province and nation and to match the new linkages between locality, province and nation created by British rule.

In 1923, the Swarajists had not been ready for legislature elections and only a handful of Swarajists had crept into the Madras Legislative Council. In 1926 they contested in force. The organisation of the Swarajist campaign, however, was loose. In the months preceding the polls, a handful of Congress leaders toured the districts seeking out candidates for the Congress slate. Influential men were invited to stand on the Congress ticket irrespective of their political antecedents; one prominent old Mylaporean and a leading Justicite were both given the opportunity of Congress candida-

[291] *Hindu* 9, 10, 12, 27 July 1927.

[292] *Hindu* 17 and 18 Mar. 1926.

tures,[293] and the party was prepared to bless the candidature of men who were campaigning in harness with Justicites in the constituency.[294] It took the Swarajist leaders four months to complete a list of candidates for the Andhra districts. Although a list for Tamilnad appeared much quicker, it underwent many changes before the polls since candidates defected in both directions. In several constituencies, the Congress had to deal with men who insisted that they were the deserving Congress candidate rather than the man who had the official nomination.[295]

After the elections, the Congress were attributed between forty and forty-eight victories, and the Justice party between nineteen and twenty-three. These figures were somewhat misleading. The Governor reckoned that only twenty should really be called Congressmen and as many as fifty-eight of those elected would fit comfortably into almost any political camp.[296] As many as thirteen of the Congress M.L.C.s had sat in previous legislatures as something other than Congressmen, and only ten old Justicite M.L.C.s had actually been defeated at the polls. It was a victory secured by sleight of hand. Yet it was enough to ensure that the Governor, who was disenchanted with the Justicites, would give the Swarajists the first option to form a ministry.[297] It was now that the differing intentions of the many elements in the ramshackle Swarajist coalition began to pull in different directions and eventually pull the alliance apart. Satyamurthi, Srinivasa Iyengar and other provincial Swarajist leaders did not feel that they could flout the all-India Congress policy. Without the prestige and backing of the all-India organisation, they believed, a Swarajist ministry in Madras would achieve little, and probably not last very long. The Governor's invitation to the Swarajists to form a ministry was therefore declined. However, when Goschen then set about erecting a coalition ministry, the Swarajists eagerly participated in the negotiations. They would not openly adhere to the coalition, but they promised their support to the ministry in return for minister-

[293] M. Ramachandra Rao and A. Ramaswami Mudaliar were the Mylaporean and the Justicite. M. Ramachandra Rao to P. S. Sivaswami Iyer, 21 Nov. 1926, Sivaswami Iyer papers NAI; Kalyanasundara Mudaliar, *Valkkaik Kurippukkal*, pp. 384–5.

[294] *Hindu* 30 Mar. 1928.

[295] *Hindu*(w) 6 and 13 May 1926, 8 July 1926, 9 Sept. 1926; AICC papers file G57(i) of 1926 NMML.

[296] Goschen to Irwin, 3 Dec. 1926, Goschen papers vol. V IOL.

[297] Goschen to Birkenhead, 2 Dec. 1926, Goschen papers vol. II IOL.

ial favours, particularly ministerial patronage and help in individual Swarajists' local political affairs.[298]

In the months following the formation of Dr Subbaroyan's nominally 'Independent' ministry, some members of the Swarajist alliance made good use of their access to ministerial patronage. But this covert arrangement did not satisfy all. The cracks in the party had been obvious enough before the elections. In July 1926, some Andhra Congressmen had exposed Srinivasa Iyengar's duplicity over his attitude to ministerships, and some important participants in the Swarajist alliance – notably T. A. Ramalingam Chetty and C. V. S. Narasimha Raju – had threatened to withdraw their support. Srinivasa Iyengar soothed them over this vital question of ministerships by promising to get all-India Congress policy changed at the next Congress session a month after the elections.[299] By that time, however, the ministry had been formed, and Srinivasa Iyengar judged it was more profitable to leave the question of ministerships alone and to concentrate on getting himself elected president of the all-India Congress for the next year. When he then invited the Congress to hold its next session in Madras in December 1927, he again made no attempt to rock the boat over ministerships. The Swarajist allies had apparently been sold right down the river.

Meanwhile in Madras itself, the Swarajists soon found in 1927 that it was very difficult to maintain influence with a ministry which, according to the all-India policy of their party, they were supposed to be obstructing and undermining. They were obliged to duck opportunities for obstruction if these might really threaten the continuation of the ministry for, if the ministry fell, Panagal and the Justicites would return and the Swarajists' influence behind the scenes would dissolve. Congress radicals in the province ridiculed the duplicity and protested to the A.I.C.C. that the Madras Swarajists were disobeying the mandate to obstruct. Srinivasa Iyengar used his position as Congress president to have the Congress Working Committee condone the Madras Swarajists, but this only made the basic deception seem worse.[300] Already, many of the prominent members

298 Rajagopalachari, Srinivasa Iyengar, Kaleswara Rao and M. Narasimha Rao were the Congress participants in the negotiations over ministry formation. G. Rudrayya Chowdary, *Prakasam: a political study* (Madras, 1971), pp. 64–6; Kaleswara Rao, *Na Jivita Katha*, pp. 440–2.

299 *Hindu* 9, 10, 12, 15, 27 July 1926.

300 AICC papers files 5 of 1927 and 6 of 1928 NMML; GOI Home Public 583 1927 NAI; *Hindu* 24 Mar. 1927, 19, 20, 27 and 28 May 1927.

of the Swarajist alliance had begun to strengthen their contacts outside the Congress, and to prepare to make personal bids for political leadership. C. R. Reddy had quit the Swarajist alliance after the ministry had been chosen in 1926, and he moved closely with Panagal.[301] R. K. Shanmugham Chetty, the Swarajists' deputy leader, quarrelled with Srinivasa Iyengar and began to cultivate Justice friends.[302] S. Muthiah Mudaliar and M. R. Seturatnam Iyer formed splinter groups within the Congress. Sami Venkatachelam Chetty approached the Justicites to bargain a change of heart in return for help in Corporation politics.[303] Panagal and the Justicite leaders teased the Swarajist by giving out that they would not accept ministries while dyarchy lasted and that thus the Swarajists' fears were unfounded.[304] No one believed them and rightly too. Panagal was already intriguing with C. R. Reddy, Venkatachelam Chetty, Muthiah Mudaliar and Seturatnam Iyer to split the Swarajists. The visit of Sir John Simon, as noted above, gave Panagal the opportunity for his coup. In March 1928, the ministry was re-shuffled, the influence of the Swarajists annulled, and the men Panagal had weaned away from the Swarajist alliance, Muthiah Mudaliar and Seturatnam Iyer, installed in the ministry.

With Panagal back in command of government patronage, many of the M.L.C.s who had withheld their support from any party over the last few months began coming home to roost. C. R. Reddy, Ramalingam Chetty, Sami Venkatachalam Chetty, R. K. Shanmugham Chetty, Dr Subbaroyan and others who had been connected with the Swarajists since 1925 took active roles in the Justice conferences and the Justicite leadership battle in 1928–30.

The Madras Nationalists were left with the shell of a party. Both the Tamil and Andhra Congresses had run out of funds early in 1928.[305] Srinivasa Iyengar went off to Europe, Satyamurthi fished for a job in Mysore state,[306] and nationalist political activity in Madras City fell to such a low ebb that Mrs Besant and her Mylaporean cronies emerged from the Adyar backwoods and threatened to steal

[301] D. Madhava Rao to M. R. Jayakar, 10 Mar. 1926, Jayakar papers file 498 NAI; C. R. Reddy to P. Narayana Rao, 6 Dec. 1929, C. R. Reddy papers file 85 NMML.

[302] *Hindu* 6 June 1927; AICC papers file 6 of 1928 NMML.

[303] FR October (1), GOI Home Political 32 1927 NAI; S. Satyamurthi to S. Srinivasa Iyengar, n.d. (probably Nov. 1927), Satyamurthi papers.

[304] *Justice* 9 Mar. 1927, quoted in Ramaswami Mudaliar, *Mirror of the Year*, pp. 12–13.

[305] AICC papers files F27 of 1926–7 and F13 of 1927–30 NMML.

[306] A. V. Ramanadham to S. Satyamurthi, 2 June 1928, 10 June 1928 and 24 Sept. 1928, Satyamurthi papers.

the political limelight. The latter organised an All-Parties Conference after which political Madras fell to debating whether Independence or Dominion status was the proper goal of the Nationalist movement, and which of the various hypothetical constitutions penned by Congress leaders (including Srinivasa Iyengar) in recent months was the best. They agreed that unity among politicians was their goal, and then argued endlessly whether the National Congress or the All-Parties Conference was the proper vehicle for achieving that unity.[307]

In early 1930, the Madras Nationalists and their allies prepared to contest the legislature elections. They did not feel that they could press Congress to change its policies over ministries, but they begged that the question should be decided by each provincial unit separately after the elections; the suggestion was ridiculed both in the province and in the all-India forum.[308] They had become extremely isolated. Both the Andhra and Tamil provincial Congress committees were being managed from Madras City, district committees had disappeared from most of the mofussil, Congress party funds had run out, and the provincial Congress membership had fallen below 8,000.[309] In 1928 and again in 1929, the Swarajist leaders had had to manipulate the rules in order to stave off attempts by other factions to take over the Congress organisation. When some students in Madras City formed a renegade Congress committee and threatened to disrupt Satyamurthi's election to the Corporation, the Swarajist leaders had to give them ten seats on the Madras district Congress Committee and four on the provincial committee to persuade them to desist.[310] The Swarajist strategy was in ruins and the City Nationalists who had built up the Swarajist alliance had apparently lost all their influence, even in Madras itself. When the all-India Congress ordered Swarajist M.L.C.s to resign from the legislatures in January 1929 as a gesture of protest, eighteen of the Madras Swarajists refused;[311] they no longer valued or respected their connection with the Congress. A few weeks later, Rajagopalachari and the Gandhians stepped forward to take over the provincial Congress – they needed to rally less than 600 supporters to achieve this coup – and carry it towards Civil Disobedience.[312]

[307] *Hindu* 4, 5, 6, 18 and 20 Oct. 1928, 5 and 28 Nov. 1928.
[308] *Hindu* 6 and 10 May 1929.
[309] AICC papers files P24 of 1929, P30(i) of 1929 and P30(ii) of 1929 NMML.
[310] *Hindu* 15 and 23 July 1929, 8, 10 and 16 Aug. 1929.
[311] FR February (1) and (2), GOI Home Political 18–3 1930 NAI.
[312] K. R. Srinivasa Iyengar, *S. Srinivasa Iyengar: the story of a decade in Indian*

THE FIRST DECADE OF DYARCHY

The Governor and the senior I.C.S. officers in Madras looked back on the 1920s with some complacency. Madras was still the peaceful province. There had been some unsettling campaigns during Non-co-operation, there had been major strikes in the Madras cotton mills in 1921 and in the South Indian Railway in 1928, and there had been an ugly demonstration to mark the occasion of Sir John Simon's visit in 1928.[313] But these incidents were the exceptions. There had been no sustained attempts to refuse taxes, no serious communal rioting and no terrorist horrors. The new Legislative Council had functioned smoothly; government had not been obliged to suspend it nor to dismiss ministers. Other provinces had not been so lucky. Government's self-satisfaction showed up in the suggestions it forwarded to the Simon Commission on the shape of future constitutional reforms. The Madras Government's memorandum to the commission stated that dyarchy had been a success and that the progress of local government in the province deserved high praise; that future reforms should follow along the lines of Montagu–Chelmsford, by transferring more subjects from the central to the provincial government and within the province giving more responsibility to elected ministers; and that there was no need to enlarge the electorate. The committee of Madras M.L.C.s invited to send their views to the Commission made virtually identical proposals; they agreed that the electorate was wide enough and they also agreed that the Governor should continue to hold an important, paternal position in the government of the province.[314] The implications of these proposals were clear. Government and its friends were quite happy with the way things were; they wanted more of the same, and no big changes.

By the limited devolution of 1920, the provincial government had offloaded many of the burdens of government and a few of its privileges onto Indians. The scheme had been successful because it enabled those who came forward to take the new ministerships to create a provincial network, woven with the strings of government patronage; no other network had such strong bonds and no other political grouping could for the meantime offer the ministers a serious challenge. The ultimate failure of the Swarajists had put the final touches to the government's mood of complacency.

politics (Mangalore, 1959), pp. 79–84; FR September (2), GOI Home Political 17 1929 NAI.

313 *Hindu* 4, 6 and 7 Feb. 1928.

314 *Indian Statutory Commission*, vol. III, pp. 10–21; vol. VI, appendix pp. 2–32.

The new institutions of local and provincial government had been lowered onto firm foundations. Although the institutions were wholly novel in the region, their introduction had done little to disturb the social fabric. Their design ensured that it was the men who already wielded power in Madras society who came to control the new levers of power. Local and provincial elections picked out local notables or their agents, local boards for the most part gave power to those willing and able to use it. These were institutions which, rather than creating new sources of power and influence, harnessed the existing influence of the leaders of local society. The networks of local notables were not damaged; in general they were strengthened and elongated. Now they could stretch out from the legislature in Madras, through the local boards, and down into the urban and rural localities. The ministers perched comfortably at the summit of this pyramid.

But while Fort St George was proud of the development of local government in the province, it had no real understanding of its political import. The British officers looked on local self-government as administration, something which was wholly different from politics. This was hardly surprising since the scheme of local government had been hatched in order to solve problems of administration. It meant, however, that government could discern little connection between, for instance, the Motheys' attempts to avoid local taxes, the Non-co-operation campaign in Ellore, the Motheys' part in the ministry shuffle in 1926, and the appearance of a Mothey in the Delhi Assembly in 1930. It meant too that government believed that the problems in the small areas which did not respond well to local government – the big towns and the deltaic tract – could be cured by administrative means – by sending in inspectors, by appointing tough Collectors to these places, by sacking unruly municipalities and, when there was any sign of serious disorder, by sending in the troops. Meanwhile in these small areas, however small and untypical of the province as a whole, were germinating many of the problems which were to confront the rulers in the coming decades. These areas had played a large part in the several minor crises of provincial politics in the 1920s, and they had been the springboard for the Swarajist campaign in the middle of the decade. In these areas, the Congress was building up a pool of leaders and an elementary framework of organisation. Once conditions in the province changed, these developments would take on significance for the province as a whole.

CHAPTER 3

Depression, Dissent and Disengagement

If the British administrators and Justicite politicians who had reported so proudly and complacently to Sir John Simon in 1929 had been asked to report again ten years later, they would have given a very different story. The events of the 1930s stood out in a stark contrast to those of the previous decade. There had been campaigns, widespread in the rural areas, demanding abolition of the zamindars and reduction of the government's revenue demand; there had been two waves of industrial strikes; several politicians, who were neither new to the political world nor men of such little substance that they could easily be dismissed, had preached revolution, and government had had to proscribe one revolutionary organisation and threaten others; the Congress campaign of Civil Disobedience had evoked a significant response in the south and the Madras Government had even asked Delhi for special powers of suppression; the electorate had returned a huge majority of Congress candidates in 1937 and placed a Congress ministry in power in Madras; the Justice party had declined and almost disappeared; there had been communal clashes in one or two towns, and small peasant jacqueries in parts of the countryside. Something very serious had evidently happened to Madras society.

The reasons for this hiatus between the decades must be sought in rural society and in shifts in the nature and purpose of government. The world depression in agriculture and trade bore down on Madras from 1929. It was the most severe shock delivered to the agrarian economy since the great famines of the last quarter of the nineteenth century, and it was a shock which, unlike the famines, was entirely new in character. Rural society had evolved no methods to cushion the blow of such a depression or to check its impact on rural relations. Thus the effects of the depression drove deep into Madras society and the province as it emerged from the slump in the middle of the decade had changed in many important respects. These changes held significance not only for the economy and society of the region but for its government as well, since the effectiveness of the frail and top-heavy edifice of British rule depended so much on the stability of its foundations in Madras society. The framework of British rule was indeed changing in the 1930s, but not in an attempt to adjust to new patterns in the society it governed. The British politicians in London and the British administrators in India had begun to pull the Raj on to a new course, dictated by difficulties which the administrators met in the details of government and by problems which the politicians faced in the changing position of Britain in the world. It was against such a background that new styles of politics took shape in the Madras Presidency.

THE DEPRESSION

Until the late 1920s, the development of the Madras economy was gradual and gentle. The most important changes in agriculture since the turn of the century had been the rapid spread of groundnut cultivation in the 'dry' districts, and the introduction of new strains of cotton plant, the 'Cambodia' and *karunganni*, which greatly increased the quality and productivity per acre of cotton grown in the Presidency. These two factors did not have great effects on other areas of the economy. Both crops were produced largely for export, groundnuts going mainly to Marseilles and cotton to Bombay or England, and after the barest minimum of processing were taken directly to the ports.[1] By the mid-1920s, the groundwork for a more extensive cotton industry was being laid – more gins and presses appeared in the countryside, and bankers in some of the major towns floated companies to build cotton mills – but these initiatives did not bear real fruit until a decade later. Amongst crops other than cotton, increases in productivity were imperceptible. Manufacture and trade continued to grow but slowly, enjoying a gentle boom on the upward trend of world prices and volume of trade in the mid-1920s. But while these developments were undramatic, one important change had been gradually creeping over the province. In the last half-century Madras had been firmly tied to the world economy. Since 1880, not only had the real value of the export and import trade of Madras roughly tripled, but that trade had become far more diverse. Whereas in 1880, the bulk of the imports into Madras, in fact three-fifths of them, were cotton goods, by the 1920s food, kerosene, railway stock, metals, machinery and motor cars had

[1] V. V. Sayana, *The Agrarian Problems of Madras Province* (Madras, 1949), pp. 24–5; A. S. Pearse, *The Cotton Industry of India* (Manchester, 1930), p. 8; *Census of India 1931* vol. XIV, pt. 1, pp. 212–13; *Report of the Indian Central Cotton Committee* (Calcutta, 1919), pp. 13–14, 118–21.

TABLE 12. *Principal articles of export*

Year	Total	Raw cotton	Cotton manufacture	Hides and skins	Oilseeds	Grain and pulse	Coffee	Tea
	Value Rs lakhs							
1895–6	1,323	160	72	337	108	85	224	21
1900–1	1,200	154	91	369	29	53	121	32
1905–6	1,576	229	94	91	100	81	172	75
1910–11	2,176	414	104	375	252	142	131	123
1915–16	2,493	174	124	450	287	406	92	173
1920–1	2,249	227	231	316	252	22	133	205
1925–6	4,405	791	293	606	1,055	137	178	353
1930–1	3,235	164	176	564	810	190	188	411
1935–6	2,729	97	114	518	580	89	101	442
1940–1	3,231	172	304	541	426	—	22	513

SOURCE: *Annual Statement of the Sea-Borne Trade and Navigation of the Madras Presidency* for the years shown. Table entitled: 'Quantities and value of principal articles of Indian produce and manufacture exported to Foreign Countries in [year] from the Madras Presidency.'

TABLE 13. *Foreign trade of Madras Presidency*

Country	Percentage share of total foreign trade				
	1904–5	1914–15	1919–20	1929–30	1939–40
U.K.	48·8	46·8	48·2	36·9	34·9
Ceylon	12·1	15·8	10·7	9·8	7·5
Straits	3·4	4·9	7·0	3·5	2·8
France	8·7	9·1	5·5	10·8	3·0
Germany	5·8	4·3	0·1	7·9	2·7
Netherlands	0·5	0·6	0·1	5·8	2·2
Belgium	5·1	2·2	1·4	3·4	2·3
Japan	3·0	3·0	7·4	3·5	3·7
America	4·6	3·4	10·9	6·1	5·3
Other	9·0	13·9	8·7	12·3	35·6

SOURCE: *Annual Statement of the Sea-Borne Trade and Navigation of the Madras Presidency* for the years shown. Table entitled: 'Value of the total exports of merchandise and treasure to foreign countries in [date] from the Madras Presidency.'

squeezed the share of cotton down to a quarter. At the same time, there had been great increases in the export of items such as cotton manufacturers, tea and groundnut which had been little in evidence in the 1880s.[2] Moreover, Britain had lost much of her dominance of the trade of the province. Between 1880–1 and 1920–1, her share of the imports into Madras had fallen from 85 to 65 per cent, and her share of the exports from Madras from 51 to 38 per cent. Japan, Germany, Russia and the United States had stepped into the gap.[3] The prices in Madras markets, even those deep in the countryside, now reflected the level of prices in the world. Madras Government departments had even thought it fit to set up machinery to ensure better dissemination of commercial information, particularly about changes in world demand and world prices, throughout the province to discourage profiteering.[4] The world slump in trade and in prices in the 1870s had had very little effect on the Madras economy, but by 1929 the position was entirely different.

In 1929–30, both the gradual rise in the volume and value of the province's foreign trade and the steady rise of primary produce prices in the province turned into sharp declines. There had been a similar

[2] See table 12. [3] See table 13.

[4] *Report of the Indian Central Cotton Committee* (annual) for 1932–3, pp. 100–6; S. Y. Krishnaswami, *Rural Problems in Madras: monograph* (Madras, 1947), p. 329.

reversal of fortunes in 1920–1, when the boom following the first world war had come to a sudden end, but that slump had not lasted for many months. What made the depression of the 1930s so swingeing was its length. The world slump in the trade and the prices of agricultural produce had its roots in the period of the first world war, when agricultural production in many of the countries on the periphery of the world economy had risen to offset the decline in the belligerent countries. By the mid-1920s, with the restoration of production in Europe and America, there was a world glut of agrarian produce, and prices might have fallen from the year 1925–6 had it not been for careful intervention by governments anxious to protect their countries' internal economies. By 1929, stocks had built up so much that prices had to fall, yet the slump that began in this way need not have been as deep or as long as it turned out if the price mechanism had been left to adjust production to demand. In the same year, however, Wall Street crashed and money-markets began to teeter in all parts of the world. As confidence ebbed, many of the leading countries in the world economy threw up protective tariffs and instigated policies of monetary deflation. These deflationary policies, a massive decline in foreign lending by Europe and America, and a downward spiral of trade ensured that agricultural prices would continue to fall. Moreover, the world economy was stranded between periods of British and American domination and thus lacked one obvious giant who would come forward and initiate policies of recovery. Thus it was not until 1933 that the slump began to 'bottom out' in the west, while in those countries with less developed economies and less resourceful governments than those of Europe and America, the depression lingered into the second half of the decade.[5]

The value of the foreign trade of Madras Presidency had climbed steadily from the early 1920s to a peak of about seventy crores of rupees per annum at the end of the decade. In the next quinquennium, it fell to about forty crores, with the most dramatic falls in the export of raw cotton, oilseeds, grain and other agricultural products.[6] As for prices, in 1930 the price of rice dropped 20 per cent on its level in the mid-1920s, and in the next three years it dropped to half of the 1930 level. The prices of cotton, millet, gram, oilseed and all other crops followed it down, and although the fall was checked after 1934–5,

[5] C. P. Kindleberger, *The World in Depression 1929–39* (London, 1973), especially ch. 3; V. P. Timoshenko, *World Agriculture and the Depression* (Stanford, 1957).

[6] *Annual Statement of the Sea-Borne Trade and Navigation of British India* for 1930.

TABLE 14. *Index numbers of prices (1873=100)*

Year	General Index	Rice	Ragi	Raw cotton
1864	111	124	141	229
1869	105	129	115	96
1874	101	118	108	82
1879	104	154	168	86
1884	91	135	103	85
1889	100	148	101	92
1894	102	152	133	84
1899	96	145	142	59
1904	101	147	124	97
1909	124	220	247	95
1914	147	254	257	114
1919	276	357	505	249
1924	221	335	380	228
1929	203	336	347	133
1930	171	273	262	97
1931	127	189	169	70
1932	126	175	197	73
1933	121	152	170	81
1934	119	152	189	78
1935	127	173	214	93
1936	125	178	189	88
1937	136	176	182	88
1938	132	173	182	63
1939	134	184	197	63
1940	168	217	220	95

SOURCE: *Index Numbers of Indian Prices 1861–1931* (Delhi, 1933, and annual addenda), pp. 1, 3, 12.

prices at the end of the decade were still lower than they had been before the first world war.[7]

The rural economy of Madras was by no means unaccustomed to disasters. The dry areas, particularly the Ceded Districts, suffered whenever the inconstant monsoon faltered, and the delta areas sometimes suffered when the monsoon was too generous and caused flooding. Both generalised and localised famines had been common throughout the nineteenth century, and more recently the Ceded Districts had suffered from serious shortages in both 1924 and 1927.[8]

[7] See table 14.

[8] *India in 1924–5*, p. 229; *India in 1927–8*, p. 6.

But the depression of the 1930s was of a quite different order. Whereas in famine years there was little for most of the people to eat, there were always good profits for those lucky or devious enough to have anything to sell. Unless they were exceptionally severe, famines reinforced rather than undermined social control in the countryside, for the village bosses, many of whom built their houses over huge grain-pits, not only suffered least but also had the opportunity to strengthen their hold over their neighbours by standing between them and starvation. In the 1930s depression, however, there was still enough for all to eat, but there were no profits for the market-oriented village boss. In the past half-century by controlling the flow of capital and the access to markets in the village, the big landlord-moneylenders had insulated their poorer neighbours from many of the effects of economic change, and had taken most of the profits from the new crops and new market opportunities for themselves;[9] now in the 1930s, they found that the full effects of the slump were visited on them rather than their neighbours. The men who were worst hit were those who had sunk capital in agriculture, particularly in the cultivation of cash-crops, and this meant the rural elite.[10] A depression such as this threatened to subvert the social and economic equilibrium of Madras.

It was not simply the incidence of the slump that proved so damaging, but also the effect it had on networks of credit and dependence. The village bosses controlled most of the liquidity in the rural economy, and this control formed one of the most important elements in their economic and political domination of their neighbours. The Madras Provincial Banking Enquiry, which collected its evidence on the eve of the depression, reckoned that the aggregate of agricultural debt in the province amounted to Rs 150 crores, averaging Rs 48 per acre and Rs 38 per rural inhabitant.[11] One informed witness told the Enquiry that 95 per cent of the rural population was indebted,[12] while another government report a few years later calculated from a sample survey that 79 per cent of landholders, 77 per cent of tenants and 64 per cent of labourers were in debt.[13] Many of the rural inhabi-

[9] D. A. Washbrook, 'Country politics: Madras 1880–1930', *Modern Asian Studies* VII, 3 (1973), 476–86.

[10] R. S. Vaidyanatha Aiyar, *A Memorandum on the Ryotwari Landholders in Madras* (Madras, 1933), pp. 13–14.

[11] *Madras Provincial Banking Enquiry Commission*, I (Madras, 1930), 54, 76.

[12] *Madras Provincial Banking Enquiry Commission*, vol. II, evidence of the Inspector of Registration Offices, p. 505.

[13] W. R. S. Sathyanathan, *Report on Agricultural Indebtedness* (Madras, 1935), pp. 41–3.

tants accepted indebtedness as part of their station, lived in continual debt, willed the burden to their heirs, and accepted a range of obligations to their creditor. Much of the debt was contracted for the purpose of marriage or other ceremonies, for building a house or for buying land or bullocks. However, a large proportion – differing considerably in different regions of the province – was contracted in the course of normal agricultural operations. At the start of the agricultural year many cultivators went, sometimes to the village merchants but more commonly to the major landholders, to borrow money for farming expenses. The security for such a loan was generally that year's crop, and commonly the moneylender took back his principal and interest in kind on the threshing floor. As one witness told the Banking Enquiry: 'It is usually the sowcar (moneylender) who buys the crop and sometimes specific conditions are entered by which the cultivator is bound to measure the crop to the sowcar in kind for the discharge of the loan. The sowcar, who is better informed about market prices, buys the crop at a price advantageous to him. If the sowcar does not purchase the crop himself he arranges for its sale so as not to lose sight of the crop till his amount is realised.'[14] The bigger landlord-moneylenders often acquired much of the village crop not only by taking from their debtors but also by buying from other cultivators who were forced to sell immediately at harvest to pay their land revenue or to pay off other loans. If the landlord-moneylender stored the grain in his barn or pit for four months or so, he could expect the price to rise, by as much as 40 per cent, and then he could either sell the grain back to the other villagers, or take it to the local market.[15] Many of those who went to the market towns used the contacts they gained there and the security of the grain they took there, to borrow more funds from urban moneylenders and to use that to swell their lending operation in the village.[16] In the case of cash-crops, some of them acted as agents for mills and exporting companies by borrowing seed and cultivation expenses from the company, distributing these to their neighbours, and effectively managing the cultivation on the lands of others.[17]

Those who made loans at the start of the agricultural year in 1929 and had calculated the level of repayment according to the prices

[14] *Madras Provincial Banking Enquiry Commission*, vol. II, evidence of B. Sitarama Raju, p. 45.

[15] *Ibid.* pp. 179, 210, 297.

[16] *Ibid.* pp. 62, 124, 210, 318.

[17] *Ibid.* pp. 36, 50–1, 62, 298–9.

they expected, were dismayed at harvest-time to find that prices had fallen so far that they had made a loss on their deals. When they then stored the crop and waited for the expected rise in market prices, they were further dismayed when prices continued to fall. The same fate was in store in 1930 and 1931 and, predictably enough, moneylenders drastically cut back on their lending activities. With so much grain locked up in barns while the rural bosses awaited some change in the market, an artificial grain shortage soon developed, and smaller cultivators found it difficult to get grain either for food or for seed for next year's cultivation.[18] In the northern parts of the province, the situation was accentuated by a bad season and here in late 1931 the grain riots started. On 6 September, a 400-strong mob attacked the house of a rich and oppressive moneylender in a village of Kistna district, robbed his granary, and fought a battle with the police when they intervened; 108 people were arrested.[19] Three weeks later a similar incident occurred in Guntur district; this time the mob was 4,000 strong and the police opened fire and shot one man.[20] In Coimbatore a large landowner was shot dead. In 1934, the year when prices reached their nadir, sporadic incidents of rioting and grain-looting were reported in Bellary, Madura, Nellore, Salem and Coimbatore districts.[21] The situation was bad enough, noted one rural politician, to force the rural inhabitants 'to countenance and cherish ideas of violent uprising against the Sahukars (moneylenders) and Banks as well as Government'.[22]

The flow of credit in many parts of the province had simply dried up. At a conference in late 1931, N. G. Ranga noted: 'None of the usual institutions which supply credit for current purposes are today willing to advance any credit to the peasants. Every one of them is still busy, in its own way, scraping up every pie that can be tapped from the ryots.'[23] Few of them were successful. In the civil courts there was a steep rise in the number of insolvency petitions, infructuous debt suits and in the imprisonment of debtors, while the number of debt suits that were settled satisfactorily declined. By 1934, a debt

[18] N. G. Ranga, *Agricultural Indebtedness and Remedial Means* (Tenali, 1933), pp. 1–9; P. J. Thomas, *The Problem of Rural Indebtedness* (Madras, 1934), p. 19.

[19] G.O. 96 (Public) 16 Jan. 1932 SAH.

[20] *Police Report* (annual) for 1931, p. 19; G.O. 1144 (Public) 6 Nov. 1931 SAH.

[21] *Police Report* (annual) for 1932, p. 15; *Police Report* (annual) for 1933, pp. 11, 13; *Police Report* (annual) for 1934, pp. 11, 14.

[22] Ranga, *Agricultural Indebtedness*, p. 19.

[23] *Ibid.* p. 9; Thomas, *Rural Indebtedness*, pp. 11–19.

suit took on average 400 days to complete and this was of little use to most lenders.[24] Most ryots could not pay their debts, as K. V. Reddi Naidu noted, 'because their land is not worth even the half of what they owe'.[25] Land was indeed the final security for a bad debt, but in most parts of the province moneylenders were reluctant to seize a debtor's lands even in normal years; they preferred to dominate their neighbours by controlling the capital they needed rather than the land on which they worked.[26] This reluctance to foreclose was reinforced in the depression since land prices fell almost as fast as grain prices, and so the volume of land transfers also contracted. The only transactions which took place, according to the Madras Registration Department, were purchases by creditors who wanted the land for a special reason or who saw no other way to recoup their losses.[27] The plight of the moneylenders was exemplified in the troubles of the Nattukottai Chetty bankers. Operating from their headquarters in Ramnad district, these wealthy bankers had spread their financial empire throughout India and other British possessions in the east. In the depression they looked on helplessly as 800 million rupees of liquid capital which they had sunk in agrarian financing in Burma solidified into two and a half million acres of land. By 1937, they owned a quarter of the agricultural acreage in Lower Burma, they did not want an inch of it, and it caused them political problems for more than a decade.[28]

The aggregate debt of the Madras agriculturists, compounded with interest that remained unpaid, gradually rose; in 1935 a government enquiry calculated that it had increased from Rs 150 crores to Rs 200 crores.[29] New loans proved difficult to find. Many of the rural moneylenders were themselves in trouble with their own creditors, the banks and urban financiers. Urban Marwari bankers, who lent at extraordinarily high rates of interest and were usually considered a last resort by prospective borrowers, did a brisk business in some dis-

[24] Sathyanathan, *Report on Agricultural Indebtedness*, p. 44; B. V. Narayanaswami Naidu and V. Venkataraman, *The Problem of Rural Indebtedness* (Annamalainagar, 1935), p. 4.

[25] K. V. Reddi Naidu to Linlithgow, 26 July 1936, Linlithgow papers vol. CLI IOL.

[26] *Madras Provincial Banking Enquiry Commission*, vol. II, pp. 36, 105; vol. IV, pp. 366, 407.

[27] Sayana, *Agrarian Problems*, pp. 120–1; *Report on the Administration of the Registration Department of Madras Presidency* (annual) for 1931, p. 4.

[28] K. V. Reddi Naidu to Linlithgow, 26 July 1936, Linlithgow papers vol. CLI IOL.

[29] Sathyanathan, *Report on Agricultural Indebtedness*.

tricts.[30] In an attempt to ease the situation in 1931, government set aside ten lakhs of rupees for rural credit and distributed it through co-operative societies. But this was only a small drop in a very large ocean. The co-operative societies also faced a liquidity crisis and they too had to join other credit agencies in the rush to realise loans. There were nearly 10,000 co-operative societies, and by 1931 nearly half of them had failed to collect more than 40 per cent of repayments due to them. Total arrears ran to 311 lakhs of rupees and over 900 societies were dissolved in two years.[31]

The Madras Government had for some time paid attention to rural credit. Frederick Nicholson, a distinguished official, had written about it in the late nineteenth century,[32] and the Banking Commission had opened its enquiries on the eve of the depression. In the early 1930s, however, rural indebtedness became a major concern for both government and moneylender, and four books were written on the subject by Indian authors.[33] While these books stressed the plight of the indebted peasant, their very appearance was testimony to the plight of the beleaguered moneylenders. Two of the authors were themselves prominent rural landowners and moneylenders, while a third was employed in the university sponsored by the Nattukottai Chetty bankers. A government report expressed the moneylender's problem: 'All lands are now either attached or mortgaged to moneylenders . . . There is a network of cross-sureties taken for pro-notes. The moneylender wants a stay of all proceedings against land for a definite period for recovery. He is eager for a settlement of debts, for he has learnt a bitter lesson.' He also cited the case of a moneylender who had lent two lakhs and who would now 'forego interest if he can get the principal in cash'.[34] Many prominent figures in rural society began to lobby government to take action to disentangle the knots in the network of rural credit. N. G. Ranga, at a 'Peasants Protection Conference', called for a moratorium on debt.[35] Reddi Naidu wrote to the

[30] Ranga, *Agricultural Indebtedness*, pp. 1–2.

[31] *Annual Report on the Working of the Madras Co-operative Credit Societies Act* for 1930–1, pp. 5–10.

[32] F. A. Nicholson, *Report regarding the possibilities of introducing Agricultural Banks into the Madras Presidency* (Madras, 1895).

[33] Ranga, *Agricultural Indebtedness*; Narayanaswami Naidu and Venkataraman, *Rural Indebtedness*; Thomas, *Rural Indebtedness*; Vaidyanatha Aiyar, *Memorandum on the Ryotwari Landholders*.

[34] Sathyanathan, *Report on Agricultural Indebtedness*, pp. 16–17.

[35] Ranga, *Agricultural Indebtedness*.

Viceroy asking for government to provide ten crores of rupees to wipe out the deadweight of agricultural debt and to get the credit system moving again.[36] Biswanath Das, one of the biggest moneylenders in the zamindari areas of the Circars, pressed for legislation. In 1935, government hurried two acts onto the statute book; the Debtors Protection Act imposed a ceiling on interest rates, and the Agriculturists Loans (Madras Amendment) Act provided funds to wipe off smallholders' debts, but neither act was equipped with adequate machinery to make it effective and the moneylenders' lobby remained unsatisfied.[37]

The problem was political as well as economic since with the constriction of credit many rural bosses were finding that their grip over the countryside had been slackened. In the Kistna–Godavari deltas, where the rural boss had long since lost the monopoly on the supply of credit and the tight control over his neighbours which many of his counterparts in the 'dry' areas still possessed, the depression exacerbated the instability which was already present. In other areas, the rural boss found his dominance called into question for the first time and in some parts, particularly the cotton tracts of Tamilnad where a small amount of economic change in recent decades had offered new opportunities for amassing wealth and influence, the effect on the pattern of rural society was very dramatic. Ramnad district, at the heart of the cotton tract, became in the 1930s almost as troublesome for government as the Kistna–Godavari deltas had been in past decades.[38]

The village elites had not only lost the weapon of credit, but they had lost some of their most reliable dependants as well. Those whose very livelihood had suffered most from the recession were those at the bottom of the village economy, the labourers and village artisans. Often they owned small plots of land, and supplemented their incomes through service to other villagers, and in the depression they could not subsist on their lands, they could not raise loans, and they felt very keenly the decline in the prosperity of other members of the village. Many felt that they might do better offering their skills in the towns, sold up their holdings and left. Professor P. J. Thomas, who in

36 K. V. Reddi Naidu to Linlithgow, 26 July 1936, Linlithgow papers vol. CLI IOL; see also *Andhrapatrika* 9 June 1931 and *Swarajya* 1 June 1931 NNR.

37 S. Y. Krishnaswami, *Rural Problems in Madras*, pp. 370–1.

38 See the riots in Ramnad recorded in the *Police Report* (annual) for the following years: 1930, pp. 16–18; 1931, p. 20; 1932, p. 14 (five incidents); 1933, pp. 13; 1934, p. 14; 1936, p. 14.

the late 1930s organised a resurvey of villages originally surveyed in the 1910s by Gilbert Slater, his predecessor as professor of economics in Madras University, found quite remarkable changes in the population of some villages. In a Tinnevelly village, there had been a big exodus of educated people, chiefly Brahmans, on the one hand, and of artisans and craftsmen on the other.[39] In a Ramnad village, the population had actually decreased because of the departure of smiths, Brahmans, shepherds and labourers.[40] In a North Arcot village, the remaining inhabitants actually cited 1932 as the year when migration had begun with the result that a quarter of the village, chiefly artisans and labourers, had left.[41] Some villages where new economic opportunities had offset the effects of the depression, had not suffered at all in this manner, but in the majority of those surveyed there had been some exodus.[42]

In many places, control of the countryside seemed to be falling apart. In 1930, the police had to deal with three times the normal number of cases of rioting and unrest, and crime figures, after a gradual decline in the 1920s, began to climb steeply.[43] Rural faction-fighting acquired new vigour; bombs were thrown in the course of local feuds in the Ceded Districts, and after similar events farther south the police uncovered a bomb factory in rural Ramnad.[44] In several places, unrest was focussed against the village leaders. In two of the villages resurveyed by P. J. Thomas, the departure of so many labourers had enabled the few that remained to press a hard bargain for their services and to assert themselves against their masters; in one of these villages the panchayat, the instrument of elite government, had completely broken down in the 1930s.[45] In Tinnevelly, low-caste Nadar Christians had refused to pay a community tax to their Hindu overlords and brought out guns to support their stand.[46] In Coimbatore in 1931, the Gounder landlords were surprised to find

[39] P. J. Thomas and K. C. Ramakrishnan, *Some South Indian Villages: a resurvey* (Madras, 1940), pp. 58–62. 93, 116.

[40] *Ibid.* pp. 1–10.

[41] *Ibid.* p. 182.

[42] For other references to migration from the villages in this period see J. Dupuis, *Madras et le Nord du Coromandel*, pp. 49–50; Sayana, *Agrarian Problems*. pp. 120–8.

[43] *Police Report* (annual) for 1931, p. 17.

[44] *Police Report* (annual) for 1931, pp. 15, 21–2; *Police Report* (annual) for 1932, p. 17.

[45] Thomas and Ramakrishnan, *A Resurvey*, pp. 141–6, 343.

[46] *Police Report* (annual) for 1930, p. 17.

that the Kulalar potters in the villages refused to perform their normal services for the village elite, and in Devakkottai in Ramnad district the Adi-Dravida labourers were similarly truculent.[47] In Anantapur, a village officer was murdered while trying to collect the revenue and a prominent local faction-leader was ambushed,[48] while in parts of Ramnad police had to be stationed between labouring and landholding communities.[49] 'In the Ramnad district generally', noted the police, 'the movement of the Adi-Dravidas towards their emancipation is almost a mass movement. At several places in the district time-honoured obligations of degradation were thrown aside and the concerted efforts of higher castes to resist and suppress the movement led to situations which were with difficulty controlled by the police.'[50] When in 1932 Gandhi undertook his fast in the cause of the political representation of the depressed classes, the response in the south was without precedent. Hundreds of meetings were held to honour and support him, numerous politicians rushed forward to espouse the cause of the depressed classes, and in several places successful attempts were made to win the right for lower castes to enter temples.[51] When Gandhi toured the province a year later to collect for his Harijan Fund, he was welcomed as never before in the province.[52]

The depressed class agitations which reached a peak in late 1933 did not usher in a social revolution and after some heady months, the lower castes found that their actual condition had changed very little. Yet in other respects, the unrest of these years had more permanent consequences. During the period of gradually rising prosperity which ended in 1929, many of the richest and most powerful members of rural society had cultivated interests outside their villages, either in commerce, the professions or politics. The growing cotton industry in the southern districts was partially founded on the capital and enthusiasm of landowning families of Gounders and Balijas from

[47] *Police Report* (annual) for 1931, p. 20.

[48] *Police Report* (annual) for 1931, p. 15; *Police Report* (annual) for 1933, p. 11.

[49] *Police Report* (annual) for 1930, pp. 16–17; *Police Report* (annual) for 1931, p. 20; *Police Report* (annual) for 1932, p. 14.

[50] *Police Report* (annual) for 1930, p. 18.

[51] *Hindu* 20, 22, 23, 24, and 26 Sept. 1932, 1, 3, 11, 12 and 17 Oct. 1932.

[52] GOI Home Political 50–1 1934 NAI; 'This mad intoxication of love must be restrained [as at Sivakasi] where in the drenching rains of that afternoon, people madly pulled the car hood and side curtains and would not let the car move till a pitched battle was fought.... The habit of falling across Mahatmaji's feet or attempting to touch him while he is walking must stop.' Statement by Dr T. S. S. Rajan, *Hindu* 2 Feb. 1934.

Coimbatore and Rajus from Ramnad. The Kasu Reddi family from Guntur had added the law and politics to their landed interests. K. Adinarayana Reddi, one of the biggest landowners of Nellore district, had acquired a mica mine. I. C. Iswaran Pillai, a prominent Tinnevelly landholder, was one of many rural leaders who had gone in for co-operative and joint-stock banking. When the depression rendered the business of agriculture virtually unprofitable for a prolonged period, it encouraged many of those who already had one foot outside the village to move even farther out. K. V. Reddi Naidu told the Viceroy that landholders 'have ceased to care whether their land is lost to them or not. In short, their proverbial love of the land is a thing of the past.'[53] Reddi Naidu was of course overstating the case, yet he himself disposed of much of his family lands in the Circars in the 1930s,[54] and many other powerful rural families followed suit. In some cases, large landholders became absentees, abandoning close control over their agricultural interests in order to pursue more closely a career in the town. In one village of West Godavari resurveyed by P. J. Thomas, twenty-two landholding families had recently become absentee,[55] and in a Tinnevelly village there had also been a large increase of absenteeism. In other cases, landholders had sold up and left. In the same Tinnevelly village, the bigger landholdings had been broken up,[56] and much the same pattern prevailed in villages surveyed in Ramnad and Tanjore.[57] The land market picked up in 1935–6, conspicuously before any easing in the credit situation which suggested that certain landholders were desperate to sell up, and in the last years of the decade, the rate of land transfer in the province accelerated rapidly and reached a new peak in the early 1940s.[58] Sample surveys suggested that it was mainly big landholders on the one hand, and artisans and labourers on the other, who were selling up. V. V. Sayana, investigating a handful of villages in the Circars, reckoned that the land boom following the depression had meant that all the land in the villages had changed hands in thirty to forty years.[59]

Land transfer gives only a crude indication of the extent of change

[53] K. V. Reddi Naidu to Linlithgow, 26 July 1936, Linlithgow papers vol. CLI IOL.
[54] Interviews with K. V. Gopalaswamy (Reddi Naidu's son), Hyderabad and Waltair July 1971.
[55] Thomas and Ramakrishnan, *A Resurvey*, pp. 216–17, 339–46.
[56] *Ibid.*, pp. 60, 64, 71.
[57] *Ibid.*, pp. 2–8, 121–4.
[58] Sayana, *Agrarian Problems*, pp. 122–36.
[59] *Ibid.*, p. 124.

in rural society yet there is other evidence of considerable disruption. The raja of Mirzapuram who, as seen above, had invested considerable energy in rural politics in the 1920s and had only just completed the construction of an enormous palace on his estates in Kistna district in the early 1930s, abandoned his rural career in favour of a commercial interest in the film business in Madras City from the mid-1930s.[60] E. Kathleen Gough and Andre Beteille, in their detailed studies of villages in Tanjore district, both noted considerable changes in the personnel and standing of the rural elite stemming from the 1930s.[61] Low profits in agriculture and the decline of old social controls cut into the position of the old rural elite, induced many to leave the villages, and left the others facing new problems of status and political influence.

'After ruin, go to the city', ran a south Indian proverb frequently quoted in the 1930s.[62] The migrations from the villages carried the impact of the depression into the towns as well, and the flight of people was accompanied by a flight of capital. In the depression, the terms of trade between agriculture and industry turned sharply in favour of the latter. World prices of industrial products fell less sharply than those of grain, demand for industrial goods held up, and input prices in many cases were noticeably reduced.[63] At the same time the fall in the volume of trade and the imposition of new tariffs gave Indian industries an important measure of protection. In the south, industry received further encouragement from low wage rates, which were probably lower than in any other part of the subcontinent[64] and which were kept low in the depression by low prices and by the flooding of the labour market with men returned from crippled estates in Burma, Malaya and Ceylon. Parts of the province also acquired cheap electrical power from the hydro projects at Pykara and Mettur for the first time in the 1930s, and this proved important for the development of nearby towns, particularly Madura and Coimbatore, as industrial centres.

60 Interview with members of the Nuzvid family, Nuzvid July 1971.

61 A. Beteille, *Caste, Class and Power: changing patterns of stratification in a Tanjore village* (Berkeley and Los Angeles, 1965); E. K. Gough, 'Caste in a Tanjore village', in E. R. Leach (ed.), *Aspects of Caste in South India, Ceylon and North-East Pakistan* (Cambridge, 1960).

62 C. W. Ranson, *City in Transition* (Madras, 1938), p. 74.

63 A. K. Bagchi, *Private Investment in India 1900–39* (Cambridge, 1972), pp. 89–99.

64 B. Shiva Rao, *The Industrial Worker in India* (London, 1939), p. 121.

The conditions for a transfer of capital from agriculture to industry had never been so good. Moreover, it had been an adequate supply of capital that had all along been so noticeably lacking in Indian attempts to industrialise. This had been due to the absence of facilities to channel capital into industry, and to the existence of enterprises other than industrial undertakings which promised a better and more secure return on investment. The funds had always been there, and as agricultural prices had risen faster than wages or land taxes since the later nineteenth century, there had been a considerable build-up of funds in the countryside. 'It is not unusual', one witness told the Banking Commission, 'to find even a lakh of rupees in cash lying in safes or buried under earth in the houses of rich rural landlords.'[65] Any new opportunity to employ this capital safely in the countryside had been quickly exploited, usually with disastrous results. Within a few years of the appearance of the first rice mills in the Cauveri and Kistna–Godavari deltas and the realisation that these mills yielded large profits, these areas were glutted with rice mills and all profit was lost.[66] In Guntur and Kistna, prosperous farmers went in for retailing, grain-trading and several small industrial enterprises in an effort to utilise spare monies, often with indifferent success.[67] Most of the rural surplus, however, was ploughed back into agriculture and moneylending. 'Indeed', wrote N. G. Ranga, 'if they [rich landholders] are not too avaricious and pay only an ordinary amount of care in choosing their customers, they can make higher profits in this rural banking than in any other business.'[68] In the more prosperous tracts, this had resulted by the late 1920s in a massive over-investment in land, inflating the price of good land to an extraordinary level.[69]

The depression injured such investors badly, and persuaded many of the rural wealthy to try and place their surplus funds in the towns. There was no immediate increase in aggregate joint-stock investment in the early 1930s, largely because the rise in serious investment was offset by the collapse of many speculative concerns set up in the boom

65 *Madras Provincial Banking Enquiry Commission*, vol. II, evidence of V. C. Rangaswami, p. 538.

66 *Minutes of Evidence taken before the Indian Industrial Commission*, vol. III, pp. 78–9.

67 N. G. Ranga, *Economic Organisation of Indian Villages*, I (Bezwada, 1926), 35–6.

68 *Ibid.*, p. 37.

69 *Ibid.* pp. 36–41; *Madras Provincial Banking Enquiry Commission*, vol. III, pp. 739–41.

years on the eve of the depression. 'The year 1933–34', reported the Madras Department of Industries, however, 'witnessed the highest number of registrations recorded since the Indian Companies Act came into force, namely 167';[70] in the next three years there were 196, 185 and 236 new registrations respectively.[71] The aggregate joint-stock capital in the province grew 37.2 per cent between 1935 and 1940, far faster than the rate in India as a whole, and five times faster than the rate per annum in Madras over the previous twenty years.[72] Whereas many of the joint-stock companies registered in the 1920s and 1930s had been old private and family businesses fitted into a better legal framework, many of the new companies of the 1930s were public flotations. *The Hindu* began to carry advertisements which announced the registration of a new company and invited readers to buy shares. Some of the first were companies set up to convey the new hydroelectric power to the towns of the province,[73] but these were soon followed by petroleum distribution companies, banks, insurance companies, cotton, sugar and jute mills and cinema enterprises. A Stock Exchange opened in Madras in the early 1920s had soon closed down through lack of interest, yet in the 1930s the level of investment and the number of freelance stockbrokers rose so rapidly that a Madras Stock Exchange Association was hurried into existence in 1937.[74] The lists of directors and investors displayed in *The Hindu* showed clearly that wealthy landholders figured prominently in this new wave of investment.[75]

Much of the investment went into intermediate financial institutions like banks, investment trusts and insurance companies, or into capital enterprises like electric supply, cement agencies and trading companies.[76] A large slice, however, went into industrial undertakings. The value of imports of industrial machinery into Madras (which A. K. Bagchi considered the most informative index of industrial in-

[70] *Report on the Administration of the Department of Industries in the Madras Presidency* (annual) for 1933–4, p. 14.

[71] See *Ibid.* for the following years: 1934–5, p. 19; 1935–6, p. 26; 1936–7, p. 26.

[72] See tables 15 and 16.

[73] See for example the announcement of electrification companies for Vizagapatam, South Arcot, Karaikkal, Cuddapah and East Ramnad, in *Hindu* 4 Sept. 1933, 14 Oct. 1933, 27 Oct. 1934, 15 Jan. 1935, 9 Jan. 1937.

[74] J. Dupuis, *Madras et le Nord du Coromandel* (Paris, 1960), pp. 500–2.

[75] See *Hindu* 6 Mar. 1934, 12 and 15 Oct. 1935, 6 and 18 May 1936, 9 Jan. 1937.

[76] See tables 15 and 16, and the flotations in *Hindu* 1 Jan. 1931, 7 Feb. 1931, 2 Jan. 1933, 8 Feb. 1933, 12 and 23 Dec. 1933, 6 Mar. 1934, 2 Apr. 1934, 17 Nov. 1934, 18 Jan. 1937; *Justice* 23 Feb. 1931.

TABLE 15. *Joint-stock capital in Madras Presidency*

Year	Number of companies	Paid-up capital (Rs lakhs)	Paid-up capital (Rs lakhs) in	
			Banking	Cotton mills
1910–11	446	469	182	90
1914–15	360	559	202	122
1919–20	435	709	247	149
1924–5	692	1,234	311	282
1929–30	746	1,533	430	269
1930–1	800	1,498	430	269
1931–2	839	1,485	430	281
1932–3	917	1,456	422	282
1933–4	1,030	1,519	429	295
1934–5	1,153	1,569	441	301
1935–6	1,292	1,365	543	372
1936–7	1,387	1,704	463	338
1937–8	1,488	1,878	540	354
1938–9	1,581	1,929	502	361
1939–40	1,577	2,208	466	332

SOURCE: *Joint Stock Companies of British India* (annual) for the years shown. Table entitled: 'Number, description, and capital of companies at work in India at the end of the year. . .'

vestment in India) stayed at a high level in the depression years despite the fall in prices, and rose quickly after 1936.[77] Cotton and sugar were the two most remarkable growth industries and while these were just as much agricultural processing concerns as the rice mills and groundnut decorticators which had spread earlier in the century, they were organised on a far larger scale. Sugar was particularly assisted by new tariff barriers, which virtually cut off imports of sugar in the early 1930s, and by the spread of new varieties of cane. The number of sugar factories in the province rose from two to eleven between 1931 and 1936, and output rose from 29,000 tons in 1934–5 to 67,400 tons at the end of the decade.[78] Meanwhile both Madura and more especially Coimbatore towns grew into major cotton manufacturing centres in the decade, profiting from protection, low wages (Coimbatore mill wages were the lowest in India) and hydroelectricity.

[77] See table 17.

[78] See *Review of the Sugar Industry of India* (annual) for the appropriate years, and *Report of the Indian Tariff Board on the Sugar Industry* (Delhi, 1938), pp. 13–18, 157–62.

TABLE 16. *New companies in the 1930s*

	Number of joint-stock companies newly registered in Madras:							
	Total	Banking and loan	Insurance	Transport	Trade and manufacture	Cotton mills	Other mills etc.	Sugar
1927–8	61	15	2	—	30	1	1	—
1928–9	64	9	5	9	20	4	3	—
1929–30	98	32	18	8	19	3	4	—
1930–1	109	27	7	11	40	—	5	—
1931–2	93	27	10	7	38	2	3	—
1932–3	146	38	33	6	48	5	3	—
1933–4	159	34	24	6	61	3	8	4
1934–5	189	44	12	17	86	8	9	2
1935–6	174	34	4	5	75	14	5	3
1936–7	235	39	8	10	112	4	8	2
1937–8	217	19	4	7	112	7	6	—
1938–9	199	7	—	48	82	6	9	—
1939–40	168	9	6	18	93	—	3	—

SOURCE: *Joint Stock Companies of British India* (annual) for the years shown. Table entitled: 'Number, description and capital of companies newly registered in the year. . .'

TABLE 17. *Imports of machinery and millwork into Madras Presidency*

Year	Value of machinery and millwork imported (Rs lakhs)	Year	Value of machinery and millwork imported (Rs lakhs)
1893–4	26	1930–1	205
1898–9	25	1931–2	135
1903–4	23	1932–3	108
1908–9	46	1933–4	145
1913–14	72	1934–5	159
1918–19	21	1935–6	167
1923–4	181	1936–7	220
1928–9	236	1937–8	240
1929–30	243	1938–9	269

SOURCE: *Annual Statement of the Sea-Borne Trade and Navigation of the Madras Presidency* for the years shown. Table entitled: 'Quantities and values of principal articles imported from foreign countries in [year] into the Madras Presidency.'

The business showed itself to be eminently profitable – Coimbatore mill companies were paying substantial dividends in the middle of the decade when companies as a whole in India were struggling[79] – and continued to attract capital. Three new mill companies were registered in Coimbatore in 1933–4 and seven more in the following year.[80] Between 1932 and 1937 the number of cotton mills in Coimbatore increased from eight to twenty and the number in the province as a whole from twenty-six to forty-seven.[81] Several towns in the surrounding cotton-growing tract also enjoyed a boom, particularly Tirruppur which emerged as the major cotton mart in Coimbatore district, and a cluster of trading towns in Ramnad including Virudunagar and Rajapalaiyam.

None of this was sufficient to drag south India into the industrial twentieth century, but it did make a significant difference to the urban aspect of the province. The development of a new industrial enclave in the north-west corner of Madras City and of new housing suburbs such as Tyagarajanagar in the west, began to transform the capital from a trade entrepot-cum-administrative headquarters into

[79] *Indian Finance Yearbook 1935.*

[80] *Report on the Administration of the Department of Industries in the Madras Presidency* (annual) for 1933–4, p. 14, and for 1934–5, pp. 19–20.

[81] See table 18.

TABLE 18. *Cotton mill industry in the Madras Presidency*

Year	Cotton mills	Looms	Spindles	Employees	Output (million lb) Yarn	Output (million lb) Woven goods
1881	3	—	48,000	1,400	na	na
1891	8	555	173,000	5,900	na	na
1901	11	1,735	288,000	12,600	27·7	na
1911	12	2,023	339,500	18,860	41·1	7·9
1921	15	2,727	423,232	24,118	41·2	13·0
1931	25	5,943	820,870	34,753[a]	76·9	19·7
1937	47	na	1,150,866	49,110	129·9	23·5

SOURCE: *Census of India 1911*, vol. XII, pt. 1, p. 207; *Census of India 1921*, vol. XIII, pt. 1, pp. 194–5; *Census of India 1931*, vol. XIV, pt. 1, p. 125; *Journal of the Madras Geographical Association*, XIV, 2 (1939), 113.

[a] 1932 figure.

a cosmopolitan city. Its population, which had grown slower than the population of the province between 1881 and 1921, picked up in the 1920s and spurted in the two decades which followed. The population of the aggregate urban areas of the province also increased more quickly from the 1930s, with growth concentrated in the centres of industrial activity.[82] The population of Madura grew by 26 per cent, of Coimbatore by 37 per cent, and of Bezwada in the Kistna–Godavari deltas by 43 per cent. In some of the smaller towns the increases were even greater. Koilpatti, one of the cotton-trading towns in Tinnevelly district, grew by a half, while Tiruppur and both Bhimavaram and Gudivada in the Kistna–Godavari deltas roughly doubled in size over the decade.[83]

This influx of people and capital into the towns gave new dimensions to the contest for political control. The artisans and labourers from the villages were joined by migrant labourers returned from the estates of Ceylon and south-east Asia and by handloom-weavers who had steadily been driven towards unemployment by the advance of the cotton mill industry, to form a sizeable class of urban poor.[84] In 1871 it was reckoned that one-eighth of the population of Madras City had lived in cheris, slum areas crowded with labourers' huts; in

[82] See table 19.

[83] *Census of India 1941*, vol. II, pp. 26–36.

[84] *Police Report* (annual) for 1933, p. 11.

TABLE 19. *Population growth and urbanisation*

Indices of population of province, urban areas of province, and provincial capital, 1891 = 100

Year	Madras Presidency	Urban areas	Madras City
1891	100	100	100
1901	107	126	113
1911	116	144	114
1921	119	155	116
1931	131	187	143
1941	146	231	171
1951	160	328	313

SOURCE: *Census of India 1921*, vol. XIII, pt. 2, pp. 4, 6, 8; *Census of India 1951*, vol. III, pt. 2 a, pp. 6, 18.

the depression years, this proportion had become a third.[85] There had been a rash of strikes in the recession following 1918 and only occasional strikes, such as the major stoppage on the South Indian Railway in 1927, throughout the 1920s. Labour organisation, which in those years was a peripheral concern of men with other political duties, was loose and intermittent. M. Singaravelu who made several attempts to get a labour movement off the ground was patronisingly referred to by government as 'our local communist'.[86] In the 1930s, things were different. There was an outbreak of strikes in 1931–2, largely as a result of some firms' attempts to retrench and cut wages in face of the fall in prices,[87] and a generally greater degree of industrial activity than in the previous decade. 1935 was another bad year, especially in Coimbatore where there were six large strikes involving over 5,000 workers. Government explained that 'with the rapid increase in industrial activity in the area, labour is unsettled and some employers are new to the problems of management'.[88] As the decade progressed, these problems induced by the rapid rate of industrialisation and urbanisation increased. 1938 was the worst year with thirty-two major strikes involving more than 25,000 labourers.[89]

85 Dupuis, *Madras et le Nord du Coromandel*, p. 519.
86 FR April (2), GOI Home Political 32 1927 NAI.
87 *Report on the Working of the Factories Act in the Madras Presidency* (annual) for 1931, p. 5.
88 *Ibid.* for 1935, pp. 5–7.
89 *Ibid.* for 1938, pp. 70–6.

In the decade a new generation of labour politicians had emerged, including men like C. Basudev, Mani Kodisura Mudaliar and T. M. Parthasarathi Mudaliar in Madras City, P. Sundararaju in Coimbatore and S. R. Varadarajulu Naidu in Madura, men who were more exclusively concerned with labour affairs than their predecessors had been.[90] Labour organisation and labour parties proliferated and there were agitations in the name of socialism or communism in Coimbatore, Salem, Negapatam, Madura, Tinnevelly, Guntur, Rajahmundry and Vizagapatam as well as Madras City.[91]

One essentially town-based political organisation which lurched into radicalism in the 1930s against this background of urban unrest was E. V. Ramaswami Naicker's Self-Respect movement. In the late 1920s it had gained notoriety through attempts to force the entry of depressed castes into temples and through public ridicule of Hindu texts which, the Self-Respecters argued, promoted an oppressive Brahmanical code, and they had gained considerable support through a series of carefully staged conferences. Yet their dependence on the patronage of certain leading Justicite politicians had ensured that the movement's radicalism remained mostly rhetorical. In the 1930s, however, the movement took deeper root in some of the towns that were being most deeply disturbed by economic change. Its headquarters was in Erode, Ramaswami Naicker's home town, deep in the cotton tracts of interior Tamilnad, and in the same region it found support in the two major manufacturing centres of Madura and Coimbatore, in Salem and Trichinopoly towns,[92] in the port of Tuticorin, in the towns of the Chettinad area of Ramnad,[93] in some of the booming trading towns of the cotton tract like Virudunagar, and in the new industrial suburb of Perambur in Madras City.[94] At its annual conference in May 1930 at Erode, the movement acquired a programme which went beyond the attack on priestcraft and religious obscurantism and included equal civil rights for depressed castes and for women and measures to redistribute wealth within society.[95] In

90 *Justice* 11 Mar. 1935; GOI Reforms 51/11 R & Kw 1935 NAI; T. V. Kalyanasundara Mudaliar *Valkkaik Kurippukkal* (Madras, 1969), pp. 512–13.

91 *Hindu* 12 Apr. 1934, 2 Mar. 1935, 19 June 1935, 3 Oct. 1936; *Tamil Nadu* 6 Sept. 1934, *Jaya Bharati* 17 Sept. 1934, *Prayabhandu* 4 Oct. 1934 NNR.

92 *Tamil Nadu* 3 Mar. 1933 NNR; *Hindu* 27 Oct. 1931, 9 May 1932, 22 Feb. 1933, 27 Nov. 1933.

93 *Hindu* 5 Dec. 1933, 15 Aug. 1934; *Justice* 6 Dec. 1934.

94 *Tamil Nadu* 19 Oct. 1934, *Samadharma* 21 Nov. 1934 NNR; *Justice* 8 July 1935, 16 May 1936.

95 *Hindu* 10 May 1930; papers on the Erode conference in Jayakar papers file 36 NAI.

1931 Ramaswami Naicker found that many of his lieutenants were attracted by the idea of agitation and political martyrdom, and some abandoned him to join the Civil Disobedience campaign or small underground revolutionary associations.[96] In 1932, he visited Europe and Russia and returned, to the astonishment and horror of his old Justicite friends, as a fervent bolshevik.[97] He preached revolution throughout Tamilnad, erected a 'Stalin Hall' to house a Self-Respect conference in Coimbatore, and gave the Self-Respect movement the litany that 'capitalism, superstition, caste distinctions and untouchability must be rooted out'.[98] In 1934, government started to bring him to heel. They jailed him for a seditious article which, among other things, accused the Justice ministers of 'sharing the spoils' of government, arrested him again for conniving in the publication of a revolutionary pamphlet, and, when they started in early 1935 to mop up all pinkish organisations in the province, forced him to a recantation of his bolshevik views.[99]

Several towns in the province experienced an unusual surge of Hindu–Muslim discord in the early 1930s. Muslims formed only 13.2 per cent of the aggregate town population of the province and, except in Vaniyambadi (North Arcot) and a handful of towns in the Ceded Districts, they were always a small minority. In most years, the Hindus and Muslims of south Indian towns moved together quite peaceably. There were occasional disputes when religious susceptibilities were deliberately ignored, but these were rarely serious. In most places, the two communities shared in one another's festivals and practised a common set of customs. At the Palni temple, one of the centres of Hindu pilgrimage in the Tamil districts, the Muslims had their own shrine inside the temple.[100] In North Arcot, a leading Muslim thought it right to donate an elephant to a Hindu temple.[101] Yet between 1930 and 1935, communal riots became a common feature of many towns. In Trichinopoly, for instance, local politics were shaped along communal lines after a Hindu lawyer, who had for many years been politically active and had never before played upon communal

[96] *Hindu* 7 Apr. 1931, 2, 3 and 7 July 1931, 27 Oct. 1931; K. Baladandayutham, *Jiva – Valkkai Varalaru* (Madras, 1966), pp. 17–24.

[97] *Hindu* 12, 21 and 29 Nov. 1932.

[98] *Hindu* 6 Mar. 1933.

[99] *Hindu* 15 Jan. 1934, 10 Apr. 1935; *Justice* 21 Feb. 1935; G.O. 1070 (Public) 22 Oct. 1934 MRO; G.O. 324 (Public) 23 Feb. 1935 MRO.

[100] R. K. Das, *Temples of Tamilnad* (Bombay, 1964), p. 97.

[101] *Justice* 16 June 1936; the leading Muslim newspaper in Tamil, the *Tarul Islam*, regularly contained articles written by Hindus.

prejudices, fought the 1931 elections on a frankly communal campaign and once elected used the municipal machinery to disrupt Muslim festivals and Muslim businesses.[102] In Salem, a Hindu–Muslim wrestling match, which was customarily an expression of communal co-existence, led to a communal riot. In the following year, the police in Salem were called in twice more and the Collector had to intervene to prevent a serious clash between the Hindu Vaisyas and the Muslims over the ownership of a piece of land which had once belonged to a mosque.[103] In Vellore, a dispute over music played before a mosque got out of hand and led to three days' rioting.[104] Many of these disputes spread outside the towns into the rural areas. Hindus and Muslims were at daggers drawn in Trichinopoly district for some months after a rumoured seduction of a Hindu woman by a Muslim. Panchayat elections in one quarter of Salem district in 1934 were conducted on communal lines, and the area of Ramnad around Kamudi saw communal tension for three years after the Hindus had accused the Muslims of wooing depressed Hindus to Islam and the Muslims had replied by looting Hindu shops. By 1935, when a major Hindu and a major Muslim festival fell on the same day, government was scared enough to impose such serious regulations to prevent trouble that many Muslims abandoned their festival in protest.[105] In the 1920s, the Muslim politicians of south India had generally worked closely with their Hindu counterparts; any specifically Muslim organisation had generally been created for a short-term end and few lasted more than a matter of months. Between 1932 and 1934, however, the province witnessed the foundation of two Muslim political organisations – the Islamic League and the Madras Presidency Muslim League – which were to become permanent features of the political landscape.[106]

In a more general sense, the upheavals of the depression years, the movements of population, the weakening of social restraints and the loosening of political bonds, encouraged the growth of new political styles. With the political dominance of village bosses and urban

[102] G.O. 3924 (LSG) 4 Oct. 1932 MRO; G.O. 2483 (LSG) 27 June 1932 MRO.

[103] *Hindu* 25 Nov. 1933.

[104] *Police Report* (annual) for 1930, p. 14.

[105] *Police Report* (annual) for the following years: 1931, p. 19; 1932, p. 14; 1933, p. 13; 1934, p. 14; *Hindu* 1 June 1931.

[106] K. McPherson, 'The social background and politics of the Muslims of Tamilnad 1901–37', *Indian Economic and Social History Review*, VI, 4 (December 1969).

magnates in partial eclipse, the way was opened for other social bonds to acquire new importance. While there had been sporadic examples of political organisation along caste lines for at least half a century, the 1930s saw a remarkable upsurge of caste associations and caste agitations. There had always been difficulties facing such associations in the social circumstances of the Madras Presidency. The region possessed many large caste groups – Vellala, Kamma, Padaiyichi and Reddi among agriculturists, Komati, Balija and Chetty among merchants, Asari and Devanga among artisans, Mala, Madiga and Paraiyar among labourers – yet these were far from cohesive groups. Indeed, above the local level, these caste groups rarely had any unifying structure. Marriage circles were generally small and inward looking, so that there were often no ties of kinship between settlements of the same caste group in adjacent districts.[107] Above the locality, there were clan organisations only among a few castes where special conditions made such organisation possible and appropriate, such as the Kallars of Madura and Ramnad who had until recently been organised as predatory tribes, and the Gounders of Coimbatore who were settled in a compact unit and who farmed a barren and unfriendly terrain.[108] There were few examples of formal caste organisation, and where there were caste tribunals they were, according to the 1911 Census Commissioner, 'an ineffectual tradition' and 'little more than a puppet show'.[109] Indeed among some of the major caste groups of the region there was little unity beyond the use of a common name. The 1891 Census, for instance, had managed to divide both the Vellala and Kapu caste groups into over 800 subdivisions,[110] and the 1921 Census noted that 'the cause of this apparent sub-division lies, not in a fissiparous tendency existing in a definite Vellala community, but rather in the general application of a quasi-social term to a number of communities, which have little or no connection one with another'.[111] The terminology of caste was very flexible; even the

[107] F. J. Richards, 'Cross-cousin marriage in south India', *Man*, XCVII (1914); L. Dumont, *Une Sous-Caste de l'Inde du Sud: organisation sociale et religion des Pramalai Kallar* (Paris and The Hague, 1957), pp. 12, 168; B. E. F. Beck, *Peasant Society in Konku: a study of right and left subcastes in South India* (Vancouver, 1972), pp. 230–2.

[108] See Dumont, *Une Sous-Caste de l'Inde du Sud*, and Beck, *Peasant Society in Konku.*

[109] *Census of India 1911*, vol. XII, pt. 1, p. 178; see also the remarks on the decline of caste tribunals in *Report of the Forest Committee (Madras)*, vol. II, p. 136.

[110] *Census of India 1891*, vol. XIII, pt. 1, pp. 232, 235.

[111] *Census of India 1921*, vol. XIII, pt. 1, p. 175.

compact Gounder community had originally been formed from the descendants of many different clans who had adopted the same honorific,[112] and the twentieth century saw an explosion of new terms adopted by some or all of the members of old caste-groups.

The spread of modern communications and the activities of government had instilled new meaning into some of these caste categories. Some trading groups and professional groups extended their activities, their circle of contacts and their marriage alliances over wider areas, and often these wider networks found expression in caste associations. Among the merchant communities, the Devangas of Salem and Coimbatore, Nadars of Tinnevelly and Ramnad, Komatis from the Andhra districts and Beri Chetties in Madras formed caste associations of this kind. They were encouraged also by government's unintentional fostering of the political importance of caste. From the later nineteenth century, the Madras Government showed itself increasingly ready to listen to political petitions couched in the language of caste, and to distribute government favours with at least one eye on caste considerations; it was not long before politicians tailored their petitions and their organisations to suit government's preconceptions.[113] In the 1920s as agriculturists were drawn strongly into local and provincial politics and, as noted above, members of the rural elite also began to widen their networks of political and marital ties, caste associations also bloomed in the countryside, particularly among the Reddis and Kammas in Andhra and the Gounders in Tamilnad. Many of the mercantile caste associations founded banks and acted like freemason brotherhoods.[114] Nearly all caste associations encouraged education, by running student hostels and funding scholarships, often in an attempt to push representatives into the public services, although this trend slackened after 1920 when the increased importance of local and provincial councils began to qualify the importance of the public services as a route to political influence.

In the 1930s, caste associations came into greater prominence. Moreover the caste associations of this decade were not simply the

[112] B. E. F. Beck, 'A sociological sketch of the major castes in the Coimbatore district', in *Proceedings of the First International Conference Seminar of Tamil Studies*, vol. I, (Kuala Lumpur, 1968), pp. 635–49.

[113] D. A. Washbrook, 'The development of caste organisation in south India 1880 to 1925', in C. J. Baker and D. A. Washbrook, *South India: Political Institutions and Political Change 1880–1940* (Delhi, 1975).

[114] R. L. Hardgrave, *The Nadars of Tamilnad: the political culture of a community in change* (Berkeley and Los Angeles, 1969), ch. 5.

children of mercantile, professional or rural elites, nor were they specifically encouraged by government, although both these factors played a part; the willingness of Sir John Simon to listen to caste representatives proved almost as fruitful for caste organisation as had Edwin Montagu's willingness a decade beforehand,[115] while the Madras Government's attention to non-Brahman demands for special representation in legislatures and public services had by the 1930s evoked demands for special representation from many different communities. In one nightmare debate in the Legislative Council in 1935, for instance, the Madras Government faced demands for special consideration in service recruitment for 'Backward Non-Brahmans', Viswa-brahmans, Settibalijas, Andhras, Rayalseema men, Chakkilas, Reddis, Telagas, Kalalis, Vannias and Christians.[116] Two sorts of caste association flourished in the 1930s, and both were to a large extent a product of the disordered times. On the one hand, there were several associations formed largely in the rural areas by men anxious to find new foundations for a political following now that old styles of political leadership had lost much of their force. One of the first of these was among the Reddis of Andhra. By 1930, the Reddis had in fact possessed a caste organisation for over a decade. This Reddi Mahajana Sabha had been the protégé of some of the most successful professional men of the Reddi caste, had concentrated its efforts on the provision of scholarships and had relied on the patronage of two wealthy men; it had reached its peak in the early 1920s and declined considerably by the end of the decade.[117] In its new incarnation in the 1930s, the Sabha had passed to new leaders in the rural areas, who organised district and taluk conferences where they called for caste solidarity at local elections.[118] There were similar associations among the Telagas of the Circars[119] and among the Kshatriya Rajus of Ramnad,[120] both of which were newly formed in the early 1930s and both of which called for electoral solidarity. In the southern Tamil districts, there was an attempt to build an entirely

115 See the evidence of several Madras depressed class associations in *Indian Statutory Commission*, vols. XVI and XVII.

116 G.O. 858 (Public) 11 Aug. 1934 MRO.

117 The workings of the Reddi Mahajana Sabha can be seen in the papers of its leading light, C. R. Reddy, especially files 6 of 1926–7, 24 of 1926–7, 52, 57 and 66 NMML.

118 *Hindu* 21 Feb. 1933, 11 Sept. 1933, 19 Apr. 1933.

119 *Hindu* 25 June 1934, 4 June 1936.

120 *Hindu* 11 and 12 June 1934, 4 June 1935.

new political force by cobbling together the three closely related castes of Kallar, Maravar and Agamudaiyar in one new association,[121] while in 1935 there was a revival in the interior of Tamilnad of the caste association of the Padaiyichis, which had first appeared in 1888 but which had lapsed since the time of Edwin Montagu's visit.[122] On the other hand, there were some energetic associations formed among low but clean castes who took the opportunity offered by the fluctuous conditions of the decade to assert themselves politically. Among the Nadars of the southern districts, a community many of whom had once been toddy-tappers but which now contained several prominent merchants, there had been since the early years of the century a caste association promoted by a handful of men who had done extremely well out of trading, planting and distilling and who were anxious to gain political favours from government. In the 1930s, however, this Nadar Mahajana Sabha was confronted by rival associations of Nadars, whose leaders were not quite as distinguished and whose members were often involved in violent battles with members of nominally higher castes in the towns of Ramnad during the decade. The most active of the new caste associations of this type were among weaving communities (particularly the Sengundars of interior Tamilnad) and artisan communities (particularly the Asaris), who had perhaps been most dramatically affected by the depression. Indeed, the Sengundar association, which was founded in 1929, gained momentum in the early 1930s, and brought out a widely read Tamil journal in the middle of the decade, flourished in the booming towns of the cotton belt,[123] while the Viswakarma sabhas of the Asaris pressed for more technical education, more government assistance to industrial development and more urban facilities, matters of great importance to the many artisans who migrated from village to town in the decade.[124]

It was not clear how effective these associations were in politics. The Kallar-Maravar-Agamudaiyar association began with a quarrel over the name of the new conglomerate (the Mukkulathur community, the Indrakula community or the Thevar Mahajana community?)[125] which did not bode well for electoral solidarity. Similarly the Padaiyi-

[121] *Hindu* 17 Oct. 1933, 7 Nov. 1933, 27 Dec. 1933, 13 July 1936.

[122] *Hindu* 23 Apr. 1934, 1 May 1935, 14 June 1935; G. O. 1532 (Public) 12 Sept. 1938 MRO.

[123] *Hindu* 7 Jan. 1928, 2 Jan. 1936, 18 July 1936; *Cenkunta Mittiran*, various issues between 1931 and 1937.

[124] *Hindu* 26 Sept. 1935, 9 Jan. 1937.

[125] *Hindu* 7 Nov. 1933.

chi, or Vannikula Kshatriya as it preferred to be known, movement was the most vociferous in calling for communal solidarity at elections, yet after the 1937 elections the association had not performed well as an electoral caucus and it complained that three Padaiyichis in the legislature was not a true representation of the political status of the community.[126] The Nadar associations could do little to wipe away the slur which their past in toddy-tapping cast upon their status, while different elements of the Viswakarmas fought bitterly over the aims of their political organisation: one faction argued that historically they were Brahmans and should be so recognised, another faction settled for the status of non-Brahman, while a third pressed government to include them in the list of depressed castes.[127]

The movement among the Sengundars was ostensibly the most successful. Although the Sengundar weavers were on the whole a poor community, they counted among their number some extremely successful merchants. Many of these were master-weavers, who had great influence in the towns of central Tamilnad and particularly in the great weaving centre of Conjeeveram. The Sengundars had supplied two municipal chairmen in Conjeeveram and one in nearby Gudiyattam, while several other Sengundars figured prominently as bankers, merchants and local politicians in towns like Coimbatore, Tinnevelly and Tenkasi. The master-weavers employed many of the other Sengundars settled in the towns, and these men formed the core of the Sengundar community organisation begun in 1928.[128] The migration of many weavers from the villages and the distress among weavers in the towns during the slump stimulated the desire for community organisation and self-help, and the Sengundar Mahajana Sangham flourished in the 1930s. Branches were formed throughout central Tamilnad and countless conferences were held. Their journal, the *Sengundar Mitran*, produced in Madras, carried articles on politics, literature and community activities and commanded a readership of 4,000 in 1935.[129] Yet as in so many cases, this prolific organisation had only a tangential effect on political views and political solidarity among the Sengundars. Numerous meetings expressing much the same aspirations for self-improvement and for communal solidarity did not mean that the Sengundars spoke with one voice. One of the most prominent members of the Sangham and one of the

126 G.O. 1532 (Public) 12 Sept. 1938 MRO.
127 *Hindu* 10 June 1933, 11 Jan. 1937.
128 *Hindu* 7 Jan. 1928, 26 Dec. 1928.
129 GOI Home Political 53/5 1935 NAI.

most influential politicians in Gudiyattam, M. V. Bhimaraja Mudaliar, blamed his repeated lack of success at Legislative Council elections on the disunity of his community.[130] Similarly in 1937, after an impressive build up of propaganda about Sengundar candidates at the elections, the *Sengundar Mitran* was distressed to announce that only one had succeeded in being elected and that this was a poor reflection on the community.[131]

The appearance of these caste movements indicated new reactions to rapid changes in political and social circumstances. They did not mean that Madras had suddenly become organised into political units built around the ties of caste where previously the diverse networks of urban and rural magnates had prevailed. They did reveal considerable uncertainty in the political leadership of locality and province. Two movements which were more directly related to the strains of the depression and which, like the caste and communal associations, gave new dimensions to political organisation in the province were the agitations against the zamindars and the campaign over land revenue. As in the caste associations so in these campaigns politicians came forward as leaders of categories which had hitherto played little part in the political life of the province – this time 'peasants' and 'tenants'. The land revenue agitation appeared after an attempt by government to resettle the revenue in the turbulent tract of the Kistna–Godavari deltas, and to raise the revenue demand at a time of falling prices. The anti-zamindari campaign arose from an extraordinary alignment of tensions within the higher levels of provincial politics, and tensions in the part of rural Madras which was still under zamindari tenure.

RURAL AGITATIONS

In 1926, certain members in the Legislative Council called for reform of the 1908 Estates Land Act to provide better protection for tenants in the zamindari proprietary estate and in the same year a zamindari ryots association was formed.[132] The issue attracted little attention. In 1929, the association was taken over by new leaders; in March 1930 it started up its own paper, the *Zamindari Ryot*; in the summer of 1931, it held a conference in Nellore district and set up a committee

130 *Cenkunta Mittiran* (1935), p. 22.

131 *Cenkunta Mittiran*, II, 3 (1937), 572.

132 A. Kaleswara Rao, *Na Jivita Katha – Navya Andhramu* (Vijayawada, 1959), p. 446.

to enquire into the conditions of zamindari ryots; towards the end of the year, another conference, in Nellore, called for tenants in the Venkatagiri estate to withhold rent from the zamindar;[133] meanwhile in zamindaris in Trichinopoly, Ramnad, Chittoor, Tinnevelly and North Arcot, police had had to intervene to quell disputes between zamindar and tenant.[134] In 1932, rural leaders organised a moderately successful campaign to withhold payment of grazing fees in the Venkatagiri estate; the zamindar took the leaders to court, but was forced to come to a settlement in which he had to agree to reduce grazing fees. Later that year, Venkatagiri tenant leaders ran for election to the Nellore district and taluk boards in opposition to the zamindar and his satellites.[135] By this time, political leaders had organised zamindari ryot conferences in many districts of the province.[136] In 1933, the report of the committee set up in 1931 was published. It alleged that rents were higher in zamindari estates than in neighbouring ryotwari tracts, that the zamindars commonly raised many other illegal dues and exacted illegal labour services, that the zamindars appropriated many of the functions of government within their estates, and that zamindari tenants were held down by terror. Although the report reviewed conditions in zamindaris throughout the province, it reserved its most violent criticism for the Venkatagiri estate.[137] Finally in 1933, a zamindari ryot conference in Ellore called for the abolition of the zamindari system.[138]

Thus the anti-zamindari campaign appeared very suddenly in the early 1930s. Its origins were complex. Although the 1933 report was able to cite with great authority cases of high rents and illegal exactions, it is clear that the ability of the zamindars to work their will on their tenants was in most cases severely qualified. The zamindari system had been introduced in the south in the early nineteenth century, and it was not discarded in favour of ryotwari before several estates had been carved out, some in the hands of ancient landed families but some grasped by opportunists and warlords who had previously had little or no claim to rural dominance. Many of the estates quickly collapsed through bad management, and many that survived

[133] N. G. Ranga, *Revolutionary Peasants* (Delhi, 1949), pp. 61–4; N. G. Ranga, *Fight for Freedom* (Delhi, 1968), pp. 138–9.

[134] *Police Report* (annual) for 1931, p. 8; *Police Report* (annual) for 1932, p. 13.

[135] Ranga, *Fight for Freedom*, pp. 150–1; *Hindu* 6 July 1932, 13 and 20 Aug. 1932.

[136] *Hindu* 26 Dec. 1930; *Zamindari Ryot* 19 Dec. 1931 NNR.

[137] N. G. Ranga, *Economic Conditions of the Zamindari Ryots* (Bezwada, 1933).

[138] Ranga, *Fight for Freedom*, p. 152.

were little better. Twenty-seven per cent of the rural areas of the province remained under zamindari tenure, most of it in the Andhra coastal districts.[139] Some of the zamindari holdings were truly baronial – in Andhra, there were six estates of over 15,000 acres with annual incomes ranging from Rs 20,000 to Rs 10 lakhs[140] – while others were only a handful of villages or less. Few of the zamindars exercised close supervision over their estates, and few maintained elaborate estate bureaucracies or possessed significant forces of retainers. Thus, like the government, they had to rely on the collaboration of the leaders of the villages in order to exercise some control over their lands, and they had to collect rent from their tenants through the agency of village officers. Most of the zamindars spent their time, and their incomes, in the towns rather than in their estates,[141] and by the end of the nineteenth century, a large number of estates were enormously indebted. One of the largest estates, Karvetnagar, had come under the auctioneer's hammer,[142] others like Ramnad, Papanad, and Singampatti were encumbered with debts which amounted to more than the annual income, and in Polavaram estate the annual revenue did not even cover the interest on the estate's debts.[143] While some of this indebtedness arose from the zamindars' profligacy and their attempts to maintain a veneer of status,[144] much of it was due to bad management and their inability to raise rents. They had experienced even more difficulty than government in raising rents to keep pace with the price-rise. V. V. Sayana noted: 'Rents are not paid regularly and it is largely the case with powerful ryots in recent years. Only the small and weak ryots pay rents regularly.'[145] The most powerful

[139] In 1911 the area under ryotwari was 61,577,420 acres, under inam 4,435,254 acres, and under zamindari 24,743,710 acres, *Settlement Report* (annual) for 1910–11, pp. 52–4.

[140] Sayana, *Agrarian Problems*, p. 91.

[141] See for instance the comments about the Venkatagiri estate by S. Wadsworth in his memoir 'Lo, the poor Indian' SAS; 'The Raja of Chettinad has not cared to visit his estate and it is wondered by many whether he or his heirs know exactly where his estate lies.' Ranga, *Zamindari Ryots*, p. 22.

[142] Wadsworth, 'Lo, the poor Indian', p. 298 SAS.

[143] Sayana, *Agrarian Problems*, p. 113; B. S. Baliga, *Studies in Madras Administration* (Madras, 1960), pp. 85–90.

[144] See the efforts of the zamindars of Kallikote and Parlakimedi to outdo one another in profligate display during a visit by the Governor, in Georgeson papers file 2 SAS.

[145] Sayana, *Agrarian Problems*, p. 110; 'The estimates of the prospective yields [for purposes of assessing rent] made when the crops are actually inspected are very much different from those made in the village after obliging the rich

tenants were able to manipulate the skeletal estate bureaucracies, tamper with assessments and tie the zamindars down with court suits. Some of the more incautious zamindars had even fallen into debt to the richer of their own tenants. In 1908, government had tried through legislation to give more order to zamindari affairs, but the act was badly drafted and its good intentions were soon sunk in a marsh of litigation.[146] The ability of the zamindar to exploit his tenants depended very little on the niceties of tenurial laws; some zamindars were able to be extortionate but many were not.

The status and the power of the zamindars depended more on their relationship to the sovereign power than on their economic base. For the British in the early nineteenth century, the zamindari system had been an answer to many of the problems of ruling a vast area with scant resources. The zamindars, they had hoped, would not only shoulder the burden of raising revenue, policing the countryside and settling disputes within their domains, but they would also be staunch allies of the Raj. In the early nineteenth century (and again during the two world wars of the twentieth when the British were again on their administrative uppers)[147] such a policy was logical if not always successful. Perhaps because the ryotwari system ordained that all ryotwari landowners were equal and thus denied government the opportunity of identifying those more equal than the rest, the Madras Government in its search for the pillars of society often turned to the zamindars. It set up a Court of Wards to bail out their debts, liberally distributed titles to them, called on individual zamindars to advise government, and tried to draft their sons into the public services. This political favour continued into the twentieth century when government was establishing new political institutions. Zamindars were given special representation in the legislature, some were appointed to the headships of local boards, and four of the five chief ministers during dyarchy were drawn from the zamindars' ranks.

But by the end of the nineteenth century, the British had begun to feel that the zamindaris stood in the way of administrative advance. Government found it difficult to improve the revenue it derived from the zamindari areas, or to improve the lot of the people within the estates. The zamindars' debts were troublesome and, as a British officer noted, 'these large estates gave the Collector a great deal of work in

and influential ryots and throwing the tax burden taken off their shoulders upon those less fortunate and influential.' Ranga, *Zamindari Ryots*, pp. 56–7.

146 Sayana, *Agrarian Problems*, pp. 107–9.

147 See the comments about Vizagapatam during the 1940s in the papers of Sir Christopher Masterman, SAS.

settling disputes between the zamindar and his tenants'.[148] Tenurial disputes clogged the courts and led one observer to surmise that 'except for the litigation the zamindars have with their tenants, their lives would be long holidays'.[149] By Independence, half of the zamindari area had still not been properly surveyed. Government had enough information, however, to see that while the ryotwari assessment system could hardly justify its original claim to be based on scientific principles, assessments within zamindari areas were often wholly absurd.[150] An officer in the Court of Wards noted: 'Often the affairs of the estates were in hopeless confusion – boxes of unlisted jewels, rooms full of records, villages unlawfully alienated to concubines, irrigation works in ruins, trust funds misappropriated and so on.'[151]

In the late nineteenth century government had considered expropriating the zamindari estates, but had dropped the scheme because of the expense and probable difficulties. It began, instead, to interfere in the administration of the estates below the level of the zamindar. By 1921, government had taken over the responsibility of paying and supervising the village officers in the zamindari tracts. The zamindars complained that although these village officers had to collect revenue for them, the officers' appointment had to be approved by government, their remuneration came from government, and all the powers to control them (other than with a three rupee fine) resided with government. Consequently, they complained, many village officers had become 'very lax in their duties to the zamindars'.[152] In 1926, K. V. Reddi Naidu noted that through the combined efforts of the village leaders and of the government, the zamindars had virtually been locked out of the administration of their own estates: 'The tenant has very little to do with the zamindar nowadays except to pay his rent. All his relations are with Government, and the Government has taken all the powers of the zamindar; the zamindar has only to pay his peishcush [revenue] and receive what he gets from the tenant.'[153] Lords of the land had become little more than tax collectors.

Government had also devised new schemes for recruiting rural

148 Papers of Sir Christopher Masterman SAS.
149 Sayana, *Agrarian Problems*, p. 111.
150 B. Sarveswara Rao, *The Economic and Social Effects of Zamindari Abolition in Andhra* (Waltair, 1963), pp. 12–15.
151 S. Wadsworth, 'Lo, the poor Indian', p. 151 SAS,
152 G.O. 521 (Revenue) 3 Mar. 1920 MRO; G.O. 351 (Revenue) 3 Mar. 1925 SAH.
153 *Royal Commission on Agriculture in India*, vol. III, p. 360.

leaders and such schemes threatened to deprive the zamindars of their political usefulness to government. The zamindars recognised only too well that they would lose their importance in the new elective constitutions, and in 1908, 1919 and 1933 they lobbied desperately for weighty representation in the new Councils.[154] 'We are losing ground gradually,' complained a zamindars' conference in 1927, 'and our position is becoming increasingly insecure.'[155] They complained of their economic decline and of the expenses of litigation brought by their tenants, and, recognising where their power had always lain, they appealed to government for more political representation to restore their position. But for government, the zamindars were now redundant. 'The zamindari system', noted a prominent member of the government in the late 1940s, 'has perpetuated an assessment which has no relation to the productive capacity of the land. It has further led to loss of contact between the Government and the actual cultivator and has acted as a brake in regard to agricultural improvement . . . . The Government are convinced that the zamindari system in force in the Province has outlived its usefulness.'[156]

Thus by the 1920s, the power of the zamindar was somewhat hollow, and in the zamindari areas, the depression had a particularly violent impact, for it provoked certain interests to take up arms against the ailing system. Firstly, many rich tenants in the estates rebelled. Most of these were the wealthy cultivators and moneylenders, similar to those we have seen in the ryotwari areas. The provision of credit in the estates had always been more difficult than in the government tracts. Tenures, subtenures and mortgages within the estates were often so complicated and land records so poor that a moneylender could not lend on the security of land without taking a great risk that the land was heavily encumbered.[157] These encumbrances, together with the risks of predations by the zamindar, also meant that land in the zamindari area was generally worth less than outside. A moneylender who lent on the security of grain in the zamindari areas also ran a risk for he might find, at the harvest, he was competing with the zamindar, who often collected rents in kind

[154] GOI Reforms Franchise A 144–61 May 1920 NAI; GOI Reforms 198-R 1931 NAI.

[155] *Hindu* 24 Nov. 1927.

[156] Kala Venkata Rao introducing the (government's) zamindari abolition bill into the Madras Legislative Assembly, quoted in Sarveswara Rao, *Zamindari Abolition*, p. 28.

[157] Sayana, *Agrarian Problems*, p. 115.

and who since the 1908 Act had first charge on the harvest.[158] Thus when the depression struck and credit became difficult, it affected the moneylenders in the zamindari estates even more disastrously than their counterparts in the ryotwari villages. To make matters worse, many village leaders in the zamindaris had, since the 1908 Estates Land Act made it easy for them, forced the zamindar to commute their rent-payments from kind to cash; while prices were rising as they were between 1908 and 1928, these fixed cash payments weighed steadily less heavily on the tenants. When prices dived from 1929, the real value of these commuted rent-payments soared. Shorn of their levers of credit and piqued at their loss of profits, the rich tenants of many zamindari villages took up arms against their overlord in the early 1930s. In Udaiyarpalaiyam and Sivaganga estates, zamindari servants and tenant groups fought one another for shares of the grain at the 1931 harvest.[159] Similar riots occurred in the Tirupati and Maniyachi estates in the following year[160] and in Mamandur in 1933 where the disgruntled tenants resorted to incendiarism.[161] The raja of Munagala had to dismiss one of his village officers for leading disaffection, and the raja of Bobbili took one of his wealthiest tenants to court. The raja of Venkatagiri found that the revolt in his estate was led by distant relatives who held tenures in the estates.[162]

Thus on the one hand, the anti-zamindari agitation grew out of tensions within the estates, precipitated by the depression. On the other hand, it gained support because it won allies within provincial politics. Although political status had gradually been ebbing away from the zamindars, they still retained disproportionate weight within the Montagu–Chelmsford constitution. The zamindars had for the most part loyally supported the Justice party and in much of the northern part of the province, particularly in the Kistna–Godavari deltas where the ministry found it difficult to secure stable allies, the Justice ministry had come to rely greatly on the zamindars as their local satellites. Many of these – the rajas of Pithapuram in East Godavari, of Mirzapuram in Kistna, of Venkatagiri in Nellore, and of Bobbili in Vizagapatam – came from the same network of Velama families as the chief minister, the raja of Panagal. With Justicite ministerial backing, these men had become unnaturally powerful in

[158] *Madras Provincial Banking Enquiry Commission*, vol. II, p. 524.
[159] *Police Report* (annual) for 1931, p. 18.
[160] *Police Report* (annual) for 1932, p. 15.
[161] *Police Report* (annual) for 1933, p. 13.
[162] Ranga, *Revolutionary Peasants*, p. 96; *Hindu* 6 Jul. 1932, 13 Aug. 1932.

their districts. Pithapuram had influence not only in the politics of East Godavari but also in the affairs of Rajahmundry and Cocanada towns. Mirzapuram, as noted above, managed under the Justicite umbrella to pursue an expansionist policy throughout the Kistna delta. But the Legislative Council also contained powerful men from the same northern areas who resented the continued power of these relics, and who were jealous of the zamindars' virtual monopoly on ministerial favours. Mirzapuram's antics, as noted above, induced other Kistna men to conspire in the establishment of the 1926 ministry largely to help bring Mirzapuram down. The irruption of the Venkatagiri family into Nellore local politics – they challenged the district board elections in the courts in 1926, interfered in the legislature elections in 1926 and in 1930 and finally put the raja's heir in as president of the district board in 1931[163] – helped to make Nellore the cradle of the anti-zamindari campaign from 1930.

B. Muniswami Naidu took up the leadership of the anti-zamindari faction. His family had formerly been in the service of the Kalahasti zamindars and he was a protégé of the raja of Panagal, yet after Panagal's death, he found that he was pitted against the Velama zamindar faction in the contest for the leadership of the Justice party. At the 1930 elections, the Velama zamindars poured funds into the Justicite election effort and expected to be rewarded with a ministership.[164] Muniswami Naidu double-crossed them. In the following months, the zamindars led by the rajas of Bobbili and Mirzapuram began manoeuvring to smash Muniswami Naidu. Muniswami Naidu moved closer to the anti-zamindari faction in the Legislative Council, helped to promote anti-zamindari meetings in the Circar districts, and introduced a bill to amend the Estates Land Act with a pro-tenant bias.[165] The chief organiser of anti-zamindari meetings was N. G. Ranga. After Muniswami Naidu was toppled from the Justicite leadership and chief ministership and replaced by Bobbili in 1932, N. G. Ranga moved the anti-zamindari movement into top gear; instead of demanding the reform of the zamindari system, they now demanded its complete abolition.[166]

By the early twentieth century the zamindari system was economically and politically redundant but, like a house of cards, it was kept in

[163] *Hindu* 10 Feb. 1928, 6 Jan. 1931.

[164] *Swadeshabhimani* 14 Oct. 1932 NNR; statement by B. Muniswami Naidu in *Evening News* (Bombay) 9 Nov. 1931, cutting in Jayakar papers file 36 NAI.

[165] *Hindu* 26 Dec. 1930, 7, 10 and 17 Sept. 1932.

[166] Ranga, *Revolutionary Peasants*, pp. 93–8.

existence through its own internal tensions. The depression, however, hit hard at one of the crucial joints in the system – the village leaders. They were already caught in a tug-of-war between government and zamindar which threatened to qualify their ability to maintain the system to their own political advantage. The fall of prices and the freezing of the credit network cut into their ability to control the villages, and threw them into conflict with the zamindar. Village leaders were encouraged to lead their villagers in agitation against the zamindars. This agitation aligned itself with tensions in local and provincial government, tensions which owed much to the unequal distribution of the prizes of dyarchy.

A similar complex of causes lay behind the other rural campaign of the early 1930s – the agitation against land revenue. The fall in prices in the depression meant that land revenue payments accounted for a far higher proportion of the cultivator's income. The Madras Government was reluctant to remit land revenue since its own financial stability relied heavily on customs and excise dues which were particularly badly hit by the depression, and any fall in land revenue returns would be disastrous. Thus Madras remitted only 2 per cent of land revenue in 1931–2, while the Punjab remitted 27·7 per cent and the U.P. 17·3 per cent.[167] The burden of collecting the same level of revenue from cultivators who had less in their pockets fell on the village officers.

In Non-co-operation, many village officers had expressed their resentment of government's measures to reduce their power and to reduce their scope to manipulate the revenue system to their own advantage. Despite these protests, government policy had continued to chip away at their privileges. The freezing of credit in the depression cut into the village officers' ability to control their rural neighbours through the power of debt. In such a situation the burden of collecting revenue during the depression became, in some areas, impossible or at least intolerable. In the 'wet' areas where, as noted above, the position of the village officers vis-à-vis their neighbours was already difficult, the problems were particularly acute. Many decided, or were forced to decide, to lead the village against the government rather than carry out government orders over the village. In Nellore, village officers were dismissed in 1930 'for disobeying . . . the orders of the Tahsildar

[167] Fazl-i-Husain to Willingdon, 12 Dec. 1933, in GOI Home Political 4/20 1933 NAI.

to attach the moveable property of a defaulter for non-payment of land-revenue and for throwing down their sticks and standing aside when told to do so by a ... rich ryot of the village'.[168] Many other village officers were dismissed for taking active part in campaigns which aimed to force the government to reduce revenue rates, and some were dismissed for urging their villages to withhold payment of the revenue.[169]

In the 'wet' area of the Kistna–Godavari deltas, the problems were compounded by the government's resettlement of the land revenue. Even before the depression struck, government anticipated that the resettlement of these districts would be troublesome, and it had made a close scrutiny of all the police and subordinate staff in the area and appointed a special police officer.[170] Even so, agitations began even while the resettlement officers were collecting information, and a Ryots Association was formed before the Resettlement Report was published.[171] In 1930, this Association set up an Economic Enquiry Committee which toured the districts, produced a report and advised government against increases in revenue rates on the ground of the great fall in prices.[172]

The government in its Resettlement Report raised the revenue demand by 18$\frac{3}{4}$ per cent. This increase was not, however, spread evenly through the districts. Since 1925, government had concluded that the revenue assessments in the province in general weighed less heavily on the more prosperous irrigated lands than on the less prosperous areas of 'dry' cultivation and that future resettlements should correct this bias. Thus the increases in the Kistna–Godavari Resettlement fell most heavily on the irrigated tracts. Moreover, the better surveys undertaken in the course of resettlement revealed how much irrigated land was in fact assessed as 'dry'. In Kistna district alone, the resettlement crew transferred 25,210 acres from the 'dry' to the 'wet' register. Thus while the overall increase in revenue demand was only 18$\frac{3}{4}$ per cent the increase in the 'wet' tracts was far more. In Kistna, the revenue demand on the wet areas rose by almost 50 per cent. Unsurprisingly, it was the regions deep in the delta which raised

168 G.O. 639 (Public) 5 June 1931 SAH.

169 G.O. 1075 (Public) 20 Oct. 1931 SAH; G.O. 980 (Public) 21 Sept. 1931 SAH; G.O.s 938 and 939 (Public) 11 Sept. 1931 SAH; G.O. 760 (Public) 16 July 1931 SAH.

170 Goschen to Birkenhead, 3 Oct. 1928, Goschen papers vol. III IOL.

171 *Hindu* 19 Jan. 1928.

172 Ranga, *Fight for Freedom*, pp. 134–6.

the greatest objection to the resettlement. Government received nearly 90,000 petitions and objections against the resettlement from Kistna, East and West Godavari districts and almost 60 per cent of these came from the six 'wettest' taluks at the heart of the deltas.[173]

It was in these tracts that a campaign against land revenue resettlement began, led in many cases by village officers and men from village officer families. N. G. Ranga was again prominent. The campaign began with conferences in 1929 and 1930, but hotted up around the time of the 1931 harvest when the effects of the depression on the credit flow became really acute.[174] November 1st 1931 was named 'Resettlement Day' and there were meetings and demonstrations throughout the Kistna–Godavari deltas. Several of these conferences discussed the idea of withholding revenue payments, and in subsequent weeks government began arresting prominent leaders of the campaign, including N. G. Ranga.[175]

The Madras Government agreed to stagger the increases in revenue rates over three years (and in a similar fashion to remit revenue in other districts which had been resettled since 1918 and whose revenue rates had then been raised in accordance with inflation). The full effect of the resettlement in the Kistna–Godavari deltas was thus delayed until 1933. This was extremely inopportune, for in that year grain prices hit their nadir, and the flow of credit virtually stopped. By this time, the agitation had spread beyond the Kistna–Godavari deltas. The depression had in fact caught government in the act of resettlement in no fewer than eleven districts. Village leaders everywhere were struggling with the problems of credit. Around the time of the 1933 harvest, revenue agitations were under way in Tanjore, Chingleput, Vizagapatam, Madura and Salem besides the Kistna–Godavari deltas.[176] The intensity of the campaign was enough to startle the Madras Government out of the complacent attitude it had so far managed to maintain through three years of agitation and Civil Disobedience. When Gandhi threatened to visit the Kistna–Godavari deltas in December 1933, the Madras Government asked Delhi for permission to arrest him if he even whispered the words 'no-tax campaign', argued that 'every day's delay will increase the danger

[173] G.O. 2233 (Revenue) 9 Dec. 1933 SAH.

[174] *Andhrapatrika* 12 May 1931, 9,19 and 20 June 1931, 17 July 1931, 28 Aug. 1931, 3 Sept. 1931 NNR.

[175] FR November(2), GOI Home Political 18-xi 1931 NAI.

[176] *Hindu* 10 Nov. 1933; R. Krishnamachariar, *Araciyal Nani Arankacami Aiyankar* (Madras, n.d.), pp. 131, 321–4.

of a mass movement', and wanted to re-enact a notorious piece of repressive legislation, the Seditious Meetings Act of 1911, and fortify it with a Special Powers Act.[177] Besides this, the Madras Government moved against some of the prominent participants in the resettlement campaign in a way that looked desperate and dangerous. They instructed revenue officials in the delta areas to cut off the supply of irrigation water to known participants.[178] Water was the essence of prosperity in these tracts and farmers commonly fought over it; government's manipulation of the supply would not win them any allies.

This wave of agitation had caught the Madras Government napping. Only a matter of months after it had boasted to the Simon Commission about the success of British rule in Madras and had registered no objection against a further devolution of power, Fort St George had gone running to Delhi for special powers of repression. Delhi refused, and in the middle years of the decade, the land agitations lost their original intensity. However, the two land campaigns had become closely allied to the Congress campaign of Civil Disobedience in the province, and had given the campaign added weight. Civil Disobedience, however, included many other agitations and drew other uncertain responses from the Madras Government.

THEMES IN CIVIL DISOBEDIENCE

Gandhi set out from Ahmedebad on 12 March 1930 to march to Dandi on the Gujarat coast and make contraband salt, thus inaugurating the Congress campaign of Civil Disobedience. Twelve months and 90,000 arrests later, the campaign was suspended after negotiations between Gandhi and the Viceroy, Lord Irwin, had resulted in a truce. For nine months, the Congress agreed to keep the campaign within the law, while the British negotiated to bring the Congress leaders into discussions on constitutional reform. In January 1932 these negotiations broke down and Civil Disobedience was resumed until July 1933 when the 'mass' campaign was called off. Finally in April 1934, Congress formally abandoned the policy of agitation. As in the Non-co-operation campaigns, the Civil Disobedience agitations in the Madras Presidency included many demonstrations organised by Gandhian followers along Gandhian lines, but also many other agitations. The latter were sporadic and were not centrally organised, but

[177] GOI Home Political 4/20 1933 NAI.

[178] *Hindu* 20 Aug. 1930.

they none the less contributed to the force of the Congress campaign. It would not be possible to give a full account of the many different elements of Civil Disobedience in a suitably short space, but it is possible to identify some of the most important themes which underlay the agitations of this period. Firstly, there were the agitations organised by Gandhi's disciples in the province, which were orchestrated to show the strength, the defiance and the moral leadership of the Congress. Secondly, there was the background of the depression, which enabled the Congress to draw on distress and disorientation to fuel their campaigns, and which threw many of those elements in the province, who were in normal years barely reconciled to the idea of government, into open revolt. Thirdly, there was the concentration of the intense and prolonged agitations either in those areas which were habitually troublesome – the deltas and the big towns and especially the towns in the deltas – or in those towns which were most affected by the economic forces and the population movements of the depression years – particularly the cotton towns of the far south. Fourthly, it was noticeable that many of the campaigns of Civil Disobedience were directed not only against the Raj but also against those who had done well out of the political dispensations of the 1920s, particularly those who had profited from the patronage and the devolutions of government. Finally, there was the acute dependence of government on its Indian collaborators when it was under attack, and the way that those collaborators attempted to make political capital out of government's embarrassment.

The Congress leaders opened their campaign in Madras with demonstrations against the salt laws to parallel Gandhi's own Dandi march. Rajagopalachari led the first salt satyagraha in the province at Vedaranyam in the south of the Cauveri delta. Many prominent Congress workers took part in the demonstration, and they were joined by volunteers from all over Tamilnad.[179] In this, and in many of the other incidents of Civil Disobedience, the provincial Congress showed that it was more capable than ever before of harnessing the idealism of students and other young workers to give organisation and weight to its show of strength. Soon after, there were also efforts to make contraband salt on the coast in Chingleput district and on the beach in Madras City,[180] while the Andhra leaders organised cam-

[179] *Hindu* issues from 3 to 17 Apr. 1930.

[180] Kalyanasundara Mudaliar, *Valkkaik Kurippukkal*, pp. 396–7; Report on Civil Disobedience in Tamilnad, dated 12 Jan. 1931, in AICC papers file G189 of 1930 NMML.

paigns in several places on the Circars coast.[181] After the police had dispersed these efforts, the Congress leaders kept up a constant stream of demonstrations by holding illegal meetings, appointing successive 'Congress Dictators' who were quickly arrested by government, and by sending out a constant stream of volunteers, including women, to court arrest. These demonstrations took place chiefly in Madras City, for thus could the Congress hope to put as much pressure as possible on the provincial government.[182]

In these demonstrations and in other scattered campaigns, the Congress was able to tap the discontent of many sectors of the population who in normal years were somewhat antagonistic to government and its impositions and who in the strained conditions of the depression were more ready than usual to lend their weight to organised dissent. In the countryside, this meant they were able to associate the anti-zamindari and resettlement campaigns with the Congress. The leader of these campaigns, N. G. Ranga, who had been identified with and patronised by the Justicites in the 1920s, was gradually drawn into the Congress in the early 1930s. In the towns, this meant they got the support of disgruntled merchants and of the mob. Masses of handloom weavers, normally held down by capitalist-managers but now thrown into unemployment, fuelled riots in Coimbatore, Gudiyattam and Kumarapalaiyam. At the time of the riot in Coimbatore in 1931, it was reckoned that there were 10,000 unemployed weavers in the town.[183] The Congress leaders imported students and agitators from all over the province to fill out the demonstrations in Madras City, and also got an unprecedented amount of support from the merchants of the local bazaars. One long-serving Congress worker who suggested that one man taking a prominent part in Congress work in the City was somewhat less sophisticated than previous Congress leaders was told that 'such were necessary in Madras City as he was a local man and well-to-do'.[184]

The temperance campaign was one of the spearheads of Civil Disobedience in the province and it drew on a multitude of different motives. Liquor was inevitably a problem in a region where it could be

[181] *Hindu* 3 and 8 Apr. 1930; *Satyagrahi* 7 Apr. 1930, *Andhrapatrika* 10 Apr. 1930 NMML.

[182] See accounts in AICC files G189 of 1930 and G116 of 1930 NMML.

[183] FR July(1), GOI Home Political 18-vii 1930 NAI; B. S. Baliga, *Coimbatore District Gazetteer* (Madras, 1966), pp. 121–2.

[184] M. Chenna Subba Rao, *Myself and Rural Life* (*Autobiography*) (Anantapur, 1951), pp. 16–20.

manufactured by the simplest of processes from the juice of palm trees which grew easily in orchards or on sandy wastelands. Abstinence was an attribute of high ritual status throughout the region, and temperance had for many years been a concern of politicians and social reformers of many different types. The Civil Disobedience campaigns gained support from these men and from the leaders of communities like the Kamma agriculturists in Kistna and Saurashtra merchants in Madura, who were anxious to raise the prestige and position of their caste fellows. The Congress organised boycotts of the government's auction of licences for liquor trading, Rajagopalachari wrote a pamphlet urging that the war against liquor was an integral part of the war of independence,[185] some liquor shops were looted and burnt and some toddy-palms were vandalised. Much of the force of the campaign, however, arose from government's policy towards liquor, in which the demands of the exchequer and the dictates of Victorian morality were inextricably confused. This confusion forced men in the liquor trade, many of whom operated at the edges of legality and were badly disposed towards government in the first place, to give support to a campaign which was apparently aimed against their own interests.

It was government's aim both to cut down the consumption of liquor, and to raise a revenue from it. Financial pressures meant that the latter motive had slightly more weight in forming excise policy, but only just. The Madras Government auctioned licences to retail liquor and levied a tax on the liquor itself. By limiting the number of licensed shops, and keeping the price of the liquor high, it hoped to check consumption. By 1921–2, when the Congress first ran a successful temperance campaign, the Madras Government realised that its policies had put an intolerable strain on the liquor retailers, who had themselves promoted the Congress campaign.[186] However, this realisation did not prevent government increasing the levies on liquor in the 1920s as a way to meet the provincial deficit. Government rejoiced that revenue rose while consumption per head apparently fell. But this was consumption, government gradually came to realise, of *licit* liquor; meanwhile side by side with the rise in taxes was an enormous rise in *illicit* brewing and distilling. 'The profits which

[185] C. Rajagopalachari, *Cuttantirap Por* (Madras, 1931); see also the Tamil pamphlet 'Remove Toddy-Cut Spathes' contained in G.O. 1194 (Public) 15 Sept. 1932 MRO.

[186] See C. J. Baker, 'Non-co-operation in South India', in Baker and Washbrook, *Political Institutions.*

the illicit distiller earns', noted the excise department, 'are so great that the profession is now preferred to other ordinary legitimate avocations.' Furthermore, they noted, competition from the bootleggers had 'become so acute that it is even suspected that the Government-licensed liquor retailers are beginning to sell illicitly distilled liquor under cover of their licences to avoid financial disaster'.[187] Following a rise in liquor tax-rates in any district, consumption would fall and cases of illicit production and sale increase. In 1927, government reacted by creating special flying squads to seek out the bootleggers.[188] The hardship of the depression raised the premium on the cheaper, illicit hooch, and made licit trade virtually uneconomic. Thus, as in 1921–2, the liquor traders themselves were happy to join hands with an agitation which was apparently aimed directly against their business. 'Bidders for liquor shops took advantage of the threatened picketing of licence auctions and kindred evils to get their shops for very low bids' noted government.[189] In Tiruppur they found that the previous licensee had himself organised the boycott of the licence auction, and in Coimbatore and other places they felt that liquor shop owners had used the excuse of Congress disruption to beg for remission of the licence-fees. Government suspected that behind the boycotts and disruptions of the licit liquor trade in many places were hooch-kings out to secure a monopoly.[190]

While the land campaigns, temperance agitations and urban scuffles were scattered throughout the province, in a few places the agitations took deeper root. In the big towns and in the Kistna–Godavari delta tract, which had been troublesome to government throughout the 1920s, agitations were more intense and more prolonged, and the towns in the deltas saw some of the most impressive campaigns of all. Agitations were also more intense in those other areas which had been most drastically affected by the economic changes of the depression years, particularly the cotton belt of Tamilnad. The Coimbatore district was the seat of the temperance agitations, while two of the small but quickly expanding cotton trading towns of Ramnad district, Virudunagar and Rajapalaiyam, saw many spurts of agitation between 1930 and 1933. Among the larger towns, Madura and Trichinopoly were the scenes of agitations over salt, temperance and defiance of repressive laws, but it was in the towns and the countryside of

[187] *Abkari Report* (annual) for 1933–4, p. 16.
[188] *Abkari Report* (annual) for 1927–8, p. 8.
[189] *Abkari Report* (annual) for 1931–2, p. 18.
[190] GOI Home Political 33/30 1931 NAI.

the Kistna–Godavari deltas that government faced the worst threat.

The Congress in the deltas found support for its agitations among the cream of local society. Wealthy landholders and prominent traders, particularly those involved with the products badly hit by the price-fall, poured funds into Congress agitation. The Rice Mill Owners Association of Guntur financed local Congress agitation, the Masulipatam Grain Merchants Association provided a free mess for Congress volunteers, and the Reddi grain traders of Nellore and the cotton merchants of Bezwada led Congress agitations.[191] A Congress demonstration in Rajahmundry was led not simply by a handful of lawyers and penniless volunteers who headed most agitations elsewhere, but by two doctors, several members of the two leading Komati merchant families, a prominent banker, two cousins of the taluk board president and about twenty substantial landlords.[192] Agitational activity was far more sustained and far more impressive than in other regions of the province. Contraband salt was manufactured throughout the delta area, liquor-giving toddy-trees were vandalised, Congress ashrams were established to train volunteers, and occasionally telegraph poles were felled and police stations were attacked.[193]

In one or two places government found that the always troublesome local boards had now gone completely out of control. In East Godavari, the district board president used the local board machinery not only for symbolic nationalist displays such as the purchase of a portrait of Gandhi and the closure of board offices for a Congress demonstration, but also to help collect Congress funds and to employ Congress volunteers on the staff.[194] In Guntur town, Civil Disobedience was particularly virulent not least because it had the entire machinery of municipal administration behind it. Pro-Congress resolutions were passed at municipal meetings and the National Flag hoisted over the municipal office; the municipal library and municipal park accommodated Congress meetings, to which municipal servants carried municipal chairs, mats and gas-lights to make it more comfortable; municipal lorries carried volunteers to make salt on the coast; municipal materials were used to construct a Congress camp and a municipal water connection was provided for it; Congress

191 K. Venkatappayya, *Sviya Caritra* (Vijayawada, 1952), p. 347; *Hindu* 31 Mar. 1930, 11 Nov. 1930, 16 Mar. 1931.

192 *Hindu* 3 Apr. 1930.

193 *Hindu* 27 May 1930, 27 Sept. 1930, 10 Dec. 1930.

194 G.O. 3081 (LSG) 31 July 1930 SAH; G.O. 459 (LSG) 25 Jan. 1934 SAH.

subscriptions were raised from factory owners and roadside shopkeepers who held licences from the municipality and from municipal contractors; and municipal employees were enlisted as Congress volunteers.[195] Government's own machinery was apparently sheltering and financing an attempt to push government itself into the Indian Ocean.

In these and in other Civil Disobedience demonstrations, the butt of the Congress campaign was not only the Raj but also those who had profited from the political circumstances of the 1920s. It was this that had in part made the campaigns more intense in the deltas and the towns for in these areas there were many people who could not find a satisfactory niche in local government and who had already in other ways shown their resentment of the local satraps who clung to the coat-tails of the ministers. In Madura town, there was a clear example of the Congress agitation conducted by those who had been left out of the politics of the 1920s against those who had controlled them. Here, Civil Disobedience was taken up by the leaders of the Saurashtra community, which formed almost a third of the town's population, dominated its commerce, and took great interest in the affairs of the Minakshi temple. Yet the Saurashtras had found themselves excluded from any significant part in the management of either temple or municipality, largely because the ministry gave support to their rivals in town affairs. Only one Saurashtra was ever nominated to the Minakshi temple committee, despite frequent petitioning, and the Saurashtra leaders did not win control of the municipal council until 1930, when government immediately suspended the municipality and installed a special officer. It was just after this débâcle that the Saurashtra leaders took up the torch of Civil Disobedience, and they moulded the campaign to their own ends. They took strongly to temperance campaigning, as it fitted in well with their plan of community uplift, and wholly ignored the idea of boycotting foreign cloth (another aim of Gandhi's programme), since they themselves dealt in it. They used agitations to embarrass the special municipal officer and to build up electoral support in anticipation of the restoration of the municipality.[196]

In Trichinopoly, Civil Disobedience was led by P. Ratnavelu Thevar, a municipal politician who for some time had been angling to replace the ministerial allies in command of town affairs and who, to this end, had until very recently been posing as a Justicite and

[195] G.O. 3683 (LSG) 15 Sept. 1930 SAH.
[196] AICC papers file G116 of 1930 NMML; *Hindu* 28 July 1930.

begging for a deflection of ministerial favours into his own camp.[197] In the towns of East Godavari, Civil Disobedience was the work of a handful of lawyers and merchants who resented the pervasive influence of the raja of Pithapuram in local politics. Everywhere these local agitators interpreted Civil Disobedience in their own fashion. The Nadars who waved the Congress flag in the streets of Dindigul demanded both self-rule and entry into the local temple.[198] The agitators of Coimbatore, where the mills turned out swadeshi cloth, stressed the need to boycott foreign textiles.[199]

Just as there were agitations directed against those whom government had accepted as the leaders of local society, so too there were agitations against those whom government had accepted as the leaders of certain communities. Since the early years of the century, the Madras Government had often distributed patronage and power to men who claimed to lead different castes, but, as government was gradually to discover, such 'leaders' could not really be taken as the representatives of their caste fellows and could not themselves count on their caste fellows' support.

In Civil Disobedience, several men came forward to protest at the way particular politicians had profited from posing as their leaders. A rural leader like J. Kuppuswami Choudhari of Guntur had done particularly well by posing as the leader of a Kamma caste movement. By 1930 he was an M.L.C., district board president and close associate of the chief minister B. Muniswami Naidu. Other Kammas resented the dominance of the Kuppuswami clique in the politics of the Kistna delta and ignored Kuppuswami's claim that Kammas were generically loyal. In 1930–3 they joined temperance campaigns, resettlement agitations and anti-zamindari outbursts, flooded into the Congress committees in Guntur and Kistna, and began fighting local elections against Kuppuswami's men.[200]

Similar moves were afoot among the Nadars of Ramnad district. The Nadars by the early twentieth century were an immensely diverse community. While many were still humbly shinning up toddy trees to tap the juice, others had become some of the wealthiest planters, distillers, wholesalers and cotton dealers in the southern districts. A small group of Nadar families centred in the cotton town of Virudunagar had, since 1920, made an extremely profitable virtue out of claiming that Nadars were both backward and loyal, and of putting

197 *Hindu* 14 June 1930.

198 *Hindu* 9 Sept. 1930.

199 AICC papers file G116 of 1930 NMML.

200 *Hindu* 27 Jan. 1932, 27 Sept. 1930; AICC papers file 7 of 1934 NMML.

themselves forward as the community's representatives. One leader of this clique, W. P. A. Soundarapandian, had been consistently nominated to one of the few reserved seats in the Legislative Council, been appointed president of Ramnad district board (although his domicile was in Madura district) and moved in ministerial circles.[201] His associates kept a strong hold on Virudunagar town. Their methods of ruling Virudunagar, however, belied their claim to the natural leadership of the Nadar community. Other Nadars in the town, alleged a petitioner to government, 'suffered by high-handed acts and partiality and arbitrary refusal of licences because they would not come into line with the clique'; at local elections, the members of the clique were not beyond 'breaking heads' of Nadar opponents, and government commonly placed extra police in the Nadar wards at election times.[202] By the late 1920s, opposition to the clique and its methods had become extreme. New associations were formed to combat the clique's own Nadar Mahajana Sabha and its claim to undisputed representation of the community. Bombs began to go off in shops and properties belonging to the clique, and the police found a bomb factory near the town.[203] Nadars also flooded into Civil Disobedience to disprove the myth of Nadar loyalty and undermine the self-imposed leaders of the community.[204] K. Kamaraj, scion of a poor Virudunagar Nadar family, became one of the most prominent Congress organisers in the Tamil districts. The dissident Nadars were not only the less fortunate, but also included some of the wealthiest Nadar merchants of the town, who seemed quite prepared to go to jail for their cause.[205] Up to now, quoted a correspondent to *The Hindu*, 'the vociferous reactionaries of the Nadar community have deceived themselves and tried to deceive others into the belief that the community as a whole is opposed to nationalist progress'.[206] In Civil Disobedience, the Nadars set out to destroy the foundations of the clique's claims to community leadership and to government patronage.

[201] Hardgrave, *The Nadars of Tamilnad*, especially pp. 176–8.

[202] G.O. 2767 (LSG) 29 June 1926 MRO; 'A Gandhite', *Kamaraj the Shrewd 1903–40* (Madras, 1961), pp. 6–8.

[203] *Hindu* 28 July 1932, 7 Mar. 1934; *Police Report* (annual) for 1932, p. 17.

[204] 'A Gandhite', *Kamaraj the Shrewd*; V. K. Narasimhan, *Kamaraj – A Study* (Bombay, 1967); R. P. Kapur, *Kamaraj – The Iron Man* (Delhi, 1966).

[205] Among those arrested were A. S. S. S. Sankarapandian Nadar, a wealthy merchant, V. T. Thangappa Nadar and R. T. P. Subramania Nadar whose personal fortunes were reckoned at thirty and fifty thousand rupees respectively; *Hindu* 21 Mar. 1932, 9 July 1932.

[206] *Hindu* 6 June 1931.

In a time of stress such as Civil Disobedience, government was especially reliant on the help of its collaborators. Many of these took advantage of government's nervousness to consolidate their position and to extend their powers. Government sought help in combatting the plague of Civil Disobedience in a very lax fashion. It asked district Collectors to compile lists of loyalists and of waverers, and to do virtually anything which might secure the support of these men and goad them into action against the agitators. In several places, local politicians took the opportunity to present themselves as loyalists, form a loyalist association, secure a licence from government to fight the Congress and then wield their associations to more individual purposes. The Motheys in Ellore and A. T. Pannirselam in Tanjore both formed loyalist associations and then moved these associations, complete with their government support and influential contacts in the local bureaucracy, into service in local elections.[207] The Muslim leaders which the government tried to cultivate in Salem tried to use government's backing to promote their own and their followers' position in local affairs and finally precipitated communal rioting in the town.[208]

It was not only government's non-official collaborators, but also many of its official handmaidens, who took advantage of government's remoteness and nervousness. Administrative change over the past half-century had managed to drag the lower echelons of the bureaucracy out of the meshes of local influence and to arm them with stronger powers; it is not clear, however, that they had been brought under strict central control, and in Civil Disobedience, many of them made use of their elbow-room. Landowners and village leaders in several Circar districts complained that subordinate revenue officials had used the cover of Civil Disobedience to settle old scores. Village officers complained that antagonistic tahsildars had framed them and had them dismissed for taking part in agitation.[209] In consequence, many agitational outbreaks were aimed directly against particular government officers or offices. The police in particular took advantage of the conditions of Civil Disobedience. The administration of the police force had changed a great deal over the previous decade. In 1920, the Madras police force was poorly manned and badly controlled. The standard of recruits, government admitted, was 'almost everywhere very low', and it was difficult to find suitable candidates for

[207] *Hindu* 27 Sept. 1931, 17 Oct. 1931.

[208] *India in 1930–1*, pp. 560–3; *Hindu* 14 June 1930.

[209] G.O. 1075 (Public) 20 Oct. 1931 SAH; G.O. 760 (Public) 16 July 1931 SAH.

promotion. There was only one policeman to 1,250 of the population, and the force was obliged to rely on the village officers and their henchmen to perform fundamental policing duties. Such a force was bound to be difficult to direct. Even the regulars were controlled not so much by strict discipline as by a system of carrots and sticks; in 1919 a third of the entire force was punished for some offence, while nearly a quarter received rewards for some meritorious act.[210] Since Non-co-operation, however, the Madras police had been thoroughly overhauled. The village police were still used, but they were meted out four times as many punishments per annum and they were reportedly more obedient. Recruits to the regulars were now far better; virtually every policeman was at least literate, and the number of punishments had fallen off.[211]

While the force was now better equipped, it was more questionable whether it was better controlled. In Civil Disobedience government was obliged to underwrite the actions of its police; yet even government had to admit that the police had run riot twice in Madras City and once in Madura in 1930–1 and that there was a definite correlation between the indiscipline of the police in Tinnevelly and the steady growth of Congress support in that district.[212] Six of the nine major riots in the Tamil districts in 1930–1 involved the police, apparently as instigators. Unsurprisingly, many agitations were directed against the police. The police were attacked in Gudivada, Ellore and Sholinganallur and police stations damaged in Tindivanam and Gudiyattam.[213] The incident in Tindivanam exemplified how an aggressive and clumsy operation by the police could create trouble. The incident, which constituted the only tremor of Civil Disobedience in South Arcot district, began when the police arrested an influential, though somewhat shady, businessman named Somu Mudaliar. The police had been after Somu Mudaliar for some time and many townspeople felt that Civil Disobedience was merely an excuse for his arrest. On the way to be tried, Somu Mudaliar was driven in a cavalcade through the bazaar with the police flourishing batons and revolvers, and no-one, not even the accused's kin, was admitted to the courthouse. After this display of arrogance by the police, the bazaar rioted, the courthouse and

[210] *Police Report* (annual) for 1919, pp. 2–9, 15.

[211] *Police Report* (annual) for 1930, 1931 and 1932.

[212] FR July(1), GOI Home Political 18-vii 1930 NAI; FR April(1), GOI Home Political 18–7 1932 NAI; *Hindu* 4 Apr. 1932, 14 June 1932.

[213] *India in 1930–1*, pp. 560–3.

police station were besieged, and several policeman were beaten up.[214]

In Rajahmundry town, the arrogation of power and the opportunism of government's official and non-official satellites provided the background for one of the most violent and sustained campaigns of Civil Disobedience in the province. One faction in town affairs who looked to the raja of Pithapuram as their chief patron and who moved closely with local officials and policemen, took the opportunity of Civil Disobedience to harass the opposing faction, which was led by a lawyer K. V. R. Sami and a doctor P. Gurumurthi, was identified with the Congress, and had recently gained control of the municipality. Police appeared at municipal meetings and made life difficult for Sami as chairman, two of Sami's allies in the municipality were beaten up by the police and then arrested on charges of sedition, and a social function organised by Sami and others was violently disrupted by a police attack. When the local Bar Association protested, it was immediately proscribed on the grounds that it was an unlawful assembly. The atmosphere at the trial of the two 'seditionists', who both belonged to prominent local families, was highly charged and the result was farcical. The judge ruled that all but one of the prosecution witnesses had 'lied profusely', and that the entire case was the product of a conspiracy between the Deputy Inspector of Police, who wanted the glory of 'bagging' prominent Congressmen, and the politicians who wanted to disrupt Sami's municipal regime.[215] The two were acquitted, but this did not deter the police from their role in town politics and two years later, in a desperate attempt to bring the affair to an end, a plot was laid to murder the senior police officer in the town.[216]

In Dindigul, the police privately admitted that their actions were not always within the law. 'Of course', said the Deputy Superintendent after he had been accused of maltreating participants in a Congress demonstration, 'we beat these people. They are only town roughs hired by the Congress party. If we were to beat them in the streets, which we are legally entitled to do, people would be very upset .... Everyone knows they are beaten in the police stations and everyone approves.'[217] Government was largely obliged to let the police have its head; as one British official noted:

[214] *Hindu* 13 Mar. 1930, 19 June 1930; B. S. Baliga, *South Arcot District Gazetteer* (Madras, 1962), pp. 102–3.

[215] Y. Venkateswarlu, *The Peddapuram Incident* (Cocanada, 1931); *Hindu* 22 Jan. 1930, 15 and 22 Jan. 1932, 16 and 18 Mar. 1932, 14 May 1932.

[216] *Police Report* (annual) for 1933, p. 12.

[217] H. Trevelyan, *The India We Left* (London, 1972), pp. 143–4.

The police were continually attacked by the Congress party, which accused them of inflicting a variety of tortures on members of the party. They treated these attacks with indifference so long as the Government supported them and did not give way to demands for inquiries into their conduct whenever they were required to suppress a riot. The Government rightly refused to give way except in the most exceptional circumstances, for it would have been impossible to keep order if police facing a rioting mob were reluctant to act for fear of a subsequent political inquiry.[218]

During the truce period in 1931, the Tamil Congress leader Rajagopalachari wrote to government complaining that the fragile peace was threatened because government could not restrain the police.[219] While government could ignore such an avowed nationalist, there were other signs of resentment of police actions. On two occasions following police actions in Madras City, the major bazaars went on strike in protest and many of the most respectable and loyal citizens came out with open complaints about police repression.[220] In Coimbatore, Justicites like Shanmugham Chetty and moderates like C. V. Venkataramana Iyengar protested after a violent police lathi charge, and in the Circars even professional loyalists like J. Kuppuswami voiced criticism of the police.[221] M. Ramachandra Rao, an old Mylaporean, attributed the severity of repression in the Circars to excesses of zeal on the part of the police and subordinate bureaucracy; although there had been many complaints, he noted, 'no member of the Government nor any responsible official has visited the districts.... To say all this is not to justify the Civil Disobedience movement or to endorse the methods or actions of those carrying on this movement, but the Government have an obvious duty to prevent an unjustifiable and injudicious exercise of their power.'[222]

The Hindu, whose editors had originally opposed the idea of Civil Disobedience and only gave the movement a reluctant and qualified support, commented that it was 'difficult to believe that Government could tolerate or countenance forms of action of the kind that have been reported ... in the name of law and order'.[223] This same editorial

218 *Ibid.* p. 143.

219 GOI Home Political 33/30 1931 NAI.

220 *Hindu* 31 Jan. 1931, 22 to 28 April 1930.

221 *Hindu* 21 June 1930, 8 July 1930.

222 *Hindu* 8 July 1930.

223 *Hindu* 26 June 1930. C. R. Reddy resigned as vice-chancellor of Andhra University in protest against government suppression; he stated: 'The measures taken by the government to crush the Civil Disobedience movement are akin to terrorism, for which there can be no justification.' *Hindu* 11 July 1930.

contrasted the liberal outlook of the Madras Government in the 1920s with the indiscriminate and unwarranted repression that was now being practised in government's name. There were many others who felt that government had over-reacted to the threat of Civil Disobedience. When Civil Disobedience was brought to a close in 1933, the Madras Government crowed that in the Presidency the movement had been a 'complete failure'.[224] And yet the Government had once been intimidated enough to ask Delhi for permission to enact draconian measures of repression; it had watched its police force harry, injure and jail thousands of people; and it had allowed District Collectors to manipulate the distribution of irrigation water, the liquid gold of Madras agriculture, to win supporters and injure opponents, which was a desperate and dangerous measure indeed. In truth, Civil Disobedience had not been particularly serious in the south. In 1930–1, only 6 per cent of the total convictions for Congress activities in the whole of British India were in Madras Presidency, and many parts of the province had barely been affected at all.[225] But the Madras Government stood at an awkward corner of the imperial system, remote from the centres of decision in London and Delhi, and increasingly more remote from the realities of provincial society.[226] During Civil Disobedience Madras Government policies had been directed both from above, by the men in Delhi, and from below, by its handmaidens.

THE POLITICS OF DISENGAGEMENT

Civil Disobedience agitations threw into sharp relief many of the problems faced by the imperial rulers, problems which had largely been brought about by changes in the nature of imperial rule over the previous half a century. As a result of a long series of administrative reforms, the writ of government now ran far deeper into society

224 GOI Home Political 4/10 1933 NAI.

225 Convictions during 1930–1: in Andhra 2,878, in Tamilnad 2,991, in India as a whole 91,124. AICC papers file G5 of 1935 NMML.

226 H. Trevelyan was given the job of deciphering 'urgent' telegrams from the Government of India during Civil Disobedience. He soon found that his colleagues in the Madras Secretariat had a proverb, 'Delhi is far away', and he noted that 'the Government of Madras looked with an indulgent or irritated sense of superiority on the antics of the men at the centre who busied themselves sending unnecessary immediate telegrams and did not understand the south.' Trevelyan, *The India We Left*, p. 121.

than it had in the first century of British rule. Agricultural and industrial departments were engaged in regulating and developing the economy; the registrar of co-operative societies and government-sponsored banks were involved in the flow of credit; new acts had given government power to control local markets; government commissions had delved into agriculture, industry, banking, forests, railways, co-operatives, fisheries, tax, cotton marketing, zamindari and inam tenures, agricultural debt and labour; taxes had risen and proliferated. This invasion had brought forth a response, partly in resentful agitation, partly in the craft of politicians anxious to have some access to the resources which government now controlled. Government now faced the problems of managing the enlarged machinery of administration, of devising means to select Indian collaborators, and of arbitrating in the disputes of Indian politicians anxious to pluck the fruits of devolution. It was not clear that the imperial rulers could deal with these problems. Civil Disobedience had been helped along by men who objected to the relentless march of government, politicians who resented the rather arbitrary way that government selected its political allies and invested them with great powers, and agitators who demonstrated government's imperfect control over its own machinery by using that machinery to embarrass government itself.

The bureaucratic load had increased enormously between 1880 and 1930. The local government department was passing about a thousand orders a year in the 1910s, and five times that number in the following decade. Administration had also become more complex. Agricultural matters, for instance, were now dealt with in four separate departments: the Board of Revenue looked after surveys and settlements, the agriculture department looked after crops, the public works department looked after irrigation and the development department looked after agrarian credit. As government had become more complex, the summit of the great pyramid of power had grown steadily more remote from the base, and it was debatable whether the attempts to centralise the administration had done much to improve the power of the rulers to control and direct their own machinery.[227] The bureaucracy had expanded greatly in size and the

[227] '[Commission member] Q. Is there any department in this presidency in which the low paid subordinate is said to be above corruption? Can you name one? [Witness] A. I cannot name one.'
Report of the Forest Committee (Madras), vol. II, p. 580.

army of petty clerks was now mammoth,[228] but government was no more sure that its orders would be justly carried out or that its attempts at reform would be successful than it had been in 1880. The report on the progress of local government submitted to the Simon Commission offered a vast array of statistics on local boards, but had to admit that on the motives and activities of the new electorates 'the material available gives practically no information', and on the local boards' use of their powers 'the picture is necessarily in the nature of a rough and incomplete sketch'.[229] The Tax Commission in 1925 wearily concluded that any attempt to devise a new tax which would fall equitably on all classes of the population could result in nothing more than a 'tax on honesty', and suggested that the vast new bureaucracy was a hindrance to good government.[230] The machinery of government had proliferated and government had become far better equipped to impose its will on society. But it was equally becoming more and more difficult for the few men perched at the summit of this machinery to manage all its parts. The Royal Commission on Agriculture in India in 1924 was struck dumb when the head of the Madras agriculture department failed to answer elementary questions about crops, tenures and agricultural practices in the province.[231] The annual reports of the departments of the Madras Government had gradually been reduced from informative essays to bare lists of statistics with few annotations. In political matters, this ignorance was even more noticeable and there were many ready to exploit it. Emerging from a meeting with the Governor in 1923, minister K. V. Reddi Naidu expressed surprise at the number of lies his colleague, A. P. Patro, had just told the Governor about the Bengali Congressman C. R. Das who was currently on a visit to Madras; Patro explained, as Reddi Naidu conferred to his diary, that after hearing these exaggerations 'these fellows (Europeans including H.E. the Governor) will not be afraid of us. We must trade on Das'.[232]

Even before the depression and the agitations lent a greater sense of urgency to these problems, the initial steps were being taken to pull

[228] See above p. 47, table 4. The number of public servants in the Madras Presidency (excluding those earning less than Rs 35 a month) had risen from 6,344 to 27,245 between 1920 and 1927.

[229] *Indian Statutory Commission*, vol. V, Memorandum on the development and working of representative institutions in the sphere of local self-government, p. 1054.

[230] *Report of the Indian Taxation Enquiry Committee 1924–5*, vol. I, p. 215.

[231] *Royal Commission on Agriculture in India*, vol. III, pp. 270–303.

[232] Diaries of K. V. Reddi Naidu, entry for 14 June 1923.

government on to a new course. The Simon Commission had begun the task of writing a new constitution for India, a task which entailed the lengthiest report on Indian affairs ever assembled by the British, three Round Table Conferences, three years in a Joint Parliamentary Committee, several subsidiary reports on the franchise, financial relations and the like, and a disproportionate amount of the British Cabinet's time and the British parliament's time. The main consideration which shaped the final result was not any detail of the Indian administration, but the changing roles of India and Britain in the world. The British government thought that the Empire needed retrenchment if it was to survive. In India itself, the declining usefulness of the outmoded Indian army, the gradual decrease of British commercial dominance, and the growing difficulties involved in the administration of Indian finance suggested to the policy-makers that a drastic solution was necessary if the military, financial and commercial interests which had for many years formed the chief justification for imperial enterprise in India were to be maintained. The solution was to dispense with as many aspects of government in India as possible, in order to be able to concentrate imperial energies on those few aspects that really mattered. By handing many responsibilities to Indians, it was hoped to win their collaboration for measures which protected Britian's financial, commercial and military interests.[233] While plans went seriously astray and Whitehall's plans for an Indian federation never got off the ground, one decision which was taken early on in the reform discussions and which was of paramount importance, was that Britain had no further interest in the government of the Indian provinces. The Simon Commission concluded that the provinces should have autonomy, and that dyarchy should be abolished in favour of unitary government.[234] The White Paper on constitutional reform in 1933 confirmed this, and added that there would be no reservation of subjects in the provinces, and no officials placed in ministerships.[235]

Other changes affected provincial government in the 1930s. These stemmed not from the global calculations of British statesmen but from the calculations of British officials in the province itself. As before, the trend of British rule in India was changed according to the wishes of those at both the top and the bottom of government, and as

[233] B. R. Tomlinson, 'Imperialism, Nationalism and Indian Politics: the Indian National Congress 1934–42', Ph.D. thesis (Cambridge, 1973), pp. 7–79.

[234] *Indian Statutory Commission*, vol. II, pp. 33–6.

[235] *Proposals for Indian Constitutional Reform* (1933), pp. 17–19, 36–9.

before the changes were made quite pragmatically to meet new problems of government. The rulers in the province were reacting to those difficulties which had been so clearly shown up in the agitations of the early 1930s – the difficulties of playing the arbiter in the politics of locality and province as those politics became relentlessly more complex. Their solution was to withdraw from the details of administration, attempting at the same time to leave behind stern bureaucratic machinery which would function without them. This new strategy in the province was essentially the same as the new strategy of London; the policy of administrative expansion was brought to an end and replaced by the policy of disengagement. The British were beginning to disentangle themselves from the difficulties of ruling India, while taking some care to set up strong institutions to leave behind. Unsurprisingly, the effects of the policy were not always those that had been intended.

The new policy of the provincial governors showed up most clearly in reforms of the administration of temples, education, co-operative societies and local boards. In place of the policy, which had reached its peak in the 1920s, of setting up bodies of non-officials to help in administration and then monitoring their activities from the capital, the Madras Government in the 1930s took steps to free itself from involvement in these complex and difficult matters, and set up stern bureaucratic machinery to take the place of the watchful eye of the provincial government.

The district education councils, committees of elected and nominated non-officials set up in the early 1920s to help in the distribution of education grants, the preparation of schemes for extending education and other educational matters, were reformed by an act in 1935. This act made them apparently more liberal, by making them wholly elective, but at the same time it deprived them of most of their powers and gave the provincial government more powers to interfere directly with local schools.[236] 'The Government', complained one education council member, 'wants a non-official body like the District Education Councils simply to cross the "t"s and dot the "i"s of the inspecting officers and the Education Department.'[237]

Temple affairs followed a parallel course. In 1932, the Advocate-General ruled that the ministers could no longer nominate members of local temple committees, and thus these committees became wholly elective.[238] At the same time, government was passing a series of acts

[236] *Hindu* 28 Jan. 1935.
[237] *Hindu* 28 Oct. 1934.
[238] G.O. 1070 (LSG) 21 Mar. 1932 MRO.

which allowed the ministry and Endowments Board to by-pass the local temple committees altogether and administer temples directly. These acts allowed the provincial government to intervene in disputes over the management of specific temples, to dissolve a recalcitrant temple committee, to frame schemes for the administration of specific temples over the heads of the local committee, and to place any temple under direct government control.[239] A separate act removed the richest temple in the province at Tirupati from the management of a committee of elected men and placed it under a new committee nominated by government.[240]

Government also changed its policy towards co-operative societies in the 1930s. Since the early years of the century, the Madras Government had promoted co-operative credit societies with great enthusiasm, and by 1930 the province had 14,878 societies with 979,745 members.[241] Their loans only amounted to a very small fraction of the total flow of credit in the province, and they were run in most cases by rich landlords and moneylenders,[242] so they made little difference to the credit market. Yet management of a co-operative society was a responsibility which gave some local patronage and influence and it was also a post that could be fought over. Co-operatives had quickly been sucked 'into the whirlpool of politics'.[243] Witnesses before the Banking Commission spoke of 'the nasty system of catching institutions for election purposes'.[244] and government noted that:

> one feature of the movement... was its dependence on local board politics... Most elections in co-operative societies are now-a-days conducted on party lines. The result has been in some places to drive out of office gentlemen who have devoted themselves to co-operation and had not taken any part in municipal or local board politics.[245]

In the early 1930s, the policy of increasing the number of co-operatives

239 *Hindu* 2 Aug. 1934, 23 Jan. 1935; G.O. 2905 (LSG) 11 Aug. 1931 MRO; G.O. 4626 (LSG) 4 Nov. 1933 MRO; Chandra Mudaliar, 'State and Religious Endowments in Madras', Ph.D. thesis (Madras, 1961), pp. 193–225.

240 *Hindu* 25 Mar. 1933; G.O. 3259 (LSG) 15 Aug. 1932 MRO.

241 *Annual Report on the Working of the Madras Co-operative Societies Act* for 1930.

242 *Report of the Forest Committee (Madras)*, vol. II, p. 462; Thomas and Ramakrishnan, *A Resurvey*, pp. 52–4, 113; *Royal Commission on Agriculture in India*, vol. III, pp. 549, 647.

243 *Hindu* 21 Apr. 1934.

244 *Madras Provincial Banking Enquiry Commission*, vol. II, p. 366.

245 *Annual Report on the Working of the Madras Co-operative Credit Societies Act* for 1931–2, p. 5.

and placing them as far as possible under the supervision of non-officials, was thrown into reverse. The number of societies fell from 14,878 to 11,110 by 1936–7, and the number of members from 979,745 to 575,817. Non-official supervisors were replaced by government officers, and revenue department officials were brought in to help collect the vast arrears of repayments.[246]

The most complex and important changes came in the administration of local self-government. Many people involved in this, particularly the I.C.S. officers in the local government department in Fort St George, had realised the inadequacy of the structure set up by the acts of 1919–20 almost as soon as it came into operation. In 1922, they had convened a meeting to consider reorganisation of local government and had initiated files on different aspects of reform,[247] yet it was eight years before these moves reached any result. The I.C.S. secretaries in the local government department wanted to reform the local bodies along two lines. On the one hand, they wanted to extricate the Secretariat from the petty local disputes which filled its files with a seemingly endless stream of petitions and allegations, and took up so much of its time. 'Myself and the office staff', wrote one local government secretary, Hilton Brown, 'have spent large portions of our time grovelling amongst the dustheaps and cesspools of Guntur and similar places.'[248] On the other hand, they wanted more powers to bring troublesome local boards and troublesome board heads into line, and they wanted to impose more official control over the minutiae of local administration.[249]

Others in the province, however, had different ideas on the direction of reform. The ministers wanted to increase their powers to meddle in local affairs, while local politicians wanted a far greater degree of local autonomy. All these different interests had a chance to put their views[250] with the result that although bills reforming municipalities and rural boards were steamrollered through the Legislative

[246] *Ibid.* for 1936–7; B. V. Narayanaswami Naidu, *The Co-operative Movement in the Madras Presidency* (Annamalainagar, 1933).

[247] G.O. 2081 (LSG) 30 Oct. 1922 MRO; G.O. 2130 (LSG) 5 Aug. 1924 MRO; G.O. 2004 (LSG) 30 May 1927 MRO.

[248] G.O. 3416 (LSG) 17 Sept. 1931 MRO.

[249] G.O. 421 (LSG) 3 Feb. 1930 MRO; G.O. 484 (LSG) 7 Feb. 1930 MRO.

[250] A conference of M.L.C.s interested in local government was called in 1928. Several private members bills on local government reform appeared in the same year and government blocked them by agreeing to incorporate some of their provisions in its own bill. *Hindu* 14 May 1928, 18 June 1928; G.O. 1753 (LSG) 15 Apr. 1929 MRO.

Council by the government in 1930, they were not as purposeful as the secretaries had originally hoped. Thus over the next four years, Fort St George followed up with a series of executive orders which completed a drastic change in the character of local government.

Through the 1930 acts local bodies were opened up to an even wider range of interests. Taxes were increased, overall expenditure of local boards rose in the 1930s to the level of one-third of Madras Government expenditure, and more responsibilities were devolved onto local boards. They were thus even more attractive. At the same time, the franchises were widened. Any tax-payer in the municipal areas and any registered landowner or tenant in the countryside qualified for the electorate. The number of seats on local bodies was increased by roughly a third, while other than in exceptional cases all local board heads were now elected. Local bodies were thus made more accessible as well.[251]

Meanwhile the head of a local board lost many of the levers with which he could control the other members. His personal command of patronage was severely limited. The 1930 Act demanded that all minor appointments had to be ratified by the whole of the local board and all major ones by the Secretariat. Then between 1929 and 1934, most of the important staff under the local board – including the engineers, sanitary officers and education officers – were drafted into a newly established cadre of the provincial civil service;[252] their appointment, promotion, punishment and dismissal were thus taken out of the hands of the board head. The board chiefs also found that their untrammelled power over the issue of contracts was severely qualified. In 1933, government began to install executive officers, known as Commissioners, in the larger municipalities. Many chairmen rebelled against this removal of their own power as executive officers, but in a series of orders government made quite clear what roles the chairman and the Commissioner should now have: 'All municipal officers and servants are subordinate to the Commissioner. If a Chairman wishes to give any instruction to them he should do so only through the Commissioner' ran one G.O., which also emphasised that 'the functions of the Chairman are primarily those relating to the meetings of the council and its committees'.[253] In the district boards,

[251] For details of the acts see V. Venkata Rao, *A Hundred Years of Local Self-Government and Administration in Andhra and Madras States 1850–1950* (Bombay, 1960), pp. 39–40, 86–8, 111, 251.

[252] G.O. 4851 (LSG) 9 Dec. 1927 MRO; *Hindu* 25 Oct. 1934.

[253] *Hindu* 12 Jan. 1935, 8 Oct. 1935; G.O. 5215 (LSG) 4 Dec. 1934 MRO.

government also considered installing Commissioners or even putting the Collector back as an executive officer, but the measures were not carried through.[254]

Besides his control over patronage, the board head also lost his control over elections. Government passed an order placing the organisation of elections under the command of special officers from the provincial civil service.[255] Then in 1934 the taluk boards were abolished and the district boards were thereafter chosen by direct election.[256] This cancelled the district board president's ability to influence the membership of his board by meddling in taluk board affairs. Finally, the board heads could now be removed by their own board through a vote of no-confidence.

These reforms had three principal effects. Firstly, they made local boards both more attractive and more accessible. Secondly, they qualified the powers of the head of a local board and made it far more difficult for him to concoct a majority and stay in power without reference to local opinion. Thirdly, they made great changes in government's supervisory role and made it far more difficult for the ministers to secure the allegiance of the leaders of local government.

The new attractiveness and accessibility of local boards prompted another rush to get inside their portals. This fact, added to the economic and social instability of these years, gave local elections a new seriousness. In the 1920s there had been only one instance of violence arising out of local elections, when a candidate for a taluk board election in Madura in 1926 was shot as he filed his nomination papers and the president of the taluk board was tried for the offence and acquitted.[257] In the 1930s, such incidents became common. In 1930, the vice-president of Anantapur district board took a gang and gunned down an enemy in broad daylight, and a Cuddapah district board member caused a riot when he went to settle an old score.[258] 1932 witnessed the first violent incidents arising directly out of local elections, when there were riots during the polls in Chittoor, Ganjam, North Arcot and Trichinopoly.[259] In the following year, 'several

[254] G.O.s 482 and 484 (LSG) 7 Feb 1930 MRO; G.O. 421 (LSG) 3 Feb. 1930 MRO.

[255] G.O. 3416 (LSG) 17 Sept. 1931 MRO.

[256] *Tamil Nadu* 29 Dec. 1934 NNR.

[257] FR September (1), GOI Home Political 12-iv 1926 NAI.

[258] *Police Report* (annual) for 1930, p. 17.

[259] *Police Report* (annual) for 1932, p. 14.

people were killed and many injured', according to the police, in 'riots and outrages' over the local elections in Kistna and West Godavari, while a member of a Coimbatore taluk board was stabbed 'as a result of local election excitement' and the Tiruppur municipal chairman was put in the dock but subsequently acquitted.[260] In 1934, district board members in Tinnevelly and Nellore and municipal councillors in Bellary and Guntur were murdered, and in 1933 the Cuddapah municipal chairman was accused of murdering a rival during local elections and there were riots at the polls in Tinnevelly, South Arcot and Kistna.[261] All the features of local elections in the past were now writ large. Trichinopoly municipal elections in 1931 sparked off a totally uncharacteristic spate of communal rioting during which a Hindu mob dismantled the minarets of a local mosque,[262] while the Kistna district board elections in 1933 occasioned 80,000 petitions against the electoral roll.[263]

The reduction of the powers of board heads brought an end to the apparent calm of the internal politics of several local boards. Many municipal chairmen and a few district board presidents fell to no-confidence motions, while others had to fight much harder to retain their powers and privileges. P. S. Rajappa, who had managed Tanjore municipality for twelve years, resigned in a hurry in 1936 to avoid dismissal by the other municipal councillors, and complained: 'Some of the councillors either directly or indirectly are interested in municipal matters ... It is surely impossible to accommodate them all.'[264] He had never found much trouble beforehand, but he was not alone among local board heads in finding it difficult to create a local following now that the patronage of the local board head had been severely diminished. Many local board heads made a desperate and often indiscreet use of the reduced array of tools at their disposal. Mallipudi Pallamraju, as president of East Godavari district board, was alleged to have flouted the district board engineer in his distribution of contracts (some of which went to his relatives), given away trees cut down by the district board, employed several new clerks and teachers for personal rather than common benefit, issued rebates to contractors he wished to woo, and spent most of the village development fund in his

260 *Police Report* (annual) for 1933, pp. 11, 13.

261 *Police Report* (annual) for 1934, p. 13; *Police Report* (annual) for 1935, pp. 13, 15.

262 *Hindu* 1 June 1931; G.O. 3226 (LSG) 13 Aug. 1932 MRO.

263 *Hindu* 24 Jan. 1933.

264 *Hindu* 3 Nov. 1936.

own constituency. He was severely censured by government.[265] Violence began to invade board meetings. After a long spate of obstruction and criticism by his opponents, the Trichinopoly municipal chairman in 1934 rolled up his sleeves in a municipal meeting and challenged his enemies to a fight.[266] Bezwada municipality dissolved in chaos in 1933 when 'in a twinkling of an eye tables were thrown aside and a councillor got upon the table and began belabouring the one sitting opposite him', another councillor threw 'his tennis bat' at the chairman, and one faction of councillors was run out of the town hall by a mob.[267]

The confusion that the reforms had caused among the upper ranks of district politicians showed up most clearly in Coimbatore where the junto which had run local politics since the early 1920s with such a firm hand fell apart in a dramatic fashion. The junto consisted in the main of rich Gounder landed families with a few financiers and merchants, and between them they had shared out the plums of district politics for almost a decade. In the early 1930s they began to disagree over who had the best claim to occupy the district's seats in the Legislative Council, and these disagreements were sharpened by a dispute over the district board. In 1933, they split into two factions over the election of the district board president. V. C. Vellingiri Gounder won, but within months his powerful supporters had become totally disenchanted with his management of the district board. Much of the fault lay not with Vellingiri Gounder but with the machinery at his disposal, but this did not allay the growth of factional anger, particularly after a sexual scandal raised the tempers of both sides. One big Gounder landlord and member of the ruling clique had a clandestine affair with the wife of one of the others. When the landlord was found out, the cuckold allegedly lured him to a remote place and extorted Rs 25,000 from him as some sort of recompense. The extortion case which followed became a local cause célèbre and also an arena for the battle of the district factions, since the protagonists were members of the opposite sides in the now divided junto. The facts of the case, the guilt or innocence of the accused extortioner and then the level of his sentence became pawns in the fight for local control as both sides deployed their con-

[265] Letter from the Collector of East Godavari dated 19 Jan. 1933 and Report of the Inspector of Local Boards dated 9 Feb. 1933, in G.O. 459 (LSG) 25 Jan. 1934 SAH.

[266] Letter from P. Khalifullah dated 27 Apr. 1934, in G.O. 2185 (LSG) 4 May 1934 MRO.

[267] *Hindu* 4 Apr. 1933; Petition dated 1 Apr. 1933, in G.O. 1387 (LSG) 7 Apr. 1933 SAH.

tacts in the police, the local bureaucracy and the provincial government to have the case decided in their favour. By the end of the affair, the two factions were at daggers drawn and two of the most revered ritual leaders of the Gounder community were not on speaking terms.[268]

Local government had become more important than it had ever been before, but it had also become far more difficult for local bosses to control. On the one hand the new electoral rules and the new procedural rules qualified the bosses' powers; this forced them to look around for new ways to build up support in the locality. On the other hand, the old system which allowed local board heads great freedom to make their own rules was rapidly being replaced with a stricter, more bureaucratised system; many of the powers once wielded by local board heads were now given to civil servants. Local politicians quickly came to resent the new order, and they showed this resentment at a conference, called in 1935 to protest against what the president called 'the reaction against the principle of de-officialisation' in local government.[269] In his speech, the president complained that in the past few years,

> Legislative amendments were resorted to, rule-making power was indented for on an unparallelled and unprecedented scale leading to the circumscribing of every conceivable act or power permitting in the body of the local boards Act by a set of hide-bound consultations or approvals or sanctions . . . resulting in the undue complication of an otherwise simple field of administration by the introduction of the cancer of red-tape dilatoriness and the evils incidental to the 'bureau' system of office routine . . . the campaign was launched of withdrawal of power and executive authority from the non-official agencies and the revesting thereof in the various departments of Government.[270]

The Government Orders which accompanied the appointment of Commissioners in municipalities he called 'a cataract of unprovoked insults'.[271] The organiser of the conference added that 'it is well known what was given by the right-hand of legislative enactment was taken away by the left-hand of Executive orders'.[272]

Many of those attending this conference had been leaders of local government for some years, and had in that time been staunch sup-

[268] *Hindu* 20 Mar. 1935, 11 and 12 July 1935, 11 Apr. 1936; *Justice* 10 Apr. 1936; Sir Owen Beasley to Erskine, 7 Apr. 1936, and N. N. Sircar to Erskine, 30 May 1936, Erskine papers vol. V IOL; Vasudevaraja of Kollengode to R. K. Shanmugham Chetty, 14, 23 and 26 Mar. 1936, Shanmugham Chetty papers.

[269] *Hindu* 18 Feb. 1935.

[270] *Hindu* 18 Feb. 1935.

[271] *Justice* 18 Feb. 1935.

[272] *Justice* 2 Feb. 1935.

porters of the Justice ministry. The president of the conference, Yahya Ali, had been president of Nellore district board and had sat on the Justicite benches in the Legislative Council. The conference showed that leaders of local government no longer looked upon the ministers as their patrons, but rather as threats to their powers and privileges. The amending acts in 1930 and subsequent government rulings had hedged the administration of local boards about with bureaucratic rules, and had replaced most of the carrots, which the ministers had once had to offer to local politicians, with a powerful array of sticks.

The ministry lost most of the powers with which in the 1920s it had been able to cajole local politicians to recognise the importance of the ministers. The ministers could no longer nominate municipal chairmen or district board presidents (except in very exceptional circumstances). They could nominate only a few men from 'minority communities' to seats in local boards. They no longer had such extensive powers to intervene in local disputes. A new grant-in-aid code had cut back the ministers' personal authority over the allocation of government grants to local bodies, while the effect of the depression on government finance in general had reduced the amount of money the ministers had to offer to local bodies. Thus the new acts and rules had reduced the ministers' patronage. Meanwhile, Hilton Brown and other officials who had a hand in framing local government reform had ensured that the ministers had more powers to punish local board politicians who went astray. 'There is nothing in the whole Bill on which I feel more strongly', noted Hilton Brown.[273] The ministers were now given the power to remove a local board head, to fine any member or head of local boards for maladministration, and to dissolve local boards at will. These powers were now their chief weapons for controlling local government. The use of such harsh weapons was more likely to alienate local politicians than to win their support.

The ministry had few opportunities to woo the support of local board heads, although it had many ways in which it could punish them. Local board heads faced greater problems then ever before over local control, but when they looked to the ministry for help, the ministry could give none. In fact the ministry was more likely to take a hand in disciplining them. The conditions which had created a close relationship between ministers and local board leaders in the 1920s had disappeared. Reform in local government, education, temple administration and co-operatives was making it far more difficult for

[273] G.O. 421 (LSG) 3 Feb. 1930 MRO; G.O. 484 (LSG) 7 Feb. 1930 MRO.

the ministers to win the support of those who commanded the resources of local south India.

In many different ways, the political opportunities that had opened up in the 1920s seemed to be closing down in the next decade. Local board heads were losing power and patronage, co-operatives were coming under stricter supervision, temple and education boards had lost much of their political significance, and the ministers were being deprived of the tools to create a local following. At the same time, there were no general elections to the Legislative Council for over six years, and only two small adjustments in the personnel of the ministry.[274] Many more people had been drawn into the political system of the province in recent years, but it now seemed to those people that the system was ossifying. Frustration fuelled several of the agitations of Civil Disobedience. The main casualty, however, was the Justice party. The party had been built up around the political opportunities and the political institutions of the 1920s, and it declined with them.

THE JUSTICE PARTY IN DECLINE

The Justice party thrived as the provincial arbiter in the constitution inaugurated in 1920. By standing firmly across the gateway to Government House, it managed to secure a monopoly over the trickle of government patronage. This enabled the party to win over the few men of power in the localities and through them to exert influence throughout the province. The failure of the Swarajist challenge in the mid-1920s showed that for the moment the Justicites were safe since no other organisation could scrape up the resources to make a substantial challenge to their position.

By the early 1930s, the props of the Justicite edifice had begun to crumble. Firstly, local politics were no longer so stable. The extension of the scope of local government had politicised many, but the devolution of power and patronage had satisfied few. The economic hardship, freeze on credit and movement of population in the depression years undermined many of the most important bonds of local society, and turned discontent with local government into powerful movements of protest. Secondly, government had relieved the ministers of many of the most important tools of local control. The trickle of patronage appeared to be drying up. The Raj was making it more difficult for its

[274] The raja of Bobbili replaced B. Muniswami Naidu as chief minister in 1932; M. A. Muthiah Chettiar replaced S. Kumaraswami Reddiar in 1936; P. T. Rajan was a minister continuously from 1930 to 1937.

ministerial collaborators to govern. Shorn of important power and patronage, the Justice ministers became increasingly reliant on an ever-decreasing circle of friends.

Panagal had moved closely with two provincial Governors, Willingdon and Goschen, but after his death in 1928, no other leading politician possessed quite such a relationship with the fount of power. Of the three chief ministers who succeeded Panagal, Dr Subbaroyan was thought to be too indecisive, Muniswami Naidu was too close to certain leading Nationalists, and the raja of Bobbili was considered a 'yes-man' who had to be commanded rather than courted.[275] None of them enjoyed the full confidence of the Governor and the senior British officers.

Government was tired of the entanglements and the anomalies of dyarchy. The division of the provincial government into two parts – one 'reserved' for the Governor and his Council, the other 'transferred' to the ministers – had caused innumerable disputes between the two halves of the executive.[276] In London it had been decided that the Raj need no longer involve itself so deeply in the government of the provinces. The men in London and the men in Fort St George expected that trusted allies like the Justice leaders would continue to dominate provincial affairs, and they believed that the Justice leaders and their ilk could now be given the freedom that they craved.

Even before the end of the 1920s, however, the withdrawing of government's steadying hand had already threatened to unleash forces which would disturb the fragile stability of the Justicite regime. The members of the party, after all, were drawn together not so much to pursue a common aim as to compete for pieces of the same cake. In 1920, 1923 and 1926, it had been the Governor who had selected the victors in this competition by personally choosing the ministers. Yet in 1929, the Governor remained aloof while the Justice party met at Nellore to fight a grim battle over who should succeed Panagal as party leader. There were at least nine contestants and no firm decision was possible. In the end Panagal's old lieutenant, Muniswami Naidu, was chosen on a temporary basis in order to prevent the party disintegrating on the spot.[277] By omitting to call a party

[275] Answers to questions put by C. A. Bayly, Sir Christopher Masterman papers SAS.

[276] 'Rigid dyarchy is a standing challenge which either ranges Ministers against the reserved half of Government or exposes them to the charge of being the subservient tools of the bureaucracy.' *Indian Statutory Commission*, vol. II, p. 33.

[277] T. A. V. Nathan (ed.), *The Justice Year Book 1929* (n.p., n.d.) pt. IV.

conference for the next three years, Muniswami Naidu offered no opportunity for another contest over the leadership and so made his temporary position more permanent. After the 1930 elections to the Legislative Council, Muniswami Naidu and Dr Subbaroyan competed for the chief ministership. As on previous occasions, the Governor knew that whoever he selected would command majority support in the Justice party and in the Legislative Council. But unlike previous occasions, the Governor decided not to determine the issue by a simple fiat. Instead, he retired to the hills for a month while the two aspirants fought it out. By the time of his return, Muniswami Naidu had persuaded enough M.L.C.s to stand forth as his supporters and he became chief minister.[278]

This contest for the chief ministership accelerated the rivalries within the Justice camp. In order to emerge successful, Muniswami Naidu had had to construct alliances and make promises. His chief alliance was with P. T. Rajan, now one of the most prominent Justice politicians in Tamilnad. He had also to woo some of the other faction leaders in the party, particularly the Nattukottai Chetty bankers and the coterie of Velama zamindars who were the financial mainstays of the electoral effort. All of these groups expected some repayment for their support. Once he had secured the chief ministership, however, Muniswami Naidu found that he could not (or need not) satisfy all his backers. He gave the other two ministerships to P. T. Rajan and his close friend S. Kumaraswami Reddiar, and ignored the Nattukottais and the Velama zamindars. The Nattukottais were for the moment quite happy to drive from the backseat, but the Velamas had expected to be offered a ministership and felt that they had been double-crossed. In the months that followed, their distrust of Muniswami Naidu grew stronger. Muniswami Naidu refused to use his powers to help one of their number, the raja of Mirzapuram, in local board affairs. Muniswami Naidu's friend N. G. Ranga began to foment an anti-zamindari campaign largely in the estates owned by members of the Velama coterie and Muniswami Naidu himself appeared on the platform at anti-zamindari meetings. Finally, Muniswami Naidu introduced a bill to amend the Estates Land Act of 1908 in a way which would strengthen the legal position of the tenants vis-à-vis the zamindars. Throughout 1931 the zamindar coterie intrigued to bring down Muniswami Naidu. They secured the support of Patro, ex-minister and party organiser, and Mohammed Oosman, an Indian mem-

[278] *Hindu* 17 and 29 Sept. 1930, 3, 23, 24 and 25 Oct. 1930.

ber of the Governor's Executive Council, and persuaded P. T. Rajan to forsake his fickle alliance with Muniswami Naidu. Rajan then helped to bring over Kumaraswami Reddiar, the third minister, and managed to place his own satellites in control of both the party organisation, S.I.L.F., and the party newspaper, *Justice*. By 1932, Muniswami Naidu was having to manoeuvre carefully in order to avoid a motion of no-confidence either in the legislature or at a party meeting.[279]

Internal party disputes, as long as they had effectively been arbitrated by the Governor, had been fairly well insulated from the political turmoil of locality and province. Even the leadership question in 1929 had been debated solely within the select circle of Justicite leaders while all outside that circle sat resolutely on the fence and awaited the outcome. Now, however, the gates were opened for local quarrels to invade and swamp the party. While the dispute between Muniswami Naidu and the Velama coterie was shaped in the mould of previous factional battles, it was substantiated by a serious battle for local control in the Northern Circars. Here Muniswami Naidu's men and the Velama zamindars faced one another in local board politics and in rural agitations. In 1932, the periphery invaded the centre. Both sides in the contest loaded special trains with their local supporters and took them several hundred miles to do battle at the annual Justice Confederation in Tanjore.[280] Some 1,500 men made this trip from the Circars to Tanjore. The Velama coterie controlled the organisation of the conference – the reception committee was in their pocket and it had elected their leader, the raja of Bobbili, as conference president – and the first riot occurred when the organisers refused to issue tickets for Muniswami Naidu's pilgrims to enter the conference tent. After a siege, and a day to cool off, the conference opened and closed again within minutes as the two sides clashed, pelted each other with mud, smashed chairs and demolished the speaker's platform.[281]

Within a month, the Governor had persuaded Muniswami Naidu to resign, and had appointed the raja of Bobbili to the post of chief minister.[282] It is difficult to underestimate the importance of the

[279] *Hindu* 1, 6 and 17 Aug. 1932; statement by B. Muniswami Naidu in *Evening News* (Bombay) 9 Nov. 1932, cutting in Jayakar papers file 36 NAI; Stanley to Templewood, 23 Nov. 1932, Templewood papers vol. X, pt. 2, pp. 23–4 IOL.

[280] *Hindu* 12 Oct. 1932.

[281] *Tamilagam* 16 Oct. 1932, *Swadeshabhimani* 14 Oct. 1932 NNR; *Hindu* 10 Oct. 1932.

[282] *Hindu* 4 Nov. 1932.

Tanjore fracas, for after it the party could never be the same again. The constituent factions drew further apart, and the range of ideological positions covered by avowed members of the party grew even greater than it had been before. Patro and Reddi Naidu urged that the party should renounce its communal origins and forget that it ever stood for the political rights of non-Brahmans. P. T. Rajan and E. V. Ramaswami Naicker became even more adamant than before that the Justice party should be the political arm of a crusade against the Brahman. The raja of Bobbili and Mohammed Oosman (a Justicite who had been appointed to the Governor's Executive Council) urged that the Justice party stood for political conservatism. Ramaswami Naicker and K. M. Balasubramaniam wanted to make Justice into the party of the new socialism. Reddi Naidu stressed that loyalty to the British was an integral part of the Justicite creed. Muniswami Naidu and T. N. Ramakrishna Reddi urged the Justice party to make common cause with the nationalist movement.

The raja of Bobbili was no more successful than Muniswami Naidu in commanding the support of the many factions inside the Justice party. Under Bobbili's command, what little party organisation there was shrank still further. The Tamil paper *Dravidian* ceased publication at the end of 1932. The company running the English paper *Justice* went into liquidation a few months later. Bobbili put his personal wealth behind the *Justice* and kept it going, but he soon faced charges that he was running the paper as a personal, rather than a party organ. Some felt that he was far too autocratic to lead a party that claimed to be democratic, and they suggested that the Justice party could more realistically be restyled as 'the Bobbili party'.[283]

Intrigue within the party rose to a new peak. The Nattukottai Chetty group and a faction from Coimbatore led by R. K. Shanmugham Chetty pressed for a place in the ministry. Bobbili was obliged to ask the Governor if he could appoint a fourth minister in order to stem the rising tide of factionalism.[284] At the time of elections to the Delhi Legislative Assembly in 1934, these intrigues came to a head. The Justice party had never shown much interest in Delhi affairs and it fielded only two candidates for the fourteen seats. Both of these candidates were important and influential party members – R. K. Shanmugham Chetty, the wealthy Coimbatore banker and industrialist, and A. Ramaswami Mudaliar, a lawyer and publicist

283 *Hindu* 20 Apr. 1933, 8 Sept. 1933, 2 July 1934.
284 *Swadesamitran* 12 Oct. 1936 NNR.

who had been described as the brains of the Justice party. Both were beaten, not so much by the strength of their opponents' campaigns, as by the intrigues of their party colleagues. The wealthy Nattukottai Chetty bankers commanded great influence in the restricted Legislative Assembly electorate, particularly in the Commerce constituency where Shanmugham Chetty was a candidate, and in the Madras City constituency where Ramaswami Mudaliar was a candidate. M. A. Muthiah Chettiar, son of the richest Nattukottai of them all, raja Sir Annamalai Chettiar, was interested in getting either the Madras Mayoralty or the prospective fourth ministership, or both. In the Commerce constituency, he influenced voters to defeat Shanmugham Chetty, since Shanmugham might have obscured his chances for the fourth ministership, and in the City constituency he bargained his votes away to Ramaswami Mudaliar's opponent in return for the help the latter could give him in the forthcoming Mayoralty elections. After the results were out and both Justicites had been soundly beaten, there was a major row over Muthiah's manipulations.[285] The idea of a fourth minister, if it had ever been serious, was quietly dropped. Muthiah was censured, dismissed from his position as party whip, and virtually drummed out of the party. There, however, the affair did not end. Four months later, Muthiah in retribution for his treatment by the party filed a motion of no-confidence in Bobbili's ministry. Muthiah's talents were financial rather than political and the Governor, Lord Erskine, was horrified to find that instead of using the time-honoured methods of party intrigue to build up support for his motion, Muthiah was systematically attempting to purchase a majority in the legislature. 'If he were to use ordinary political methods', noted Lord Erskine, 'nobody could object, but he has set about getting his revenge by what can only be described as mass bribery . . . He is reputed to have spent Rs 30,000 up to now and to be quite prepared to spend another Rs 30,000 as well.' M.L.C.s proved to be too expensive, even for a Nattukottai Chetty banker, and the ministry survived the no-confidence notion. But Erskine was shaken. He noted: 'I must say that I thought I knew something about playing funny politics but I must take off my hat to these Indians. They are

[285] S. Guruswami and T. S. Kunjithan to R. K. Shanmugham Chetty, 19 Dec. 1934, raja Annamalai Chettiar to R. K. Shanmugham Chetty, 4 and 22 Dec. 1934, statement by R. K. Shanmugham Chetty dated 6 Dec. 1934, Shanmugham Chetty papers; GOI Home Public 311 1934 NAI; GOI Home Political 136 1934 NAI; *Hindu* 11 Dec. 1934; FR December (1), GOI Home Political 18-12 1934 NAI.

past masters at the art. The last few days have been an orgy of corruption and intrigue.'[286]

The tides of party factionalism changed so quickly that before the year had ended Bobbili and Muthiah were re-united in the face of threats from other members of the party, and Bobbili made Muthiah Chettiar a minister when Kumaraswami Reddiar had to retire because of failing health in 1936. In that year, Bobbili took a trip to England, to Erskine's despair, for now his colleague and kinsman the raja of Pithapuram led an attempt to supplant him as chief minister.[287] Bobbili in fact survived this, and throughout this period Bobbili himself was actively manoeuvring to make political alliances which would have displeased many of his friends. In mid-1934 he advocated entry of Brahmans into the party, privately floated the idea of a conservative coalition between his group and the Mylaporeans, and invited a leading Mylaporean to the annual party confederation.[288] Opposition to Mylapore had of course been the original raison d'être of the party. Then in 1935 he contemplated ditching his current ministerial colleagues for an alliance with Dr Subbaroyan (who was now almost in the Congress) and some Muslim leaders.[289] Finally in 1936 he tried, through the mediation of C. R. Reddy, to negotiate an alliance with some of the younger members of the Congress;[290] they presumably had no less in common with him than several current members of the Justice party.

The decline of the Justicites in the 1930s was exemplified in the failure of the Justice ministry to pass any important legislation. There were many amending acts, several of which cleared up difficulties in the administration of temples and local government, but in their passing the Justice ministers were little more than the tools of the Secretariat. Besides these, much time was spent on the bill to protect zamindari tenants, originally introduced by Muniswami Naidu. After Bobbili had replaced the latter as chief minister, he managed to change the character of the bill entirely. The measures for tenants were entirely

[286] Erskine to Willingdon, 11 Mar. 1935, Erskine papers vol. V IOL.

[287] *Times of India* 3 June 1936, cutting in Jayakar papers file 36 NAI; Erskine to R. A. Butler, 9 May 1936, Erskine papers vol. XIX IOL.

[288] *Hindu* 1 June 1934, 29 Nov. 1934.

[289] Erskine to Willingdon, 27 Apr. 1935 and 6 June, 1935, Erskine papers vol. VIII IOL.

[290] C. R. Reddy to Bobbili, 7 July 1936, C. R. Reddy papers file 31 of 1935–42 NMML.

emasculated, and new clauses introduced which served to bring tracts of land under inam tenure under the provisions of the 1908 Estates Land Act. By being omitted from the 1908 Act and thus being almost untroubled by legislation, inam lands in the province had become very valuable. To many contemporary observers, this Inams Bill, as it became known, seemed little more than an act of spite on behalf of Bobbili and his zamindar allies who had suffered from the 1908 Act, against all the inamdars who had luckily escaped.[291]

Justice, it seemed, could not prevail for much longer. The foundations on which the party had been built were fast falling away, and there seemed little possibility that the party could be rebuilt to suit the new circumstances of politics in the 1930s. Similarly, it did not seem that the imperium of the British in India could continue as it had done in the past. The policy-makers in London had admitted the need to draw in their horns; the administrators in Fort St George had thrown the policies of the past half-century into reverse. The crumbling of the old order made way for the new.

[291] *The Mirasidar* 12 Oct. 1936; correspondence on the Inams Bill in Erskine papers vol. V IOL; *Hindu* 22 Mar. 1934, 4 Oct. 1934, 4 Sept. 1936.

CHAPTER 4

The Ascent of the Congress

The changes in the structure of power between 1920 and 1940 sent reverberations throughout the province. The important corridors of power were creations of the British Raj, and until 1930 or thereabouts the British took some trouble to control access to them. The allocation of important jobs in the public services and the gift of ministerships under dyarchy were closely monitored by the provincial Governor and his aides. To seek favour and advancement, men had to present themselves to the rulers. But as the British began to disentangle themselves from affairs of locality and province, the ingredients of political success changed rapidly. In local government, the amendment acts of 1919–20 saw a considerable withdrawal by the Raj, yet the lingering influence of the ministers ensured that local politicians still had to focus their attention on the fount of imperial power. In the early 1930s the Raj started to withdraw from the provinces. The Governor stood aloof from the political intrigues of the ministers and their circle; he and the leading I.C.S. men took a smaller part in the affairs of the Legislative Council; and finally in the Government of India Act of 1935 the Raj virtually withdrew altogether from provincial government. Politicians who had before looked to please their masters, now had to look to please their constituencies. This was not a sudden change; for many years politicians had had to strive to please both the rulers and the ruled. Yet the 1930s was a time of crucial change.

Local politicians faced a decline in old systems of influence. In local government it had previously been imperative to have ministerial support; the constituency could be brought into line through alliance, bargain and threat, but no position of local power was safe without ministerial acquiescence. Similarly, it was an important ingredient of success at legislature elections to prove that one would be a useful delegate to the provincial forum and to do so a candidate had to display a network of contacts in high places; no constituency wanted to elect a man who could not deliver the goods. In the 1930s, the facts of political life were changing. The ministers were tied to old friends and shorn of many of their powers, the local boss could no longer hold down a constituency with ease and more people were anxious for a foothold in local and provincial politics. The old systems of alliance and transaction would no longer suffice.

There were two main implications of these changes. In the first place, they lent new significance to agitation, organisation and ideology as means to marshal political support; the proliferation of movements among labourers, tenants, castes and other social groups in the 1930s and the leadership of many of these movements by men who had once participated in the old style of politics were testimony to the new order of things. The career of N. G. Ranga encapsulated the changes in the circumstances facing political organisers. In the 1920s he adhered to the Justice party and won favours from the ministers; in the early 1930s, however, he gradually cut his links with the Justicites and by leading the anti-zamindari and resettlement campaigns, by helping with Congress organisation, and by promoting a new socialist ideology for Indian peasantry, he became one of the most prominent politicians of the decade.[1]

In the second place, it had become clear that it was no longer adequate simply to master and exploit the political rules made by the Raj, for these rules might and did change suddenly and traumatically. Nor was it enough just to bargain with the British who were making the rules. The story of constitutional reform by the Raj in India was full of anti-climaxes for Indian politicians; the biggest came in the 1930s when the process of reform began with no Indian on the Simon Commission, continued with the moulding of the new constitution to placate British rather than Indian politicians, and ended with the unimaginative and abortive scheme for an Indian federation. Indian politicians could see that nothing would suffice except complete control over the ordering of politics in India. It was this that had led the all-India Congress to resolve at its 1927 session in Madras that its goal was complete independence. Even the Justice party, for all its provinciality, had felt that it was necessary to seek political power on an all-India basis. Those Justicites who called for party members to enter the Congress in 1927 and 1928 in part justified this strategy by arguing the need for all-India organisation, while in 1930 the Justicites joined hands with non-Brahman politicians from Bombay to hold an all-India Non-Brahman Conference.[2] The Justicites returned to their provincial concerns in the 1930s and their all-India pretensions languished, yet the consultations over constitutional reform again

[1] N. G. Ranga, *Fight for Freedom* (Delhi, 1968).

[2] *Telagasanghabhwardhini* 29 Feb. 1930 NNR.

stressed the need for a national perspective; unlike Montagu who in 1918 had listened to deputations from provincial organisations, Sir John Simon listened mainly to petitions from groups which could claim to have an all-India significance, and in the Round Table Conferences in the early 1930s the stress was on the need for all-India prescriptions for reform.

The way was being opened up for the Congress. Its stated aim was to take over the entire structure of the Raj, and beyond that its ideology was eclectic and uncontroversial. It promised to provide a framework for organisation at every level of the political process from locality to nation, even if the framework was as yet more potential than actual. Thus in the mid-1930s, the Congress was invaded by many who felt the need for new styles of political organisation and who saw the Congress as the appropriate vehicle. It would be misleading to say that the Congress recruited these new members; they entered the Congress and shaped it to suit their own ends.

THE PROVINCIAL CONGRESS

The Congress had a fitful and uneven history in south India. Before 1920, it had been led from Madras City by a cluster of some of the most successful Indian lawyers and administrators, and the barometer of its activity had risen and fallen according to the willingness of the rulers to admit these men into the corridors of power. In the period 1916–22, the irruption of new forces into the world of provincial politics, the indecision of the old Congress leaders over the new legislatures, the arrival of Gandhi on the all-India stage and the explosion of Non-co-operation agitation had equipped the provincial Congress with new aims, new policies and new leaders. C. Rajagopalachari led a batch of leaders from the Tamilnad mofussil – men like the clan head and doctor P. Varadarajulu Naidu, the banker T. Adinarayana Chetty, the businessman and ex-chairman of Erode municipality E. V. Ramaswami Naicker, the doctor T. S. S. Rajan and the publicist T. V. Kalyanasundara Mudaliar – into control of the newly established Tamilnad provincial Congress. In the new Andhra provincial Congress, old leaders like Konda Venkatappayya and A. Kaleswara Rao and new men like Dandu Narayana Raju and Bikkani Venkataratnam came together and for two years helped to organise the campaigns of Non-co-operation.

Meanwhile Gandhi wrote for the Congress a new constitution which included an all-India working committee capable of keeping

Congress active throughout the year, a scheme for membership with a four-anna subscription, and a hierarchy of committees reaching down from the all-India working committee to the province, district, taluk and village.[3] But while these important years grafted new elements onto the Congress, the old were not entirely superseded. Many of the old leaders, who had apparently been pushed aside by the Gandhians, returned to the Congress in the mid-1920s. Gandhian agitation had to take its place as only one weapon in the Congress armoury, and the old constitutionalist strategies returned from time to time. The new Congress constitution provided the framework for an elaborate organisation but could not ensure that this framework would be filled. As in the years before 1920, periods of intense nationalist activity were interspersed with periods of stagnation. In the years 1923–5 and 1927–9 the Congress organisation was as skeletal and as sketchy as at any time in its history. Even in the years of activity, the Congress made little progress towards the acquisition of a firm organisational base. Throughout the decade the Andhra and Tamil provincial Congress committees found it difficult to collect subscriptions, and in years like 1923–4 and 1928–9 the coffers were empty.[4] The most important decisions on Congress policy were still taken in small gatherings. Only 218 persons came to the meeting which swung the Tamilnad Congress into Non-co-operation in 1920. Roughly the same number went to the conference which abandoned agitation in favour of the Swarajists' constitutional strategy, and only 600 were present when the Tamilnad Congress turned back to Civil Disobedience in 1929.[5] By the end of the decade only 7,500 Tamils and Andhras, around 0.02 per cent of the population, claimed membership of the Congress.[6]

Yet the years 1916–22 had broken the Congress loose from its old moorings and left it to be blown along on the prevailing winds. Thus the twists and turns of the Congress policy in the decade re-

[3] Gopal Krishna, 'The development of the Indian National Congress as a mass organisation, 1918–23', *Journal of Asian Studies*, XXV, 3 (1966).

[4] AICC papers files 5 of 1926, 7 of 1920–6, P24 of 1929, P30 (i) of 1929 NMML; *Hindu* 5 Aug. 1924; D. Gopalakrishnayya, after seeing Sambamurthy elected president of the Andhra Congress in 1924, wrote to a friend: 'God be with him. It is a thoroughly bankrupt throne ... I am just wondering how the big guns fell off the office in such an unchivalrous manner, in time of its dire need, after having enjoyed all its weather and warmth in the days of all-round plenty. There is no money, no members, no methods.' D. Gopalakrishnayya, *Letters* (Bezwada, 1934), p. 73.

[5] *Hindu* 21 and 28 July 1921, 6 Sept. 1923, 2 Sept 1929.

[6] AICC papers file P30(i) of 1929 NMML.

flected not merely factional, ideological and tactical battles within the Congress but rather movements in the affairs of province and nation. In the 1920s, the Congress did not have the organisational resources to create and direct the trends of politics in the province. The Congress was able to mould, interpret and express movements which originated outside the organisation. In 1921–2, the Congress capitalised on several loosely related agitations to create the Non-co-operation movement. These agitations grew out of changes in administrative practices, disappointment at the constitutional reforms, economic dislocation, changes in taxation and changes in local government; they were only very indirectly related to the cause of nationalism. Congressmen and Congress funds, however, helped to organise and direct these agitations, and the Congress press gave them a wide hearing.[7] Again in 1924–6 the success of the Congress Swarajists in local board and legislature elections was built on the widespread feeling in the localities that new methods and new resources were necessary to mount a challenge to the interests that were rapidly becoming entrenched in positions of local and provincial power. The Swarajists provided a provincial and national platform, offered some organisational assistance and promised to deliver the goods.

Similarly the Congress was returned to an agitational strategy in 1930 not simply because of the machinations of a handful of leaders, but because of broader developments in the province. The demand for a return to agitation had been building up amongst political workers for three years, while the Congress leaders had actively tried to resist the trend. The first signs of frustration at the course of provincial politics had come in 1927, when young political enthusiasts in Madura had decided that the statue of a British officer who had been active in suppressing the 1857 revolt in northern India was an irksome symbol of imperial domination and they had demonstrated against it.[8] In the same year, others in Madura had marched through the streets carrying decorative swords to protest against the act which forbade Indians to carry weapons.[9] In 1928, other political organisers had helped to foment a strike among workers on the South Indian Railway,[10] and to stage demonstrations against the visit of the Simon Commission. After the first Simon demonstration in Madras City ended in an embarrassing display of violence, the Congress leaders

[7] C. J. Baker, 'Non-co-operation in south India', in C. J. Baker and D. A. Washbrook, *South India: Political Institutions and Political Change 1880–1940* (Delhi, 1975).

[8] *Hindu* 22 Sept. 1927.

[9] *Hindu* 17 June 1927.

[10] *Hindu* 4, 6, 8 and 31 Oct. 1928.

kept the capital quiet, but in many mofussil centres there were large demonstrations against the all-white commission.[11] In 1929, a Tinnevelly politician noted that although the provincial organisation of the Congress was dormant, 'there are signs of revolt everywhere which show that the [nationalist] movement is progressive'.[12] When the gathering of 600 in November 1929 voted for the provincial Congress to resume agitation, it was mounting a bandwagon that had already begun to roll.

The continuity of the provincial Congress in the 1920s was maintained less by any organisational framework than by the activities of a small number of Congress leaders. Men like Rajagopalachari and Satyamurthi in the Tamil districts, Konda Venkatappayya, Kaleswara Rao and Tanguturi Prakasam in the Andhra districts, were firmly committed to the idea of a Congress movement. Beyond these small circles of Congress leaders, however, the support for the Congress differed very widely from year to year. Many of the village officers, temperance reformers and local politicians drawn into the Non-co-operation agitations had no part in the Swarajist Congress. Many who had been elected to local bodies and legislatures in the name of Congress in the mid-1920s withdrew gracefully when the Congress turned back to unconstitutional methods. Nor was this simply a split between constitutional and agitational support; Civil Disobedience and Non-co-operation drew on very different areas of support. E. V. Ramaswami Naicker was one of Rajagopalachari's leading lieutenants in Non-co-operation, and he organised one of the most impressive temperance campaigns in the province in 1921. By 1925 he had moved away from the Congress and in 1930–3 he and his followers helped government and Justicites to counter the Congress agitations. Similarly the Mothey family of Ellore, who celebrated Non-co-operation with great éclât, helped government to organise loyalist associations during Civil Disobedience.

Congress in the 1920s was little more than the sum of its parts. It was continually being recreated by its ever changing bases of support and it differed not only from time to time but also from place to place. At the provincial level, this was obvious in the difference between the Andhra and Tamilnad organisations. In Tamilnad, the agitational and constitutional parties in the Congress were fairly distinct. The agitational cadre was a legacy of the Non-co-operation years. After the close of the movement, a small group of leaders and party workers

[11] *Hindu* 30 Jan. 1928, 4, 6, 7 and 8 Feb. 1928. [12] *Hindu* 15 Aug. 1929.

wholly committed to Congress work retired into ashrams, 'National education' institutions and khaddar organisations. C. Rajagopalachari, their acknowledged leader, set up a Congress ashram near Tiruchengodu in Salem.[13] Much of the energy of this group went into the development of the khaddar industry. They spun yarn by hand, organised schemes for collecting hand-spun yarn from outlying rural areas and made arrangements for marketing.[14] With the great promotion of khaddar as a symbol of national regeneration, the khaddar industry was soon a financial success.[15] Khaddar profits, and the benefactions of wealthy patrons, allowed the cadre of Gandhians to continue their 'constructive work'.[16] They developed the Congress ideology, kept up a constant flow of Congress propaganda in newspapers, journals and pamphlets, undertook projects of social reform and village uplift, and participated in occasional agitations. The Gandhians had little interest in the politics of dyarchy, and for most of them it was true that even if they had an interest, they did not command the resources necessary for entry into that world. Thus these agitational leaders battled hard to hold on to the Tamilnad provincial Congress organisation and keep it out of the hands of the constitutionalists who wished to use Congress in local and legislature elections.

The constitutionalist faction was led by men like S. Srinivasa Iyengar, Satyamurthi and A. Rangaswami Iyengar who were stationed in Madras City, who had good contacts among the local political elite of the province, and who could from time to time get elected to the legislatures. They believed that with the backing of a strong constitutionalist Congress, they could force their way into the halls of government. They drew support from men involved in the affairs of locality and legislature and their tactics, as the Swarajist campaign showed, mirrored those of the Justicites.

In Andhra, the Congress was not divided into two such distinct parts. Andhra too had its agitational cadre and there was an ashram at

13 Kausikan, *Rajaji* (Madras, 1968); N. Perumal, *Rajaji* (Madras, 1953); K. Baladandayutham, *Jiva – Valkkai Varalaru* (Madras, 1966), pp. 8–20.

14 For accounts of khaddar work see S. Ramanathan, *Gandhi and the Youth* (Bombay, 1947); M. Chenna Subba Rao, *Myself and Rural Life* (*Autobiography*) (Anantapur, 1951), pp. 9–11.

15 See report of the Tamiland branch of the All India Spinners Association for 1925–6; khaddar sales in Tamilnad in 1924–5 were worth Rs 737,356, in 1925–6 Rs 877,628, and in 1929–30 Rs 1,616,524. *Hindu* 26 Nov. 1926, 25 Sept. 1932.

16 *Hindu* 1 Aug. 1936.

Seetanagram outside Rajahmundry, a fine national school in Masulipatam, and khaddar organisations in several towns. But these activities were not set apart from other political concerns. Konda Venkatappayya who ran the khaddar organisation, was involved in local politics in Guntur for thirty years;[17] Dr Subramaniam, who ran the Seetanagram ashram, sat on municipal councils and local boards in East Godavari; and Bulusu Sambamurthy who cultivated a Gandhian image just as ardently as Rajagopalachari was up to his neck in the torrid politics of Rajahmundry town. The Andhra Congress in other words was not split down the middle like that of Tamilnad. The reason for this difference lay in the fact that the Andhra Congress was almost the exclusive property of the Kistna–Godavari tract, and in this 'wet' area the problems of political control were entirely unlike those in the 'dry' region which characterised most of Tamilnad. Here there was no firm control over the countryside by rich landlords and moneylenders, local politics were unstable, agitations common, and political organisations of all kinds were an intrinsic part of everyday political life. In such a region, the Congress already in the 1920s functioned as a useful vehicle for the protagonists of local politics. For some time, the name of the Congress had been bandied about in local elections both in town and countryside. In many of the towns the faction fights of local politics already took place within the Congress organisation; elections to local Congress committees, allocations of Congress candidatures at elections, the choice of delegates to the provincial Congress committee were all matters for acute competition between local parties. It took, for instance, twenty-two hours to choose the executive committee of the Andhra provincial Congress in 1924 and even longer to debate whether the provincial Congress should have a cabinet system in the executive or not.[18] Questions of Congress strategy, such as the motion on 'complete independence' which the Andhras discussed relentlessly between 1925 and 1927, taxed the Andhra Congress leaders in a way that their Tamil counterparts would not have understood.[19]

Organisation and agitation played a large part in the local politics of the deltas. There was thus little distinction in the Andhra Congress between an agitational and a constitutional party. The ashramites took part in local politics, and local politicians patronised the ashra-

[17] K. Venkatappayya, *Sviya Caritra* (Vijayawada, 1952 and 1955), passim.

[18] *Hindu* 10 July 1924, 23 Oct. 1924.

[19] M. Venkatarangaiya, *The Freedom Struggle in Andhra Pradesh (Andhra)*, vol. III (Hyderabad, 1965), passim.

mites and deployed them and their agitational resources in the politics of local boards. It was thus that in 1931 the Madras Government came to find the institutions of local government in the Andhra deltas littered with men practising Civil Disobedience with the help of local board machinery. The sources for support for the Congress in Andhra were as fluctous as elsewhere, yet the organisation here had marginally more elaborateness and more permanence.

While the years of Civil Disobedience placed Congress firmly in the centre of the political stage, the involvement in agitation did not automatically equip Congress with a better substructure of organisation. Only 200 persons attended the meeting in Madras City to mark the start of Gandhi's salt march.[20] The agitational leaders were so afraid that the movement in the south might be a fiasco that they resolved to concentrate their efforts in a small area. Rajagopalachari planned a salt satyagraha on the Tanjore coast and arranged for committed Congress workers from all the towns of Tamilnad to converge on the spot,[21] while Andhra leaders planned a similarly concentrated demonstration in Guntur.[22] The provincial Congress organisations in both Tamilnad and Andhra were out of pocket and issued desperate appeals for funds.[23] District and taluk Congress committees had fallen into disarray; a report compiled by the Congress leaders themselves after six months of Civil Disobedience revealed that Congress organisation was still in a depressing state. Coimbatore district had no Congress committee; in Ramnad, North Arcot and Tinnevelly there were committees but no funds and no offices; in Chingleput there were only twenty Congress workers; in Salem and Tanjore there was no activity at all; as for Madras City, the report stated: 'Today there is not one man in Madras City who though he may have full sympathy with the Congress and would like to do some work for it has got the courage of his convictions. . . . Prominent men have chosen to remain in the background and with them their followers who are a good number.' Many blamed the apathy on organisers of the salt satyagrahas, for these agitations had allowed the government to arrest the cream of the province's Congress workers in convenient batches. Rajagopalachari's plan was called 'tactless', and Nageswara Rao noted that following government's arrest of a few leaders in Andhra 'there is

[20] FR March (1), GOI Home Political 18–3 1930 NAI.

[21] T. V. Kalyanasundara Mudaliar, *Valkkaik Kurippukkal* (Madras, 1969), pp. 396–7.

[22] Venkatappayya, *Sviya Caritra*, pp. 348–50.

[23] *Hindu* 17 Mar. 1930, 1 Apr. 1930.

a complete dearth of workers and the movement has come to a standstill'.[24]

These reports were in fact compiled only a few weeks before the 1930 harvest, when the depression began to bite and the tensions that were to make Civil Disobedience a success in the province came to the surface. In 1931 and 1932, Congress activity and organisation reached new levels. When the resettlement campaign began, Congress membership in Andhra jumped from 4,500 to 30,000 in two months,[25] and later Kistna Congress workers noted how the coincidence of falling prices and government's resettlement operations helped them to enrol 5,000 new members in a few months.[26] During the truce in 1931, Congress leaders in both Tamilnad and Andhra sped round the districts enrolling members, setting up committees and finding new local leaders.[27]

But this rapidly established organisation was equally rapidly smashed. When the truce between Gandhi and Irwin collapsed in early 1932 the government proscribed all these committees, ransacked their offices and impounded whatever funds and papers they possessed.[28] Thus in the end, the organisation of Civil Disobedience was even more localised than the organisation of Non-co-operation had been. Most of the peripatetic organisers and other members of the Congress agitational cadres (who had helped give some unity to Non-co-operation) spent most of the period of Civil Disobedience behind bars. Whereas the organisational machinery in 1921–2 had been oiled with generous grants coming from Gandhi's Tilak Swarajya Fund and from the A.I.C.C. and distributed by the provincial Congress leaders, the funds for Civil Disobedience agitations had to be found locally. The Madura agitations for instance, were supported by the big Saurashtra patrons, one of whom was said to be pouring Rs 1,500 a month into the agitation while he himself sat in a jail.[29] The provincial leaders found it difficult to control and direct the agitation. Rajagopalachari was annoyed to find that his wish for a concentrated salt satyagraha

[24] Report on satyagraha in south India, in AICC papers file G116 of 1930 NMML.
[25] Reports from the Andhra provincial Congress dated 4 July 1929 and 14 Sept. 1929, in AICC papers files P30(i) and P30(ii) of 1930 NMML.
[26] Report on Congress work in West Kistna district, in AICC papers file P2 of 1932 NMML.
[27] *Hindu* 9 Mar. 1931, 23 and 30 Apr. 1931, 1 and 16 May 1931.
[28] FR January (1), GOI Home Political 18–1 1932 NAI; FR January (2), GOI Home Political 18–2 1932 NAI; FR February (2), GOI Home Political 18–4 1932 NAI.
[29] AICC papers file G116 of 1930 NMML; for other examples of local fund raising see *Hindu* 1, 4, 7, 12 Apr. 1930.

in Tanjore was ignored and that other leaders started their own demonstrations in Madras City and in South Arcot.[30] Similarly in Andhra the idea of a unified and concentrated campaign collapsed and salt was made illegally at many places up and down the coast. The code of non-violence advocated by Gandhi and many of the provincial leaders of the agitation received little respect. There were several violent riots, assaults on the police, on officials and on official buildings, arson of liquor shops, and minor terrorist outrages. One Tamil pamphlet published in the cause of the temperance campaign showed on its cover a cartoon of the Mahatma in a scarcely non-violent mood laying waste to toddy trees with an outsize axe.[31]

FROM AGITATIONS TO ELECTIONS

'The movement', crowed the Madras Government as Civil Disobedience was brought to a close, 'had proved a complete failure and the local Congress party was well aware of it.' This was not even smugness, but sheer bravado, for the Madras Government had never before been so successfully intimidated. However, government went on to point a finger of ridicule at the fickleness of Congress tacticians by noting that *The Hindu* had in recent weeks 'in a sudden volte face confessed the hollowness and failure of the tactics that had hitherto been employed and invited a free discussion on the course which a reorientated Congress policy should pursue'.[32] But paradoxically, and to government's ultimate dismay, the Congress grew rather than lost in stature with the collapse of its agitational campaign.

When the Congress dropped its policy of defying government and defying the law, it quickly became respectable because there were so many people who wanted to use it for respectable and constitutional ends. From the early years of the decade, some of the most influential and experienced politicians in the province had shown their disillusionment with the Justice party by cutting their ties with the party and starting out to seek a vehicle more suited to the political circumstances of the decade. Many of these had been reliable followers of the ministry for some years, and several of the defections evidently came after the ministry had been faced with a difficult decision over the distribution of local patronage. M. K. Reddy had been head of the district board and a Justicite satellite in Chingleput in the 1920s,

[30] Kalyanasundara Mudaliar, *Valkkaik Kurippukkal*, pp. 396–7.
[31] Pamphlet enclosed in G.O. 425 (Public) 24 Apr. 1931 MRO.
[32] GOI Home Political 4/10 1933 NAI.

but in the early 1930s when he had a row with his local lieutenant and the ministry backed the latter, Reddy crossed the floor.[33] Other local politicians were distressed to find that the ministry could no longer control them with gifts, and so was trying to continue to control them with coercive powers. Yahya Ali of Nellore moved away from the Justicite benches and chaired the conference that criticised the changes in government policies towards local boards after the ministry had tried to bring him into line with threats of disciplinary action.[34] By 1932, a nationalist party had come together in the Legislative Council. It was led by old Swarajists and by Justicite defectors, and although its members abjured any connection with Civil Disobedience they pressed motions in support of temperance and other aspects of the Congress agitation, and fulminated against the excesses of the police and other officials. In parallel with the Congress policy to boycott foreign cloth and other foreign products, several of the nationalist M.L.C.s began a 'Buy Indian League'. While this was chiefly engaged in promoting Indian products and establishing marketing outlets for them, government suspected that it also helped raise funds for the Congress agitation.[35]

While such men were not prepared to give their immediate allegiance to an illegal organisation, it was clear where their sympathies lay. In other areas of political life, the movement towards the Congress was more direct. Both in the truce period of 1931 and following the lift of the government ban on organisations in 1933, new Congress committees sprang up in many localities. In the 'dry' region, district Congress organisations appeared in many places where they had never or only very intermittently existed before. In the deltaic region, where local Congresses were more firmly established, the local organisation bulged at the seams. In West Godavari there was a long battle for the control of the district Congress between men from the district headquarters who had run the committee in the 1920s and men from the rural areas many of whom were new adherents.[36] In Guntur, the irruption into the Congress simply could not be contained; in 1931 three, and in 1933 two separate district Congress committees appeared simultaneously and argued with one another over their claims to legitimacy.[37]

[33] G.O. 3342 (LSG) 20 Aug. 1930 MRO; *Hindu* 20 Mar. 1930.
[34] *Hindu* 17 Sept. 1932.
[35] FR March (1), GOI Home Political 18–5 1932 NAI.
[36] *Hindu* 13 Jan. 1935.
[37] AICC papers file G29 of 1934 NMML; *Hindu* 16 Aug. 1931.

During the truce in 1931, Satyamurthi urged that the Congress should get involved in local elections as it had in 1925–6. The recent reforms of local government, he noted, 'have abolished nomination and indirect election, have made all [tax-] assessees voters, and have vested the right to conduct elections in revenue officers. Therefore elections to these bodies have recently become easier for a democratic organisation like the Congress.'[38] In 1931 Satyamurthi and other Congress leaders helped in local elections under the new rules. Even the Gandhian die-hard Rajagopalachari took a hand in municipal elections in Coimbatore.[39] In East Godavari, local elections in 1932 were conducted under the Congress banner, although the Congress organisation was under a ban at the time, and the Congress candidate for district board president was defeated by the narrow margin of a single vote.[40]

In 1933 Satyamurthi and his allies took their argument a stage further and proposed that the Congress should again invade the legislatures. They were encouraged to take this step not only because tremors in the political life of locality and province intimated that such a step would gain support, but also because announcements by government on the course of constitutional reform revealed that Indian politicians would soon be entering a new, bewildering era in which the Congress could assume unprecedented significance. In March 1933, government published a white paper outlining its proposals for constitutional reform in India.[41] Although this document contained no details on such matters as the franchise, it showed that London was planning to hand provincial government over to Indian ministers responsible to enlarged provincial legislatures. Following this publication, Satyamurthi's polemics became more pointed and more persuasive:

> Swadeshi, removal of untouchability and khaddar are all right in their place, but they cannot take the place of real live political work. It is also ideal to speak of or write of economic and social Utopias unless they are related to everyday political work in the country . . . these reform proposals represent perhaps the last attempt of the foreign bureaucracy to try and govern this country, as long as possible, with the help of communal die-hards. . . . The practical question then is, how to harness all progressive political and national forces . . . so as to revive political life in the country, and to replace communalism by robust nationalism in all our affairs. The only practical

[38] *Hindu* 5 June 1931. [39] *Hindu* 24 Nov. 1931.
[40] *Hindu* 25 Sept. 1932, 23 Jan. 1933.
[41] *Proposals for Indian Constitutional Reform* (London, 1933).

solution seems to be to organise the thirty and odd million electors who will most probably be enfranchised under the reform proposals. No political party dare ignore this electorate and hope to carry on an effective political or economic programme. . . . To attempt to ignore the Councils while paying the taxes levied by them, obeying the laws made by them, is to attempt to play at revolution.[42]

In the mid-1920s the transformation of the Congress after Non-co-operation from an agitational to a constitutionalist organisation had been laborious; it took three years, innumerable meetings and innumerable speeches. In comparison the similar transformation at the end of Civil Disobedience was almost effortless. Satyamurthi began his council entry propaganda in March 1933. Rajagopalachari and other Civil Disobedience leaders meeting in August were reluctant to try and carry on further Civil Disobedience agitation, and reluctant to mount an opposition to Satyamurthi.[43] In September a group of old Mylaporeans and dissaffected Justicites proposed forming a party to enter the new constitution in the name of nationalism.[44] Spurred on by the fear that he might be beaten to the draw by such relics of the political past, Satyamurthi formed a Tamilnad Congress Swarajya Party in October and issued a manifesto. Among the fifty signatories of the manifesto were many important mofussil politicians as well as Satyamurthi's usual friends from Madras City.[45] After the issue of the manifesto, Satyamurthi and his lieutenants set out on tours of the mofussil, forming branches of their party. By the end of the year Andhra also had a Swarajya party armed with district branches,[46] while Satyamurthi had begun to forge contacts with potential allies in other provinces. One of these, Dr Ansari of Delhi, agreed to hold a meeting of like-minded men in early March and to discuss with Gandhi the relationship of these new Swarajist parties to the Congress. Even before Satyamurthi met Ansari and the others in Delhi in March, Gandhi let the Swarajists know that he would not stand in their way.[47] Rajagopalachari was dismayed by Gandhi's blessing of the Swarajists not so much because he wanted the Gandhians to stand and fight them, but because he was afraid lest the Swarajists should operate outside the Congress organisation

[42] S. Satyamurthi, 'Capture the Councils', *Indian Review*, XXXIV (December 1933), 790–1.

[43] FR August (1), GOI Home Political 18–9 1933 NAI.

[44] FR September (2), GOI Home Political 18–10 1933 NAI.

[45] *Hindu* 30 Oct. 1933.

[46] *Hindu* 13 Feb. 1934.

[47] GOI Home Political 4/19 1933 NAI.

and thus fragment the nationalist movement. Rajagopalachari as much as Satyamurthi realised that Congress must mould itself to popular wishes and that popular feeling was quickly focussing on the opportunities inherent in the new constitution. The Swarajists finally met at Ranchi at the beginning of April and founded the all-India Swarajya party. This party existed for less than two weeks because the A.I.C.C. meeting at Patna on 14 April formally accepted the idea of invading the legislatures, absorbed the Swarajya party into the Congress, and set up a committee of the Congress to deal with elections.[48]

By 1934, there had been no legislature elections for four years. Government in Delhi, expecting the new constitution to be inaugurated in the near future, thought it neither wise nor necessary to dissolve the provincial legislatures and hold new elections. Elections to the Central Legislative Assembly in Delhi, however, would be less disruptive and the results would hopefully help government to gauge trends within the Indian body politic. On 1 May 1934, Delhi announced that there would be general elections to the Central Assembly in October.[49] The campaigns leading up to these elections gave the first indication of how rapidly the Congress was changing.

The Congress had only six months between the Patna decision and the Assembly polls, and this gave little time to consolidate any formal Congress organisation in the districts to carry out the election campaigns. Where Congress committees were in existence, they were used; elsewhere individual Congress leaders worked off their own bats. The Tamilnad provincial Congress committee met at the start of July and appointed an election organiser for each district. These men were to consult with the important men in the constituencies and find suitable candidates.[50] In similar fashion, the leaders of the Andhra Congress toured the outlying districts to find candidates. In the aftermath of elections, government noted that the eleven Congress candidates 'were men of local reputation and influence'.[51] This of course was the reason for their selection.

Indeed the manner in which the Legislative Assembly candidates were selected throws light on the internal organisation of the Congress in this period. Examples from three different constituencies show how far the pre-poll bargaining which had always formed a large

[48] GOI Reforms 10/34-R 1934 NAI.
[49] GOI Reforms 10/34-R 1934 NAI.
[50] *Hindu* 1 and 7 July 1934.
[51] GOI Home Public 311 1934 NAI.

part of election contests was being brought inside the framework of Congress organisation.

In the Ceded Districts constituency, the Congress leaders knew that C. R. Reddy was thinking of offering himself as a candidate. This influential educationalist and politician had good contacts both inside and outside government circles, moved closely with both leading Congressmen and with Justicite ministers and, as his tortuous career in Madras politics since he quit Mysore state service in 1920 had shown, he was a man of easy political virtue. In 1934, Congress leaders pressed him to sign the Congress pledge, a declaration of allegiance to Congress aims and strategies which was the only stricture the Congress imposed upon its electoral representatives, and to be a Congress candidate. They were anxious to point out that any differences between Reddy's views and the details of Congress dogma were relatively unimportant. One of the most influential rural leaders and satellites of the Justice party in the Ceded Districts had already announced his candidature for the Assembly, and the Congressmen believed that C. R. Reddy, an old associate of this man, was the only person who could press the rural leader to withdraw. Reddy chose instead to ask this rural leader to sign the Congress pledge and be the Congress candidate in his stead, but the rural leader refused to wear the Congress colours. The Congress leaders then decided that he must be beaten. C. R. Reddy, however, who had much at stake in provincial politics and was loath to be shot down in the Congress front line, shirked the idea of an electoral battle with this man. He urged the leader of the Chittoor bar to stand, and the latter, feeling that he was too old for such antics, put forward his most brilliant junior. C. R. Reddy then threw all his influence behind this Congress candidate.[52]

In the Salem–Coimbatore constituency the situation was similar. Dr P. Varadarajulu Naidu, a clan head, local politician and agitational leader who had been closely associated with the Congress until the eve of Civil Disobedience, offered his candidature. Congress leaders pressed him to sign the pledge. Varadarajulu Naidu had good contacts with Justice leaders both in the locality and at the provincial capital; he had always been an elusive man and at this point preferred the Justicites to the more cloying embrace of the Congress. He offered to stand down in favour of Mrs Subbaroyan, wife of the chief

[52] A. Kaleswara Rao to C. R. Reddy, n.d. (probably 1934), C. R. Reddy papers file 53 NMML; C. Doraisamy Iyengar to C. R. Reddy, 28 July 1934; B. Gopal Reddy to C. R. Reddy, 6 July 1934; M. Anantasayanam Iyengar to C. R. Reddy, 12 July 1934; C. R. Reddy papers file 55 NMML.

minister of the years 1926–30, if Congress would withdraw from the constituency. The Congress leaders proffered the pledge to Mrs Subbaroyan, but she too refused to sign and become a Congress candidate. The Congress had now, however, secured the allegiance of V. C. Vellingiri Gounder, one of the most influential magnates in the constituency. With his backing they chose Avanashilingam Chetty, cousin of the rich banker T. A. Ramalingam Chetty, the man who had been a thorn in the Justicite side in the 1920s. Before the massed influence of this banker and this magnate, Mrs Subbaroyan quailed and withdrew her candidature.[53]

In the deltaic region, the selection of candidates was predictably different. Here the problem of the Congress leaders was not to persuade the right man to accept the torch, but to arbitrate between the many who sought it. For the Guntur–Nellore constituency there were three claimants. The first, N. V. L. Narasimha Rao, was Guntur municipal chairman. He had been imprisoned for Civil Disobedience yet it was now thought that, in order to retain his municipal chair, he had sold his political allegiance to the Justicite chief minister, the raja of Bobbili. The second claimant, Bezwada Gopala Reddi, came from one of the richest rural families in Nellore district. Like many such families, they had good contacts on both sides of the political fence, but were beginning in the early 1930s to come down more firmly than before on the Congress side. Finally there was N. G. Ranga, a Justicite in the 1920s who had organised the anti-zamindari and resettlement campaigns in the early 1930s and had brought them into the Congress agitation. As the final date for the selection of candidates drew near, government noted that although Congress organisational activity in the province as a whole was slight, 2,000 new members had been enrolled in Guntur within a fortnight – a sure sign that the various factions were drumming up support for a battle royal in the Congress committees. Indeed, there were ugly scenes at the Congress selection meeting and a retributive campaign in the press thereafter. Gopala Reddi dropped out to avoid getting hurt in the fray, and some of the Andhra leaders who knew of Narasimha Rao's compact with the Justicite ministry ensured that Ranga got the nomination. Narasimha Rao retorted by putting up an influential man to oppose Ranga as an independent candidate.[54]

[53] *Hindu* 18 and 19 Oct. 1934.

[54] *Hindu* 22 Oct. 1934, 10 Dec. 1934; A. Kaleswara Rao to J. Kripalani, 4 Jan. 1935, AICC papers file 7 of 1934 NMML; FR July (1 and 2), GOI Home Political 18–7 1934 NAI.

The eleven Congress candidates gave a good picture of the newly emergent Congress. They fell into three groups. The first group included P. S. Kumaraswamy Raja, K. Nageswara Rao and Dr T. S. S. Rajan who were all easily identifiable as Gandhians. Rajan had been one of Rajagopalachari's closest associates for twenty-five years, Nageswara Rao had been one of the foremost disciples of the Mahatma in Andhra since 1920, and all three had won their colours in Civil Disobedience. Their involvement in the elections exemplified the rapprochement between Gandhians and Swarajists, and the growing conviction among all politicians, even the most fervent advocates of Gandhian methods, that elections and councils could no longer be ignored. The second group, which included Satyamurthi, C. N. Muthuranga Mudaliar and Sami Venkatachelam Chetty, had all been Swarajists in 1926 and had all been somewhat equivocal about the idea of Civil Disobedience. Satyamurthi had rather grudgingly taken part in the agitation, but Muthuranga Mudaliar had kept right out of it and had continued to sit in the Legislative Council during the agitations. Venkatachelam Chetty, who had always moved smoothly between Congress, Justice and independent attachments, had also taken no part in Civil Disobedience. The last group consisted of men who were new adherents to the Congress cause. N. G. Ranga, the rural agitator, and V. V. Giri, a trade unionist who had spent most of his political life outside the province, were politicians who had made their mark outside the Congress and were now crossing the threshold. Samuel Aaron, a Christian businessman from the West Coast, was entirely new to Congress politics, M. Anantasayanam Iyengar had some contact with the Congress through his legal senior who had been a Swarajist, and T. S. Avanashilingam Chetty had previous political connections only through his uncle, T. A. Ramalingam Chetty, who since 1920 had been a Justicite or an independent. The adoption of these men showed how the gates of the Congress were easing open to admit new men.

The Congress leaders took pains to play down all divisive issues during the election campaign. The central government in Delhi was contemplating legislation on Hindu marital customs and on the right of all castes to enter temples, and both these issues were causing a considerable stir. Many orthodox religious associations insisted that such matters should form the crux of the election, since they were soon to be debated in the Central Legislative Assembly. 'In seeking the votes of the electorate', said Rajagopalachari however, 'Congress has taken care to eliminate all issues at the ensuing elections other than the constitutional political issue between the Government and the Congress.'[55] The election in other words, was to be about the place of the Congress in the political systems of nation and province and nothing else. 'If they succeed,' wrote an opponent, 'they become intolerable. Even now as it is the bearing of the prison-returned Congressmen is bad enough and it will be much worse after their success in the elections.'[56]

The electioneering followed well-tried lines. The candidates toured their constituencies and contacted the most important controllers of votes, and it was significant how many of these fell in with Congress. Dr Rajan was entertained by the ex-chairman of the municipality in Trichinopoly, by a man who sat on the Justicite benches in the legislature in Srirangam, by the municipal chairman, by a leading landowner who had once presided over the taluk board and by a manager of the town bank in Mannargudi, and by a leading landowner and scion of the premier Muslim trading family in Nagore.[57] Avanashilingam Chetty toured round Salem and Coimbatore in company with a leading zamindar, was entertained by past municipal chairmen in both Salem and Tiruppur, and relied on his banker uncle to arrange things in Coimbatore town.[58] Satyamurthi toured his constituency of Madras City in the company of the trustee of one of the most important temples.[59] K. Nageswara Rao met with district board members, the leaders of the Vaisya Seva Sadanam and the Vaisya youth organisation, and held campaign meetings at the temple gates in the towns of his Circars constituency.[60]

But in many ways the campaigns were new and more rigorous. Efforts were made to ensure that supporters appeared on the electoral roll. Satyamurthi put in 4,000 claims (equivalent to a third of the existing electorate) for admission to the City electoral roll.[61] The Congress used prominent provincial leaders in the district campaigns, and even brought in Congress notables from other parts of India to lend a wider dimension to the campaigns.[62] Moreover, where the old vote-brokers would not fall in line with the Congress, the Congressmen resorted to more direct forms of electioneering than had been

[55] Quoted in FR September (2), GOI Home Political 18–9 1934 NAI.

[56] C. V. S. Narasimha Raju to C. R. Reddy, 19 July 1934, C. R. Reddy papers file 55 NMML.

[57] *Hindu* 10, 12 and 16 Oct. 1934, 5 and 8 Nov. 1934.

[58] *Hindu* 22 Sept. 1934, 22 Oct. 1934, 7 Nov. 1934.

[59] *Hindu* 4 Oct. 1934.

[60] *Hindu* 10 Oct. 1934, 1 Nov. 1934.

[61] *Hindu* 25 July 1934.

[62] *Hindu* 20 Nov. 1934.

tried previously. 'Hundreds of young men and students and lawyers', said Anantasayanam Iyengar, 'distributed themselves over the polling stations and carried the message of the Congress and the call of the leaders to the home of every voter.' Dr Rajan, wrote a Madras editor, 'practically lived in his car during the last three months and covered hundreds of miles every day. This method of direct approach and appeal to the voter led to important and interesting reactions. The election bosses in the district found the pressure of their following increasingly difficult to resist and were forced into the open. The more far-sighted among them fell into line with the Congress.'[63] Finally the Congress was better organized on polling day. They arranged transport for the voters and they posted agents at all the polling booths.[64] All eleven of the Congress candidates romped home.

In itself, the victory at the polls held no great significance. The electorate for the Delhi Assembly was small and the deliberations of the Assembly had only peripheral importance in the affairs of province and nation. In only two constituencies did Congressmen face any serious opposition, and there, as noted above, Justice factionalism had undermined any chances of candidates defeating the Congress. Yet the provincial Congress leaders and the successful candidates made good use of their victory. They held triumphal meetings and parades for weeks afterwards, and went on laps of honour round their constituencies receiving the plaudits of caste associations, local boards, chambers of commerce and individual local leaders.[65] Many of those who joined in these celebrations had lent no support to the Congress before the elections, and indeed at several of these triumphal meetings men stood up and announced that now that the potential of the Congress had been revealed to them they were switching their allegiance to it.[66] In some ways, the Congress 1934 campaign, like the Swarajist coalition in 1926, had been something of a confidence trick; the Congress banner had been carried to the polls by a variety of different politicians who differed greatly in outlook and ambitions, many of whom had only recently lent their name to the Congress cause. Yet it was a landmark. It had begun to show that the Congress could act as a vehicle for gaining power, and there were many around who needed such a vehicle.

[63] *Hindu* 12 Nov. 1934.

[64] *Madras Mail* 12 Nov. 1934; GOI Home Public 311 1934 NAI.

[65] *Hindu* 17, 18, 19, 21, 23 and 28 Nov. 1934.

[66] See the miraculous conversion of A. Lakshminarayana Reddy, *Hindu* 17 Nov. 1934.

In the next few years, Congress absorbed much of the energy and many of the personnel of the agitational campaigns of the early 1930s. The resettlement campaign had already become a Congress cause, Satyamurthi had organised a 'Land Revenue Day' in 1933,[67] and Ranga's adoption as a Congress candidate in 1934 had sealed the alliance between the Congress and the anti-zamindari campaign. In 1936 the Self-Respecters debated whether they should join the Congress en masse and when their leader E. V. Ramaswami Naicker hesitated and then declined, many of his followers abandoned him and joined the Congress anyway.[68] In 1934, Muniswami Naidu's faction in the Justice party also debated a wholesale defection to the Congress camp and only narrowly rejected the idea.[69] The bandwagon had begun to roll.

CONGRESS AND LOCAL ELECTIONS

Addressing a conference of mirasidars (landholders) in Tanjore in early 1935, a prominent Madras journalist and politician impressed on his audience the intimate connection between their specific political interests, and the aims of nationalism:

> The time has arrived when mirasidars, not merely as Indians but as mirasidars, should line up with the nation in its fight for Swaraj. There was a time when big business in India kept itself aloof from political agitation ... but the time arrived soon enough for them to realise that big business trenched on high politics when they had developed up to a limit; you find them now in the front rank of politics. You have now reached a similar impasse ... I am asking you to create live organisations, all over this district, link them with similar organisations in the province, and put forth your demands with one voice.[70]

It was probable that he was preaching to the converted, for in many districts by this time local leaders had begun to take a new interest in nationalism.

By the early 1930s, considerable pressure had built up within the politics of local government. Many different interests were anxious to gain some purchase in local affairs, but few could find satisfaction within the shaky framework of local government boards. These boards were losing some of their powers under the provincial govern-

[67] *Hindu* 28 Nov. 1933.
[68] Baladandayutham, *Jiva*, pp. 22–5; *Hindu* 2 June 1936.
[69] *Hindu* 22 Dec. 1934.
[70] *Hindu* 7 Jan. 1935.

ment's new reform policies, and what remained was, in most local boards, jealously guarded by a few individuals. Indeed at the start of the decade most local boards possessed fairly stable regimes, which had won favour from the ministers and now seemed unshakeable. As reform of local government threatened to undermine the position of these satraps and the ability of the ministers to assist them, the ministers clung desperately to the friends that remained and invested more and more of their diminishing stock of power and patronage in keeping them in power. Opponents of these entrenched regimes grew steadily more and more indignant, and at the same time looked around for more and more effective levers with which to unseat their enemies. Between 1933 and 1936, many local groups which had once been simply opposition factions became, gradually and almost imperceptibly, local Congress parties. Of course in the big towns and the deltaic districts, the Congress had played a significant role in local politics for some years, but in the other areas which formed the majority of the province, the party labels of provincial and nationalist politics had not previously been invoked in local affairs in anything but the most fleeting fashion. At the district board elections in South Arcot in 1934, the alignment of local factions followed very closely the pattern that had existed for some years; the only difference was that one side fought this election as a Congress party.[71] In Salem, the years 1930–3 saw a massive build-up of opposition to the regime of S. Ellappa Chetty who, as lieutenant to the district board president and then president himself, had dominated local politics since 1920. The opposition, which included prominent zamindars and landowners as well as merchants and financiers from Salem town, had tried many different techniques of opposition; they had organised ratepayers associations and conducted local agitations on the one hand, and on the other they had put one of their number into the Legislative Council in the hope that he would be able to influence the ministry. Yet they had failed to unseat Ellappa Chetty, who was an accomplished politician and who could count on ministerial support to the extent that the ministers repeatedly refused to listen to allegations of corruption and mismanagement in Salem affairs. In 1933, the opposition ran at the local elections simply as enemies of the current regime, but at the next elections they ran as Congressmen.[72]

In Madura town, the interventions of the ministry to keep their

[71] *Hindu* 4 Dec. 1934.

[72] G.O. 3402 (LSG) 23 Aug. 1933 MRO; G.O. 1272 (LSG) 14 Mar. 1934 MRO; *Hindu* 3 Apr. 1933, 9 June 1936.

satellites in power in spite of swelling opposition in the locality, were perhaps more blatant and more galling than in any other locality. The clique led by R. S. Naidu dominated the politics of the municipality and of the Minakshi temple for over a decade. In 1930 their ambassador in the provincial capital, P. T. Rajan, became a minister in the Justicite government, and this proved vital for the clique. By 1933, P. T. Rajan's influence had been felt in all aspects of local government; he had been present during municipal crises, had helped engineer a change in the district board regime and had intrigued to have the Minakshi temple committee prorogued when it fell into enemy hands.[73] There had been two main factions pitted against the Naidu–Rajan clique for many years. Firstly, there were a handful of lawyers and merchants interested in temple affairs, led by the lawyer K. R. Venkatarama Iyer. They had conducted local agitations, sent innumerable petitions to government and filed innumerable court suits concerning temple affairs, all to little avail. Venkatarama Iyer had been twice elected to the Legislative Council as an independent. Secondly, there were the leaders of the Saurashtra community. Their community dominated local trade and manufacture, particularly in cotton goods, and were among the most devout worshippers at the Minakshi temple. Nevertheless, despite numerous attempts they had never succeeded in gaining a strong hold over the municipality, and despite numerous petitions they had only ever had one member put on the temple committee. The Saurashtra leader N. M. R. Subbaraman had expressed his frustration by joining Civil Disobedience, going to jail, and financing the agitational activities of his many caste fellows. After Civil Disobedience he led his followers into municipal politics under the Congress banner, and was joined by Venkatarama Iyer and his followers.[74]

In many smaller towns as well, local politicians took on a Congress mantle. Chidambaram was in fact the scene of one of the first of the Congress local campaigns in 1935. In this town local politics had, since 1925, been dominated by one man, P. Venugopala Pillai, a local landowner and businessman who had surpassed almost any other local magnate for lack of scruple. The opposition to him, led by the two most prominent families in the local bar, a young doctor and a handful of local merchants, had changed little since his advent. They had

[73] G.O. 1684 (LSG) 2 May 1935 MRO; G.O. 3572 (LSG) 8 Aug. 1934 MRO; *India* 18 Aug. 1932 NNR; *Hindu* 3 Oct. 1935.

[74] *Hindu* 15 July 1935, 30 Aug. 1935, 7 Sept. 1935; FR October (1), GOI Home Political 18–10 1935 NAI.

unseated Venugopala Pillai in 1928 but the latter had resorted to intimidation (the doctor who became the municipal chairman was stabbed) and had deployed his contacts in the ministry to raise himself back to the municipal chair by 1931.[75] The political temperature of the town had always been high and at the 1929 municipal elections the rival parties had written scurrilous novels about one another.[76] There had been a Congress committee in the town but it was run by students and poor vakils, it functioned intermittently and it had little to do with local politics. However, only three days after Venugopala Pillai had manoeuvred his way back to municipal power in 1931, a new Congress committee was formed by this municipal opposition.[77] This Congress committee lay low during Civil Disobedience, but re-emerged in 1935[78] and ran a highly successful municipal election campaign against Venugopala Pillai and his cronies. 'Some of the old councillors', wrote a rather jaundiced Venugopala Pillai after the Congressman Dr Jatabhavallar had been elected municipal chairman, 'called themselves Congressites which name they clutched at as an easy weapon to hoodwink the voters ... Dr Jatabhavallar who was afraid of even uttering the name of Congress till then was made to sign the Congress creed and to loosen his purse for the love of power.'[79]

By 1936, even a district like Ramnad which had previously been considered a political backwater, had a flourishing Congress committee deeply involved in local politics. Several very different elements in the district had come together in this committee – some Nadar traders from Virudunagar, some Raju landowners and merchants from Rajapalaiyam, some wealthy Nattukottai Chetty bankers from the Chettinad area, and some Maravar agriculturists. All had found in recent years that they had good reason to resent the power of government in general, and the power of the ministry and its ally in the district, the raja of Ramnad, in particular. The Rajapalaiyam merchants had been brought up against the intrusive power of the government early in the century when they found that they no longer had unfettered control

75 *Hindu* 10 and 11 Nov. 1931.

76 'As an offshoot of this election, a scurrilous novel has been recently published attacking the integrity of Raghupathi Sarma and his friends who, according to the opposition, figured prominently in the elections, although the names of the several characters have been slightly changed to give the appearance of a novel. This novel has been freely distributed and has caused a profound sensation in the town. The affected party are said to be contemplating the issue of another novel as a counterblast.' Report of the Collector, G.O. 5710 (LSG) 19 Dec. 1929 MRO.

77 *Hindu* 14 Nov. 1931.

78 *Hindu* 29 July 1935.

79 *Hindu* 11 June 1936.

over markets and other important institutions in their home town.[80] The Maravar landowners had suffered far more recently when the newly aggressive police force had begun to interfere in their local feuds and, as a result, government had placed the Maravars under the jurisdiction of the notorious Criminal Tribes Acts.[81] Both the Rajapalaiyam men and the Nattukottai Chetties had complained loudly in the 1920s when the raja of Ramnad had used local board machinery to interfere with their businesses and with their influence over local temples and markets.[82] The Virudunagar men were annoyed that the ministry and the raja colluded with their enemies in the town. The raja, with ministerial help, had broken the hold of the Rajapalaiyam men over their local temple committee and, working with one faction of Nattukottais led by Annamalai Chettiar, had packed another temple committee with placemen and kept many other Nattukottais out.[83] The attempts to counter these indignities had all been frustrated. All of these groups had deluged the Secretariat with petitions; the Rajapalaiyam men had flirted with the Swarajists; and some of the Rajapalaiyam men led by P. S. Kumaraswamy Raja[84] and some of the Virudunagar men, led by K. Kamaraj,[85] had heartily joined in Civil Disobedience. The disgruntled Nattukottais had financed a local paper, the *Ooliyan*, which focussed criticism on Annamalai Chettiar and the raja of Ramnad. The raja sued its editor for defamation.[86] By 1935, P. S. Kumaraswamy Raja, Kamaraj and the editor of the *Ooliyan* led the new district Congress committee, and they attached the support of the Maravars when they helped to make the trial of the leader of the Maravars, U. Muthuramalinga Thevar, for his resistance to the implementation of the Criminal Tribes Act, into a cause célèbre.[87]

The backwardness of Ramnad and the extreme domination of the raja and his cronies, meant that the political alignments in this district were particularly stark and the movement of opposition politicians

[80] G.O. 1462 (LSG) 26 Feb 1923 MRO; G.O. 1984 (LSG) 7 Sept. 1923 MRO.

[81] G.O. 1098 (LSG) 18 Mar. 1936 MRO; *Hindu* 10 Dec. 1935, 2 Apr. 1936.

[82] G.O. 783 (LSG) 3 May 1922 MRO; G.O. 811 (LSG) 9 May 1922 MRO; G.O. 1462 (LSG) 20 June 1923 MRO; G.O. 1984 (LSG) 7 Sept. 1923 MRO; G.O. 104 (LSG) 9 Jan. 1925 MRO; G.O. 4139 (LSG) 25 Sept. 1926 MRO; *Hindu* 8 and 9 Apr. 1921, 9 Aug. 1921.

[83] G.O. 4905 (LSG) 11 Dec. 1927 MRO; G.O. 704 (LSG) 22 Feb. 1930 MRO; G.O. 4833 (LSG) 16 Dec. 1930 MRO.

[84] See P. S. Kumaraswamy Raja, *My Induction as a Gandhite* (Rajapalaiyam, 1956).

[85] 'A Gandhite', *Kamaraj the Shrewd 1903–40* (Madras, 1961).

[86] *Hindu* 24 July 1926.

[87] *Hindu* 7, 10 and 23 Oct. 1935, 21 Jan. 1936, 2 Apr. 1936.

into the Congress was clearly noticeable. Elsewhere, factional alignments were more complex and the development of local politics in the 1930s far less straightforward. Even so, there was a general pattern in which groups with long experience of opposition in local boards organised themselves as local Congress parties. In many cases they were joined by politicians who had had more success in local government but who now felt they no longer needed to curry favour with the ministry but should instead concentrate on securing a firm local base.

The local board reforms of 1930 made it easier for opposition factions to dislodge the old operators. Local boards and municipalities now had more places, wider electorates, and fewer nominated members. From 1932, temple committees also became elected rather than nominated. The first elections under these new rules took place between 1931 and 1933 and in several places the results were dramatic. In Tanjore district board, the old Justicite ally A. T. Pannirselvam lost control,[88] and in Kistna district board, the raja of Mirzapuram was dislodged.[89] In Madura, the Minakshi temple committee changed hands for the first time since 1920.[90] Even in some of the small municipalities which had seemed secure in the hands of a small clique, there were dramatic reversals of fortune.

Few local politicians had anticipated the upshot of the 1930 reforms, however, and there had been little concerted organisation at these first elections. It was at the second set of elections which took place between 1934 and 1936 that people began to organise to take advantage of the new circumstances. In 1934, a few local election campaigns were conducted under the name of the Congress, and provincial Congress leaders visited the areas concerned and assisted these campaigns. There were some Congress successes in municipal elections in Tanjore district, in rural board elections in West Godavari and in a handful of other places, but for most of the year many of the provincial and local Congress leaders were involved in the Legislative Assembly election campaign. It was in 1935 that the provincial Congress organisations resolved that it was an official part of the Congress programme to 'capture local bodies', and set up machinery to organise local election campaigns.[91] Following this there were numerous Con-

[88] *Hindu* 10 Mar. 1933.

[89] 'The whole city has been placarded with posters declaring the end of the "Justice" regime in the district and heralding the commencement of democratic rule.' *Hindu* 1 and 2 June 1936.

[90] G.O. 1684 (LSG) 2 May 1935 MRO.

[91] AICC papers file P19 of 1934–6 NMML; *Hindu* 9 July 1935.

gress successes. In late 1935 there were Congress campaigns in the district board elections in South Arcot, Trichinopoly, Anantapur, Kurnool, Tinnevelly and South Kanara, and in the municipalities of Madura and Chidambaram, all of which resulted in elevating Congressmen to positions of power, and also slightly less successful campaigns in Bellary and West Godavari boards.[92] In early 1936, Congress won control of several municipalities, and of the Guntur and North Arcot district boards, and towards the end of the year there were Congress successes in Salem, Chingleput, Tanjore, Nellore, and Ramnad district board elections, and less successful campaigns in Kistna, West and East Godavari districts.[93] By the end of 1936, Congress controlled over two-thirds of local government bodies in the province.

The Justice ministry fought back gamely but hopelessly. Shorn of the old levers in local government, the ministry fashioned new ones. Their new weapons were, however, punitive rather than palliative and they alienated more people than they won. Firstly, they took advantage of the new acts which allowed them to by-pass and even to abolish temple committees in order to rescue temples which had fallen into enemy hands. The Minakshi temple, where the committee was abolished in 1934 and R. S. Naidu appointed sole manager by the ministry, was the first and most flagrant instance. To save the richest temple of the province at Tirupati from going astray, a new act was passed setting up an entirely new Tirupati temple committee appointed by government.[94] Secondly, Bobbili passed new electoral rules. Though apparently innocuous, these rules allowed Bobbili to force municipalities that had fallen into Congress hands to submit themselves to new elections within a matter of months. The new rules were used, for instance, to bring about new elections in Madura municipality only a matter of weeks after Congress had won control and were settling down for a long spell in command.[95] Thirdly, Bobbili made a point of appointing strict officials as Commissioners in municipalities where Congress had won control, and there were inevitably fights between the Commissioner and the Congress chairman. In Madura again, the Congressman N. M. R. Subbaraman found that he had to do battle with the Commissioner to implement any municipal decision, while the Commissioner made a point of enforcing unpopular municipal regulations (which had hitherto been neglected) which promised to

[92] *Administration Report of the Government of Madras* (annual) for 1934–5, pp. viii–x.
[93] Erskine to Linlithgow, 1 Dec. 1936 and 6 Jan. 1937, Erskine papers vol. VIII IOL.
[94] G.O. 3259 (LSG) 15 Aug. 1932 MRO; *Hindu* 25 Mar. 1933.
[95] *Hindu* 1 Aug. 1934.

turn popular feeling against the chairman and other leaders of the council.[96] Lastly, Bobbili dissolved the municipalities in many of the major towns when they became rowdy or unfriendly. In the early thirties, the municipal councils in Tinnevelly, Trichinopoly, Guntur, Bezwada, Madura and Rajahmundry were all dissolved and suspended for some period of time. In three years, Bobbili suspended more local boards than all the other chief ministers together.

In the district boards, ministerial activities were even more flagrant. In 1933, Bobbili delayed the elections in the Kistna district board while his henchmen the raja of Mirzapuram played around with the electoral roll.[97] In the same year, when the East Godavari Board was captured by a Congress regime, Bobbili contemplated using the excuse that much of the region north of East Godavari was about to be ceded to the new Orissa province, to redraw the East Godavari district boundaries in a way that might well alter party fortunes in district board politics.[98] Bobbili's biggest weapon, however, was bifurcation, the division of an old district board into two new boards. With the abolition of taluk boards in 1934, it was argued that there were good reasons for reducing the areas of many of the district boards for simple reasons of administrative convenience. Bobbili, however, found that bifurcation was convenient in many other ways. In the reconstitution of district boards after bifurcation lay the only chance under the new rules for the ministry to nominate members to a district board, and this power was wielded in a partisan fashion. Districts could also be divided in a way that favoured certain factions and prejudiced others. Moreover, bifurcation also brought in its wake fresh elections which, if they came soon after the last set, could severely strain Congress electoral resources. Tanjore district board was divided in 1934, soon after the Justicite favourite, A. T. Pannirselvam, had lost control to a Congress regime; Congress retained command of one of the two new boards, but the other went to a man who had been Pannirselvam's lieutenant.[99] When district boards started sliding into Congress hands in 1935, Bobbili started bifurcating wildly. Nellore, Salem, Kistna, East Godavari and Coimbatore district boards were bifurcated even while elections were in progress and the Congress appeared to be doing well. North Arcot was divided on the eve of the elections, and Chingleput

[96] G.O. 3572 (LSG) 8 Aug. 1934 MRO; G.O. 1600 (LSG) 25 Apr. 1935 MRO; *Hindu* 2 June 1936.

[97] *Hindu* 24 Jan. 1933.

[98] *Hindu* 14 July 1933.

[99] *India* 22 Dec. 1934 NNR; *Hindu* 19 Dec. 1934.

immediately after a Congress regime had been installed. The Chingleput case was particularly flagrant since the Secretariat advised that the division into two new boards would be financially disastrous.[100] By the end of the year, sixteen district boards had been bifurcated. The Governor, Lord Erskine, had begun to realise that something was up in late 1935 and had written to the Viceroy describing the ministry's strategy:

If the Congress wins the election then the Minister postpones, as he has power to do, the entry into office of the new Board and issues an order allowing the old Board to carry on for a month or so. During this period attempts are made to induce various members of the new Board who have been elected as Congress candidates or independents to change their allegiance and vote for a Justice Party President when the time comes for the new Board to be installed. If these blandishments fail then the Board is bifurcated in such a way that the Justice Party make sure of one President out of the two. Again there is power, when a Board is bifurcated, for the Government to nominate persons to represent minorities if the circumstances require it. This power of nomination has been used far more in the interests of the political party to which the Minister belongs than in the interests of the minorities. The power has in fact been used to alter the political complexion of the new Board and then upset the results of the election.[101]

Lord Erskine summoned Bobbili and told him to stop it, but Bobbili was desperate and was not going to be stopped even by the Governor. He continued to wield the weapon of bifurcation for another year.

Shorn of many of its powers to win new friends in the localities, the ministry became increasingly dependent on its old faithfuls. In many cases in which the ministry deployed the weapon of bifurcation and other administrative powers, it was clearly acting in the service of its old friends. As noted above, the Minakshi temple committee was abolished in order to accommodate the old ministerial satellite, R. S. Naidu, as sole manager of the prestigious temple. Salem district board was divided even while elections were in progress and the local empire of Ellappa Chetty seemed to be threatened. Kistna district board was divided in an attempt to rescue the fortunes of the raja of Mirzapuram, and East Godavari was divided just when the Congress had launched a campaign to run the old Justicite satellite and cousin of Bobbili, the raja of Pithapuram, out of the local boards. The finale came in the Ramnad district board elections in 1936 when all

[100] *Jaya Bharati* 5 Nov. 1935, *Prajabhandu* 2 Dec. 1935 NNR; G.O. 4916 (LSG) 28 Nov. 1935 MRO; *Hindu* 6 Dec. 1935.

[101] Erskine to Willingdon, 23 and 29 Dec 1935, Erskine papers vol. V IOL.

the weaknesses of the ministry – its use of inflammatory techniques to retain control, its reliance on an ever decreasing circle of friends – were starkly evident.

Both the Congress and the Justice parties organised large campaigns at the Ramnad district board elections. The Justice leaders who normally stood slightly aloof from these contests, were closely involved because raja Annamalai Chettiar (whose son Muthiah was now a minister) was greatly interested in the outcome and was grooming his son-in-law for the district board presidentship. Justice leaders came down from Madras City to give speeches in the Pallathur constituency where Annamalai's son-in-law was standing. Meanwhile the police were set to work to obstruct the Congress campaign. Congress workers were harassed by the police; one was arrested for making a slanderous comment about Annamalai; one Congress meeting was dispersed by a police lathi charge; another Congress meeting was disrupted by a car driven through the crowd, and a hundred Congress workers were arrested in one batch. Half way through election day, Bobbili ordered that polling be suspended in Pallathur constituency on the ground that he feared a breach of the peace. When the election was re-run a few days later, tempers ran high and there were numerous skirmishes around the polling stations. The son-in-law won, but the overall result in the district was in Congress' favour. Thus even before the full result had been compiled, Bobbili announced that the board was to be bifurcated and that the elections would have to be run again.[102] Not surprisingly, the reaction was enormous. Nilkan Perumal, a Madras journalist, who visited Ramnad a few months later, met many Nattukottai Chetties who told him that the Pallathur fiasco had revolutionised the extent of Congress support in the district.[103]

The organisation of local board election campaigns by the Congress struck a nice balance between flexibility and discipline, and between provincial direction and local control. The provincial Congress leaders provided the framework, while local men filled in most of the details. The Tamilnad Congress set up a provincial civic board in May 1935. This body was empowered to constitute district civic boards, which would do all the work of selecting candidates and conducting the election campaign. The Andhra Congress established a similar organisation in August.[104] In neither case did the provincial Congress

[102] *Justice* 10 and 12 Dec. 1936; *Hindu* 12, 13, 14, 15 and 16 Dec. 1936.

[103] N. Perumal, *Chettinad* (Madras, 1938), pp. 26–8.

[104] *Hindu* 13 May 1935; AICC papers file P3 of 1934–6 NMML.

dictate how the local election board should be set up; in fact the organisation was far looser than the Congress resolutions implied. In the following months, provincial Congress leaders (particularly Satyamurthi in Tamilnad, Prakasam and Sambamurthy in Andhra) toured the districts where local elections were due. They consulted with established Congressmen and influential men in local politics, and if it was decided that a Congress local election campaign was a good idea, a local election board was conjured up.[105] If there was a district Congress committee in existence the local election board tended to be a duplicate. But in many districts (including a third of those in Andhra) there were still no district Congress organisations, and thus election boards were constituted on an ad hoc basis.[106] In mid-1936, the Tamilnad Congress changed the format of the local electoral organisation, not however to make it tighter, but to make it even more flexible; the civic boards were replaced by ad hoc election committees which generally consisted of a few men chosen by the local Congress committee and one appointed by the provincial Congress.[107]

Besides helping to set up this skeleton organisation, the provincial Congress leaders used their influence to pressure a few magnates who were hesitant about putting their weight behind the Congress, gave speeches in the constituencies, and published details of the campaign and results in the provincial press. Beyond this, however, the campaigns were the work of the local leaders. Although the provincial civic boards were supposed to help settle disputes over candidatures and the like, the provincial leaders were generally well aware of the dangers of interfering in local faction fights. N. V. L. Narasimha Rao, who wielded more influence in the Andhra provincial Congress (where his close friend Prakasam was president) than in the local Congress in Guntur (where there were many who had suffered from his handling of the Guntur municipality in the past years), wanted the provincial Congress to vet all local election candidates in Guntur, but the Andhra provincial leaders would not fall in with his wishes.[108] In a few cases, the provincial Congresses tried to influence the leadership of local campaigns, but generally with little effect.

The conditions for being accepted as a Congress candidate were simple: one had to sign the Congress pledge, a formula in which the signatory promised allegiance to the Congress programme and goals. There was rarely any close scrutiny of the political antecedents of

[105] For some such activity in Andhra see *Hindu* 2 Aug. 1936.

[106] AICC papers file P3 of 1934–6 NMML; *Hindu* 20 Aug. 1935.

[107] *Hindu* 30 Apr. 1936.

[108] *Hindu* 14 Mar. 1936.

candidates. It was evident that the Congress was primarily interested in winning and the door to the organisation had been opened as wide as possible to ensure victory. The Congress local election boards did not start off by selecting candidates; rather they invited anyone in the district to apply for a Congress candidature.[109] Those who were then accepted were asked to contribute towards Congress funds; candidates claimed to have paid amounts ranging between one hundred and one thousand rupees. After this they still had to bear the costs of electioneering themselves, although they might receive the propaganda assistance of Congress leaders and they might find that the provincial and district leaders helped to clear away their opponents and bring them in unopposed. In some districts, it was later alleged that the local Congress had virtually invited people to bid for the Congress ticket; one West Godavari man claimed to have paid Rs 100 into Congress funds, only to find that the Congress were offering the ticket for his constituency to another man if he paid Rs 1,000. But if the Congress organisation was fickle about its candidates, the candidates were equally fickle about their party allegiance. This West Godavari man, along with many others who were thwarted in their applications for Congress tickets, went on to stand at the elections as a Justicite.[110]

The Congress local election committees were often flooded with applications. The Chittoor committee received 100, over twice the number of seats available.[111] Many of these applicants were rejected, largely on the ground that they had little chance of victory at the polls; eighty applied for the fifty-two candidatures in Anantapur, but only twenty-seven were accepted. After this, Congress leaders toured the district seeking out more promising candidates.[112] In many cases, sitting members of the district board, who had little or no previous association with the Congress, were pressed to sign the pledge and stand forth as Congress candidates. Many who were easily identifiable as Justicite satellites were invited to become Congressmen, and many influential men who had hitherto held aloof from local government were lured into the Congress. A Tanjore headmaster wrote to his employer, an influential Mylaporean, about the district board elections in 1936, saying: 'The Congress Party is sure to win . . . today a deputation of the Tanjore Taluk Congress Committee saw me and requested me to stand as a candidate on the Congress ticket. I am not a

109 See invitation issued by Dandu Narayana Raju asking prospective candidates for the West Godavari elections to sign the pledge and hand it in to Congress officials, *Hindu* 5 Sept. 1935.

110 *Justice* 27 and 30 May 1936.

111 *Hindu* 12 Sept. 1935.

112 *Hindu* 19 Sept. 1935.

member of the Congress Party and the idea of standing as a candidate never struck me at all.'[113] In other cases, men who had already filed their candidature for the district board elections were pressed to become Congressmen; some were told that they would face the opposition of a Congress candidate unless they signed the pledge.[114] In some districts such as Bellary, local politicians resented the way party labels and provincial party disputes were being forced on to district politics, but in general few politicians felt constrained to resist; at best the Congress label might bring some electoral assistance, and at worst it could do little harm. Meanwhile the Congress leaders were zealous that they should be seen to win.

During the North Arcot district board election campaign in early 1936, government noted that 'there have been numerous and locally important defections from the Justice Party to the Congress'.[115] These included two men who had in recent years served as ministerial allies in local government and had stood for election to the Legislative Council as Justicites. In many other local campaigns, there were dramatic defections into the Congress camp. In Anantapur, the mainstays of the Congress campaign were two rural bosses who had been in local politics for some years and had until recently enjoyed the good favour of the ministry.[116] In elections to the Madras Corporation, Congress absorbed many men who until recently had counted as Justicites including the labour leaders V. Chakkarai and G. Selvapathi Chetty, and the Gujarati gems merchant, Laldoss Govindoss.[117] Govindoss had good reason, for the Justice leaders had just double-crossed him over elections to the board of the wealthy Pachaiyappa's charity.[118] Chakkarai, who had been associated with the Congress in the dim past but had been a Justicite for over a decade, gave good grounds for his conversion which, he said, 'is no doubt a fertile subject for denunciation [by] opposing party politicians . . . but it is the future that must fill our minds with faith, hope and charity. Can it be said that there is any movement in India that can compare with the Congress for rallying and organising the national strength for the struggle?'[119] Politicians looked to the future not the past, and they appreciated opportunities not antecedents.

[113] V. Guruswami Sastri to P. S. Sivaswami Iyer, 6 Nov. 1936, Sivaswami Iyer papers NAI.

[114] See Bobbili's statement in *Hindu* 24 Dec. 1935.

[115] FR February (2), GOI Home Political 18–2 1936 NAI.

[116] *Justice* 24 Dec. 1935.

[117] *Hindu* 6 Sept. 1935.

[118] *Hindu* 29 Oct. 1934.

[119] *Hindu* 17 Sept. 1935.

Many of the old members of the Congress, however, were apprehensive about this influx of new talent, particularly when they were themselves shouldered aside in the contest for Congress candidatures. Disgruntled Congress workers in the City pointed out that Congress candidates in the City included Ramanatha Goenka, 'a non-Congressman, Dubash of the Bombay Company that has been carrying on trade in foreign cloth', who had been pressed to stand because 'he was a benevolent rich man who had been helping with monies in the Congress cause', and K. Venkataswami Naidu, an extraordinarily wealthy merchant and patron who was plainly a Justicite.[120] Similarly workers in Guntur complained that the Congress were running Upputuri Rama Rao who was 'known only for his wealth'[121] and V. V. Punniah who was 'in the habit of presenting Christmas cakes and other presents to officials', and had neglected many men who had served Congress in jail and picket line.[122] T. V. Kalyanasundara Mudaliar who went to help in the elections in North Arcot was so distressed by the influx of dubious local politicians, by the neglect of Congress workers and by the inability of the local Congress organisation to enforce any sort of discipline, that he threatened to form a breakaway 'New Congress' and began a campaign to 'clean up' the national movement.[123] In Cuddapah, the editor of a Congress paper and veteran of three jail sentences resigned from the Congress 'as it has become impossible to fight the moneyed class on one side and new converts from the Justice Party... on the other'.[124]

The Cuddapah dissident added that in his district there was 'no organisation of the Congress except in the newspapers', but in other districts the Congress local election campaign was remarkably well organised. A local politician who had worked against the Congress in one district later wrote rather ruefully:

> The Congress organisation managed to spread its network among important villages long before the elections, with the result that, as soon as the nomination papers were filed, it was able to put into the field a very large number of volunteers and workers to address public meetings, visit the countryside and canvass votes. You might visit any village even in outlying and out-of-the-way areas and you were sure to come across groups of urchins wearing Congress khaddar uniforms and Gandhi caps and holding aloft the tri-coloured

[120] Sambamurthy to R. Prasad, 28 July 1935, AICC papers file P33 of 1935 NMML.
[121] *Justice* 18 Jan. 1937.
[122] Ch. Suryanarayana to R. Prasad, 15 July 1936, AICC papers file P3 of 1936 NMML.
[123] Kalyanasundara Mudaliar, *Valkkaik Kurippukkal*, pp. 403–5.
[124] *Justice* 18 Nov. 1936.

banner. Nearly eighty per cent of these workers and volunteers had been drawn from the voteless propertyless unemployed hundreds of the urban and villages areas ... In one circle it was my experience that a candidate was helped by no fewer than two hundred such volunteers and workers ... In quite a large number of places we found the village headman helping the Congress. In one village it had been announced by beat of tom-tom that all should vote for the Congress.[125]

The Congress leaders brought into the contest the experience they had gained in previous elections to the legislatures. They ensured that several nomination papers were filed (to prevent the common practice in which candidates tried to get their opponents' nominations invalidated because of procedural errors), helped to patch up the electoral rolls, harnessed the idealism of students and youths in order to spread propaganda, and made elaborate arrangements to transport voters to polling booths. Since they knew that many voters when they cast their vote were hoping to be on the winning side, they knew it was important to appear confident and poised for victory. Often they published, a few days before the polls, lists of Congress candidates returned unopposed. In West Godavari they posted a list of sixteen Congressmen returned unopposed on the gate of the local school; local opponents protested that only six candidates were unopposed, and not all of these were Congressmen anyway.[126] Moreover, right up to the last minute candidates were canvassed to become Congressmen; in Chittoor, several candidates on their way to poll their own vote were accosted by Congress leaders and persuaded to sign the Congress pledge.[127]

Moreover, the attempts to widen the Congress net did not cease once the district went to the polls. As soon as the results were in Congress leaders began to lobby those who were still outside the fold. Men who had applied for the Congress ticket, been refused, had stood anyway and had been elected, were now welcomed back with open arms.[128] Figures showing Congress successes, figures which were often disputed by their opponents, were posted in the press in the hope of persuading the newly elected members still outside the Congress that they should come over to the winning side.[129] Offers were made to prominent faction leaders to transfer to Congress in return for a

[125] *Justice* 16 and 23 July 1935.

[126] *Justice* 22 Oct. 1935.

[127] *Justice* 1 Nov. 1935.

[128] For instance A. R. V. Achar and Shaffee Mohammed in the Madras Corporation elections. *Hindu* 22 Oct. 1936.

[129] See the wrangle in Chittoor; the Justice party claimed a victory by 27 seats to 19, while the Congress claimed they had won 'not less than twenty-five'. *Hindu* 4 Nov. 1935; *Justice* 1 and 8 Nov. 1935.

suitable reward, and often these blandishments were effective. K. Sarabha Reddi, who had sat on the Justicite benches in the Legislative Council throughout the 1920s, led eight members elected to the Kurnool district board on a Justicite ticket over into the Congress camp and was rewarded with the office of vice-president of the district board a few weeks later.[130] Similarly, six Justicite members in Anantapur transferred their allegiance to the Congress after the polls and their leader was subsequently elected vice-president by the Congress party in the board.[131] Some of these defections were quite dramatic. M. D. T. Kumaraswami Mudaliar, an extremely wealthy businessman and property owner in Tinnevelly whose family dominated Tinnevelly politics and who moved closely with the raja of Bobbili,[132] ran at the district board elections against the Congress but underwent a miraculous conversion only a few days before the date for the election of the board president, and was then elected president in the name of the Congress.[133] In Chittoor matters were even more complex. C. R. Reddy was originally elected president of the district board on a Congress ticket, but resigned a few weeks later in order to become vice-chancellor of the new Andhra University. Immediately, two influential rural leaders, both of whom had been M.L.C.s associated with the Justice party, rushed to join the Congress and fill the vacuum C. R. Reddy left. One of them V. Raghunatha Reddi, had in fact led the Justicite campaign against C. R. Reddy and the Congress only a few weeks beforehand. The other, T. N. Ramakrishna Reddi, had just been omitted from the ministry's list of appointments to the new Tirupati temple committee and had reason to feel slighted. These two, Raghunatha and Ramakrishna Reddi were two of the biggest faction leaders in the district and were old enemies; because of this, not despite this, they had both previously been in the Justice party and were now both in Congress. Ramakrishna Reddi got the Congress nomination and was elected president of the district board. Raghunatha Reddi did not, so he re-defected and worked against the Congress again. This prompted yet another local Justicite, a man who had once been a close friend of the chief minister Muniswami Naidu, to go over to the Congress and bid for the vice-presidentship.[134]

130 *Hindu* 31 Dec. 1935.

131 *Justice* 16 Nov. 1936; *Hindu* 10 Nov. 1936.

132 B. J. M. Kulasekhara Raja and M. Anandanarayanam, *Tirunelveli Talavay Mutaliyar Kudumpavaralaru* (Madras, 1925); M. D. T. Ranganatha Mudaliar to R. K. Shanmugham Chetty, 5 June 1935, Shanmugham Chetty papers.

133 *Hindu* 26 Nov. 1935.

134 C. R. Reddy to Bobbili, 7 July 1936, C. R. Reddy papers file 31 of 1935–42

After the election results were known, both Congress and Justicites negotiated with local leaders to ensure that the president would be elected under their flag. In most cases the Congress, by being more zealous and more flexible, was the most successful. In the Ongole district board (half of bifurcated Guntur), the Congress leaders converted a minority of four into a majority by promising a small group of Reddis that they would be allowed to choose the presidential candidate. In North Arcot, once the elections were over there were four distinct and rival factions within the Congress party in the district board, and the negotiations over the choice of a presidential candidate were long and tricky. Once the choice of presidential candidate was made, it was problematic whether the ramshackle parties would stay together long enough to get the Congressman elected president.[135] In Chittoor, as noted above, the party started to fall apart almost as soon as the choice was made, and in several other boards factions which failed to get their leader appointed as the Congress presidential candidate quit the Congress immediately.[136] Thus in several districts, members of the Congress party in the district board were made to swear a solemn, semi-religious oath that they would stay loyal to the party before a picture of the Mahatma.[137] In West Godavari once the presidential candidate was chosen, the Congress district board members were kept under lock and key and then escorted to the district board office in the care of a professional wrestler, to ensure that no intruder could try and influence their party loyalty.[138]

Despite these precautions, many local Congress parties began to fall apart. In Tinnevelly, a prominent ex-Justicite whose defection to the Congress a few weeks before the election would, it was thought, 'greatly facilitate the success of the Congress',[139] was narrowly rejected as the

NMML; *Justice* 21 Oct. 1935, 1 Feb. 1937; *Hindu* 21 Sept. 1935, 20 Dec. 1935, 27 May 1936, 5 Dec. 1936.

[135] K. Kasipathi, *Tryst with Destiny* (Hyderabad, 1970), pp. 36–7; *Justice* 18 Feb. 1936.

[136] 'Tactical success at any cost became the sole and chief concern of the Congress... Opportunists, self-seekers and place-hunters were labelled as Congress candidates and the credulous elector was exploited to a degree by the Congress. All sorts of persons with no community of interest, with little team spirit and with less esprit de corps were herded together and proclaimed to the world as Congress parties. The Congress is now reaping the fruits of its blundering. Defections and disciplinary actions consequent thereon have become the order of the day.' Statement by G. Lakshminarayan, resigning as leader of the Congress party in the Guntur district board, quoted in FR August (1), GOI Home Political 18–8 1936 NAI.

[137] *Hindu* 10 Nov. 1936, 8 Jan. 1937.

[138] *Justice* 23 May 1936.

[139] *Hindu* 11 Sept. 1935.

Congress presidential candidate and a few weeks later resigned from the Congress. He took his followers with him and formed a new Justicite branch.[140] In Chittoor the Congress boasted a large majority after the polls but at the presidential election there was a tie and the Congress candidate won by lot. In North Arcot, Congress claimed twenty-six members of the district board, but at the presidential election their candidate was defeated; this meant ten Congressman had voted for the rival candidate.[141] In West Godavari there was a big Congress majority on paper, but the presidential election was 'touch and go' according to local observers, and in the elections to important district board committees a few weeks later several leading Congressmen were soundly defeated.[142] In the Guntur district board these committee elections touched off squabbles in the local Congress which split the party in two halves.[143] In South Arcot, thirteen members of the Congress party in the district board broke away after a few months and formed a separate party in the district board.[144]

But the casualties did not outweigh the achievements. As in the aftermath of the Legislative Assembly election success in 1934, each victory in a district board election was followed by triumphal tours in the districts and much trumpeting in the press. Even where the Congress campaign had not been a success, the Congress leaders did not seem daunted. After the Congress presidential candidate had been defeated in North Arcot, Satyamurthi blithely suggested that the victor, C. Abdul Hakim, and the local Congress might be able to come to some arrangement.[145] The raja of Bobbili pretended to be unworried by the Congress victories; after all, he pointed out, many of those carrying the Congress torch were in fact his followers.[146] But this was either bravado or blindness, for they were men who followed the scent of power, not some particular party. By the end of 1936 the resources of two-thirds of the district boards in the province were in Congress hands.

CONGRESS ORGANISATION

The local election campaigns had brought much of the intrigue, faction-fighting, personal squabbles and transactional bargaining of

[140] *Hindu* 23 Dec. 1935.
[141] *Hindu* 20 Dec. 1935.
[142] *Justice* 23 and 30 May 1936; *Hindu* 27 Apr. 1936, 6 June 1936.
[143] *Justice* 8 Aug. 1936; *Hindu* 8, 13 and 17 Aug. 1936.
[144] *Justice* 5 Oct. 1936.
[145] *Hindu* 2 May 1936.
[146] D. Kotaiah to Gandhi, 3 Oct. 1936, AICC papers file P3 of 1936 NMML.

local politics inside the Congress organisation. In particular, the process of selecting Congress candidates for local elections began to replace the old pre-poll bargaining. The Congress organisation took on an importance in day-to-day politics that it had never had before and this was reflected in membership figures. By the end of 1936, the Tamilnad Congress had 65,105 members on its rolls, and the Andhra Congress 50,865 compared to the combined total of 7,500 in 1929.[147] These were the largest figures to date. Moreover the organisation was also more elaborate than ever before. In Tamilnad, there were 123 primary Congress committees and all the districts other than Tinnevelly had a district Congress committee. The provincial Congress maintained a permanent office in Madras with a secretarial staff of four persons.[148] In both Tamilnad and Andhra, elections to new Congress committees had been held in mid-1936 while the local board elections were in full swing, and there had been considerable rivalry to get on the Congress committees in many districts.

Congress was facing new difficulties; rather than propaganda and recruitment, discipline and control were now its chief problems. In 1936 the provincial and national Congress committees began to be inundated with disputes and complaints originating from the localities. There were disputes over the elections to district Congress committees, disputes over the choice of local election candidates, disputes over the rightful membership of Congress, and complaints about activities unbefitting to Congressmen in local bodies.[149] Already in 1934 the all-India Congress Committee had noted with 'deep regret' that people had begun to manipulate elections to Congress committees.[150] In October of that year, the Congress had acquired a new constitutional framework. This constitution laid down a procedure for elections, fixed strict quotas for the size of provincial committees and provincial delegations to the all-India sessions, imposed a six-month membership qualification for voting in elections of delegates and Congress committee executives, required all delegates and members of Congress committee executives to be habitual wearers of khaddar and to have performed a manual labour service for six months, and

[147] Tamilnad Congress Committee report dated 4 Dec. 1936, AICC papers file P25 of 1937 NMML; *Hindu* 17 Oct. 1936.

[148] AICC inspection report in Tamilnad, AICC papers file G56(Kwi) of 1935 NMML.

[149] See AICC papers files P3 of 1936, G65 of 1936, 7 of 1934, P3 of 1937, P19(ii) of 1937 NMML.

[150] Proceedings of the Working Committee meeting at Benares on 27 July 1934, *The Indian National Congress 1934–6* (Allahabad, 1936), pp. 22–3.

stressed that the Congress leaders had the authority to discipline wayward members of the party.[151] This new constitutional framework was designed to check any abuse of the name and prestige of the Congress, yet the volume and nature of the disputes and complaints about Congress organisation in 1936 suggest that this constitution imposed little check on matters. A few Congress committees, particularly in the turbulent deltaic area in Andhra, were almost torn apart by internal rivalries. Guntur already possessed rival Congress committees in the early years of the decade, and this disputation continued right through until 1937. Mediators from the Andhra Provincial Congress Committee (A.P.C.C.) spent many months in Guntur trying to beat out some formula for reconciliation.[152] The district board elections in West Godavari in 1935 split the local Congress down the middle, and again Andhra leaders had to devote a lot of time to arranging a compromise.[153]

The reason for the ineffectiveness of the new Congress constitution lay in the loose and flexible nature of the existing Congress organisation, that is, in the very factors which the constitution was supposed to change. A constitution full of strict conditions, sanctions and coercive powers had little effect when the body wishing to enforce it had few powers of authority.[154] In some places, the new constitution was simply ignored. When the South Arcot district Congress met to elect its executive in January 1936, for instance, it first voted to disregard the clause of the constitution which demanded that all executive members should have performed a manual labour qualification.[155] In Andhra, when the provincial organisation was reconstituted according to the new rules, the provincial leaders found that the Congress agents in many districts and localities had completely failed to understand the new constitution; the numbers elected to the provincial Congress bore no relation to the quotas (fixed according to the number of Congress members enrolled in the district) that should have been elected; the elections of the executives of the district Congress committees had taken no account of the manual labour qualifications laid down in the

151 *Indian Annual Register 1934*, vol. II, pp. 208–17; for amendments to the constitution see AICC papers file 31 of 1936 NMML.

152 See numerous letters about Guntur affairs in AICC papers files P3 of 1936, G65 of 1936, G29 of 1934, 7 of 1934 NMML; *Hindu* 14 Mar. 1936; *Justice* 6 Feb. 1933; Ranga, *Fight for Freedom*, pp. 226–30.

153 *Justice* 8 June 1936; *Hindu* 15 Jan. 1935, 18 Mar. 1935, 6 June 1936.

154 See B. R. Tomlinson, 'Imperialism, Nationalism and Indian Politics: the Indian National Congress 1934–42', (Cambridge, 1973) pp. 187ff.

155 *Hindu* 21 Jan. 1936.

constitution (often because strict attention to these qualifications would have meant that there were simply not enough 'qualified' Congressmen to fill the executives).[156]

As well as being easily ignored the constitution could also be easily manipulated. It had to be implemented by those already in command of Congress committees, and at both the district and provincial level the opportunities for manipulation were enormous. District Congress leaders organised the committee elections, and had the power to decide who fulfilled the qualifications on khaddar wearing and manual labour. The A.I.C.C. was inundated with complaints from people who claimed elections had been organised with the deliberate aim of keeping them out, and from Young Turks who found that they were excluded from Congress executives on the ground that they were not 'habitual khaddar wearers'.[157] In 1936 there were complaints that those in command of the Andhra provincial Congress committee were rigging the district quotas of delegates to the provincial Congress so that they could include friends and exclude enemies.[158]

Command of the provincial Congresses had always been a matter for factional dispute, but now these disputes took on a new fervour and bitterness. Ever since 1920, Rajagopalachari and Satyamurthi had represented two different strategic views in the Tamilnad Congress. Rajagopalachari, the Gandhian, had led the agitations, khaddar organisation and the Congress 'constructive programme' and had shunned involvement in local and provincial government; Satyamurthi, the Swarajist, had co-operated reluctantly in the Gandhian agitations and had consistently urged that the Congress should invade the governmental framework. The continuing battle for leadership between these two and their respective followings had been essentially a battle over Congress policy. In 1934, however, Rajagopalachari and the Gandhians acquiesced in the Congress' new electoral strategy. After this there was no fundamental disagreement on policy and the leadership battle focussed simply on control of the Congress organisation. Satyamurthi masterminded the Legislative Assembly and the district board campaigns in 1934–6, and thus for the moment dominated Congress organisation in Tamilnad. However, at the Tamilnad provincial conference in January 1936 his leadership was challenged. His opponent was C. N. Muthuranga Mudaliar, a Chingleput politician whose

156 *Hindu* 24 Feb. 1936.

157 AICC papers files P3 of 1937 and P19 (ii) of 1937 NMML.

158 A. S. Chalapati Rao to R. Prasad, n.d., and A. Kaleswara Rao to R. Prasad, 30 June 1936, AICC papers file P3 of 1936 NMML.

political views closely followed Satyamurthi's own and who had once been a lieutenant of S. Srinivasa Iyengar, before the latter retired from Congress politics in 1930. Satyamurthi defeated Muthuranga Mudaliar in this presidential contest,[159] but by the time of the next contest in December the political temperature was far higher and Satyamurthi was accused of rigging his success in January. He had, it was alleged, wooed supporters with promises of patronage from the Madras Corporation, where Satyamurthi had influence, and with complementary tickets to the Congress Exhibition and Musical Festival which Satyamurthi had recently helped to stage in Madras. In December, Muthuranga Mudaliar defeated Satyamurthi.[160] Satyamurthi still hoped to lead the Congress party in the provincial Legislative Assembly after the 1937 elections, and he had secured the Congress nominations for the only 'pocket borough', the University constituency. At the eleventh hour however, such political pressure was brought to bear that Satyamurthi was obliged to give up the seat to his old foe Rajagopalachari, and allow Rajagopalachari to lead the party which he, Satyamurthi, felt he had done so much to establish.[161]

In Andhra, where the Congress already loomed large in local politics before 1934 and where consequently control of the organisation had already been a matter for personal and factional disputes for some years, the position was far more complex. Different individuals, different factions and different districts had long been scrapping over the A.P.C.C., but now the fights became more bitter and the alignments more hardened. The Congressmen of Guntur district were eliminated from the contest in 1935 when other Congressmen decided to hold the A.P.C.C. executive elections while the Guntur men were embroiled in their district board elections.[162] This left two factions. That of Prakasam and Sambamurthy which was based in East Godavari, and that of A. Kaleswara Rao and K. Nageswara Rao, which was based in the Kistna district. While Prakasam was president in 1935 and 1936, Kaleswara Rao and others consistently criticised his handling of local elections and constantly demanded that his 'cabinet' should be elected rather than appointed. Factional disputes in district Congresses became aligned around this battle; the rival parties in Guntur district, for example, arrayed themselves behind the rival parties in the A.P.C.C.[163]

[159] *Hindu* 26 Jan. 1936.
[160] *Justice* 24 Jan. 1936, 7 Dec. 1936.
[161] Narasimhan, *Kamaraj – A Study*, pp. 20–1; *Hindu* 19 Jan. 1937.
[162] A. S. Chalapati Rao to R. Prasad, n.d., AICC papers file P3 of 1936 NMML.
[163] Letters from Venkatappayya, Kaleswara Rao, Chalapati Rao and Prakasam in AICC papers file P3 of 1936 NMML.

The Congress organisation grew in importance at this time largely because it provided a forum in which disputes of this sort, which were an inevitable by-product of the increased significance of local and provincial politics, could be played out. The tiered structure of Congress committees, in which disputes could be passed upwards, provided a machinery for settling conflicts. The provincial Congress sent down mediators to arbitrate in disputes within local Congress committees, and even occasionally an emissary came from the all-India body to settle differences at provincial level. Moreover the provincial Congress tried to discipline Congressmen who transgressed Congress policies in local government; for instance they tried, with some success, to force the resignations of Congress district board members who voted against the party ticket in presidential elections.

Moreover, these factional disputes became one of the most important mechanisms through which the Congress machinery was extended. Congress politicians sought to bring new elements within the Congress in order to bolster their following within the organisation. This was particularly noticeable in Andhra. N. G. Ranga, who since his conversion to the Congress in the early 1930s had never got the purchase within the organisation which he wanted, attempted to build up a following in the Congress by recruiting new members from areas where the Congress had previously had little presence. To begin with he brought many of his contacts from the resettlement and anti-zamindari campaigns into the Congress, and he lobbied for changes in the Congress constitution which would please many of his rural contacts who were still dubious about joining the Congress.[164] Next he concentrated his recruiting drives in the districts outside the Kistna–Godavari deltas (Vizagapatam in the north, and Anantapur, Bellary, Cuddapah and Kurnool in the Ceded Districts) where hitherto little interest had been shown in the Congress.[165] Another Congressman who started to recruit in new areas was Dr. B. Pattabhi Sitaramayya, Masulipatam businessman and official Congress historian, who since 1920 had been remarkably unsuccessful at gaining influence in the Andhra provincial Congress. In the mid-1930s, he too began to plumb the uncharted waters of the Ceded Districts. One result of these efforts was to give new life to the Rayalseema movement which had for some years entered occasional protests

[164] N. G. Ranga to R. Prasad, 25 July 1936, Prasad papers file I/36; N. G. Ranga to J. Doulatram, 18 May 1936, Prasad papers file IX/36.

[165] Ranga, *Fight for Freedom*, pp. 204–7.

against the political domination of the coastal areas of Andhra over the Ceded Districts in the interior.[166]

There were some Congressmen, however, who felt that the Congress had grown at the expense of its dignity. The list of defectors into the Congress had by late 1936 grown long and impressive – it even included men like Dr Subbaroyan who had once been a chief minister[167] – but so was the list of old Congressmen who had been pushed aside in the rush to claim the fruits that the Congress could now offer and who now feared that the national movement would be torn apart by internal feuds. 'There are a number of Justicites', wrote one observer, 'who have sought election to the local boards and Legislative Councils under the cloak of Congress membership and these wolves will cast off their cloaks soon after their election.'[168] In late 1936 while Congress was preparing for the inauguration of the new constitution a Tanjore Congressman noted: 'You can find instances of one and the same individual being a member and office-bearer of a Taluk Congress Committee, a District Congress Committee and the Provincial Congress Committee, a member and office-bearer of a district board, a member and office-bearer in a municipal corporation and with all these having a sure chance of being selected for a seat in the Legislative Assembly elections.'[169] There were many who called for a halt to the interpenetration of Congress and the constitutional structure. In Andhra, these groups gravitated towards the new Congress Socialist party, which had been founded in 1934,[170] and which grew in strength in the Andhra province in 1936.[171] The C.S.P., which did not gain much weight in Congress affairs before 1937, did not try and stop the Congress involvement in elections; it argued that Congressmen should not adopt ministerships but should invade the constitution wholly in order to wreck it. In Tamilnad, few went into the C.S.P., yet many old Congress workers argued for a reform of the Congress constitution along strict Gandhian lines so as to exclude many of the new blatantly opportunistic members, and for far stricter controls over

166 K. V. Narayana Rao, 'The Emergence of Andhra Pradesh', Ph.D. thesis (Madras, 1966), pp. 229–62; *Hindu* 5 Sept 1935.

167 *Hindu* 12 July 1936.

168 *Justice* 12 Oct. 1936.

169 E. Krishna Iyer to J. Nehru, 21 Nov. 1936, AICC papers file G5(a) of 1936 NMML.

170 FR June (2), GOI Home Political 18–6 1934 NAI.

171 *Prajabandhu* 14 Oct. 1936, *Andhrapatrika* 6 June 1936 NNR.

Congress election campaigns in the localities.[172] These groups in Tamilnad and Andhra saw that power within the Congress was quickly passing from those who cherished nationalistic ideals to those who already wielded some power in society and government and who wanted more. The fears which they cherished over the resulting effect on the Congress itself seemed to be confirmed by the events in Trichinopoly in 1936.

Local elections in Trichinopoly in 1935–6 highlighted all the most questionable features of current Congress strategy. Trichinopoly had for many years been a centre of Congress activity. Dr T. S. S. Rajan, who was the undoubted 'Gandhian' leader in the town, had been in Congress politics since 1910 and was one of Rajagopalachari's closest and most enduring associates. But Trichinopoly was also the scene of extremely turbulent local government politics. The municipality changed hands every one or two years, local elections were often violent, and the ministry had been obliged to supersede the municipality in 1933. When Congress entered the local fray in 1934–6 the local Congress organisation was put under great strain. P. Ratnavelu Thevar, a lawyer and one of the most prominent figures in local politics, neatly sidestepped into Congress. He had flitted between parties in 1920 and had once been secretary of the local Justicite branch. In 1930 he had espoused Gandhism and had helped in Civil Disobedience, but in 1932 he had mounted a blatantly anti-Muslim campaign at the municipal elections. Such a campaign was unusual in south India, and it was unusually violent, but Thevar was successful and once installed in the municipal chair he used the municipal machinery to continue his communalist strategy. In 1934, the ministry removed Thevar from the municipal chair chiefly on the ground of maladministration, but partly because the leader of the local Muslim community had influence with the raja of Bobbili.[173] When Thevar slid into the Congress a few weeks later, there were many in the Trichinopoly branch who felt that Thevar's antecedents ought to disqualify him from Congress membership and who doubted Thevar's motives for joining the Congress. Their fears seemed to be confirmed when in a short space of time Thevar managed to dominate the local Congress, to use it to return himself to power

[172] *Hindu* 12 and 22 Oct. 1936.

[173] G.O. 571 (LSG) 31 Jan. 1934 MRO; G.O. 1126 (LSG) 8 Mar. 1934 MRO; G.O. 2185 (LSG) 4 May 1934 MRO; G.O. 3041 (LSG) 19 June 1934 MRO.

in the locality and to seek revenge on Bobbili. Within weeks of joining the Congress, Thevar stood as a Congress candidate at a by-election for the Trichinopoly–Srirangam seat in the Legislative Council, and was elected.[174] In 1935, he led a Congress campaign to capture the district board and was elected president.[175] In July 1936, he led a Congress campaign to capture the municipality and put himself forward as candidate for the municipal chair.

With the influx of Thevar and other local politicians into the local Congress in Trichinopoly, many of the old Congress workers were squeezed out. In February 1936, two of the local leaders of Civil Disobedience resigned from the district Congress committee in disgust.[176] In June, after failing to be elected either as a member of the provincial Congress committee or as the district's delegate to the next Congress session, Dr T. S. S. Rajan stated that he too wanted to resign as a protest against the manipulation of the local Congress machinery by such a well-known communalist.[177] Dr Rajan tried to keep the Congress aloof from the municipal election in Trichinopoly, but he failed. Then he threatened to stand as an independent, but Thevar and his lieutenants promised to set up a Congress candidate in opposition to him unless he accepted the Congress ticket.[178]

When the municipal elections were complete, there were four distinct factions in the local Congress – Thevar's, Rajan's and two others. Each wanted its own leader to get the Congress nomination for the chairmanship. Since a deadlock was likely, the provincial Congress took a hand in the selection process and gave the nomination to Thevar. Dr Rajan was scandalised:

> I found that the Tamil Nad Congress Committee, in carrying on its campaign of capture of local bodies, were bent on securing somehow a majority under the Congress label regardless of the consideration whether the candidate who signed the pledge, generally at the last moment, sometimes on the understanding that he would be selected often to secure his own interests, understood the implications of the pledge or would add to the strength of the Congress. . . . Mr Thevar's strong hates and bitter communalism are very well known. I, in common with others, felt that his becoming Chairman with the help of the Congress machinery would re-open old sores and develop a very unhealthy situation. . . . Pledges were got from all and sundry. Candidates

174 *India* 24 Dec. 1934 NNR; *Hindu* 14 Dec. 1934.
175 *Hindu* 2 Nov. 1935, 8 Jan. 1936.
176 *Hindu* 19 Feb. 1936.
177 *Justice* 1 June 1936; *Hindu* 17 Aug. 1936.
178 *Hindu* 10 Aug. 1936.

were arrayed under Congress label inside and outside with an eye to expediency in regard to the chances of Chairmanship. People in Trichinopoly alone can know the methods employed during the election, how Congressmen were found working for non-Congress candidates, how candidates opposed to some Congress nominees were threatened and their movements restrained, how so-called Congressmen behaved indecently towards ladies at polling booths, how rowdyism of a kind not cognisable by law was indulged in and how foul and vulgar language about communities and persons was used by persons who ought to know better.... The Congress claimed to have secured 21 seats, a fictitious majority.... It contained at least four aspirants to the Chairmanship, each with a following outside this group.... If the ballot box could tell its secrets, it would reveal that among the 21 Congress Councillors, leaving the two candidates and the non-voting member, the remaining eighteen were equally divided in the casting of their votes. A hotch potch group like this should not be allowed to parade as a party. To convert this position into a majority for Mr Thevar by the fiat of the Working Committee, while an unseen hand has been all along deftly manoeuvring the Congress election for the vindication of personal prestige, is not a service which, in my opinion, an honest Congressman whose views as to the functions and ideals of the Congress are different, should be compelled to undertake in the name of discipline.[179]

In defiance of the provincial leaders, Dr Rajan set up his own candidate for the municipal chair and, with the votes of ten Congressmen and five other longstanding opponents of Thevar, Rajan's candidate was elected chairman.

On the following day Rajagopalachari announced that he was resigning from Congress. He told Gandhi that he had seen Dr Rajan before the municipal elections; 'I had pleaded with him', Rajagopalachari went on,' that his threatened conduct would lead to tragic results and break up the Congress. Still he has done this. I have now lost all faith in this business. I have no heart to be pretending any longer that we can build up organised work on party discipline. A man of Dr Rajan's position having done this I cannot lift my head and speak the language of party politics, collect funds or take pledges or do anything now in the elections or in the Congress Committees.... It is worse than a vote of censure.'[180]

The Trichinopoly débâcle sent reverberations throughout the Congress. Thevar's local opponents crowed. The Justice press in Madras City pointed to the internal disorganisation of the Congress

[179] *Hindu* 15 Aug. 1936.

[180] C. Rajagopalachari to Gandhi, 11 Aug. 1936, Prasad papers file VIII/36.

and prophesied that the movement would soon tear itself apart. Madras Congress leaders were shaken by Rajagopalachari's resignation, for his personal prestige, his network of contacts in the mofussil and his personal standing with the youthful volunteers who did much of the donkey-work of Congress organisation and electioneering, were considered vital for Congress victory in the coming elections under the new constitution. The resignation also shook the all-India Congress. Rajagopalachari was not only one of Gandhi's closest disciples, but also in recent years he had been an important mediator between the Gandhians and the Swarajist side of Congress and had helped to reconcile Gandhi to the whole idea of Congress involvement in elections. Besides this, there were many in the upper reaches of the Congress who hoped that Rajagopalachari would become president of the all-India Congress that year and would lead the Congress into the era of the new constitution.[181]

The reasons which lay behind Rajagopalachari's resignation summed up the difficulties of Congress politics in this crucial period. It had been the Gandhians who had urged stricter control and greater discipline in Congress election campaigns; it was ironic that now the Gandhians found that, in the name of Congress discipline, they were after the blood of one of the most prominent Gandhians in the province. It was this irony that had in part prompted Rajagopalachari to resign. He saw that the trend of Congress politics was likely to place old workers like Dr Rajan and Rajagopalachari himself in a cruel dilemma like this one. But Rajagopalachari was further prompted by other fears. He knew that the rising tide of the Congress was to a great extent sustained by the belief that the Congress would ultimately triumph; men were prepared to hitch their wagon to the Congress star because they saw that Congress was becoming a route to power and influence. Congress recruitment depended greatly on an appearance of efficiency and success. The Trichinopoly débâcle might cast doubts on the usefulness of the organisation. In the aftermath of the Trichinopoly affair, Rajagopalachari wrote to Rajendra Prasad: 'I think the encouragement to revolt and rebellion that disgruntled and mischief-making Congressmen in the south have received owing to a variety of circumstances has made success in the elections very problematical in this province.' He added, 'the rot is not only in Tamilnad. It is all over India', and suggested that it would be 'useless' for him to become president of the all-India Congress.[182]

[181] C. Rajagopalachari to Gandhi, 11 Aug. 1936, Prasad papers file VIII/36.
[182] C. Rajagopalachari to R. Prasad, 7 Sept. 1936, Prasad papers file VIII/36.

Rajagopalachari did not wish to go down as the captain of a ship that seemed already to be sinking.

If the genesis of the Trichinopoly affair was significant of developments in the Congress, the conclusion was even more instructive. Rajagopalachari's worst fears turned out to be unfounded, and the whole matter was smoothed over remarkably quickly. Dr Rajan rejoined the Congress and took a leading role in the organisation in the years to come. At the same time Ratnavelu Thevar retained his position in the Trichinopoly Congress and was chosen as the Congress candidate for the Trichinopoly constituency at the 1937 elections. Rajagopalachari himself was drafted back into the Congress to lead the party into these elections. The easy settlement of the affair was conclusive proof of the ability of the Congress to absorb different and often conflicting elements.

THE 1937 ELECTIONS

The long and arduous process of amending India's constitution culminated in the Government of India Act of 1935. In six 'Governor's provinces', including the Madras Presidency, the act bestowed provincial autonomy. Finance and other aspects of provincial administration were added to the list of subjects transferred to provincial control, dyarchy was abolished and provincial government was vested in a Council of Ministers responsible to a bicameral legislature. The Governor remained the titular head of the provincial government, and retained certain safeguards to protect the interest of the civil service and the rights of minorities, and to maintain law and order should it come under threat. Beyond this, the Council of Ministers – there were to be ten ministers in Madras – was in command.

The new provincial Legislative Assembly was to replace the old Legislative Council. The number of elective seats rose from 98 in the old council to 215 in the new; nominations were abolished and depressed castes and minorities were represented through reserved seats. Sixty-nine seats were filled by special electorates of Muslims, Christians, landholders, commerce representatives, registered graduates of the University, women and labour; backward or 'scheduled' castes were allotted reserved seats in the general constituencies. The general constituencies for the old Legislative Council had each covered a district, had each returned two or three members, and the voter had possessed as many votes as there were candidates. The new general constituencies were smaller – there were five or six to a district, five returned two members, thirty returned one ordinary member and one 'scheduled caste' member in a reserved seat, and the other seventy-four constituencies returned one member only. There was plural voting only in the constituencies returning two candidates. The franchise was considerably widened. In the rural areas the qualification was lowered from a payment of Rs 10 in land revenue (or equivalent) to payment of any sum. This brought the legislature electorate almost exactly into line with the local board electorates set up in 1930, and expanded it from roughly one and a half millions to roughly six and a quarter millions, or from 3.1 to 13.2 per cent of the population. The average number of voters per seat was roughly doubled. There was also a second chamber – the provincial Legislative Council – to which forty-six members were elected on a narrower franchise (electorate: 24,979).[183] The first elections under this new constitution were scheduled for February 1937.

This constitution clearly opened up vast new possibilities in provincial politics. Even though the all-India Congress was not until July 1936 finally committed to contesting the first elections, there had for some time been little doubt in Madras Presidency that the Congress would be involved. Satyamurthi had of course been campaigning for a return to a Council strategy ever since it was abandoned in 1929. By 1936, the leaders of Civil Disobedience from Andhra, Prakasam and Kaleswara Rao, were firmly in favour of contesting the elections, while Rajagopalachari had stated: 'My own view is that . . . as much benefit should be wrung out of the Councils as possible for strengthening the prestige and position of the Congress.'[184] Since 1935, the Congress in Madras had contested all the five by-elections to the old Legislative Council that had occurred because of the death or retirement of sitting M.L.C.s; they had won every one, largely because of the lack of interest – the percentage polls were very low – and the lack of any concerted opposition to the Congress candidates.[185] Nevertheless these victories, like those in the local election campaigns, were loudly trumpeted by Congress and they added to the organisation's prestige and to the likelihood of success in 1937.

The attraction of the Congress in the province depended very

183 GOI Reforms Franchise 9/1-F 1935 NAI; GOI Reforms 102R & Kw 1932 NAI.

184 C. Rajagopalachari to R. Prasad, n.d., Prasad papers file VIII/36.

185 By-elections: Madras City, 5,224 votes, a poll of 24 per cent; Madras City again, 9,010 votes, a poll of 39 per cent; Chittoor, 6,281 votes, a poll of about 15 per cent; Trichinopoly, 4,511 votes; Anantapur, no details but low poll reported. *Hindu* 19 Jan. 1935, 8 and 10 Apr. 1935, 11 Feb. 1936; *Justice* 23 Jan. 1935.

much on its potential for capturing the new positions of power that were becoming available. In 1926, the Madras Congress contested the legislature elections with great success but all-India concerns prevented the Congress assuming ministerial office, and soon after the Congress party that had been cobbled together before the elections fell apart. Madras leaders felt it was important that these events should not be repeated. In early 1935, Satyamurthi began to campaign for a firm statement by the all-India Congress leaders that, if successful in the elections, they would accept ministerial office. In May he tackled members of the Congress High Command on the issue.[186] In June, other Madras leaders made motions to start a new Swarajist party to ginger the Congress into a strategy of office-acceptance, and in August a similar party was floated in the Andhra districts.[187] At a conference in Madras City in July, a motion was passed urging office-acceptance, in August the Madras press came out wholeheartedly in support of the idea, and at the Andhra Conference in early 1936 the idea was backed by most of the Andhra Congress leaders.[188] At the next Congress session in Lucknow in April 1936, however, the issue was left in the air. As in 1926, the situation in the all-India Congress was complex and thorny. For many of Gandhi's lieutenants, who were still effectively in control of the Congress High Command, the idea of accepting ministerial office was anathema. They were joined in this opinion by many other Congressmen who feared that the acceptance of ministerial office would place undue influence in the hands of the few Congressmen who got elected and became ministers, and would put the integrity and the unity of the Congress at great risk. In provinces where Congress showing at the elections was highly uncertain, these views were common. The Congress Socialist party, which wanted Congress to sabotage the new constitution, included many who feared that ministerships would place new powers in the hands of their rivals within the Congress organisation.

Yet ever since the Gandhian leaders had in 1934 accepted the

[186] S. Satyamurthi to V. Patel, 21 May 1935, intercepted and kept in GOI Home Political 32/3 1935 NAI. It was widely reported in Madras that many prominent politicians, particularly M.L.C.s, were awaiting the Congress decision on office acceptance before announcing their future political loyalties; see FR June (2), GOI Home Political 18–6 1935 NAI.

[187] *Hindu* 23 June 1935, 25, 26 and 27 Aug. 1935.

[188] *Andhrapatrika* 10 Feb. 1936 NNR; FR July(2), GOI Home Political 18–7 1935 NAI.

notion of contesting elections of any sort, they had stepped onto a slippery slope. Now they found that they must bow to the opinion of the mass of Congress members, or abdicate the leadership just as the Congress was growing massively in size and importance. The all-India Congress parliamentary board asked all the provincial branches to give their views on office-acceptance; when all but Bengal and the Punjab declared in favour, the secretary, J. Kripalani, exclaimed that 'nobody could have imagined that there was such a strong opinion for accepting office'.[189] Open discussion on the question of office might easily have damaged Congress unity in the vital months before the elections; it was thought far better that those who did not want Congress to accept ministries, as well as those who did, should all vote for the Congress candidates at the elections. Moreover it was thought far better than the decision on office-acceptance should be deferred until the elections were over and the Congress standing in the new legislatures was clearly known. Under pressure from the all-India leaders, the Madras politicians agreed to observe a moratorium on the question of office-acceptance. At the Tamilnad provincial conference in January 1936, the issue was carefully sidestepped.[190]

Many Madras politicians who were anxious to be told that the Congress vehicle was to be driven right into the halls of power were disappointed. When pressed, however, Satyamurthi declared that there was no discussion of the office-acceptance question because there was no disagreement on the problem in the province and hence it was not worth mentioning.[191] The Governor Lord Erskine reported to Delhi in June 1936 that Satyamurthi was 'cooing like a dove' and that the Madras Congress leaders were 'panting for office'. In November Satyamurthi paid him a visit and promised that the Congress would not try and wreck the constitution in the province.[192]

Thus in July 1936, with no formal decision on the question of office-acceptance but with a widespread belief in the province that office would be accepted, the Congress opened its election campaign. The working committee of the all-India Congress Committee set up a parliamentary board to oversee the election effort, and following suit the working committees of the Tamil and Andhra Congresses established provincial parliamentary boards and instructed the

[189] J. Kripalani to R. Prasad, 15 Feb. 1936, Prasad papers file III/36.

[190] *Hindu* 27 and 30 Jan. 1936.

[191] *Justice* 7 Dec. 1936.

[192] Erskine to Linlithgow, 14 June 1936, Linlithgow papers file 116 IOL.

district branches to form special committees to help in the selection of candidates and the organisation of electioneering.[193] The selection process followed closely the pattern used in the local board campaigns. The provincial parliamentary boards invited aspiring candidates to apply for the Congress nomination; in Tamilnad they were asked to enclose Rs 50 with this application.[194] Then in October and November, the provincial leaders toured the district to settle any disputes and to help make the final selection. Prakasam and Sambamurthy led the selection organisation in Andhra, while the committee which toured Tamilnad consisted of Satyamurthi, P. S. Kumaraswamy Raja, C. N. Muthuranga Mudaliar, T. S. Avanashilingam Chetty and O. P. Ramaswami Reddi. The Tamilnad leaders asked district and taluk Congress committees to select candidates but to keep their decisions secret until they had been visited.[195] The all-India Congress parliamentary board officially made the final decision on candidate selection, but in fact it only rubber-stamped the lists sent by the provincial leaders and refused to arbitrate in the disputes over candidatures. The selections were made by the men in the locality, under the aegis of the visiting provincial leaders.

As in the local campaigns, the Congress placed a priority on winning. The all-India Congress parliamentary board laid down only three conditions to guide the selection of candidates: that they should have signed the Congress pledge, that they could provide their own finance, and that they had a good chance of winning.[196] Dissidents in the provincial Congress tried to add other conditions – that they were habitual wearers of khaddar, that they had been a member of the Congress for a prescribed period – in order to ensure that the candidates were 'good Congressmen', but in the selection process these conditions were largely ignored. The future of the Congress rather than the antecedents of its standard-bearers was the vital issue, or as Prakasam put it: 'It is a mistake to think that non-Congressmen were not patriots. Swaraj was intended for all, both [for] those who went to jail as well as those who stood aloof from the Noncooperation movement.'[197] Throughout 1936 sudden conversions continued. Dr P. Varadarajulu Naidu returned to the Congress after ten years of association with the Justice party; a year

[193] *Hindu* 12 July 1936, 1 Aug. 1936.
[194] FR August(2), GOI Home Political 18–8 1936 NAI.
[195] *Hindu* 21, 22 and 30 Oct. 1936.
[196] R. Prasad, *Autobiography* (Bombay, 1957), p. 427.
[197] *Hindu* 1 Aug. 1936.

before he had been trying to persuade the Justicite leaders to finance him to edit a paper for the Justicite cause and only weeks before, pointed out the *Justice* newspaper, he had issued an appeal to politicians to start a new party to oppose the Congress.[198] J. L. P. Roche-Victoria, a Catholic community leader and leading businessman of Tuticorin, who had led local government bodies in his region for over a decade, slid into the Congress and was nominated as a Congress candidate just two weeks before the polls.[199] In December 1936 T. A. Ramalingam Chetty, the Coimbatore banker and aspirant for Justice leadership in the 1920s, disowned the honorary title bestowed upon him by the British and applied for the Congress nomination.[200] George Joseph of Madura, another stray from the Congress camp, also returned to the fold and was given the Congress nomination for a Christian constituency. Dr Subbaroyan, independent chief minister and aspirant for Justicite leadership late in the 1920s, also became a Congressman and was nominated for a Salem seat; Rajagopalachari, whose brother managed Subbaroyan's estate and who himself was a close friend of Subbaroyan, smoothed his entry and announced in public in July 1936 that although only a recent convert, Subbaroyan was already 'a very good Congressman' and should not be accused of merely hunting for office.[201] K. Sitarama Reddi, who had been the lieutenant of the first Justice chief minister and a Justicite satellite in South Arcot for many years, crossed the fence and was made Congress candidate in Cuddalore. S. Ramanathan who had quit the Congress in 1925 to follow E. V. Ramaswami Naicker into the Self-Respect movement and who since that date had fulminated against Gandhi, the Congress and the khaddar industry in books and pamphlets, returned to take up a Congress candidature in Tanjore. V. I. Muniswami Pillai who had been nominated by the Governor to sit on the Justicite benches in the old Legislative Council, now presented himself to be nominated by the Congress for a scheduled caste seat in South Arcot.[202] Not everyone was pleased by these additions to the Congress camp. One veteran of Congress agitations wrote scathingly of 'the adoption of pseudo-penitent prodigal sons of India by the Parliamentary Boards' and suggested that 'the spectacular resignations of Kaiser-i-Hind medals, Rao Bahadur sanads, of Dewan Bahadur sanads and the wide publication given to these

[198] Dr P. Varadarajulu Naidu to R. K. Shanmugham Chetty, 12 Jan. 1935, 18 Feb. 1935, and 26 July 1935, Shanmugham Chetty papers; *Justice* 10 Sept. 1936.

[199] *Hindu* 10 Feb. 1937.

[200] *Justice* 18 Nov. 1936.

[201] *Hindu* 1 Aug. 1936.

[202] *Hindu* 2 Feb. 1937.

marvellous somersaults, rather wonderful metamorphoses on the eve of the coming elections must have opened the eyes of the public in general ... to the cantankerous disease from which the Congress is suffering'. He also analysed the causes: 'The result of the [1934] Assembly elections, the idea of getting an easy walkover without much electioneering expense as a Congress candidate, the fond hope of getting a ministership in the unguarded optimism of Congress taking up office under the new Constitution, have tempted many men to become political renegades.'[203]

In the election campaign, the provincial leaders provided a skeletal framework of organisation, and local men filled in the details. In May–June 1936, the provincial leaders toured the districts helping to ensure that the newly enfranchised voters registered themselves.[204] In July they initiated a membership drive and appointed committees of five to eight prominent local Congressmen in each area to tour round the villages.[205] They devoted special attention to registering voters, enrolling Congress members and finding candidates for the newly established special constituencies – those for women, labour and scheduled castes. This was followed in November by elections to the local, district and provincial Congress committees. Coming as they were only weeks before the Legislative Assembly polls these elections attracted great interest. The provincial leaders also brought down prominent all-India leaders to make tours – Rajendra Prasad in November 1935, Jawaharlal Nehru in August 1936 and Vallabhai Patel in December 1936 – and they themselves sped round the province in the weeks before the polls giving speeches in every constituency. They also made a propaganda film, the first political film in south India, although the government did not allow them to show it.[206]

In the localities, the Congress campaign followed very much along the lines of elections during the dyarchy period. Congressmen now had a grip on a majority of the local boards in the province and these were put to electioneering use just as they had been before. In Chidambaram, the new Congress regime quickly reduced property tax and built a new market in the few months before the election.[207] In Guntur, N. V. L. Narasimha Rao ignored government instructions to raise taxes, while he raised municipal expenditure by over 50 per

[203] *Justice* 9 Jan. 1937.
[204] FR May(2), GOI Home Political 18–5 1936 NAI.
[205] *Hindu* 11 July 1936, 30 Oct. 1936.
[206] *Hindu* 1 Feb. 1937.
[207] *Justice* 11 June 1936.

cent; when government asked how he proposed to balance the budget he replied that he would make it up in later years by spending nothing on roads, sanitation and other public works.[208] In the Ellore district board it was alleged that the Congress president had distributed favours to contractors and to presidents of village panchayats with an eye on the elections, and had transferred 700 teachers.[209] Teachers were useful election agents; transfers were often used both to set up an election network, and to intimidate teachers who were hesitant about electioneering for their boss. In Guntur, the Congress district board regime transferred 172 teachers in the space of two months, employed Congress workers on the district board staff and spent lavishly in the months before the elections. The vice-president, who was a Congress candidate at the Legislative Assembly elections, appointed six new teachers, all men from his constituency, and built a new school in his constituency.[210] In the Ongole district board, it was alleged that the president had transferred 200 teachers 'simply to satisfy the members of his party in the Board and secure votes to his own brother who intends to contest in the ensuing Madras Legislative Assembly elections', and that he 'expected all the elementary school teachers to be ready with the votes of the respective villages in the polling area'.[211]

The bargaining before the poll was as important a part of the contest as it had been in recent elections. Much of it revolved around the Congress nomination but it continued after this had been settled. In Coimbatore rural constituency, C. S. Ratnasabhapathi Mudaliar signed the Congress pledge and applied for the Congress candidature; seeing that his old enemies Ramalingam Chetty and Vellingiri Gounder now dominated the local Congress and that this lessened his chances, he offered to withdraw his application in return for a free passage in the neighbouring Erode seat. The Congress refused, and so Ratnasabhapathi Mudaliar offered his candidature as an Independent in the Coimbatore constituency and the negotiations had to begin again.[212] Finally, he was prevailed upon to withdraw. Meanwhile in Erode, the Congress nomination was originally given to K. S. Periaswami Gounder but when the Gounder clan-head the Pattagar of Palaiyakottai announced his intention to stand, a handful of local Congress leaders pressed Periaswami Gounder to withdraw in the

[208] G.O. 1753 (LSG) 2 May 1936 SAH; G.O. 3586 (LSG) 14 Aug. 1936 SAH.
[209] G.O. 1240 (LSG) 31 Mar. 1937 SAH; G.O. 3698 (LSG) 21 Aug. 1936 SAH.
[210] G.O. 3149 (LSG) 17 Aug. 1937 SAH.
[211] G.O. 3181 (LSG) 20 Aug. 1937 SAH.
[212] *Hindu* 5 Jan. 1937.

Pattagar's favour to avoid an expensive clash.[213] In many seats the Congress leaders succeeded in getting some opponents to withdraw before the polls, and in eight the Congress candidate was returned unopposed. The apotheosis of pre-poll bargaining came in the elections to the upper house from Coimbatore district where, on the eve of the polls, Congress slyly persuaded its two opponents to withdraw in favour of one another thus giving the Congressman the seat unopposed.[214]

In the manner of past campaigns, too, the Congress candidates lobbied known vote-banks. A Tinnevelly candidate paid a special visit to the head of the influential Nanguneri *math* at the outset of his campaign, and later held campaign meetings in the premises of a Tinnevelly temple.[215] Candidates in Tanjore commonly held their election meetings at the gates of the temples.[216] Big rural magnates were lobbied. V. C. Vellingiri Gounder, one of the richest landholders, moneylenders and rural businessmen of Coimbatore, did not stand himself but he toured round every one of the rural constituencies in Coimbatore district with the respective Congress candidates.[217] Candidates tried to ensure that village officers, rich landlords or panchayat presidents chaired meetings held in villages and that they received addresses from big merchants and merchant associations in the towns. In Tiruppur they received the open support of the old municipal chairman, and of the cotton merchant association.[218] In Guntur, the leaders of the Vaisya merchant community declared in favour of Congress, and in Ellore the merchants decided to close the bazaars on polling day.[219]

In many districts, the Congress candidates sought the support of caste and community leaders. Conferences of castes which had never conferred before issued approvals of the Congress. A meeting of Nattukottai Chetties in Ramnad declared support for the Congress and announced that the established Nattukottai Nagarathar Association, which was dominated by raja Annamalai Chettiar and thus was emphatically Justicite in complexion, was unrepresentative of the community. A new Maravar association was formed solely to give support to the Congress.[220] In South Arcot and adjacent areas, the

213 *Hindu* 7, 18 and 20 Jan. 1937, 8 Feb. 1937.

214 M. Sambanda Mudaliar to R. K. Shanmugham Chetty, 26 Jan. 1937, Shanmugham Chetty papers.

215 *Hindu* 1 and 8 Feb. 1937.

216 *Hindu* 1 Feb. 1937.

217 *Hindu* 7 and 18 Jan. 1937, 2 Feb. 1937.

218 *Hindu* 13 and 15 Feb. 1937.

219 *Hindu* 16 and 20 Feb. 1937.

220 *Hindu* 2 Feb. 1937.

Congress seized the opportunity offered by government when it placed a small section of the Vannikula Kshatriya community under the Criminal Tribes Act, to set up Vannikula Kshatriya conferences and associations to fulminate against government.[221] In Melur taluk of Madura district, the headman of the Ambalan community issued a 'Nattu Olai' enjoining members of the community to vote for the Congress.[222]

More than ever before, however, the Congress attempted a direct approach to the voters. K. Brahmananda Reddi, whose brother contested Narasaraopet constituency in Guntur district, claimed to have gone from door to door visiting every voter.[223] In other constituencies, lorries full of Congress volunteers toured the villages, while songs, dramatic performances and processions were used to rouse support. 'As the elections proceeded,' reported the Governor to Delhi, 'it became clear that the Congress organisation was of the most efficient character. They had committees in every large village and town, whilst even in the smaller hamlets, they had agents and canvassers.' Moreover, the Governor added, the Congress made good use of election promises; he went on: 'Although, so far as I can make out, the responsible Congress leaders themselves never said anything of the sort, their agents and canvassers made all sorts of wild promises. So far did they go that many of the ryots have been left with the impression that not only will there be no more taxes after April 1st, but also that hospitals, wells, roads etc. will be improved and built in every village.'[224]

The Justicite leader A. P. Patro echoed this feeling; he claimed that: 'Congressmen captured the imagination of the ryots and poisoned the rural areas by false and mischievous propaganda.... Processions and songs attracted the rural population; slogans such as "Ryot versus Rajah, no rent to be paid, no rent higher than a rupee for one plough, down with landlords and government who were responsible for the crushing poverty of the ryots – the [Justicite] party is the handmaid of Government for oppression of the poor, Congress could only redeem them from poverty and distress and burdens of taxation." This poison worked to a dangerous extent.'[225]

Congress paid great attention to the new, less wealthy and less literate, voter. They helped to ensure he was registered, they sought

221 *Hindu* 12 Feb. 1937.

222 *Hindu* 15 Feb. 1937.

223 Kasipathi, *Tryst with Destiny*, p. 40.

224 Erskine to Linlithgow, 1 Mar. 1937, Erskine papers vol. VIII IOL.

225 Patro to Erskine, 4 Mar. 1937, Erskine papers vol. XIX IOL.

his vote, and they offered him transport to the polls. Partly because of the wider electorate, partly because of the lingering effect of the depression on social and political relations, the old methods of electoral bargaining proved useful but inadequate. It was not simply that the electorate was new; it had never before voted at provincial elections but it had voted at local elections since 1930. Nor was it the case that the constituencies were larger and less manageable; the franchise was much wider but the constituencies were much smaller and the turn-out in 1937 much lower than in the legislature elections during dyarchy; thus the number voting in each constituency in 1937 was little different from what it had been in previous elections. Even so, the electorate was not as amenable to the election bosses as it had been a decade before. Several influential candidates opposing the Congress pulled out of the election half way through the campaign. The zamindar of Seithur, for instance, abandoned the Srivilliputtur constituency, and V. V. Ramaswamy, an influential businessman, abandoned Virudunagar to the young Congress worker, K. Kamaraj. The local response to V. V. Ramaswamy's withdrawal revealed how much the electorate had turned against the men who had once been called election bosses: shops and properties belonging to Ramaswamy and his clique of wealthy friends were attacked and looted, and their lawyer's car was smashed up.[226] A. P. Patro, a Justicite candidate who did not withdraw, told how his election campaign had fallen to pieces: 'My constituency comprised in six zamindaris; the tenant revolt however became conspicuous only towards the very last [of the campaign period] when it was impossible to combat this evil. The leaders became powerless against the revolt of their own people.'[227]

Yet it was not just the case of the tenant against the zamindar, commoner against boss. In many places, the Congress fielded zamindars and old ex-Justicite election bosses as its own candidates. In its ideology the Congress was as flexible as in its recruitment policy. While the official Congress manifesto, penned by Jawaharlal Nehru, conveyed an unmistakably socialist message and while this was adopted by several Congress campaigners, the majority of Congress leaders were at pains to explain that not all Congressmen were of such opinions. While in many of the constituencies in the Circars where the Congress was opposed by zamindars or zamindars' agents, the Congress used anti-zamindari slogans and campaigned through

[226] *Justice* 22 Jan. 1937.
[227] Patro to Erskine, 4 Mar. 1937, Erskine papers vol. XIX IOL.

zamindari tenant associations, in one constituency in the centre of this area the Congress fielded the zamindar of Jayantipuram. Similarly in Ramnad, where the chief opponents were the acolytes of the raja of Ramnad, tenant associations were again in evidence in the Congress election campaign. In nearby Tiruchengodu, Dr Subbaroyan, the zamindar of Kumaramangalam, ran on the Congress slate. In some constituencies, the Congress was opposed by Sanatanist candidates who feared that Government would trample on orthodox religion, and in these places the Congress candidates urged that religious orthodoxy was not an electoral problem.[228] Yet in great centres of orthodox culture, such as Kumbakonam, the Congress candidate attended Sanatanist meetings and gave carefully worded addresses about Congress and religion.[229] The Congress electoral appeal was tailored to local conditions.

In 1926, one of the chief reasons for the Swarajists' electoral success had been that it was predictable; many had believed that the Swarajists would win the elections and form a ministry, and this belief helped to secure the success. In the same manner, by the time of the polls in February 1937 there were many in the ranks of the Congress who thought it would win, and whose massed support would ensure victory. To many it already seemed that the route to influence and power lay through the Congress. The issue of office-acceptance had again been put on the shelf at the all-India Congress session in December, but the mass of opinion in Madras was clear on the subject. As Erskine told the Viceroy after the results were in: 'The present Congress majority are in no way a cohesive mass. Many of them are men who till quite lately were Justicites or Liberals, and the Party as a whole will be quite furious if they are not allowed to accept the ministerships.'[230] Since 1934, the Congress press had trumpeted every electoral victory and ignored every setback in order to give an illusion of unbroken success. This policy was continued right up to the moment of the polls. Owing to the staggering of elections in the different provinces, the Orissa results were published before Madras went to vote, and the Congress victory there gave a great boost to the

[228] This was particularly common in Madras City, see for instance *Hindu* 1 Feb. 1937.

[229] *Hindu* 2 and 16 Feb. 1937.

[230] Erskine to Linlithgow, 10 Mar. 1937, Erskine papers vol. VIII IOL; Rajagopalachari visited Erskine fifteen days before the polls and told him that Congress would accept office, see Erskine to Linlithgow, 3 Feb. 1937, Erskine papers vol. VIII IOL.

last days of the Congress campaign in Madras.[231] As the election campaign hotted up in late 1936, Erskine had complained bitterly that he was ham-strung by the all-India government policy to appear strictly neutral at the elections and that he could therefore do nothing to counteract the Congress propaganda that they were going to win. 'We are being strongly attacked by the moderate parties', he complained, 'for allowing seditionist statements to be made without prosecuting the speakers and it is being said that the government are abdicating in favour of the Congress and have deserted the Justice Party and the other moderates who have always been supporters of the British Raj.' Even worse in Erskine's view was the Congress attempt to use governmental power before they had really got their hands on it. 'In certain cases,' wrote Erskine, 'threats have publicly been made to the Police that if they do their duty and prevent Congress hooliganism, they will be individually punished by dismissal after April 1st.'[232]

The Justice party could not match the new methods employed and the new prospects promised by the Congress. The party had never possessed the machinery for conducting a public campaign throughout the province, and being in such disarray in the 1930s it could take only feeble steps towards creating one. In early 1935, pro-Justice groups in the mofussil urged Bobbili and other party leaders to resuscitate the party to meet the growing Congress challenge.[233] In 1935–6, as old Justice satellites faced the Congress campaigns in local board elections, these exhortations became more frequent and more desperate. Virudunagar, Salem and Trichinopoly – all places where Congress campaigns scored notable successes – led the movement to press Bobbili into action. The Nadar clique in Virudunagar finally called a conference on their own authority in March 1935 and discussed party organisation.[234] This was followed by a conference of Justice leaders from the Tamil districts at Coimbatore in June,[235] a meeting of Justicites from Andhra at Guntur in October,[236] and several smaller meetings. The Virudunagar meeting appointed two paid propagandists. The Coimbatore conference voted a subsidy to Ramaswami Naicker to use his paper *Viduthalai* as a party

[231] *Hindu* 1 Feb. 1937.

[232] Erskine to Linlithgow, 14 June 1936, Linlithgow papers vol. CXVI IOL.

[233] *Justice* 4 Feb. 1935; *Hindu* 7, 10 and 17 Jan. 1935, 13 Feb. 1935.

[234] *Justice* 30 Mar. 1935, 1 Apr. 1935.

[235] *Hindu* 17 June 1935.

[236] *Justice* 7 Oct. 1935.

organ and agreed that the paper should come out as a daily as soon as sufficient finance could be found; it also started a drive to enrol party members. At the Guntur conference, claimed the *Justice*, 'for the first time in the history of the Party, a Party fund has been inaugurated, to which over a lakh of rupees has been subscribed, the Hon. the Rajah Saheb of Bobbili leading with a donation of Rs 25,000.'[237] In the following months, the Justice leaders set up a central committee for the first time, appointed district organisers and opened a party office in Madras City. Branch organisations were newly established or revived in Ramnad, Anantapur, Tenkasi and a few other mofussil centres.[238] A Young Justicite League and a Non-Brahman National Youth League were established in the City with branches in some mofussil towns,[239] and both P. T. Rajan and Bobbili went off on long tours to revive support. Bobbili also tried to patch up quarrels among party members. He brought the erring Muthiah Chettiar back into the fold, and made a settlement with Muniswami Naidu and his followers who were still smarting from the insult delivered at the Tanjore conference in 1932.[240] Finally on his tour of Andhra he managed to patch up an agreement between the raja of Mirzapuram and the raja of Chellapalle, whose private feuding was threatening to give the Congress an easy run at the local elections in the Kistna–Godavari deltas.[241] He also tried to win back the support of the raja of Pithapuram who was threatening to leave the party and take his considerable financial support elsewhere.[242] The party also acquired a manifesto; some of the zealous party workers in Tamilnad dusted off the programme that E. V. Ramaswami Naicker had written for the Self-Respect movement at its 1931 conference at Erode and urged the Justice leaders to adopt it. Meanwhile other Justice leaders took up a more defiant stance towards the Congress. S. Kumaraswami Reddi railed:

> The Justice Party is given the dignified name of job-hunters. Yes we are all job-hunters. Is there anybody amongst you, Congressmen included, who does not care to have a job for himself or his relatives? If we ask for a ministry, it is job-hunting; and if Congressmen ask for it, it is patriotism![243]

[237] *Justice* 7 Oct. 1935.
[238] *Hindu* 25 Dec. 1935, 16 Mar. 1936; *Justice* 16 Dec. 1935, 7 Jan. 1936, 8 Apr. 1936.
[239] *Justice* 4 and 13 Feb. 1935, 15 Aug. 1935; *Hindu* 17 Sept. 1935.
[240] *Justice* 25 Mar. 1935; *Hindu* 22 Mar. 1935, 11 Dec. 1935.
[241] *Justice* 7 Oct. 1935.
[242] *Hindu* 20 Dec. 1935.
[243] *Hindu* 28 June 1935.

Just as the party was moving into a higher gear, however, the raja of Bobbili left for a tour of Europe,[244] the organisational impetus faltered and the party leaders returned to their old concern with petty intrigue. In early 1936, a committee consisting of E. V. Ramaswami Naicker, V. V. Ramaswamy, W. P. A. Soundarapandian and C. D. Nayagam toured the Tamil districts and a few conferences were held in Andhra, but the party leaders, as one disillusioned party worker complained, 'are not in touch with the supporters in the City or elsewhere' and the party had 'ceased . . . to function as a political entity'.[245] Bobbili refused to give the party a policy, and Muthiah Chettiar refused to let the party workers have the resources of the Tamil newspaper the *Dravidian* to use for campaign purposes.[246] There was simply too wide a gap between the entrenched leaders of the party and the new hopefuls. Bobbili and his cohorts were wary of Ramaswami Naicker and his radical ideas, but it was Ramaswami Naicker and his adherents who provided much of the impetus for a revival of the party. Reluctantly, Bobbili agreed to adopt Ramaswami Naicker's electoral programme,[247] but thereafter it was studiously ignored. His paper was not given enough funds to make it into a daily until the Justice leaders had looked around for other possible party organs,[248] and so the *Viduthalai* did not appear as a daily until a few weeks before the polls.[249] The committee set up to select Justicite candidates for the Assembly elections consisted of Patro, Mohammed Oosman and the kumararaja of Venkatagiri, all old party stalwarts, and none of the energetic new party workers.[250] The *Justice*'s main propaganda onslaught focussed on an analysis of the administration of the Congress Tilak Swarajya Fund during Non-co-operation, an issue which was now a piece of ancient history and which could only be used with some difficulty since one of the chief villains of the piece, Ramaswami Naicker, was now on the *Justice*'s own side and had to be written out of the account.[251]

Lord Erskine and his advisers viewed the Justice party with dismay. The Madras Government had since 1929 looked on the idea of constitutional reform with equanimity since they fully expected

244 *Hindu* 4 Apr. 1936.

245 *Hindu* 16 May 1936.

246 *Justice* 4 and 6 May 1936.

247 *Justice* 19 Nov. 1935.

248 See the flirtation with Dr P. Varadarajulu Naidu: Dr P. Varadarajulu Naidu to R. K. Shanmugham Chetty, 12 Jan. 1935, 18 Feb. 1935 and 26 July 1935, Shanmugham Chetty papers.

249 *Justice* 4 Jan. 1937.

250 *Justice* 30 Nov. 1936.

251 See issues of *Justice* in December 1936 and January 1937.

their Justicite friends to maintain their dominance over provincial affairs; but now they were beginning to have doubts. Indeed, they had become nervous enough to use governmental influence to help the Justicite cause. In 1936, it was rumoured, Erskine had been persuaded by Justice leaders to use his influence to get the government in Delhi to reduce and then to remit altogether a stiff prison sentence passed on an influential Justicite magnate in Coimbatore; local Congress organisers had been very annoyed about the effect such a blatant display of government favour could have on popular political loyalties.[252] Erskine had also tried to get the India Office to change the electoral rules; the Justicite leaders felt that they would have more chance of retaining influence if the new legislatures were chosen by indirect rather than direct election and Erskine had canvassed, unsuccessfully, for London to introduce indirect elections.[253] A senior I.C.S. officer in Madras wrote to the old Justicite, Shanmugham Chetty, who had recently found a more comfortable nest as Dewan in the native state of Cochin, and begged him to use his influence to help the ailing Justice party on the eve of the elections.[254] But despite the efforts of Governor and senior civil servants, the Justice party refused to be revived. 'I regret to say,' wrote Erskine to London in May 1936, 'that the Justice Party are all asleep and, kick their leaders as I may, I have not yet succeeded in affecting their lethargy.'[255] Bobbili still felt he could rely on his old allies and his old methods. In the dying days of 1936, he made a desperate attempt to rescue Justicite fortunes by using the machinery of local government, by bifurcating four district boards. The Ramnad affair, as noted above, caused a major furore, meanwhile in three districts of Andhra Bobbili bifurcated, delayed elections and snatched all of the boards from the clutches of the Congress. It was the last straw. After the Assembly polls, Erskine wrote:

[252] Erskine to Linlithgow, 1 Mar. 1937, Erskine papers vol. VIII IOL.

[253] Erskine to R. A. Butler, 25 July 1935, Erskine papers vol. XVIII IOL; Patro, while in London in 1935, also had a try: 'Patro made a great song when he was at home last and tried to suborn Sam [Hoare] by telling him that the new franchise would redound to the disadvantage of the Justice Party. I never believed it . . . He attempted to suborn me by saying, "My dear R. A. Butler, men with a future are those who have the courage to change their minds, and you could now restrict the franchise and give indirect election."' R. A. Butler to Erskine, 23 May 1935, Erskine papers vol. XVIII IOL.

[254] L. Graham to R. K. Shanmugham Chetty, 26 Apr. 1936, Shanmugham Chetty papers.

[255] Erskine to R. A. Butler, 9 May 1936, Erskine papers vol. XIX IOL.

The class who run the district boards and generally take an interest in local self-government have shown their resentment at Bobbili's conduct of affairs by voting against his candidates. In fact I have seen a good many electors of this category in Madras City, and most of them have openly told me that they voted for the Congress nominees for two reasons: firstly because they had received private assurances from Congress leaders that they would be prepared to accept office and behave reasonably, and secondly because they wished to register their dislike at Bobbili's conduct of his department.[256]

In May 1936, a new party was formed in the province. It consisted almost entirely of politicians who had decided that the Justice party was bankrupt and that, as its manifesto stated, 'there is a great necessity for a well-organised constitutional party'.[257] This People's party was led by the raja of Pithapuram, the East Godavari zamindar and politician, who had been a supporter and financier of the Justice party since its foundation in 1916, and who had recently been intriguing unsuccessfully to replace Bobbili at the head of the Justice party. The core of the party was Pithapuram's allies in the politics of the Circar districts, and allies of its other chief organiser S. Muthiah Mudaliar, the Tanjore politician who had been made a minister under Panagal's auspices in the late 1920s. Pithapuram and Muthiah Mudaliar toured round the province in September and October and attracted many politicians who saw no future in loyalty to the Justice party but who, unlike many others, felt they could not transfer their allegiance to the Congress. The leaders established some branch organisations and found a handful of willing election candidates, yet as a political organisation it fell between all the stools. The Congress press called it a 'party of political orphans who are doubtful about becoming Ministers if they remain in the Justice Party',[258] while the *Justice* proclaimed that 'our party will always prefer Congressmen who are our open enemies to unprincipled jobhunters [like the] mongrel puppy, whelp and hound and curs of low degree' who formed the new party.[259] Predictably the Justice party spent more of its energies attacking these renegades than countering the Congress in the months before the election.

Those who joined the People's party were just the last in a long line of deserters from the Justicite camp. Many of the most prominent

256 Erskine to Linlithgow 1 Mar. 1937, Erskine papers vol. VIII IOL.
257 *Hindu* 16 May 1936.
258 *Jaya Bharati* 22 July 1936 NNR.
259 *Justice* 2 Nov. 1936, 12 Jan. 1937.

opponents of the Congress had abandoned the battlefield before the province went to the polls. R. K. Shanmugham Chetty, for instance, had chased after jobs in Delhi and abroad before securing the post of Dewan in Cochin.[260] A. Ramaswami Mudaliar had sought a job in Delhi and had finally got a place on the new Council of India there, and Patro had also fished for a job outside Madras. Less than a third of the members of the old Legislative Council chose to risk their reputations before the new electorate.

The Congress faced little enthusiastic opposition in 1937. The new electorate had not rushed to claim the franchise. Despite widespread government advertisement and well-organised Congress registration campaigns, by the date fixed for the completion of the preliminary electoral roll only six of the twenty-five districts had yielded up the 15 per cent of the population that government expected would register.[261] On polling day, only half of these came forward to cast their votes. The percentage poll of 51.6 in Madras was lower than that in any other province except Bengal.[262] 'Both Congress and Justice', wrote Erskine a few weeks before the polls, 'seem to be disliked by the population. I suppose that the party that is disliked least will do best, but there is no real enthusiasm for either side.'[263]

In the 109 general constituencies (returning 146 members) Congress fielded 138 candidates, the Justice party 90 and the People's party 45.[264] In many constituencies, the opposition to the Congress candidate was only nominal, as the margin of the Congress victories suggested. In two of the general constituencies the Congress did not put up a candidate and in five they were not opposed. In the remainder, they polled over 60 per cent of the vote in eighty-six constituencies, over 75 per cent in forty-four, and over 90 per cent in fifteen.[265] Polling day was quiet. There were ructions only in Pallathur, where the memory of the recent fiasco at the Ramnad district board elections was still fresh, and in the raja of Bobbili's constituency where the chief minister employed every possible device to try and retain control.[266] There was little of the fervour or the violence that had

[260] S. G. Jog to R. K. Shanmugham Chetty, 2 Mar. 1935; Vasudevaraja of Kollengode to R. K. Shanmugham Chetty, 9 June 1935, Shanmugham Chetty papers.

[261] *Hindu* 15 July 1936.

[262] GOI Home Political 129 1937 NAI; GOI Reforms 20-F 1936 NAI.

[263] Erskine to Linlithgow, 14 June 1936, Linlithgow papers vols. CXVI IOL.

[264] FR January(1), GOI Home Political 18–1 1937 NAI.

[265] Calculated from results in GOI Home Political 129 1937 NAI.

[266] *Hindu* 2, 23 and 24 Feb. 1937.

TABLE 20. *The Madras Legislative Assembly election results 1937*

Constituency	Total	Congress	Justice	People's party	Muslim League	Muslim Progressive party	Independent or no party
General (open)	116	111	3	—	—	—	2
General (scheduled castes)	30	26	2	—	—	—	2
Mohammedan	28	4	8	—	9	1	6
Christian	8	3	4	—	—	—	1
European and Anglo-Indian	5	—	—	—	—	—	5
Women	8	7	—	—	—	—	1
European commerce, etc.	4	—	—	—	—	—	4
S. Indian Chamber of Commerce	1	—	—	—	—	—	1
Nattukottai Nagarathars	1	—	1	—	—	—	—
Landholders	6	—	3	1	—	—	2
Labour	6	6	—	—	—	—	—
University	1	1	—	—	—	—	—
Backward tribes	1	1	—	—	—	—	—
Total	215	159	21	1	9	1	24

marked local government elections in recent years. Congress had won by default.

CONGRESS VICTORY

The result surprised even the most optimistic Congressmen. They won all but 9 of the 146 general seats, and 159 of the 215 seats overall. The raja of Pithapuram, contesting a landholders' seat where only fifty-eight voters polled, was the only candidate returned for the People's party, and the Justice party got only twenty-one seats, more than half of these in the special Muslim and Christian constituencies. The raja of Bobbili, P. T. Rajan, the kumararaja of Venkatagiri and A. P. Patro were all defeated. Only twelve Congress candidates were defeated, five of them in Muslim constituencies where Congress faced two Muslim parties. Congress polled 64.5 per cent of the vote and won 73.8 per cent of the seats. It was the most striking Congress victory in any of the provinces.[267]

The widening of the franchise, and the increase in the number of seats did not radically change the character of persons elected.[268] Indeed thirty-two of the members of the Legislative Assembly (M.L.A.s) elected in 1937 had sat in the legislature during dyarchy. Few were new to politics. Three-fifths of them had been in local government – a quarter had been in local boards for at least ten years – and most of these had held an executive position in local government at some time. In each successive election under dyarchy, a larger proportion of the seats was filled by landlords and agriculturists, while the remainder was made up of merchants, lawyers and other professionals. The M.L.A.s of 1937 followed a similar pattern. The vast majority were landed, many with a sideline interest in commerce or rural industry. Meanwhile ninety-four of them possessed B. A.s, sixty-four

[267] GOI Home Political 129 1937 NAI.

[268] This survey of the M.L.A.s elected in 1937 is based on a wide variety of sources including: T. N. Satchit, *Who's Who in Madras* 1935 and 1938 editions; *Directory of the Madras Legislature*, published by the Madras Legislature Congress Party (Madras, 1938); C. Ranga Rao, *Andhra Desa Directory and Who's Who* (Bezwada, 1939) GOI Reforms Franchise B 34–99 March 1921 NAI; GOI Home Public 953 1924 NAI; GOI Home Public 325 1930 NAI; GOI Home Public 311 & Kw 1934 NAI; GOI Reforms 50/2-R 1946 NAI; details on membership of local boards taken from *Madras Civil List* and the files of the LSG department; other details from many of the biographies and commemoration volumes listed in the bibliography.

were drawn from the legal profession and another twenty-two from medicine, journalism and teaching.

The Congress contingent was not markedly different from the overall pattern. Seventy-seven of the 137 Congressmen returned by the general constituencies had been in local government, and almost half of those had ten years' experience there. Thirty-one were involved with co-operative societies and local banks. This was not an army of men totally new to the politics of locality and province.

The 159 M.L.A.s of the Congress Assembly party fell into three roughly equal groups. The first group was the hard core who had been closely involved in the Congress work for several years; fifty-five had been to jail for the cause. The hard core included both men like A. Kaleswara Rao, who had been consistently involved with the Congress in Andhra for twenty years but who simultaneously had maintained many political interests outside the Congress, and men like C. P. Subbiah, a party worker who had been involved in every agitation since 1919, whose organising abilities had won him a place on the Tamilnad Congress and on the all-India Congress Committee, and who had been backed at the elections by prominent Coimbatore magnates despite his low status and minimal influence in the locality.

The second group was more varied. Some were established politicians, often from remote areas of the presidency, who had not hitherto been called upon to identify themselves with political alignments outside their neighbourhood. Such was B. Anantachar of Bellary, who had been prominent in the local bar, banks and municipality politics for twenty years but had never before ventured into wider political worlds. Some were young men who had only stepped into politics as Congress began its rapid rise. Such was Arunachalam Chettiar of Ramnad, scion of a rich Nattukottai banking family, who had made his debut in local politics in 1936 at the age of twenty-eight. Others were representatives of the new special electorates – labour, women and scheduled castes – whom the Congress alone had taken the trouble to recruit and assist at the elections.

The final group was the recent adherents, men who had switched their political horses since 1934. About one-third of the party fell into this category. Fourteen had sat in previous legislatures under a non-Congress flag; such was K. Sitarama Reddi of Cuddalore who had been an acolyte of the first Justicite chief minister, who had presided over the South Arcot district board for nine years, and who since 1930 had been appointed by the Justice ministry first to the Hindu Religious Endowments Board and then as the first Commissioner of the Tirupati temple. Some had been Justicite satellites in local government; such was R. B. Ramakrishna Raju who came from an old zamindari family in Chittoor district, was well received by the local gentry (including the family of the raja of Panagal), had spent fifteen years in local boards, and had been local henchman of the Justicite chief minister Muniswami Naidu.

The Madras Congress was anxious to form a ministry. The all-India Congress committee was inundated with records of resolutions passed by Congress gatherings urging the Congress to enter the ministries.[269] Government too was anxious. If Congress did not assume office, it would be difficult to work the Madras Assembly and the province would have to be governed much as before. Besides, the Congress victory had touched off a wave of euphoria, resulting in a rash of strikes and demonstrations. 'Once we can get a Ministry into office,' wrote the Viceroy to Erskine, 'we may hope to see the trouble makers adequately dealt with by their own countrymen.'[270] But the all-India Congress had to placate Congressmen throughout India. The Congress Socialists were set against office, and the Congress parties in Maharashtra, U.P., Bengal and Punjab, where the Congress had been less successful at the polls, were not as keen on office as the Congressmen of Madras were.

As a compromise formula, the all-India Congress leaders demanded certain reassurances that the Governor's safeguards would not be used. The Governor demurred, the Congress refused to form a ministry and the Governor was obliged to form a caretaker cabinet. In the following weeks Congress leaders in Madras capitalised on the wave of euphoria to stage demonstrations and processions, while Rajagopalachari negotiated with Lord Erskine on one hand and the all-India Congress leaders on the other. Finally in July, without any significant concession by the Governor, the Congress gave way.[271] Rajagopalachari became chief minister and selected nine other Congressmen for his cabinet.[272] The Congress was in power.

The success of the provincial Congress in the 1930s was founded

[269] AICC papers file G62 of 1937 NMML.

[270] Linlithgow to Erskine, 29 Dec. 1936, Linlithgow papers file CXVI IOL.

[271] See the FRs between March and July 1937, GOI Home Political 18-3, 18-4, 18-5, 18-6, 18-7 1937 NAI.

[272] The other ministers were: Dr P. Subbaroyan, Dr T. S. S. Rajan, V. I. Muniswami Pillai, V. V. Giri, Yakub Hassan, S. Ramanathan, K. Raman Menon, B. Gopal Reddi, T. Prakasam; AICC papers file PL3(i) of 1937 NMML.

upon its openness, its eclecticism and its flexibility. The organisation was loose. There were few people who had invested their political future wholly in the organisation and would thus fight hard to keep it to one policy, and there was not such a strong control from the top that policies and strategies could not be moulded to the wishes of a wide section of the people. The Congress was pushed towards elections in the mid-1930s because enough people required the facilities which an organisation like the Congress could provide for electoral purposes.

The strength of the Congress was based, as it always had been, on the accumulated strength of its constituent members. The Congress grew to be so important in the decade because so many of the influential men in the province entered the organisation. Most of the leaders of the Congress were men who commanded much the same sort of resources as previous political leaders in the province; they were rich landlords, merchants and financiers or the professional men who worked with them. There were a few who had found their way to influence through 'institutional' rather than 'personal' means: B. Pattabhi Sitaramayya, who had risen to importance through his skill in managing new financial institutions, banks, co-operative societies and insurance companies and in organising new political associations, Congress committees and local pressure groups, was the prime example, but he was still in very select company.

With the entry of so many men with personal influence, the provincial Congress had acquired firmer foundations. It had spread its network of committees far wider and deeper into provincial society; it had acquired more permanent bureaucratic existence; and it had forged contacts with groups ranging from students to zamindars. With the success in 1937 these foundations became even firmer. It was in the months after the capture of the ministry that the provincial Congress gained a network of Congress committees which covered every district and taluk in the province. It was in the two years when the Congress ministry was in power that every local politician had to review his attitude to the Congress. Congress membership in Tamilnad and Andhra which had stood at 115,971 in 1936 had risen to 594,397 two years later.[273] The provincial Congress, like the Justice party before, had come of age by attaching itself to the governmental system laid out by the Raj. But the Congress did not simply become a part of this governmental system, it also added to it. The Congress

[273] See table 21.

TABLE 21. *Congress membership*

Date	Andhra Pradesh	Tamilnad	Total	
April 1923	1,562	8,836	10,398	i
December 1925	2,678	2,250	4,928	ii
July 1929	4,531	3,135	7,666	iii
December 1929	36,087	29,685	65,772	iv
Late 1935	45,103	55,004	100,107	v
Late 1936	50,866	65,105	115,971	vi
1938	334,030	260,367	594,397	vii

SOURCES: i – *Hindu* 19 Apr. 1923; ii – *Indian Annual Register 1925*, vol. II, p. 17; iii – AICC papers files P24 and P30(i) of 1929 NMML; iv – *Indian Annual Register 1929*, vol. II, p. 264; v – AICC papers file G36 of 1935 NMML; vi – AICC papers file P25 of 1937 NMML and *Hindu* 17 Oct. 1936; vii – AICC papers file P19(ii) of 1937–8 NMML.

provided machinery for selecting leaders, settling disputes and for deciding policies which supplemented the formal institutions of representative government.

POSTSCRIPT

South India changed rapidly in the years following 1937. The potential of the Congress government was barely realised. Its many acts of legislation included a measure of debt relief which helped to untie the knots in the credit system, but its most ambitious measures on education and land tenure never reached the statute book. Education reforms were sunk when the bureaucracy proved too inflexible to implement them and when opponents of the Congress regime chose to make the issue of education a political casus belli. The desire of both government officials and many Congressmen to abolish the zamindari system or at least impose drastic reforms on it was overtaken by the influx of zamindars and their agents into the newly influential Congress.[274] The Madras ministry resigned, along with the Congress ministries in other provinces, in 1939; ostensibly it was because of Britain's attitude to India in wartime, but partly at least it was because the machinery of Congress had proved too raw and too weak for the demands which were put on it when it became part of the

[274] N. S. Venguswamy, *Congress in Office* (Bombay, 1940).

administrative machinery of the province.[275] During the war, the constitutional machinery was put on the shelf and Madras was returned to direct rule through officials and hand-picked Indian helpers. When hostilities had ceased and the constitutional machinery was resurrected and refurbished, the Congress came forward to occupy its old position in it and to carry south India into the independent state of India.[276] Although the Congress was formed out of its local and provincial parts, and although much of its impetus came from parochial and regional loyalties, it was built around the unities of Imperial India and it would preserve most of those in the independent state. The men who dominated the Congress governments in the first twenty years of independence in the south were mostly drawn from the ranks of those who had emerged to the front in the dyarchy period. The triumph of the Dravida Munnetra Kazhagam (D.M.K.) in Tamilnad in 1967 and the rise of the Telangana movement in Andhra Pradesh soon after that ushered in a new period.

Meanwhile the aftermath of the depression and the changes of the 1930s brought new factors into the politics of the region. In some areas, the rural dislocation made way for new movements of class conflict. In deltaic Andhra, the rural protests of the 1930s were followed by the foundation and spread of revolutionary parties.[277] In Tanjore, a movement of protest had already taken root among the labouring castes in the 1930s, and in the next thirty years it would grow gradually stronger. In the towns and particularly in Madras City and other big towns of the region, the influx of people from the land brought new problems, new political conflicts and new political leaders. Demonstrations against the Congress government in 1938–9 drew on a new and more violent strain of urban radicalism than had been seen before. Student leaders and trade union organisers played a large part in these agitations, while new urban media such as the cheap press, the satirical journal and the cinema film helped to fan political feelings.[278]

The fortunes of non-Brahmanism differed in the north and the south of the province. Although Telugus had provided most of the leadership and finance for the Justice party, after 1937 the non-Brahman issue faded into insignificance as the Telugus were con-

[275] Tomlinson, 'Nationalism and Indian politics', pp. 310–17, 423–4.
[276] For the post-war election results see GOI Reforms 94/4-R 1945 NAI.
[277] S. Harrison, *India – the most dangerous decades* (Princeton, 1960), pp. 181–210.
[278] B. S. Baliga, *Tanjore District Handbook* (Madras, 1957), pp. 112–17. T. M. Parthasarathy, *Ti. Mu. Kalaka Varalaru* (Madras, 1961), pp. 22–6.

sumed with the formation of their own state of Andhra Pradesh and, after this had been achieved in 1956, with the problems thrown up by the very different features and historical experiences of the component parts of the new state. In Tamilnad too, the main political concern was with statehood but here it sustained rather than swamped the politics of caste. 'By adding to the tepid enthusiasms of rationalism the more fiery urges of sub-nationalism', as one observer of Tamilnad politics noted, non-Brahman politics were given new vigour as part of the defence of Tamil interests in a sovereign state ruled from north India.[279]

The Justice party virtually died with dyarchy. After the 1937 defeat, some of the leaders including Bobbili withdrew gracefully from politics while others looked round for opportunities outside the province. The rump joined more closely with Ramaswami Naicker and his followers and were on the point of choosing the demands of the Andhras for a separate state as an issue with which to embarrass the Congress ministry when Rajagopalachari's government made the study of Hindi compulsory in Madras schools. Rajagopalachari did not want the measure but it was a concession he had to make to the leaders of the all-India Congress and to the truly nationalist aspirations of the freedom movement. Nor, indeed, did the measure have much impact since there were few Hindi teachers.[280] Yet it was the first sign of north Indian domination and it enabled Ramaswami Naicker and the Justicite rump to join hands with student politicians, trade unionists and agitational leaders and stage a long and impressive agitation in which 1,000 people were arrested.[281] The shaky alliance of Justicites and Ramaswami Naicker's Self-Respect followers continued into the early 1940s until first the Self-Respecters threw off the patronage of the Justicites (many of whom had been drafted in to help government in the wartime administration), and then Ramaswami Naicker himself was squeezed out by younger agitators and student leaders led by C. N. Annadurai.[282] In the next twenty years, their new organisation, the Dravida Munnetra Kazhagam, became the chief focus of opposition to the Congress regime in Tamilnad. The D.M.K. fostered at different times and in different permutations the non-Brahman cause, movements among the politically and socially under-

[279] P. Spratt, *D. M. K. in Power* (Bombay, 1970), p. 31.

[280] Papers of Sir Christopher Masterman (who was secretary of the education department in Madras in 1938), SAS.

[281] Parthasarathy, *Ti. Mu. Kalaka Varalaru*, p. 23.

[282] *Ibid.* pp. 25–36.

privileged, the promotion of Tamil culture, and resentment of north India. By the time it achieved office in 1967, however, subnationalism had finally swamped communalism, non-Brahmanism had been almost completely left behind, and the D.M.K. resembled the many other pragmatic parties on the Indian subcontinent.[283]

[283] See Spratt, *D.M.K. in Power*, and T. V. Sathyamurthy, 'The Dravida Munnetra Kazhagam in the politics of Tamil Nadu 1949–71', paper presented to the seminar on leadership in South Asia, School of Oriental and African Studies London, January 1974.

Conclusion

The British government in south India in the mid-nineteenth century was perched over a society which was closely controlled by those with mastery over its slowly developing economy. Between the governors and the mass of the governed was interposed a stratum of local leaders and subordinate Indian administrators. This stratum insulated the government from the problems and protests of local society, and helped to give to south India an appearance of enduring calm; but it also locked government out of its own administrative system and hindered government attempts to encourage change.

Towards the end of the century, under the pressure of financial and administrative needs, government was forced down more firmly on the society. Government took on many new roles and government intruded into the backyard of many more of the population. Government also became far more important as a controller of men and resources. An equal and opposite reaction was bound to follow.

The new administrative machinery tied together in a much firmer fashion than before the parts of what had been an immensely disparate and fragmented province; it united the Madras Presidency as a political unit centred on the provincial capital. Power had been withdrawn from the districts and relocated in the institutions in Madras City. Thus in the early years of the twentieth century, the political temperature of the provincial capital rose dramatically. Government provided opportunities for Indians to spread their political influence over an area which, until the British had created the province and now pulled it together, had never existed as a unit before. The first opportunities were given to government's non-official advisers, and were monopolised by a close-knit group of the most successful legal and service families in Madras City. With the inauguration of the Montagu–Chelmsford reforms in 1920, however, these positions of influence were formalised in an elected legislature with Indian ministers. The prizes now passed to the only group to pose as the leaders of a political party prepared to work the new constitution, the Justicites. Balanced still on stable social foundations, this new administrative structure functioned smoothly for a decade.

Yet the new administration attracted more interests than it could accommodate. The Raj was now governing south India more closely than it had ever been governed before; but it was also governing by devolving power on to a few Indians whom, it hoped, it could cajole into trusty collaboration. The uneven nature of this devolution of power soon rankled. The institutions of local and provincial government were soon filled up by those who controlled the wealth and resources of the society, and the contests to occupy the few places of power and privilege grew more dramatic and more bitter. Yet for the moment there was nothing which could compare with government's stock of power and patronage as a focus of political ambitions and political loyalties. Those who stood across the corridors leading in and out of the governmental machine seemed unassailable.

In the 1930s, the situation changed dramatically. The world depression in trade and agriculture delivered an unprecedented blow to the agrarian economy and rural society of the province. The firm foundations on which the smooth administration of Madras had for so long been mounted were shaken and in some places dissolved. Political rivalry took on new dimensions, and began to overflow the machinery provided by the Raj. At the same time, government was changing yet again. In line with a world-wide policy of withdrawal from unnecessary commitments, the British disentangled themselves from the affairs of Indian province and locality in order to concentrate on those aspects of the Indian empire which were more immediately important to Britain's position in the world. The machinery of the provincial leviathan was left intact, but the imperial rulers abandoned their role as the immediate arbiters of power in the province and withdrew to loftier heights.

The loose structure of provincial control managed by the Justicites departed with them. The race for power now required wider and more elaborate methods and institutions. In the 1930s, men of influence in provincial and local society rebuilt the Congress to suit their needs, and drove it into the vacuum left by the withdrawing rulers.

The administrative changes begun in the late nineteenth century had made government loom very large in the life of the region. No previous government had controlled men and resources to such an extent. Moreover, the governmental machine, although it was often manipulated from the bottom, concentrated much of the power to make decisions and to distribute resources at the very top. The power to divide up the purse was jealously guarded. Under dyarchy, it was held by the Governor; even under provincial autonomy from 1937, Delhi retained enough power over expenditure; and in independent India, the central government has retained enough financial powers in the armoury of weapons it can wield against the states.

Politicians thus always had to propitiate their masters. The Mylaporeans fell from favour and lost much of their influence when they dared to snub the Governor. The Justice leaders were glad to be part of the 'Happy Family' of Lord Willingdon, and even the Congress ministry installed in 1937 sought a similarly cosy position in the imperial household. 'His Excellency the Governor', noted a Congress minister, 'has assured us every cooperation and sympathy and I am not letting out any secret of the cabinet in informing you that His Excellency has been our friend, guide and philosopher.'[1]

This position enabled the British rulers to dictate the form but not the content of Indian politics. Political groupings adopted the vocabulary of British politics. Political leaders expressed their demands in language that they expected the rulers would understand and would respond to. It was no coincidence that political caste associations appeared soon after government began to use caste considerations in important facets of its administration. In the same manner, the non-Brahman movement appeared in part at least because it gratified British expectations. In one sense the quarrel between Brahman and non-Brahman arose from the brief concentration of political interest on the affairs of the public services and of the provincial capital, where rivalries could with advantage be squeezed into the communal model. But in other senses, it was the rulers' own fear of the dominance (and then the dissidence) of a handful of Brahmans in Mylapore, that ensured that a petition for admission into positions of power and influence would be couched in communal terms.

The rulers dictated the shape of political groupings in another way, a way which ensured that the non-Brahman movement would never acquire the substance which it professed. Government was creating unities where before there had only been disparity. It had cobbled together the varied localities of south India within the anomalous outline of the Madras Presidency. This was the unit which administrative institutions straddled, and this was the unit which political

[1] Venguswamy, *Congress in Office*, p. 71.

movements would have to encompass. The variety of the province defied any attempt to mount a political movement on any social base. It would have to be eclectic in its outlook, eclectic in its choice of supporters. This was particularly true of a body such as the Justice party which spanned the region by moving through the only channels which tied the region together, that is, the channels of government administration.

The Raj linked not only locality to province but also province to nation. The Congress spanned the same range. The appearance of the Indian National Congress in the late nineteenth century reflected the way that certain matters in the government of the various provinces were decided on an all-India scale, and an all-India organisation was necessary if politicians wished to gain influence over such decisions. The spread of the Congress into the localities in the 1920s and 1930s reflected the way that the localities had been merged more firmly into the province. When the Swarajists in the mid-1920s and the Congress in the mid-1930s set out to invade the constitutional structure, they had to stretch the skein of their organisation right over the framework tacked together by government; they had to encompass both the imperial capital and the locality and thus even more than the Justice party, the Congress had to resolve great differences within its ranks.

Political parties were not built around their ideologies. In the case of the Justice party, it was its functions that attracted support not its attributes. Similarly, it was not merely the fervour of patriotism that drew so many into the Congress in the 1930s. That is not to say that members of the Congress did not believe in the goals of nationalism, which of course they did. Yet by the period of this study, the problem which faced politicians was not the rightness or wrongness of nationalism as the ultimate goal of politics, but the priority that nationalism should have among other political goals and the strategies that were correct for the nationalist movement. Circumstances in the 1930s brought nationalist aspirations and the more immediate goals of the local and provincial politician close together.

Nor were political parties built out of units of caste. The vocabulary of south Indian politics has led many commentators to suggest that caste was the creative force in the region's affairs, and these suggestions couched so often in the language of warfare – unit, conflict, mobilisation – have painted a picture of communal armies marching across the political map of the region. In this period at least, the evidence to support such a view is slight. In so far as considerations of lineage, clan and ritual status permeate local society, as every anthropological study in the region has shown, politics were founded on caste. Yet neither castes nor subcastes functioned as constituencies or pressure-groups in anything but the most ephemeral fashion. South Indian society did not consist of a series of family, clan, subcaste and caste units each aware of its own extent and each nesting within the one above – a Spenserian view which the early anthropologists wished to confirm. 'The whole social edifice', as Brenda Beck suggested, 'is built not so much on the entities themselves as on the various oppositions used in its construction.' There were no 'units' of caste waiting to be 'mobilised'.

The penetration of government into Indian society, the growing governmental control over the society's resources and the gradual integration of the region were most clearly seen in south India in the history of local government. Historians have neglected the importance of local boards in the overall study of political development and, indeed, have largely neglected its importance at all, pointing to the inauguration of panchayati raj in independent India as the only real expansion of government's scale in the localities. While the proliferation of boards and the channelling of development funds in panchayati raj represented a considerable advance on the structure of local government under the British, this does not devalue the significance of local boards since at least the beginning of the twentieth century. Indeed the inauguration of panchayati raj was perhaps less abrupt in the south than in other regions of India since local government had developed further in Madras than elsewhere. In 1934–5, for instance, when the total expenditure of the central and provincial governments in the Madras Presidency was Rs 18.2 crores, the local boards and municipalities spent Rs 6.2 crores (of which some Rs 83.5 lakhs came from government grants).[2] In other words local boards commanded the equivalent of a third of total government expenditure.

The British looked on local government as 'administration', something which was entirely divorced from 'politics', and their handling of local boards often reflected this view. Yet local administration and political organisation were intimately connected, not least because the participants were often the same. Nearly all of the prominent figures in provincial and nationalist politics in this period had some

[2] *Finance and Revenue Accounts of the Government of India* for 1934–5; *Report on the Working of District Municipalities in the Madras Presidency* for 1934–5; *Report on the Working of Local Boards in the Madras Presidency* for 1934–5.

interest in local government. Local boards were both an interest – since they controlled such extensive resources – and a constituency – since they could act as a springboard of aspiring politicians. The changing relationship between provincial government and parties and local boards formed one of the keys to the political history of this period.

This study of the province illuminates important facets of the dialogues between rulers and ruled at one of the turning-points of empire. British policy underwent a drastic change in the 1930s. The Montagu–Chelmsford reforms were the footnote to an era in which the British had tried to recapture the peace and stability of earlier years while at the same time improving the quality of their government with the help of powerful, informed and amicable Indians. This era had drawn the British deeper into the complexities of Indian society, and by the 1930s the British had started to recoil and to retreat from this policy. The twists and turns of British policy were not just the indulgences of men in Westminster, nor were they merely the upshot of the dialogue between Viceroys and a handful of Indian leaders. When they were turning to the policy of administrative expansion in the later nineteenth century, and again when they were throwing that policy into reverse half a century later, the British were trying to find answers to practical problems in the government of India. In both cases, the impulse for change came not only from the policy-makers in the imperial capitals, but also from the many lesser officials who were obliged to implement policies once they were made. In the 1930s, for instance, the decision of Westminster to retreat from the provinces to the safer and strategically more important heights of Delhi, was mirrored by the moves of Indian civil servants in Fort St George to extricate themselves from the tiresome details of local and provincial administration.

In this sense the opposition to imperial rule was truly a mass movement. The British were withdrawing not because their will to rule had collapsed, nor merely because the chess-board diplomatists in London could see a better move. They were finding it increasingly difficult to stay on. The attempts to tighten up British rule, to expand the administration and eliminate the glaring faults of the nineteenth century, had foundered. Government had become larger in scope but thus more difficult to manage. The increasing despair of those in charge of the local government department in the Madras Secretariat was eloquent testimony to this. The British had installed better machinery for running the province, but now found it was slipping through their fingers. The Governor and his inner circle were at first surprised about the annihilation of the Justice party in 1937, but surprise soon turned to fatalism. Imperial rule had met its limitations.

The provincial Congress went through three phases, matching the contortions of British policy. Until the years 1916–20, it was an exclusive club for some of the most successful men in provincial society. In the 1920s and early 1930s, it became a channel for dissidence of all kinds. In the late 1930s, it took over the aspects of government which the British had decided to neglect. Until the 1930s, the importance of the Congress as an institution was little more than the sum of the men who gave it support. Those who rose to positions of leadership in the provincial Congress were, with a few very important exceptions, men whose importance was established outside the Congress. In the 1930s, the Congress became much more important in its own right. From then on, people rose to importance through the organisation itself. Men became leaders by serving the organisation, not through lending it their personal prestige. Self sacrifice and loyalty to the institutions took on a new significance in Congress affairs. Men like Dr B. Pattabhi Sitaramayya, who had served the Congress well for many years before the 1930s but who had not been rewarded with positions of authority in the organisation, suddenly emerged into the front rank of Congress leaders in the late 1930s.

BIOGRAPHICAL NOTES

Key to abbreviations

C	Chairman
DB	District board
DEC	District education council
MC	Municipal council
M.L.A.	Member of the Legislative Assembly
M.L.C.	Member of the Legislative Council
P	President
TB	Taluk board
TC	Temple committee
VC	Vice-chairman
VP	Vice-president

Raja Sir ANNAMALAI CHETTIAR b. 1881, fourth son of Muthiah Chettiar, wealthy and munificent banker and leader of Nattukottai Chetty community; expanded banking business in India, Burma, Ceylon etc; estates in Ramnad and elsewhere; countless benefactions including renovation of Sri Nataraja temple, Chidambaram, and foundation of Annamalai University; recognised head of community; a Governor of the Imperial Bank; M.L.C. 1916; Council of State 1920–30.

R. N. AROKIASAMI MUDALIAR b. 1870 in Christian family; entered public services and rose to be superintendent engineer in public works department; M.L.C. 1926–30, minister for development 1926–8.

Raja of BOBBILI b. *c.* 1902 in one of leading Padmanayak Velama families of Northern Circars; private education; married daughter of Zamindar of Telaprole; estate in Vizagapatam, 920 sq. m., population 213,241, revenue Rs 6½ lakhs; father was first Indian on Governor's Executive Council 1910; defeated Justicite candidate 1926; M.L.C. 1930, chief minister 1932–6; defeated Justicite candidate 1937.

Kasu BRAHMANANDA REDDI b. 1908 in village officer family in Guntur; legal education in Madras and Trivandrum; big criminal practice in Narasaraopet, patronage of local zamindar; DB 1934; brother Venkata elected Congress M.L.A. 1937.

Sankara ELLAPPA CHETTY Landowner (value over Rs 4,000), merchant and a moneylender (family payed income tax on Rs 8,700) in Salem; PTB 1920; VPDB 1922–7; MC; PDEC 1923; PDB 1927–36.

Paidupati Curasulu ETHIRAJULU NAIDU b. 1871; son-in-law of Hyderabad judge; landowner, contractor and leading tobacco merchant in Guntur town; CMC 1918–20; PDB 1920–8; TC; M.L.C. 1920, 1923, 1926, defeated 1930.

G. F. F. FOULKES Member of adventurous European family with land and plantations in the region; forest service; succeeded to Salem zamindari; brother Robert and uncle Robert Fischer prominent in Madura; PDB Salem 1920–8.

Varahagiri Venkata GIRI b. 1894, son of leading barrister in Ganjam; Dublin University 1913–16; jail for liquor agitation in Non-co-operation; labour organiser, largely among railwaymen in N. India; led Bengal–Nagpur Railway strike in 1927; Congress M.L.A. (Delhi) 1934; M.L.A. 1937, minister for labour.

Ayyadevara KALESWARA RAO b. 1881 in Brahman village officer family in Kistna; owned 124 acres of land; legal education, turned down career in services, barrister in Bezwada 1908–21; jail for Non-co-operation; Swarajist M.L.C. 1926; CMC Bezwada 1927–30; jailed three times in Civil Disobedience; leading Congressman in Andhra and India for many years; M.L.A. 1937, council secretary to the chief minister.

T. V. KALYANASUNDARA MUDALIAR b. 1883 son of small businessman and eminent Tamil scholar; Tamil teacher in Madras City; joined Gandhian agitations in late 1910s, edited *Desabhaktan* for C. Rajagopalachari 1917–20; edited *Navasakti* from 1920; leading Tamil journalist and prose stylist, acknowledged father of modern Tamil journalism; labour organiser.

K. KAMARAJ b. 1903 in poor Nadar family in Virudunagar; Non-co-operation, Vykom satyagraha, leading organiser for agitational cadre of Congress; jailed 1930; became lieutenant for Satyamurthi; M.L.A. 1937.

O. KANDASWAMI CHETTY b. 1868, Christian Beri Chetty, half-brother of O. Tanicachalam Chetty; senior lecturer in English at Madras Christian College 1915–24; editor *Social Reform Advocate*; publicist for Justice party in early stages.

S. KASTURIRANGA IYENGAR b. 1859 in Brahman service family in Tanjore; lawyer and local boards member in Coimbatore in 1880s and 1890s; to Madras 1894, member of Egmore faction; worked for *The Hindu*, bought it in 1905 and made it the leading English daily in the region; active in 'Nationalist' branch of the Congress, late convert to cause of Non-co-operation; d. 1923.

Poosapati Sanjeevi KUMARASWAMY RAJA b. 1898 in leading mercantile and landed family (land worth Rs 20,000) in Rajapalaiyam, Ramnad; TB and DB 1922–31; TC 1928; ran co-operative bank; jail 1932; VPDEC 1933–6; M.L.A. (Delhi) 1934; M.L.A. 1937; leading member of Tamilnad Congress from 1930s.

S. KUMARASWAMI REDDIAR b. 1879 in rich and renowned landed family in Tinnevelly; leading lawyer in Palamcottah; CMC 1911–21; PDB 1924–30;

M.L.C. 1926, 1930; minister for education 1930–6 in Justicite government.

Jagarlamudy KUPPUSWAMI CHOUDHARY b. 1892, son of biggest landowner-moneylender in Guntur; paid Rs 8,000 in kist and Rs 480 in income tax; M.L.C. throughout dyarchy; PDB 1928–35; defeated Justicite candidate 1937; recognised leader of local Kammas.

Raja of MIRZAPURAM Member of Nuzvid family of Velamas which owned extensive zamindari lands in Kistna delta, and were related to other Velama zamindari families; PTB Kistna 1914–17; PDB 1924–6; M.L.C. 1926, 1930.

MOTHEY family Dominant Komati mercantile family in Ellore; extensive interests in moneylending and general trading, jute, cotton, paper and rice mills, bus companies, zamindari and other lands paying annual revenue over Rs 5,000; Mothey Narasimha Rao, b. *c.* 1900, paid income tax on Rs 6,000 in 1929, CMC 1930, promoted Non-co-operation, M.L.C. 1926, active in formation of Subbaroyan ministry, M.L.A. (Delhi) 1930; Mothey Narayana Rao, b. 1875, studied engineering in England, Congressman in 1930s; Mothey Krishna Rao, PTB 1931; Mothey Gangaraju, b. *c.*1875, ran loyalist association during Civil Disobedience, on 60th birthday 'weighed himself with gold, silver and precious stones and distributed the value for public institutions and various other charities' (*Who's Who in Madras 1938*).

Bollini MUNISWAMI NAIDU b. 1885, son of lessee of Karvetnagar zamindari; leader of civil side of bar in Chittoor from 1920; family moneylending business with Rs 20,000 capital; groundnut and rice mills; M.L.C. throughout dyarchy; PDB 1922–6; sometime CMC; interest in co-operative societies; chief minister 1930–2; d. 1935.

M. A. MUTHIAH CHETTIAR b. 1904, first son of raja ANNAMALAI CHETTIAR; leading businessman in Madras City; Pachaiyappa's Trust from 1928; Madras Corporation from 1929; Mayor of Madras 1932; president of S. Indian Chamber of Commerce 1932–6; board of Imperial Bank, president of Indian Bank; M.L.C. 1930, minister 1936–7.

S. MUTHIAH MUDALIAR b. 1888 in very orthodox Thondamandala Mudaliar family in Tanjore; landowner in Tanjore; legal practice in Madras; director of Triplicane Urban Co-operative Bank; M.L.C. 1923 (Justicite), 1926 (Swarajist); minister in independent government 1928–30; a leader of the People's party in 1936, defeated in 1937 elections.

R. S. NAIDU b. 1883; married daughter of big Dindigul lawyer; legal education in England, practice in Madura from 1921, and business interests; CMC 1923–30; TC 1928–31; defeated at 1926 elections; first manager of Minakshi temple appointed by government 1935.

Chintalapat Venkata Surya NARASIMHA RAJU b. 1876; zamindar in Vizagapatam (peishcush Rs 1,200); legal practice; M.L.C. 1916, 1920, 1923, 1926; sometime PDB; a Governor of Imperial Bank.

Nadimpalle Venkata Lakshmi NARASIMHA RAO Son of rich and successful

Guntur lawyer, member of one of premier Brahman families of town; legal education in England, but more interested in business and politics; ran Andhra Traders Co.; jail in Non-co-operation; CMC 1922–30, 1933–6; jail in Civil Disobedience; failed to get Congress candidature in 1934 and 1937, so stood against Congress in 1937 and was defeated.

Dandu NARAYANA RAJU b. 1899 in prominent Kshatriya landed family of West Godavari; legal practice in Ellore from 1918; Non-co-operation, and thereafter prominent Andhra Congressman, jailed three times in Civil Disobedience; M.L.C. 1926; PDB 1936; M.L.A. 1937.

Dr C. NATESAN b. 1875 in prominent Thondamandala Mudaliar service family in Madras City; teacher, dubash and then doctor; active in helping non-Brahman youths to get education and service jobs; ran *Madras Dravidian Association*, a forerunner of the Justice Party; M.L.C. 1923, 1930 (defeated 1920, 1926); prominent in Madras Corporation but never realised ambition to be Mayor; active but disgruntled Justicite; d. 1937.

Raja of PANAGAL P. Ramarayaningar, assumed title in 1922; b. 1866 in prestigious Velama zamindari family connected to Kalahasti; estate income of Rs 60,000 but rumoured to be indebted; 6 years on DB in N. Arcot; M.L.C. 1920, 1923, 1926; chief minister 1921–6; patron of Sanskrit learning; early leader of Andhra Movement; d. 1928.

A. T. PANNIRSELVAM b. 1888, Christian Udaiyar family; educated at Cambridge and Gray's Inn; practice at Tanjore; CMC 1918–20; PDB 1924–30; PDEC 1922–4; leading Justicite in locality; M.L.C. 1930; delegate to Round Table Conference; Home Member of Governor's Executive Council 1934–7; M.L.A. (Justicite) 1937.

Annepu Parasurandoss PATRO b. 1875; large landowner, advocate of agricultural improvement, author of books on local government and rural economics; landowner, leader of Ganjam bar for a decade; TB, DB, sometime CMC; Liberal League 1916–20, moved to Justice party; M.L.C. throughout dyarchy; minister for education 1921–6, responsible for Madras University Re-organisation and Andhra University Acts; chaired All-Parties Conference, Delhi 1931; Round Table Conference and Joint Select Committee on the reforms; defeated Justicite candidate 1937.

Penumetcha PEDDIRAJU b. 1886 in landed Kshatriya family in Kistna delta; Ellore district munsiff; legal practice in Ellore from 1913; PTB 1920–32; PDB 1927–32; prominent in co-operative banks; bought land and built expensive house in 1930s; M.L.C. 1923, 1932; Congress M.L.A. 1937.

Raja of PITHAPURAM b. 1885, Velama zamindar; estate of 400 sq. m., much of it in Godavari delta and thus rich and troublesome, with population of 280,317; Brahmo Samajist and patron of many Brahmo projects; many other benefactions included College at Cocanada; dominated East Godavari politics from behind the scenes; influential member and financier of Justice party until he started People's party in 1936 and became its only M.L.A. elected in 1937; lent money to other zamindars.

Tanguturi PRAKASAM b. 1872, Brahman village officer family in part of

Venkatagiri estate in Guntur district; legal practice in Rajahmundry, CMC 1903–4; legal education in England 1904–7, caused furore by refusing to do penance for overseas travel; criminal practice in Madras City; purchased *Madras Law Times 1911*; Non-co-operation; started *Swarajya* in 1921; M.L.A. (Delhi) 1926; bared chest to police bayonets during Simon Commission demonstrations 1928; jail during Civil Disobedience; active in cause of zamindari ryots; dominated Andhra provincial Congress committee 1934–7; M.L.A. 1937 and minister for revenue 1937–9; styled the 'Lion of Andhra' for contribution to national movement.

Chakravarti RAJAGOPALACHARI b. 1879, son of 50-acre landholder, village officer and Sanskrit scholar; did well at Salem bar and owned first car in the town; CMC 1917–19; quit Salem after wife's death, became political leader in Madras City, and was important lieutenant of Gandhi at 1920 Congresses; jail 1921; edited Gandhi's *Young India* 1922; established ashram at Tiruchengodu, acknowledged Gandhian leader of province, prominent khaddar organiser; jail 1930; M.L.A. 1937, chief minister 1937–9.

Ponnambala Tyaga RAJAN b. 1892, Thondamandala Mudaliar family, ward of Uttamapalaiyam zamindar (peishcush Rs 8,000), influential in Madura district; educated at Oxford; Madura bar from 1919; M.L.C. throughout dyarchy; active in Justice party, minister 1930–7.

Dr T. S. S. RAJAN b. 1881 in Brahman family, educated in England; large private medical practice in Trichinopoly, built own 40-bed, well-equipped hospital in 1927; invested money in land and electric companies in 1930s; one of most prominent Gandhians in Tamilnad, active in swadeshi and harijan work; M.L.A. (Delhi) 1934; M.L.A. 1937, minister for health 1937–9.

Tiruppur Angappa RAMALINGAM CHETTY b. 1881, son of leading banker and merchant in Tiruppur with properties all over Coimbatore district; inherited one-sixth of estate, worth Rs 7 lakhs, in 1910, and paid kist of Rs 1,000 and income tax on Rs 25,000 in 1920; leader of civil side of Coimbatore bar; director of three cotton mills, and several banks and co-operative societies; VPDB 1913; PDB 1916–22; VCMC 1919; CMC 1919; Congressman, switched allegiance to Justice party, became party renegade in 1920s; M.L.C. 1920, 1923, 1930, defeated 1926; president of Tirupati temple committee 1933–5; renounced government title to re-join Congress in 1936; Congress M.L.A. 1937.

C. Ramalinga REDDY b. 1880 in prominent Chittoor service family associated with local zamindars; educated at Cambridge; vice-principal of Maharaja's College, Baroda 1908, principal 1916–18; inspector-general of education in Mysore state 1918–20; M.L.C. 1920, 1923, rather intransigent Justicite; moving spirit of Reddi Mahajana Sabha; first vice-chancellor of Andhra University 1926–30, resigned as protest against police repression; flirtation with Congress and local politics in Chittoor 1934–6; returned to vice-chancellor's post 1936–40.

J. N. RAMANATHAN Son of district munsiff and renowned Tamil scholar J. Nallaswami Pillai; leading journalist and propagandist for Justice party, sometime editor of *Dravidian*; led non-Brahman associations and agitations in Madura and was almost rewarded with seat on municipal council; disillusionment with party leaders led him to rebel briefly in 1920s.

Chetpat Pattabhirama RAMASWAMI IYER b. 1879, son of Madras judge; apprenticed to top Mylapore lawyer, inherited large practice from brother-in-law, and quickly became a leading civil lawyer in Madras; general-secretary of Congress 1917–18; Madras Corporation; Moderate delegation to England 1919; M.L.C. 1920; Advocate-General 1920–3; Law Member of Governor's Executive Council 1923–8; Indian representative at League of Nations 1926–7; reverted to the bar in 1928; Law and Commerce Member in Government of India for short periods in 1930s; Dewan of Travancore 1936.

Arcot RAMASWAMI MUDALIAR Member of Thondamandala Mudaliar family with many members in the public services; legal education; Justicite delegation 1919; secretary of S.I.L.F.; secretary to minister Patro and then lieutenant of Panagal; M.L.C. 1920, 1923, defeated 1926; editor of *Justice* 1926; Mayor of Madras 1928; Council of State 1930; M.L.A. (Delhi) 1930, defeated 1934.

Erode Venkatappa RAMASWAMI NAICKER b. 1879, son of leading merchant in Erode; after wayward youth, inherited father's position and became leader of Erode affairs; CMC 1917–19; joined Rajagopalachari in Congress 1919, active in temperance campaigns in Non-co-operation; hero of Vykom satyagraha 1923; quit Congress in 1925; started *Kudi Arasu* and later other Tamil journals; initiated Self-Respect movement; visited Europe and Russia 1931–2; socialist propaganda and jail 1933–4; helped Justicite election campaign 1936–7.

Raja of RAMNAD Estate of 2,104 sq. m. and 700,000 population, comprising most of Ramnad district; family is one of recognised leaders of Maravars, and one of foremost patrons of religion and scholarship in southern districts; b. 1889; M.L.C. 1915; helped in war effort, but also a Home Ruler; president of Kumbakonam temple committee 1915; PDB Ramnad 1921–8; M.L.C. 1920, 1923, 1926; life president of Madura Tamil Sangham and proprietor of journal *Sen Tamil*; d. 1928, son came of age and took title of raja in 1931; elected PDB 1933.

N. Gogineni RANGA b. 1900 in Kamma landowning (150 acres) and village officer family in Guntur; Oxford 1920; professor of history and economics at Pachaiyappa's College 1926–30; on various government advisory boards 1928–31; leader of resettlement and anti-zamindari campaigns in 1930s; M.L.A. (Delhi) 1934 for Congress; joined Congress socialists; prolific writer on economics and socialism.

Arcot RANGANATHA MUDALIAR b. 1879 in Bellary family with two generations of service in army; entered government service 1901, rose to Deputy Collector and resigned 1915; follower of Mrs Besant and theosophy; edited

Telugu journal *Prayabandhu*; interest in co-operatives; DB from 1923; M.L.C. throughout dyarchy; minister for development 1926–8.

A. RANGASWAMI IYENGAR b. 1877 in Tanjore landed (20 acres) and service family; successful legal practice in Tanjore from 1902, began long agitation over land settlement in Cauveri delta; to Madras in 1905 when uncle Kasturiranga Iyengar bought *The Hindu*, worked as assistant editor; acquired *Swadesamitran* in 1915, made it Tamil sister of *The Hindu*; leading member of Madras Nationalists; M.L.A. (Delhi) 1923, 1926; general-secretary of Congress during Swarajist phase 1925–7; editor *The Hindu* 1928; d. 1934.

P. RATNAVELU THEVAR b. *c.* 1888; lawyer and businessman in Trichinopoly; VCMC 1922–6; CMC 1926, 1932–4; defeated Justicite candidate 1926; joined Congress 1935; M.L.C. 1935; PDB 1936; M.L.A. 1937.

Kurma Venkata REDDI NAIDU b. 1875 in landed (two villages) and service family in East Godavari; legal practice at Rajahmundry from 1900, built up family lands with profits and reputedly worth Rs 75,000 by 1921; MC 1901–5; PTB 1902–5; DB 1901–5; moved to Ellore 1904; MC 1907–20; PTB 1911; DB 1912–20; interest in co-operatives; attended several Congress sessions; disavowed use of Brahman priests 1917; M.L.C. 1920, 1923, defeated 1926; minister for development 1920–3; very active in Justice party, but elbowed out by Panagal; formed Justice Democratic party and later Justice (Constitutionalist) party; Law Member of Governor's Executive Council 1934–7; acting Governor during Erskine's leave in 1936.

Bulusu SAMBAMURTHY b. 1886 son of Brahman Vedic scholar; teacher and then successful criminal lawyer at Cocanada from 1911; gave up practice for Non-co-operation, and became a leading Congressman in Andhra; organised Congress session at Cocanada 1923; jail three times in Civil Disobedience; involved in local boards; M.L.A. 1937, speaker of Assembly.

S. SATYAMURTHI b. 1887, son of vakil in Pudukottai state; not very successful at Madras bar, but patronised by S. Srinivasa Iyengar and K. Srinivasan because of his services to Indian politics; leading member of Madras Nationalists, organiser of Swarajist party in 1920s and of Congress campaign in mid-1930s; remarkable orator and parliamentarian; jail in Civil Disobedience; Madras Corporation; stood down for Rajagopalachari at 1937 elections.

M. R. SETURATNAM IYER b. 1888 in landed family in Trichinopoly; paid revenue of Rs 3,522; chairman of Kulittalai Union 1912–17; VPTB 1917; PTB 1918; interest in co-operatives; M.L.C. 1920, 1923, 1926; wavering allegiance; minister for development 1928–30.

Ramaswami Kandaswami SHANMUGHAM CHETTY b. 1894 in wealthy, moneylending family in Coimbatore; legal education and practice in 1920s but primarily a businessman after inheriting family interests in 1916; reckoned in 1921 to have capital of Rs 6 lakhs and incomes of Rs 6,000 from house properties and of Rs 8,000 from investments in seven banks, two cotton mills etc; family built Vasantha Mills in 1928; VCMC 1920; M.L.C. 1920, secretary to minister Reddi Naidu; M.L.A. (Delhi) 1923, 1926, 1930, speaker 1931; delegate to Ottawa Imperial Economic Conference 1932; Dewan of Cochin 1935.

T. N. SIVAGNANAM PILLAI b. 1861, son of superintendent of customs at Tuticorin; entered public service 1885, rose to Deputy Collector and resigned 1917; fanatical loyalist; appointed PDB Tinnevelly 1919–23; M.L.C. 1920, 1923; minister for development 1923–6; connected to Ettaiyapuram zamindari family, and worked for some time as dewan.

S. SRINIVASA IYENGAR b. 1874 in orthodox Brahman family in Madura; legal apprenticeship under his father-in-law, a leading Mylaporean; quickly acquired lucrative civil practice; bought zamindari land in Madura; many benefactions; Advocate-General 1916–20; M.L.C. 1920, resigned 1921 and joined Non-co-operation; leader of Madras Swarajists 1923–7; president of Madras Corporation 1925; M.L.A. (Delhi) 1926; president of Congress 1927; withdrew from political front-line after clash with Gandhians 1928–30.

N. M. R. SUBBARAMAN b. 1905 in one of leading Saurashtra mercantile families of Madura; several investments in cotton enterprises; active in community; jail twice in Civil Disobedience; CMC 1935; M.L.A. 1937.

A. SUBBARAYALU REDDIAR b. 1853; very big landlord (over 10,000 acres) in South Arcot; legal practice in Cuddalore from 1880; MC 1899; CMC 1904–20; PTB 1911–16; PDB 1917–20; president of temple committee 1910–20; M.L.C. 1913; chief minister 1921, resigned owing to ill-health; d. 1922.

Dr Paramasiva SUBBAROYAN b. 1889; zamindar of Kumaramangalam, highly respected among Gounders of Coimbatore; legal education at Oxford, Dublin and Inner Temple; estate of 39,385 acres with income of Rs 80,211 in 1926; lent money to tenants; somewhat impoverished by sending three sons to Eton; friend of Rajagopalachari; married West Coast Brahman's daughter, educated at Oxford; M.L.C. throughout dyarchy; secretary to minister Panagal 1921–2; chief minister 1926–30; patron of Self-Respect; joined Congress 1935; M.L.A. 1937; minister for education 1937–9.

Ottilingam TANICACHALAM CHETTY b. 1874 in wealthy Beri Chetty mercantile family with interests in some of the important temples and markets of Madras City; short period in government service before apprenticeship in European firm of solicitors and then own legal practice; chief judge of small causes court 1928; prominent in Madras Corporation, president in 1926; M.L.C. 1920, 1923, defeated 1926; leading Justicite in Madras City; d. 1929.

Pitti THYAGARAJA CHETTY b. 1852 in respectable Devanga family; large landowner in Madras City and environs; moneylender, banker, leading entrepreneur in the handloom industry, and many other business interests which made him the premier Indian businessman of the province; founder of the South Indian Chamber of Commerce; forty years on Madras Corporation, three years as president; M.L.C. from 1912 until his death in 1925; early Congressman, then co-founder of Justice party; patron of Telugu revival.

Dr P. VARADARAJULU NAIDU b. 1887, head of clan of Balijas in western Tamilnad; built up successful practice in indigenous medicine until he had income of Rs 24,000; founded Tamil journal *Prapancha Mitran*, later edited newspaper *Tamil Nadu* and other journalistic exploits; active in agitations in 1908, arrested for sedition at Madura Mill strike in 1918 and his trial became a political cause célèbre; joined Rajagopalachari Congress, jailed three times in Non-co-operation; offered a ministership by Panagal in 1925; quit Congress in 1929 and concentrated on labour organisation; looked for Justicite patronage in mid-1930s.

Vellaikinar Chinnappa VELLINGIRI GOUNDER b. *c.* 1880, one of largest landholders in Coimbatore district; active in Gounder community associations and in temperance work; interest in co-operative societies and in agricultural innovation; M.L.C. 1920, 1923; PDB 1933; family had large interests in expanding cotton industry in Coimbatore; Congress campaigner 1937.

Sami VENKATACHELAM CHETTY b. 1887 in Komati family from Guntur; became one of province's most prominent businessmen, working chiefly as a commission agent in chillies and gram, a dealer in cotton goods, an agent for oil, coal and cement companies, and a director of banks and insurance companies; Madras Corporation from 1919, president 1925; M.L.C. 1923, 1926; active in Vaisya associations; M.L.A. (Delhi) for Congress in 1934.

Raja of VENKATAGIRI One of largest estates in province, with 2,200 sq. m. mostly in Nellore; one of leading Velama houses (Bobbili is an offshoot) and hence president of the Madras Landholders Association; son, kumararaja, active in Justice party; M.L.C. 1926, 1930; PDB 1931–4; organiser for 1937 election campaign, but defeated at polls.

Konda VENKATAPPAYYA b. 1886 in conservative Brahman family in Guntur, son of clerk in a Vaisya firm who owned thirty acres; legal practice at Masulipatam and then Guntur where he was very successful; volunteer at 1897 Madras Congress, and thereafter a leading Congressman and promoter of the Andhra movement; gave up practice for Non-co-operation, organised No-Tax campaign, jailed; jailed twice in Civil Disobedience; M.L.A. 1937; styled 'Desabhakta' (the patriot) for contribution to the nationalist cause.

GLOSSARY

abkari: *manufacture or sale of liquor; hence, excise.*

Adi-Dravida: *term coined for the untouchable castes of Tamilnad.*

Andhra: *the country of the Telugus.*

Asari: *the artisan caste, otherwise known as Kammalan.*

ashram: *a spiritual retreat.*

Balija: *Telugu merchant caste, often found in Tamilnad.*

bidi: *cheap cheroot.*

Brahman: *the priestly and scholarly varna.*

Ceded Districts: *Anantapur, Bellary, Kurnool and Cuddapah; the region ceded to the British by the Nizam of Hyderabad in 1801.*

cheri: *hut quarter, usually for untouchables.*

Chetty: *name of several Tamil merchant castes.*

Circars, or Northern Circars: *historically derived term for the coastal districts of Andhra.*

crore: *a unit of ten million.*

Devanga: *Telugu weaver caste, found throughout Presidency.*

Dewan Bahadur: *honorary title, conferred by British government.*

Dharmarakshana Sabha: *an association founded by the Mylaporeans to play a part in the management of temples.*

dubash: *an interpreter or intermediary, especially in European business houses.*

durbar: *a public audience held by a ruler or official.*

dyarchy: *dual rule; term applied to the form of provincial government under the Montagu–Chelmsford constitution.*

Egmore: *suburb of Madras City which gave its name to a political faction opposed to Mylapore.*

Fort St George: *site of government offices in Madras City.*

Gounder: *title and caste-name used by respectable Vellala cultivators in western Tamilnad, otherwise known as Kongu Vellala.*

hartal: *a form of strike.*

inam: *land held wholly or partially free of revenue.*

jamabandi: *the annual settlement of the land revenue with the cultivators.*

Kallar: *caste of southern Tamilnad, traditionally given to stealing, now largely cultivators.*

Kamma: *respectable cultivator caste of Andhra, dominant in Kistna delta.*

Glossary

Kapu: *respectable cultivator caste of Andhra, common in Godavari delta, closely allied to Reddis.*

karnam: *village accountant*

khaddar: *hand-spun yarn and the cloth made from it.*

Khilafat: *name given to movement among Muslims to defend the Khalifah, the successor to the Prophet as ruler of the Muslims, after end of first world war.*

kisan: *north Indian word for peasant.*

kist: *land revenue payment.*

Komati: *Telugu merchant caste with aspirations to be restyled as 'Arya Vaisya'.*

Kshatriya: *the warrior varna; caste-name claimed by several landed groups, particularly in Godavari, Chittoor and Ramnad.*

kumararaja: *son and heir of a raja.*

lakh: *a unit of one hundred thousand.*

lathi: *baton or riot-stick used by Indian police.*

Maravar: *cultivator caste of southern Tamilnad, formerly warriors.*

math or mutt: *a monastic institution, seat of a religious leader and his disciples.*

mirasidar: *originally the holder of a hereditary and privileged land tenure ('mirasi') in certain parts of Tamilnad.*

mofussil: *upcountry; the hinterland as opposed to the city.*

Morley–Minto: *term applied to the constitution for India in force between 1909 and 1920.*

munsiff: *a native judge; term also applied to the village headman in his capacity as an arbitrator.*

Mylapore: *suburb of Madras City which gave its name to the most powerful faction in Madras politics in the late nineteenth and early twentieth centuries.*

Nadar: *Tamil caste of toddy-tappers, many of whom had become landowners and merchants.*

Nattukottai Chetty: *caste of wealthy bankers, with headquarters in Ramnad district and business throughout British possessions in the east.*

Padaiyichi: *respectable cultivator caste of north-east Tamilnad, with aspirations to be restyled 'Vannikula Kshatriya'; otherwise known as Palli or Vanniyan.*

panchayat: *a local council or court, traditionally of five persons.*

Paraiyar: *largest untouchable caste of Tamilnad.*

patta: *land deed.*

peishcush: *revenue paid by a zamindar.*

Raj: *the British empire in India.*

raja: *ruler; hereditary title used by principal zamindari families.*

Raju, or Razu: *Telugu cultivator caste claiming Kshatriya status, with some migrants resident in Tamil districts.*

Rao Bahadur: *honorary title conferred by British government.*

Rayalseema: *historically derived term for the southern Deccan, comprising roughly the Ceded Districts, Chittoor and adjacent areas of Bombay Presidency.*

Reddi: *respectable cultivator caste of Andhra, dominant in Rayalseema.*

ryot: *cultivator.*

ryotwari: *land revenue system under which assessments are made on individual landholdings.*

sabha: *an association or assembly.*

sanad: *a deed or certificate.*

Sanatanist: *a follower of Sanatana Dharma, orthodox religious observance.*

satyagraha: *truth-force; Gandhi's term for his technique of passive resistance.*

Saurashtra: *caste of dyers and weavers, migrant from Gujarat into the towns of Tamilnad.*

Sengundar: *name adopted by Tamil weaver caste previously called Kaikkolan.*

sheristadar: *head Indian official in a Collectorate or court.*

swadeshi: *produced in one's own country.*

swaraj: *self rule.*

tahsildar: *subordinate Indian official in revenue service.*

taluk: *subdivision of a district.*

Telaga: *respectable cultivator caste of Andhra.*

toddy: *country beer, brewed from the sap of palm trees.*

Udaiyar: *largely cultivator caste of Tamilnad, numerous in South Arcot and Tanjore.*

Vaisya: *the merchant varna; name claimed by several trading castes.*

vakil: *an agent, usually applied to a legal representative.*

Vannikula Kshatriya: *caste name claimed by the Padaiyichis.*

Velama: *cultivator caste of Andhra, among whose members are the zamindari houses of Pithapuram, Bobbili, Venkatagiri and Nuzvid.*

Vellala: *name for respectable cultivator castes in Tamilnad.*

Viswakarma: *name claimed by the Asari artisan castes.*

zamindar: *landholder paying permanently-settled revenue directly to government.*

BIBLIOGRAPHY

NOTE. The Bibliography is arranged under the following heads:

Government Records
Official Publications
    (1) Parliamentary Papers
    (2) H.M.S.O.
    (3) Government of India
    (4) Government of Madras
    (5) Madras District Manuals and Gazetteers
    (6) Annual Reports
Private Papers
Newspapers and Periodicals
Unpublished Dissertations
Congress Publications
Published Books, Articles, Pamphlets

GOVERNMENT RECORDS

Proceedings of the Secretary of State for India. India Office Library.
    Public and Judicial Department
Proceedings of the Government of India. National Archives of India.
    Home Department
    Education, Health and Lands Department
    Reforms Department
    Judicial Department
    Finance Department

Proceedings of the Government of Madras. Madras Record Office (Tamilnadu Archives) and State Archives Hyderabad.
    Law Department
    Revenue Department
    Local and Municipal Department
    Local Self Government Department
    Public Department
    Education Department

OFFICIAL PUBLICATIONS

(1) PARLIAMENTARY PAPERS

Royal Commission on Decentralisation. Vol. II *Report.* 1908 Cd. 4360. Vol. II *Evidence taken in Madras.* 1908 Cd. 4361.

Royal Commission on the Public Services in India. Appendix, vol. II *Minutes of Evidence relating to the Indian and Provincial Services taken in Madras from 8 to 17 January 1913.* 1914 Cd. 7293.

Report on Indian Constitutional Reform. 1918 Cd. 9109.

Report of the Indian Industrial Commission 1916–8. 1919 Cmd. 51; *Minutes of Evidence taken before the Indian Industrial Commission.* Vol. III *Madras and Bangalore.* 1919 Cmd. 236.

Report of the Committee appointed by the Secretary of State for India to enquire into questions connected with the division of functions between the Central and Provincial Governments and in the Provincial Governments between the Executive Council and Ministers (Chairman: Mr. R. Feetham). 1919 Cmd. 103.

Report of the Committee appointed by the Secretary of State for India to enquire into questions connected with the Franchise and other matters relating to constitutional reform (Chairman: Lord Southborough). 1919 Cmd. 141.

Report of the Committee appointed to advise on the question of the Financial Relations between the Central and Provincial Governments in India. 1920 Cmd. 724.

Return showing the results of the elections in India. 1921 Cmd. 1261.

Return showing the results of the elections in India in 1923. 1924 Cmd. 2154.

Report of the Reforms Enquiry Committee 1924 and connected papers. 1924–5 Cmd. 2360.

Views of Local Governments on the Working of the Reforms, dated 1923. 1924–5 Cmd. 2361.

Views of Local Governments on the Working of the Reforms, dated 1924. 1924–5 Cmd. 2362.

Return showing the results of the elections in India in 1925 and 1926. 1927 Cmd. 2923.

Report of the Royal Commission on Agriculture in India. 1928 Cmd, 3132.

Indian Statutory Commission. Vol. I *Survey.* 1929 Cmd. 3568. Vol. II *Recommendations.* 1929–30 Cmd. 3569. *Reports of Committees appointed by Provincial Legislative Councils to cooperate with the Indian Statutory Commission.* 1929–30 Cmd. 3572.

Government of India's Despatch, 20 September 1930, on proposals for constitutional reform. 1930–1 Cmd. 3700.

Despatches from Provincial Governments in India containing proposals for constitutional reform. 1930–1 Cmd. 3712.

Report of the Royal Commission on Labour in India. 1930–1 Cmd. 3883.

Return showing the results of elections in India in 1929 and 1930. 1930–1 Cmd. 3922.

Report of the Indian Franchise Committee vol I. 1931–2 Cd. 4086.

Proposals for Indian Constitutional Reform. 1932–3 Cd. 4268.

Proposals for Indian Constitutional Reform. 1933 Cmd. 468.

Return showing the results of the general election to the Legislative Assembly in India 1934. 1934–5 Cmd. 4939.

Report of the Committee on the Delimitation of Constituencies and connected matters. Vol. I *Report.* 1935–6 Cmd. 5099. Vol. II *Proposals for the delimitation.* 1935–6 Cmd. 5100.

Financial Enquiry Report by Sir Otto Niemeyer. 1935–6 Cmd. 5163.

Return showing the results of the elections in India 1937. 1937–8 Cmd. 5589.

(2) H.M.S.O.

Royal Commission on Agriculture in India. Vol. III *Evidence taken in Madras and Coorg.* London, 1927.

Indian Statutory Commission. Vol. V *Memoranda submitted by the Government of India and the India Office.* Vol. VI *Memorandum submitted by the Government of Madras.* Vol. XV *Extracts from Official Oral Evidence.* Vols. XVI and XVII *Selections from Memoranda and Oral Evidence by Non-Officials.* London, 1930.

Royal Commission on Labour in India. Evidence Vol. III *Madras and Coorg.* London, 1931.

(3) GOVERNMENT OF INDIA

Evidence taken before the Reforms Committee (Franchise) vol. II. Calcutta, 1919.

Report of the Indian Cotton Committee. Calcutta, 1919.

Minutes of Evidence taken before the Indian Cotton Committee vols. I–VI. Calcutta, 1920.

Indian Economic Enquiry Committee 1925. Vol. I Report, Vol. II Evidence. Calcutta, 1925–6.

Report of the Indian Taxation Enquiry Committee 1924–5 vol. I. Madras, 1926.

Report of the Indian Tariff Board on the Sugar Industry. Delhi, 1938.

Census of India 1891 vol. XIII. Madras, 1892.

Census of India 1901 vol. XV. Madras, 1902.

Census of India 1911 vol. XII. Madras, 1912.

Census of India 1921 vol. XIII. Madras, 1922.

Census of India 1931 vol. XIV. Madras, 1932.

Census of India 1941 vol. II. Delhi, 1942.

(4) GOVERNMENT OF MADRAS

Report of the Forest Committee (Madras) vols. I–II. Madras, 1913.

Handbook of Commercial Information. Madras, 1916.

A Statistical Atlas of the Madras Presidency. Madras, editions in 1913, 1924, 1936.

Report of the Tamil University Committee. Madras, 1927.

Report on the Survey of Cottage Industries in the Madras Presidency by D. Narayana Rao. Madras, 1929.

The Madras Provincial Banking Enquiry Commission. Vol. I Report. Vols. II–V Evidence. Madras, 1930.

Economic Enquiry Committee vols. I–III and connected papers. Madras, 1931.

Village Officers and Ryots Manual. Madras, 1931.

Report on Agricultural Indebtedness, by W.R.S. Sathyanathan. Madras, 1935.

Madras Legislative Council Proceedings.

Selections from Madras Government Records.

(5) MADRAS DISTRICT MANUALS AND GAZETTEERS

Baliga, B.S. *Tanjore District Handbook.* Madras, 1957.

Madura District Gazetteer. Madras, 1960.

South Arcot District Gazetteer. Madras, 1962.

Coimbatore District Gazetteer. Madras, 1966.

Brackenbury, C.F. *Cuddapah.* Madras, 1915.

Francis, W. *Bellary.* Madras, 1904.

Madura. Madras, 1906.

South Arcot. Madras, 1906.

Vizagapatam. Madras, 1907.

Nilgiri District Gazetteer. Madras, 1908.

Hemingway, F.R. *Tanjore*. Madras, 1906.
Godaveri. Madras, 1907.
Trichinopoly. Madras, 1907.
Mackenzie, G. *A Manual of the Kistna District*. Madras, 1883.
Nicholson, F.A. *Coimbatore District Manual*. Madras, 1898.
Pate, H.R. *Tinnevelly*. Madras, 1917.
Richards, F.J. *Salem*. Madras, 1918.
Stuart, H.A. *North Arcot District Manual*. Madras, 1895.

(6) ANNUAL REPORTS

Agricultural Statistics of British India.
Administration Report of the Corporation of Madras.
Administration Report of the Government of Madras.
Annual Report on the Working of the Madras Co-operative Credit Societies Act.
Annual Statement of the Sea-Borne Trade and Navigation of the Madras Presidency.
Finance and Revenue Accounts of the Government of India.
India in ...
Joint Stock Companies in British India and in the Indian States.
Report of the Indian Central Cotton Committee.
Report on the Administration of the Abkari Department in Madras Presidency.
Report on the Administration of the Department of Agriculture in Madras Presidency.
Report on the Administration of the Department of Industries in the Madras Presidency.
Report on the Administration of the Estates under the Court of Wards in the Madras Presidency.
Report on the Administration of the Income Tax in the Madras Presidency.
Report on the Administration of the Police in the Madras Presidency.
Report on the Administration of the Registration Department of Madras Presidency.
Report on Public Instruction in the Madras Presidency.
Report on the Settlement of the Land Revenue in the Districts under the Madras Presidency.
Report on the Working of District Municipalities in the Madras Presidency.
Report on the Working of Local Boards in the Madras Presidency.
Report on the Working of the Factories Act in the Madras Presidency.
Report on the Working of the Forest Department of the Madras Presidency.
Review and Returns of Sea-Borne Trade and Navigation of the Madras Presidency.
Review of the Sugar Industry of India.
Season and Crop Report of the Madras Presidency.
Statement exhibiting the Moral and Material Progress and Condition of India.
Statistical Abstract for British India and the Indian States.
The Quarterly Civil List for Madras.

PRIVATE PAPERS

All-India Congress Committee papers. Nehru Memorial Museum.
Erskine papers, Mss Eur D 596. India Office Library.
W. W. Georgeson papers. South Asian Studies Centre, Cambridge.
Goschen papers, Mss Eur F 93. India Office Library.
Halifax papers, Mss Eur C 152. India Office Library.
M. R. Jayakar papers. National Archives of India.
P. Kesava Pillai papers. Nehru Memorial Museum.

Linlithgow papers, Mss Eur F 125. India Office Library.
T. I. S. Mackay papers. South Asian Studies Centre, Cambridge.
Madras Mahajana Sabha papers. Nehru Memorial Museum.
Sir Christopher Masterman papers. South Asian Studies Centre, Cambridge.
G. A. Natesan papers. Nehru Memorial Museum.
Motilal Nehru papers. Nehru Memorial Museum.
Rajendra Prasad papers. Microfilm with Dr A. Seal, Cambridge.
K. V. Reddi Naidu papers. Andhra University, Waltair.
C. R. Reddy papers. Nehru Memorial Museum.
Satyamurthi papers. Microfilm with Dr A. Seal, Cambridge.
R. K. Shanmugham Chetty papers. With R. Sunderraj, Coimbatore.
P. S. Sivaswami Iyer papers. National Archives of India.
V. S. Srinivasa Sastri papers. National Archives of India.
Templewood papers, Mss Eur E 240. India Office Library.
Sir Richard Tottenham papers. South Asian Studies Centre, Cambridge.
Sir Sydney Wadsworth papers. South Asian Studies Centre, Cambridge.
Willingdon papers, Mss Eur F 93. India Office Library.

NEWSPAPERS AND PERIODICALS

Ananta Pōṭṭini (Tamil). 1927–33.
Ceṅkunta Mittiraṉ (Tamil). 1931–7.
Fort St George Gazette. Occasional copies.
The Hindu. 1916–37.
Indian Patriot. Occasional copies.
Indian Review. Occasional copies.
Justice. 1934–7 and occasional cuttings.
Madras Mail. 1921–37.
The Mirasidar/Mirācutār (English and Tamil). 1935–7.
Tarul Islām (Tamil). 1925.

Reports on English Papers owned by Natives examined by the Criminal Investigation Department Madras, and on Vernacular Papers examined by the Translators to the Government of Madras.

UNPUBLISHED DISSERTATIONS

Baker, D. E. U. 'Nation and region in Indian politics: a study of the Swarajya party 1922–6', M.A. thesis, University of Western Australia, 1966.
Bayly, C. A. 'The Development of Political Organisation in the Allahabad Locality 1880–1925', D.Phil. thesis, University of Oxford, 1970.
Chandra Mudaliar. 'State and Religious Endowments in Madras', Ph.D. thesis, University of Madras, 1961.
Gordon, R. A. 'Aspects in the history of the Indian National Congress with special reference to the Swarajya Party 1919 to 1923', D.Phil. thesis, University of Oxford, 1970.
Kesavanarayana, B. 'Political and Social Factors in Andhra from A.D. 1900 to A.D. 1956', Ph.D. thesis, Osmania University, 1970.
Leonard, J. G. 'Kandukuri Viresalingham: A biography of an Indian Social Reformer 1848–1919', Ph.D. thesis, University of Wisconsin, 1970.

Narayana Rao, K. V. 'The Emergence of Andhra Pradesh', Ph.D. thesis, University of Madras, 1966.

Saraswathi, S. 'Minorities in Madras State: a study of group interests and their organisation in Madras politics since 1890', Ph.D. thesis, University of Madras, 1965.

Suntharalingam, R. 'Politics and Change in Madras Presidency 1884–1894: a regional study of Indian nationalism', Ph.D. thesis, University of London, 1966.

Tomlinson, B. R. 'Imperialism, Nationalism and Indian Politics: the Indian National Congress 1934–42', Ph.D. thesis, University of Cambridge, 1973.

Visalakshi, N. R. 'Growth of Public Services in Madras State', Dissertation, University of Madras, 1962.

Washbrook, D. A. 'Political Change in the Madras Presidency 1880–1921', Ph.D. thesis, University of Cambridge, 1973.

CONGRESS PUBLICATIONS

The Indian National Congress 1920–1923: Being a collection of the resolutions of the Congress and of the All India Congress Committee and the Working Committee of the Congress from September 1920 to December 1923. Allahabad, 1922.

The Indian National Congress 1924. Allahabad, 1925.

The Indian National Congress 1926. Madras, 1927.

The Indian National Congress 1927. Madras, 1928.

Report of the Civil Disobedience Enquiry Committee, appointed by the All-India Congress Committee. Allahabad, 1922.

The Indian National Congress 1928. Allahabad, 1929.

The Indian National Congress 1930–1934. Allahabad, 1934.

The Indian National Congress 1934–1936. Allahabad, 1936.

The Indian National Congress 1936–1937. Allahabad, n.d.

Secretaries' Report for the Year 1927. Madras, 1928.

Report of the Thirty-Fifth Indian National Congress, held at Nagpur on 26th, 28th, 30th and 31st December 1920. Nagpur, n.d.

Report of the Forty-First Indian National Congress, held at Gauhati on 28th, 29th, 30th and 31st December 1926. Madras, n.d.

Report on the Forty-Second Indian National Congress, held at Madras on 28th, 29th, 30th and 31st December 1927. Madras, n.d.

Report of the Forty-Eighth Indian National Congress, Bombay, October 1934. Bombay, n.d.

Report on the Forty-Ninth Session of the Indian National Congress, Lucknow, April 1936. Allahabad, 1936.

PUBLISHED BOOKS, ARTICLES, PAMPHLETS

Acharya, M. K. *The Struggle for Swaraj.* Madras, 1923.

'An Admirer.' *Periyar E. V. Ramaswami – A Pen Portrait.* Erode, 1962.

Ahluwalia, S. *Anna – The Tempest and the Sea.* Delhi, 1969.

All Parties Conference 1928: Report of the Committee appointed by the Conference to determine the Principles of the Constitution of India. Allahabad, 1928.

Almanack and Directory of Madras and Southern India. Madras, 1933.

Annasami Sastri, K. A. *Caurāstira Pirāmanā Carittiram* (Tamil – History of the Saurashtra community). Madura, 1914.

Bibliography

Anuntha Row Pantulu, V. *An Old Man's Family Record and Reference.* Madras, 1916.

Appa Rao Naidu, K. *Communal Representation and Indian Constitutional Reforms.* Cocanada, 1918.

Arokiaswami, M. *The Kongu Country.* Madras, 1956.

Arttanarica Varma *Vaṉṉikula Ksatriya Capai Upatēcankal* (Tamil – Origins of the Vannikula Kshatriya Association). Madras, 1927.

Arumuga Pillai, T. M. *Cuyamariyātaikku Ōr Cuddukkōs* (Tamil – Against the Self-Respect movement). Madras, 1929.

Bagchi, A. K. *Private Investment in India 1900–39.* Cambridge, 1972.

Baker, C. J. and Washbrook, D. A. *South India: Political Institutions and Political Change 1880–1940.* Delhi, 1975.

Baladandayutham, K. *Jivā – Vālkkai Varalāṟu* (Tamil – Biography of Jiva). Madras, 1966.

Balasubramaniam, K. M. *South Indian Celebrities.* Vol. I Madras, 1934. Vol. II Madras, 1939.

The Life of J. M. Nallaswami Pillai. Trichinopoly, 1965.

Baldwin, G. B. *Industrial Growth in South India.* Glencoe, 1959.

Baliga, B. S. *Studies in Madras Administration.* Madras, 1960.

Barlow, G. *The Story of Madras.* London, 1921.

Beaglehole, T. H. *Thomas Munro and the Development of Administrative Policy in Madras 1792–1818: the origins of the Munro system.* Cambridge, 1966.

Beck, B. E. F. 'A sociological sketch of the major castes in the Coimbatore district', in *Proceedings of the First International Conference Seminar of Tamil Studies* vol. I. Kuala Lumpur, 1968.

Peasant Society in Konku: a study of right and left subcastes in South India. Vancouver, 1972.

Berna, J. J. *Industrial Entrepreneurship in Madras State.* New York, 1960.

Beteille, A. *Caste, Class and Power: changing patterns of stratification in a Tanjore village.* Berkeley and Los Angeles, 1965.

Castes Old and New. Essays in Social Structure and Social Stratification. London, 1969.

Bhargava, G. S. *A Study of the Communist Movement in Andhra.* Delhi, 1955.

V. V. Giri. Delhi, n.d.

Bhavaiah Chowdary, K. *A Brief History of the Kammas.* Sangamjagarlamudi, 1955.

Bhimasankara Rao, S. *The Indian National Congress – Then and Now.* Rajahmundry, 1929.

Bhushayya Chowdary, P. *A Memorandum of the Real Indian National Congress Party Bezwada submitted to the Government of India regarding the Temple Entry Bill.* Bezwada, 1934.

Boag, G. T. *The Madras Presidency 1881–1931.* Madras, 1933.

Bobbili, Maharajah of, *Bobbili Zamindari.* Madras, 1907.

Broomfield, J. H. *Elite Conflict in a Plural Society.* Berkeley and Los Angeles, 1968.

Butterworth, A. *The South Lands of Siva.* London, 1927.

Chakravarti, N. R. *The Indian Minority in Burma: the rise and decline of an immigrant community.* Oxford, 1971.

Chandrasekhar, S. 'Growth of population in Madras City 1639–1961', in *Population Review* (Madras) (1964).

Chandrasekharan, K. *V. Krishnaswami Aiyar.* Masulipatam, 1963.

Chenchayya, D. *Nēnu Nā Dēśamu* (Telugu – Myself and my country). Vijayawada, 1952.

Chenna Subba Rao, M. *Myself and Rural Life (Autobiography)*, part I. Anantapur, 1951.

Chettiar, C. M. R. 'Growth of modern Coimbatore', *Journal of the Madras Geographical Association*, XIV, 2 (1939).

Chidambaranar, *Tamilar Talaivar* (Tamil – The Tamil's leader). *Erode, 1960.*

Chiefs and Leading Families in the Madras Presidency. Madras, 1915.

Coopooswamey *Everyday Life in South India: The Story of Coopooswamey, an Autobiography*. London, 1885.

The Cult of Incompetence: being an impartial enquiry into the record of the first Madras ministry. Reprinted from *Swarajya*. Madras, 1923.

Das, C. R. *The Way to Swaraj*. Madras, 1923.

Das, R. K. *Temples of Tamilnad*. Bombay, 1964.

Davies, Kingsley *The Population of India and Pakistan*. Princetown, 1951.

Devanandan, P. D. *The Dravida Kazhagam: a revolt against Brahminism*. Bangalore, 1959.

Dharmapuram Adhinam Mutt and Temples. Madras, n.d.

Directory of the Madras Legislature. Published by the Madras Legislature Congress Party. Madras, 1938.

Dumont, L. *Une Sous-Caste de l'Inde du Sud: organisation sociale et religion des Pramalai Kallar*. Paris and The Hague, 1957.

Dupuis, J. *Madras et le Nord du Coromandel: étude des conditions de la vie indienne dans une cadre geographique*. Paris, 1960.

Elliott, C. M. 'Caste and faction among the dominant caste: the Reddis and Kammas of Andhra', in R. Kothari (ed.), *Caste in Indian Politics*. New Delhi, 1970.

For and Against the Andhra Movement. Masulipatam, 1914.

Frykenberg, R. E. *Guntur District 1788–1848: a history of local influence and central authority in south India*. Oxford, 1965.

(ed.). *Land Control and Social Structure in Indian History*. Madison, 1969.

Collected Works of Mahatma Gandhi, vols XV, XXI, XXVI. Ahmedebad, 1965–6.

'A Gandhite'. *Kamaraj the Shrewd 1903–40*. Madras, 1961.

Geddes, Sir P. *Report on the Towns in Madras Presidency*. London, 1915.

Gopalakrishnayya, D. *Letters*. Bezwada, 1934.

Gopal Krishna. 'The development of the Indian National Congress as a mass organisation 1918–23', *Journal of Asian Studies*, XXV, 3 (1966).

Gopala Menon, N. *A Short Sketch of the Life of Dr T. M. Nair*. Madras, 1920.

Gopalaratnam, V. C. *A Century completed. A History of the Madras High Court 1862–1962*. Madras, n.d.

Gough, E. K. 'Brahman kinship in a Tamil village', *American Anthropologist*, LVIII (1956).

'Criteria of caste ranking in south India', *Man in India*, XXXIX (1959).

'Caste in a Tanjore village', in E. R. Leach (ed.), *Aspects of Caste in South India, Ceylon and North-East Pakistan*. Cambridge, 1960.

Govindarow Naidu, P. *The Legislative Council Elections (1920): a critical study of party programmes*. Rajahmundry, 1920.

Gowda, M. S. L. *Indian Economic Census: economic planning special volume*. Madras, 1936.

Gurunatham, J. *The Andhra Movement*. Guntur, 1913.

Hardgrave, R. L. *The Dravidian Movement*. Bombay, 1965.

The Nadars of Tamilnad: the political culture of a community in change. Berkeley and Los Angeles, 1969.

Harisarvothama Rao, G. *Spiritual Swadeshi or Humanitarian Nationalism*. Madras, 1923.
Harrison, S. *India – the most dangerous decades*. Princeton, 1960.
Hilton Brown. *'The Civilian's South India*. London, 1921.
Parry's of Madras: A Story of British Enterprise in India. Madras, 1954.
Hjejle, B. 'Slavery and agricultural bondage in the nineteenth century', *Scandinavian Economic History Review*, XV, 1 and 2 (1967).
Irschick, E. F. *Politics and Social Conflict in South India: the Non-Brahmin Movement and Tamil Separatism 1916–29*. Berkeley and Los Angeles, 1969.
Iswara Dutt, K. *Sparks and Fumes*. Madras, 1929.
Pen-portraits of Andhra Leaders. Madras, n.d.
Iyengar, A. S. *All Through the Gandhian Era*. Bombay, 1950.
Jagadisan, T. N. *Letters of Srinivasa Sastri*. London, 1944.
Jayakar, M. R. *The Story of My Life*. Vol. I, Bombay, 1958. Vol. II, Bombay, 1959.
Jayaraman, K. *A Study of Panchayats in Madras*. Bombay, 1947.
Justice Party Golden Jubilee Souvenir. Madras, 1968.
Kaleswara Rao, A. *Nā Jīvita Katha – Navya Āndhramu* (Telugu – My life and the new Andhra). Vijayawada, 1959.
Kalyanasundara Mudaliar, T. V. *Tamil̠ Ten̠ral*. (Tamil – A breeze through Tamilnad). Madras, 1925.
Man̠itavāl̠akkaiyum Kantiyadikalum (Tamil – Gandhi and current problems). Madras, 1928.
Vāl̠kkaik Kur̠ippukkaḷ (Tamil – Autobiography). Madras, 1969.
Kandasami Pillai, V. *Tiruvāvaduturai Kurican̠am* (Tamil – Visit to Tiruvadathurai). Madras, 1921.
Kannappar, J. S. *Cūttirarkaḷ Yār?* (Tamil – Who are the Sudras?). Madras, 1926.
Kapur, R. P. *Kamaraj – The Iron Man*. Delhi, 1966.
Karvannan, Muthu *Cuyamariyātai Camattuva Pādalkaḷ* (Tamil – Songs on the power of Self-Respect). Madura, 1931.
Kasipathi, K. *Tryst with Destiny*. Hyderabad, 1970.
Kausikan. *Rājājī* (Tamil). Madras, 1968.
Kindleberger, C. P. *The World in Depression 1929–39*. London, 1973.
Kistna District Association. *Troubles of the Ryots of the Kistna Eastern Delta*. Masulipatam, 1917.
Kodanda Rao, P. *The Right Hon. V. S. Srinivasa Sastri. A Political Biography*. London, 1963.
Krishna, K. B. *The Problem of Minorities*. London, 1939.
Krishna Ayyar, R. V. *In the Legislature of Those Days*. Madras, 1956.
Krishnamachariar, R. *Araciyal Ñān̠i Araṅkacāmi Aiyaṅkār* (Tamil – Political genius Rangaswami Iyengar). Madras, n.d.
Krishnamurthi Mudaliar, C. *Life and Activities of K. Chidambaranatha Mudaliar*. Shiyali, 1938.
Krishnaswami, S. Y. *Rural Problems in Madras: monograph*. Madras, 1947.
Kulasekhara Raja, B. J. M. and Anandanarayanam, M. *Tirun̠elvēli Taḷavāy Mutaliyār Kudumpavaralār̠u* (Tamil – Family history of the Dalavoy Mudaliars of Tinnevelly). Madras, 1925.
Kumar, D. *Land and Caste in South India. Agricultural labour in the Madras Presidency during the nineteenth century*. Cambridge, 1965.
Kumaraswamy Raja, P. S. *My Induction as a Gandhite*. Rajapalaiyam, 1956.
Lakshmi Narasu, P. *A Study of Caste*. Madras, 1922.

Leonard, J. G. 'Politics and social change in south India: a study of the Andhra Movement', *Journal of Commonwealth Political Studies*, v, 1 (1967).

'Urban government under the Raj: a case study of municipal administration in nineteenth century south India', *Modern Asian Studies*, VII, 2 (1973).

Mackenzie, A. T. *History of the Periyar Project*. Madras, 1899.

McPherson, K. 'The social background and politics of the Muslims of Tamilnad 1901–37', *Indian Economic and Social History Review*, VI, 4 (1969).

Madhavaiah, A. *Thillai Govindan*. Madras, 1913.

Lieut. Panju: A Modern India. Madras, 1924.

Madhavan Nair, C. *A Short Life of C. Sankaran Nair*. Madras, n.d.

Madras Mahajana Sabha Diamond Jubilee Souvenir. Madras, 1946.

The Madras Tercentenary Commemoration Volume. Madras, 1939.

The Madras Year Book 1924. Madras, 1924.

Mandelbaum, D. G. *Society in India*. Berkeley and Los Angeles, 1970.

Maniparathi, R. S. *Maddappārai Ciṅkam R. S. Veṅkadrāmayyar Jīviya Carittiram* (Tamil – Biography of R. S. Venkataramier, the lion of Mattaparai). Dindigul, 1956.

Marakayyar, Ahmed Thambi *Cadda Capaiyil Eddu Varuca Vēlai* (Tamil–Eight years' work in the Legislative Council). Madras, 1920.

Mencher, J. P. 'A Tamil village: changing socioeconomic structure in Madras State', in K. Ishwaran (ed.), *Change and Continuity in India's Villages*. New York and London 1970.

Menon, K. P. S. *Many Worlds: an autobiography*. London, 1965.

C. Sankaran Nair. Delhi, 1967.

Mitra, N. N. *Indian Annual Register*. Calcutta, annual.

Molony, J. C. *A Book of South India*. London, 1926.

Montagu, E. S. *An Indian Diary*. London, 1930.

Mukherjee, N. *The Ryotwari System in Madras*. Calcutta, 1962.

Muni, A. K. *The Moral Victory*. Proddatur, 1925.

Munikulaju, S. *The Non-Brahmin Peril and Blasted Brahminism*. Udipi, 1930.

Murton, B. J. 'Key people in the countryside: decision makers in interior Tamilnad in the late eighteenth century', *Indian Economic and Social History Review*, x, 2 (1973).

Murugappa Chettiar, S. *Namatu Palacarakkukkadai* (Tamil – Our grocery shop). Karaikudi, 1922.

Muthulakshmi Reddy, S. *Autobiography*. Madras, 1964.

Naga Gopala Rao, A. *Homage*. Ellore, 1960.

Nair, A. A. *Peeps at the Press In South India*. Madras, n.d.

Nair, B. N. *The Dynamic Brahmin*. Bombay, 1959.

Nair, T. M. *Evolution of Mrs Besant*. Madras, 1918.

Nancharya, B. V. *Biography of Lodd Govindoss Varu*. Madras, 1942.

Nanda, B. R. *The Nehrus – Motilal and Jawaharlal*. New York, 1963.

Narasimhan, K. L. *Madras City – A History*. Madras, 1968.

Narasimhan, V. K. *Kasturi Ranga Iyengar*. Delhi, 1963.

Kamaraj – A Study. Bombay, 1967.

Kasturi Srinivasan. Bombay, 1969.

Narasu Raju, D. *et al. A Beautiful Life – an appreciation of Sir Mutha Venkatasubba Rao*. Secundarabad, 1960.

Narayanaswami Naidu, B. V. *The Co-operative Movement in the Madras Presidency*. Annamalainagar, 1933.

Bibliography

Rajah Sir Annamalai Chettiar Commemoration Volume. Annamalainagar, 1941.
Madras Finance. Madras, 1948.

Narayanaswami Naidu, B. V. and Venkataraman, V. *The Problem of Rural Indebtedness.* Annamalainagar, 1935.

Natarajan, B. *Food and Agriculture in Madras State.* Madras, 1953.

Nathan, T. A. V. (ed.). *The Justice Year Book 1929.* n.p., n.d.

Nethercot, A. H. *The First Five Lives of Annie Besant.* Chicago, 1960.
The Last Four Lives of Annie Besant. Chicago, 1960.

Owen, H. F. 'Towards nationwide agitation and organization: the Home Rule Leagues 1915–18', in D. A. Low (ed.), *Soundings in Modern South Asian History.* London, 1968.

Padmanabha Ayyar, V. S. *A Short Account of the Tinnevelly District.* Palamcottah, 1933.

Padmanabha Iyer, K. V. *A History of Sourashtras in South India.* Madras, 1942.

Pandya, A. L. *Biography of Sriman Lodd Govindoss Maharaj – the Hindu Hero.* Madras, 1942.

Parthasarathy, R. T. *Dawn and Achievement of Indian Freedom.* Salem, 1953.

Parthasarathy, T. M. *Ti. Mu. Kaḻaka Varalāṟu* (Tamil – History of the D.M.K.). Madras, 1961.

Patro, A. P. *Studies in Local Self-Government, Education and Sanitation.* Madras, n.d.
'The Justice Movement in India', *Asiatic Review,* XXVIII (1932).

Pattabhi Sitaramayya, B. *The History of the Indian National Congress.* Vol. I Madras, 1935. Vol. II Bombay, 1947.

Pearse, A. S. *The Cotton Industry of India.* Manchester, 1930.

Pentland, Lady *The Right Honourable Sir John Sinclair; Lord Pentland G.C.S.I.* London, 1918.

Periyār Irāmacāmi Avarkalaip Paṟṟi (Tamil – All About Periyar Ramaswami). *Erode,* 1960.

Perumal, N. *Contemporary South Indians.* Madras, 1934.
Jamal Mohammed. Madras, 1936.
Two Important Men. Madras, 1936.
Chettinad. Madras, 1938.
Rajaji. Madras, 1953.
Talented Tamils. Madras, 1957.

Pillai, K. K. *History of Local Self-Government in the Madras Presidency 1850–1919.* Bombay, 1953.

Playne, S. *South India: its history, peoples, commerce and industrial resources.* London, 1915.

Prakasam, T. *Nā Jīvita Yātra* (Telugu – My life's path). Rajahmundry, 1957.

Prakash, A. *Sir C.P.* Madras, 1939.

Prasad, R. *Autobiography.* Bombay, 1957.

Pulavar Arasu. *V. Vē. Cu. Aiyar* (Tamil). Madras, 1951.
Tiru. Vi. Kaliyāṇacuntaraṉār (Tamil). Tinnevelly, 1961.

Purnalingam Pillai, M. S. *Tamil India.* Tinnevelly, 1945.

Raghavachendrayya Sastri, D. *Brahmin–Non-Brahmin Hindu Problem.* Madras, 1938.
Congress Brahmins' Nationalism. Madras, 1957.

Raghavan, T. S. *Makers of Modern Tamil.* Tinnevelly, 1965.

Raghavayya Chowdary, S. *Brahmaṇettara Saṅgha Dhārasyan.* (Telugu – Aims of the Non-Brahman Association) Bapatla, 1927.
Brahmanettara Vijayamu (Telugu – Non-Brahman victory). Kollur, 1925.

Raj, V. P. *Dr Sir R. Venkataratnam*. n.p., 1929.
Rajagopalachari, C. *Chats Behind Bars*. Madras, 1931.
Indian Prohibition Manual. Madras, 1931.
Cuttantirap Pōr. (Tamil – War of Independence). Madras, 1931.
Rajaji's Jail Life: a day to day record of Sri C. Rajagopalachariar's life in Vellore Jail in 1920. Madras, 1941.
Rajah, M. C. *The Oppressed Hindus*. Madras, 1925.
Rājāji (Tamil). Madras, 1949.
Ramachandra Aiyar, V. G. *An Address to the Brahmans*. Palamcottah, 1920.
Ramachandra Rao, D. S. *Dhannavada Anantamu 1850–1949*. (Telugu – History of the Dhannavada family). Calcutta, 1956.
Ramachandra K. S. 'The Andhra Movement', *Modern Review* (1916).
Ramakrishna Aiyar, V. G. *The Economy of a South Indian Temple*. Annamalainagar, 1946.
Ramadas, V. *Memorandum on Andhra Province*. Madras, 1939.
Ramalingam Chettiar, T. A. 'The Legislative Council', *Indian Review*, XXIII (1922).
Raman Rao, A. V. *Economic Development of Andhra Pradesh 1766–1957*. Bombay, 1958.
Raman Rao, M. V. *Development of the Congress Constitution*. Delhi, 1958.
Ramanatha Iyer, P. *Madras Hindu Religious Endowments Act*. Madras, 1946.
Ramanathan, J. N. *Ākātu: Tīya Acārankaḷ* (Tamil – It is unbecoming: evil customs). Madras, 1926.
Ramanathan, S. *Gandhi and the Youth*. Bombay, 1947.
Ramanathan, S. *et al. The Superstition of Khadi*. Erode, 1931.
Ramanathan Chettiar, L. P. K. *Aṇṇamalai Aracār* (Tamil – Raja Annamalai). Madras, 1965.
Ramarao, R. V. M. G. *Of Men, Matters and Me*. London, 1961.
Ramaswami Iyer, C. P. *'C.P.' by his Contemporaries*. Madras, 1959.
Biographical Vistas: sketches of some eminent Indians. Bombay, 1960.
Ramaswami Mudaliar, A. (ed.). *Mirror of the Year: being a collection of the leading articles in 'Justice', 1927*. Madras, 1928.
An Indian Federation – its constitutional problems and possible solution. Madras, 1933.
Ramaswami Sastri, K. S. *The Present Crisis in Hindu Society*. Madras, 1918.
Professor K. Sundarama Aiyar: his life and work. Srirangam, 1944.
Vita Sua. Madras, 1945.
Sri N. Subramanya Aiyar: a biography. Madras, 1956.
Ramaswami Sastri V. S. and Swamin, Dhurta *The Brahmins*. Madras, 1929.
Ramaswamy Tatachariar, D. *The Vanavamalai Temple and Mutt*. Tinnevelly, 1937.
Ramesan, N. *Temples and Legends of Andhra Pradesh*. Bombay, 1962.
Ranga, N. G. *Economic Organisation of Indian Villages*. Vol. I Bezwada, 1926. Vol. II Bombay, 1929.
Agricultural Indebtedness and Remedial Means. Tenali, 1933.
Economic Conditions of the Zamindari Ryots. Bezwada, 1933.
The Modern Indian Peasant. Madras, 1936.
Revolutionary Peasants. Delhi, 1949.
Fight for Freedom. Delhi, 1968.
Ranga Rao, C. (ed.). *Andhra Desa Directory and Who's Who*. Bezwada, 1939.
Rangachari, K. *Sri Vaishnava Brahmins*. Madras, 1931.
Rangaswami Aiyangar, A. *The Land Revenue Problem in Southern India*. Madras, 1919.

Ranson, C. W. *City in Transition*. Madras, 1938.
Reddy, C. R. 'Dyarchy and after', *Indian Review*, XXIII (1922).
Richards, F. J. 'Cross-cousin marriage in south India', *Man*, XCVII (1914).
Row, C. S. *The Confessions of a Bogus Patriot*. Madras, 1923.
Row, M. V. S. *Our President Pattabhi*. Masulipatam, 1949.
Rudolph, S. H. and L. I. *The Modernity of Tradition: Political Development in India*. Chicago, 1967.
Rudrayya Chowdary, G. *Prakasam: a political study*. Madras, 1971.
Ruthnaswamy, M. *The Political Philosophy of Mahatma Gandhi*. Madras, 1920.
Some Influences that made the British Administrative System in India. London, 1939.
Sambanda Mudaliar, P. *Eṉ Cuyacaritai* (Tamil – Autobiography). Madras, 1963.
Sankar Linge Gowda, M. *Zemindari Taxation Enquiry Committee Report, Vol. I*, Trichinopoly, 1936.
Sankaran Nair, C. *Gandhi and Anarchy*. Madras, n.d.
Autobiography. Madras, 1966.
Santanam, K. *Caddiya Camājam* (Tamil – Social reform). Madras, 1931.
Sarma, S. K. *Towards Swaraj: being the exposition of a scheme for responsible government*. Madras, 1928.
Sarveswara Rao, B. *The Economic and Social Effects of Zamindari Abolition in Andhra*. Waltair, 1963.
Sastri, K. R. R. *The Madura Sourashtra Community: a study in applied economics*. Bangalore, 1927.
Sastri, V. L. (ed.) *Encyclopedia of the Madras Presidency and Adjacent States*. Madras, 1921.
'Satabisha'. *Rashtrapathi Dr Pattabhi*. Madras, 1948.
Satchit, T. N. (ed.). *Who's Who in Madras*. Cochin, annual.
Sathyanathan, W. R. S. *Report on Agricultural Indebtedness*. Madras, 1935.
Satyamurthi, S. 'Capture the Councils', *Indian Review*, XXXIV (1933).
Satyanarayana, Ch. *Āndhra Ratnamulu* (Telugu – Heroes of Andhra). Palacole, 1930.
Saunders, A. J. 'The Sourashtra community of Madura, south India', *American Journal of Sociology*, XXXII (1926).
Sayana, V. V. *The Agrarian Problems of Madras Province*. Madras, 1949.
Schamnad, M. *A brief sketch of the work done by Mr Mahmud Schamnad MLA during his three years' tenure in the First Indian Legislative Assembly 1921–3*. Mangalore, n.d.
Seal, A. *The Emergence of Indian Nationalism: Competition and collaboration in the later nineteenth century*. Cambridge, 1968.
Sesha Ayyangar, M. S. *Madura Resettlement 1915*. Madura, 1915.
Madras Village Panchayats. Madura, 1916.
Shanmughasundaram, L. *Di. Ke. Ci. Varalāṟu* (Tamil – Biography of T. K. Chidambaranatha Mudaliar). Madras, 1955.
Sharma, D. S. *From Literature to Religion*. Bombay, 1964.
Shenoy, J. P. L. *Madura, the Temple City*. Madras, 1955.
Shiva Rao, B. *The Industrial Worker in India*. London, 1939.
Singaravelu, M. *Camatarma Upanyācam* (Tamil – Socialist discourse). Erode, 1942.
Singer, M. *When a Great Tradition Modernises*. London, 1972.
Sitrasu, S. P. *Dākdar P. Varatarāculu Nāyutu: Avarkaḷin Vālkkai Varalāru (Tamil* – Biography of Dr P. Varadarajulu Naidu). Madras, 1957.

Sivakolundu Mudaliar, A. *A Short Brochure on the Kallars.* Tanjore, 1926.
Sivayya, K. V. *The Trade Union Movement in Visakhapatnam.* Waltair, 1966.
Sivertsen, D. *When Caste Barriers Fall.* New York, 1963.
S. K. N. *Non-Brahmin Letters.* Madras, 1915.
Slater, G. *Some South Indian Villages.* Oxford, 1918.
Southern India: its political and economic problems. London, 1936.
Somasundaram Pillai, S. A. *Dr T. M. Nair M.D.* Madras, 1920.
South Indian Maharashtrians. Madras, 1937.
South Indian Mohammedan Educational Association Golden Jubilee Souvenir, 1902–52. Madras, 1954.
Spate, O. H. K. and Learmouth, A. T. A. *India and Pakistan: a general and regional geography.* London, 1967.
Spratt, P. *D.M.K. in Power.* Bombay, 1970.
Srinivas, P. R. *Indian Finance Yearbook 1935.* Calcutta, 1935.
Srinivasa Iyengar, K. R. *S. Srinivasa Iyengar: the story of a decade in Indian politics.* Mangalore, 1939.
Srinivasa Iyengar, S. *Swaraj Constitution.* Madras, 1927.
Srinivasa Raghavaiyangar, S. *Memorandum on the Progress of the Madras Presidency during the Last Forty Years of British Administration.* Madras, 1893.
Srinivasa Rao, V. N. *Tirupati Sri Venkatesvara-Balija.* Madras, 1949.
Srinivasachari, C. S. *A History of the City of Madras.* Madras, 1939.
Staal, J. F. 'Notes on some Brahman communities of South India', *Art and Letters,* XXXII (1958).
Subba Rao, G. V. *Sree Gopalakrishnayya.* Amalapuram, 1935.
Gopalakrishnayya's Essays and Addresses. n.p., n.d.
Life and Times of Sir K. V. Reddi Naidu. Rajahmundry, 1957.
Subba Rao, K. *Revived Memories.* Madras, 1933.
Subbaramaiah, S. *Finances of an Indian Temple: A case study of the finances of the Tirumalai-Tirupathi Devasthanam 1951–63.* Jullundur, 1968.
Subramania Aiyar, M. S. *Cuyarājya Pērikai* (Tamil – The cream of the national movement). Madras, 1931.
Subramania Aiyar, N. 'Party politics in India', *Indian Review,* XXI (1920).
Subramaniam, S. (ed.). *Dr A. Ramaswami Mudaliar and Dr A. Lakshmanaswami Mudaliar Eighty-First Birthday Commemoration Volume.* Madras, 1967.
Sundaraja Iyengar, S. *Land Tenures in the Madras Presidency.* Madras, 1922.
Sundaraja Iyer, V. M. *Tirun̲elvēli Jilla Carittaram* (Tamil – History of Tinnevelly district). Tinnevelly, 1933.
Suryanarayana, K. *Sir R. Venkataratnam.* Rajahmundry, 1952.
Suryanarayana, V. *Sūryanārāyaṇīyamu* (Telugu – A family history). Kovvur, 1936.
Swami Subramania Thambiran. *Tiruvāvatturai Atin̲ak Kuruparamparai* (Tamil – Succession in Tiruvadathurai *math*). Chidambaram, 1925.
Thomas, P. J. *The Problem of Rural Indebtedness.* Madras, 1934.
The Growth of Federal Finance in India 1833–1939. Oxford, 1939.
Thomas, P. J. and Ramakrishnan, K. C. *Some South Indian Villages: a resurvey.* Madras, 1940.
Thurston, E. *Castes and Tribes of Southern India.* 7 vols. Madras, 1909.
The Madras Presidency with Mysore, Coorg and the Associated States. Cambridge, 1913.
Timmayya, M. *Is India Fit for Swaraj?* Bezwada, 1929.

Tiruvenkataswami, V. (ed.). *Pachaiyappa's College Centenary Commemoration Book 1842–1942*. Madras, 1942.
Trevelyan, H. *The India We Left*. London, 1972.
Vadivelu, A. *The Aristocracy of Southern India*. n.p., 1907.
Ruling Chiefs, Nobles and Zemindars of India. Madras, 1915.
Vaidyanatha Aiyar, R. S. *A Memorandum on the Ryotwari Landholders in Madras*. Madras, 1933.
Vaiyapuri Pillai, S. *History of Tamil Language and Literature*. Madras, 1956.
Varadarajan, M. *Tiru. Vī. Kā* (Tamil). Madras, 1968.
Varadarajulu Naidu, Dr P. *The Bugle Call – Speeches and Writings of Dr P. Varadarajulu Naidu*. Madras, 1934.
The National Dharma – Life, Speeches and Writings of Dr P. Varadarajulu Naidu. Salem, 1948.
Dr P. Varadarajulu Naidu Commemoration Volume. Madras, 1955.
Varadarajulu Naidu, T. *The Justice Movement 1917*. Madras, 1932.
Veerabhadra Rao, M. *Dēśabhakta Jīvita Caritra* (Telugu – Life of K. Venkatappayya). Hyderabad, 1966.
Venguswamy, N. S. *Congress in Office*. Bombay, 1940.
Venkata Raju, A. K. D. *A Brief Life Sketch of P. S. Kumaraswamy Raja*. Rajapalaiyam, 1964.
Venkata Rao, V. *A Hundred Years of Local Self-Government and Administration in Andhra and Madras States 1850–1950*. Bombay, 1960.
Venkatappayya, K. *Svīya Caritra* (Telugu – Autobiography). Vijayawada, 1952 and 1955.
Venkatarama Aiyar, K. R. *The First Trichinopoly District Conference*. Trichinopoly, 1914.
M. Venkatarama Iyer Centenary Celebration Souvenir. n.p., 1965.
Venkatarama Sastri, T. R. *Historic Roots of some Modern Conflicts*. Kumbakonam, 1946.
Venkatarangaiya, M. *The Development of Local Boards in the Madras Presidency*. Bombay, 1939.
The Freedom Struggle in Andhra Pradesh (Andhra). Vol. I Hyderabad, 1965. Vol. II Hyderabad, 1969. Vol. III Hyderabad, 1965.
Venkataratnam, M. *The Non-Brahmin Origin of the Brahmins*. Madras, 1922.
Reform of the Brahmins. Madras, 1924.
Venkateswara Rao, K. *Ṭanguṭūri Prakāśaṃ* (Telugu). Tanuku, 1958.
V. Venkateswarlu Sastrulu Commemoration Volume. Madras, 1941.
Venkateswarlu, Y. *The Peddapuram Incident*. Cocanada, 1931.
Venu, A. S. *Life of Annadurai*. Madras, 1953.
Dravidasthan. Madras, 1954.
'Victor Trench'. *Lord Willingdon in India*. Bombay, 1934.
Viswanatha Sastri, C. V. *Biographies of a Grandfather and a Grandson*. Madras, 1939.
Waley, S. D. *Edwin Montagu*. London, 1964.
Washbrook, D. A. 'Country politics: Madras 1880–1930', *Modern Asian Studies*, VII, 3 (1973).
Whitehead, H. *Village Gods of South India*. Calcutta, 1921.
Yakub Hassan. *Hindu-Muslim Problem*. Madras, 1917.

INDEX

SUDIPTA KAVIRAJ
OXFORD 28.11.81.